BIBLICAL NOTES
FOR THE
SUNDAY LECTIONARY

BIBLICAL NOTES
FOR THE
SUNDAY LECTIONARY

By

James Gaffney, Ph.D.

PAULIST PRESS
New York/Ramsey/Toronto

Copyright © 1978 by
The Missionary Society
of St. Paul the Apostle
in the State of New York

All rights reserved. No part of this book may be reproduced or transmitted in any form or by any means, electronic or mechanical, including photocopying, recording or by any information storage and retrieval system without permission in writing from the Publisher.

Library of Congress
Catalog Card Number: 77-93011

ISBN: 0-8091-2071-2

Published by Paulist Press
Editorial Office: 1865 Broadway, New York, N.Y. 10023
Business Office: 545 Island Road, Ramsey, N.J. 07446

Printed and bound in the
United States of America

CONTENTS

Introduction 1

ADVENT SEASON

1st Sunday of Advent, A 4
1st Sunday of Advent, B 5
1st Sunday of Advent, C 7
2nd Sunday of Advent, A 9
2nd Sunday of Advent, B 11
2nd Sunday of Advent, C 13
3rd Sunday of Advent, A 14
3rd Sunday of Advent, B 16
3rd Sunday of Advent, C 18
4th Sunday of Advent, A 20
4th Sunday of Advent, B 21
4th Sunday of Advent, C 23

CHRISTMAS SEASON

Christmas Midnight, A, B, C 26
Christmas Day, A, B, C 27
Holy Family, A 29
Holy Family, B 31
Holy Family, C 32
Octave of Christmas, Solemnity of Mary, Mother of God, A, B, C 33
2nd Sunday after Christmas, A, B, C 34
Epiphany, A, B, C 36
Baptism of the Lord, A 37
Baptism of the Lord, B 39
Baptism of the Lord, C 40

LENTEN SEASON

1st Sunday of Lent, A 42
1st Sunday of Lent, B 43
1st Sunday of Lent, C 45
2nd Sunday of Lent, A 47
2nd Sunday of Lent, B 48
2nd Sunday of Lent, C 50
3rd Sunday of Lent, A 52
3rd Sunday of Lent, B 53
3rd Sunday of Lent, C 55
4th Sunday of Lent, A 57
4th Sunday of Lent, B 58
4th Sunday of Lent, C 60
5th Sunday of Lent, A 62
5th Sunday of Lent, B 64
5th Sunday of Lent, C 65
Passion (Palm) Sunday, A 67
Passion (Palm) Sunday, B 68
Passion (Palm) Sunday, C 69

EASTER SEASON

Easter Sunday, A, B, C 72
2nd Sunday of Easter, A 73
2nd Sunday of Easter, B 75
2nd Sunday of Easter, C 77
3rd Sunday of Easter, A 79
3rd Sunday of Easter, B 80
3rd Sunday of Easter, C 82
4th Sunday of Easter, A 84
4th Sunday of Easter, B 85
4th Sunday of Easter, C 87
5th Sunday of Easter, A 89

5th Sunday of Easter, B	**90**
5th Sunday of Easter, C	**92**
6th Sunday of Easter, A	**94**
6th Sunday of Easter, B	**95**
6th Sunday of Easter, C	**97**
Ascension, A	**99**
Ascension, B	**100**
Ascension, C	**101**
7th Sunday of Easter, A	**101**
7th Sunday of Easter, B	**103**
7th Sunday of Easter, C	**104**

PENTECOST

Pentecost, A, B, C	**108**
Trinity Sunday, A	**109**
Trinity Sunday, B	**111**
Trinity Sunday, C	**113**

SEASON OF THE YEAR

2nd Sunday of the Year, A	**116**
2nd Sunday of the Year, B	**117**
2nd Sunday of the Year, C	**119**
3rd Sunday of the Year, A	**120**
3rd Sunday of the Year, B	**122**
3rd Sunday of the Year, C	**123**
4th Sunday of the Year, A	**125**
4th Sunday of the Year, B	**127**
4th Sunday of the Year, C	**128**
5th Sunday of the Year, A	**130**
5th Sunday of the Year, B	**132**
5th Sunday of the Year, C	**133**
6th Sunday of the Year, A	**135**
6th Sunday of the Year, B	**137**
6th Sunday of the Year, C	**138**
7th Sunday of the Year, A	**140**
7th Sunday of the Year, B	**142**
7th Sunday of the Year, C	**144**
8th Sunday of the Year, A	**145**
8th Sunday of the Year, B	**147**
8th Sunday of the Year, C	**149**
9th Sunday of the Year, A	**150**
9th Sunday of the Year, B	**152**
9th Sunday of the Year, C	**154**
10th Sunday of the Year, A	**155**
10th Sunday of the Year, B	**157**
10th Sunday of the Year, C	**159**
11th Sunday of the Year, A	**160**
11th Sunday of the Year, B	**162**
11th Sunday of the Year, C	**163**
12th Sunday of the Year, A	**165**
12th Sunday of the Year, B	**167**
12th Sunday of the Year, C	**168**
13th Sunday of the Year, A	**170**
13th Sunday of the Year, B	**171**
13th Sunday of the Year, C	**173**
14th Sunday of the Year, A	**175**
14th Sunday of the Year, B	**177**
14th Sunday of the Year, C	**178**
15th Sunday of the Year, A	**180**
15th Sunday of the Year, B	**182**
15th Sunday of the Year, C	**183**
16th Sunday of the Year, A	**185**
16th Sunday of the Year, B	**187**
16th Sunday of the Year, C	**189**
17th Sunday of the Year, A	**190**
17th Sunday of the Year, B	**192**
17th Sunday of the Year, C	**194**
18th Sunday of the Year, A	**195**
18th Sunday of the Year, B	**197**
18th Sunday of the Year, C	**199**
19th Sunday of the Year, A	**200**
19th Sunday of the Year, B	**202**
19th Sunday of the Year, C	**204**
20th Sunday of the Year, A	**205**
20th Sunday of the Year, B	**207**
20th Sunday of the Year, C	**208**
21st Sunday of the Year, A	**210**
21st Sunday of the Year, B	**212**
21st Sunday of the Year, C	**213**
22nd Sunday of the Year, A	**215**
22nd Sunday of the Year, B	**217**
22nd Sunday of the Year, C	**218**

23rd Sunday of the Year, A	220	29th Sunday of the Year, B	251
23rd Sunday of the Year, B	222	29th Sunday of the Year, C	253
23rd Sunday of the Year, C	224	30th Sunday of the Year, A	255
24th Sunday of the Year, A	225	30th Sunday of the Year, B	256
24th Sunday of the Year, B	227	30th Sunday of the Year, C	258
24th Sunday of the Year, C	229	31st Sunday of the Year, A	260
25th Sunday of the Year, A	231	31st Sunday of the Year, B	261
25th Sunday of the Year, B	232	31st Sunday of the Year, C	263
25th Sunday of the Year, C	234	32nd Sunday of the Year, A	265
26th Sunday of the Year, A	236	32nd Sunday of the Year, B	266
26th Sunday of the Year, B	237	32nd Sunday of the Year, C	268
26th Sunday of the Year, C	239	33rd Sunday of the Year, A	270
27th Sunday of the Year, A	241	33rd Sunday of the Year, B	271
27th Sunday of the Year, B	242	33rd Sunday of the Year, C	273
27th Sunday of the Year, C	244	Christ the King, A	275
28th Sunday of the Year, A	245	Christ the King, B	276
28th Sunday of the Year, B	247	Christ the King, C	278
28th Sunday of the Year, C	248		
29th Sunday of the Year, A	250	Biblical Index	281

To

My Mother

". . . with all the ceremonies of joy."

INTRODUCTION

The purpose of this book is simple and prosaic. It is to provide, especially for those who preach or teach about the Sunday liturgical readings, but also for those who privately reflect upon them, a very elementary time-saving device.

The Sunday lectionary, in the form that has become familiar to us during the past seven years, confronts priest and people each week with three short passages of Scripture, one from the Gospels, one from elsewhere in the New Testament, and one from the Old Testament. Inevitably, the selections have only rarely any close literary relationship with one another, although in a number of cases they are chosen with a view to some common theological or ethical theme. All of them are, of necessity, detached from their literary and historical contexts, and most of them can in no sense be considered independent literary units.

Given the kind of lectionary that was, for good pastoral reasons, judged to be desirable, and given the kind of book that the Bible is, such limitations as these cannot possibly be avoided. But at the same time some of the difficulties they raise can scarcely be ignored. Under the circumstances, only a reader whose familiarity with the entire Bible is quite out of the ordinary could have any hope of reading or hearing these passages with more than occasional awareness of the biblical contexts from which they have been drawn.

Indeed, for an adequate appreciation of their contexts, most readers, however literate and intelligent, would have to refer to more than simply a full text of the Bible. They would have to consult commentaries and introductions that provide historical and literary information derived either from extra-biblical sources or from refined methods of analyzing the biblical text. Even with an amply annotated Bible and a very comprehensive commentary, many pages usually have to be turned and other books often have to be opened before any satisfactorily clear sense emerges of where and how a given reading fits into a distinct portion of the Bible.

At the same time, to preach, teach, or reflect on a liturgical reading without having at least a rough idea of its biblical context leaves one, and certainly ought to leave one, with the uneasy feeling that one may be interpreting in a highly subjective and potentially misleading manner.

What this book undertakes is to provide a bare minimum of background commentary necessary for basic relief from that uneasy feeling, so that one's time and thought can be devoted to discovering and developing whatever relevant message a liturgical selection may contain for a reader or congregation.

The book, therefore, is not intended in any sense to provide prefabricated homilies or pre-digested meditations. A great deal of what the book contains seems entirely inappropriate to include explicitly in a homily. It is rather the kind of background information that seems necessary to prevent homilies, lessons, or reflections on the liturgical readings from straying too far from directions of thought that are plainly indicated by the biblical context.

As a result, the use of this book is understood as altogether preliminary to the task of constructing a homily or extracting a lesson. Presumably, it would even be best to replace a book like this on one's shelf before directly undertaking that sort of task. By the same token, the book deals only occasionally and incidentally with liturgical themes as such, since themes of that kind are brought out precisely by the selection and combination of texts in the lectionary. A liturgical theme that cannot be discovered merely by an attentive reading of the lectionary can scarcely be accounted a liturgical success, and is unlikely to be a very helpful topic for instruction.

This kind of book is plainly predestined to superficiality. If the notes are to serve as time-savers, they must be brief and yet reasonably self-contained. More ample reference works and extensive bibliographies are now abundantly available, and as often as one has time to consult them a book like this should be unhesitatingly discarded. Nevertheless, experience has taught most of us who preach or lecture on the liturgical readings that the requisite leisure for such research, even on a quite modest scale, is often lacking, and that the sort of compromise this book represents can be at times a helpful resource.

The material contained in the following pages represents a revision and expansion of notes on the Sunday readings that were issued originally in serial form over the course of the past three years in the quarterly publication *Service: Resources for Pastoral Ministry*. During its first year, some of these notes were prepared by my former teacher, Matthew J. O'Connell, whose fine contributions, incorporated with trivial modifications in the present text, I acknowledge most gratefully. I owe equal appreciation to Bernadette Kenny, of Paulist Press, whose editorial skills organized, improved, and carried forward that whole project from start to finish. A number of specific suggestions that have led to notable improvements in the present version came from my wife Kathleen, of the theology faculty at Xavier University in New Orleans, who critically reviewed the entire manuscript.

James Gaffney

Loyola University
New Orleans

ADVENT SEASON

FIRST SUNDAY OF ADVENT

Cycle "A" Readings: Is. 2:1-5; Rom. 13:11-14; Mt. 24:37-44

The book of Isaiah, from which the first reading is taken, far from being the simple work of a single author, has been aptly described as a collection of collections. The verses selected for the reading are the opening passage of one of the smaller collections. The first words introduce this subsection as a distinct prophetic vision of Isaiah concerning the southern kingdom, Judah, and the capital city, Jerusalem. However, the verses which follow this introduction and constitute most of the reading also appear identically in the book of Micah, and thus seem to have circulated as a separate passage of unknown authorship. These verses express a vivid anticipation of a glorious new age in which Jerusalem is to assume a central role in the history of the non-Jewish nations, bringing them the law of God as a basis for justice and peace. The spirit of this passage is hard to associate with Isaiah's own lifetime, the period of Assyrian imperial expansion, when Jerusalem's prospects looked anything but bright. The mood of the passage more nearly suggests the period of high optimism during reconstruction after the return from the exile. But whatever its original historical setting may have been, the passage has been much quoted to express a hope that has timeless pertinence, the hope that God's salutary revelation should be extended to all mankind, and overcome the hostilities that subordinate basic peacetime pursuits to the exigencies of war. The prophecy looks for a reversal of this sorry pattern of human history, symbolized by refashioning the instruments of destruction into tools of peaceful productivity.

The second reading, from the letter to the Romans, reintroduces a theme more characteristic of Paul's earlier writings, that of the proximity of the Day of the Lord. This traditional expression designates the ancient Israelite expectation of an historical climax, when God's sovereignty, and his people's recognition of that sovereignty, would be vindicated in accordance with absolute justice. The Day of the Lord was anticipated, therefore, as judgment day. But since the judgment it was to bring would be God's judgment, it was awaited eagerly as a day of salvation by those who considered themselves loyal to God. In the New Testament, this day of judgment and salvation was identified with the second coming of Jesus Christ, and thus represented the focal point of Christian hope. In the passage that constitutes the reading, Paul develops an association of ideas by taking the word day, in Day of the Lord, in the sense of daytime, and not simply of a chronological date. Thus to look forward to the Day of the Lord can be likened to the expectation of dawn, when darkness gives way to light and sleep to waking. The time before Christ's coming is thus conceived as a nighttime, already so far advanced that the hour is at hand for waking up and getting ready. It is probable that another association of ideas leads Paul to think of night not simply as a time for sleeping, but as the time of Roman nightlife, so much satirized in the ancient world for its excesses of lechery, drunkenness, and the fighting that went with them. Thus Paul's warning of the imminent Day of the Lord serves to introduce the familiar biblical symbolism of light and darkness as representing moral and religious antitheses of good and evil.

The third reading is from the portion of the Gospel according to Matthew which describes Jesus' last words and actions in Jerusalem, ending with the account of the passion. The two chapters just before the passion narrative are filled with warning, anticipating the future. First, the destruction of the temple is foretold, to be followed by a time of international warfare and persecution of the disciples, when false prophets would appear with messianic pretensions, supporting their claims by displays of wonder-working. All this is to take place before a final cosmic cataclysm heralds the coming of the Son of Man, who will convoke all the peoples of the earth to their final destiny. These ominous predictions, whose details derive from Jewish apocalyptic tradition, constitute the background of the Gospel reading, which makes it a basis for urgent exhortation. The seriousness of the coming crisis is emphasized by likening it to the legendary crisis of the deluge, when God's judgment fell upon a heedless, helpless humanity of whom only Noah and his family proved worthy of salvation. The point of the exhortation is brought out in the concluding verses, with their warning to stay awake, and their reminder that judgment will come upon the world as suddenly and unexpectedly as a burglar comes upon his victim. Thus, the dire apocalyptic events earlier foretold are not to be relied upon as a series of warning signs that might justify postponing readiness. The life of a Christian must be one of habitual readiness.

FIRST SUNDAY OF ADVENT

Cycle "B" Readings: Is. 63:16-17, 19; 64:2-7; 1 Cor. 1:3-9; Mk. 13:33-37

Today's reading from the book of Isaiah comes from a psalm contained within that book. The psalm is thought to have been introduced either toward the end of the Israelites' Babylonian captivity or a little later, during the difficult early stages of their re-establishment in their homeland. In either case, the circumstances it reflects are painfully frustrating ones. The psalm begins, "The favors of the Lord I will recall, the glorious deeds of the

Lord because of all he has done for us." As it proceeds, however, this remembering of God's kindness to his people becomes, in one respect, a bitter memory. For what the miserable conditions of the time appear to signify is that the long history of God's kindness to Israel has come to an end, that human wickedness has so affronted divine goodness that God has, at last, left his people to their own devices. And their devices, unsupported by God, are found to be utterly futile. The basic prayer of the psalm is for God once again to guide and protect his people. But the prayer is impeded by an acute awareness that the sinfulness they have allowed to corrupt their lives alienates them from God. And worst of all, this too is something they are unable to cope with when left to their own devices. So, in effect, the psalm asks God to do everything—not only to love and care for them, but to re-form them, making them into the kind of people who can truly accept God's love and care. This is a psalm of absolute despair of man's self-sufficiency. It is also a psalm of absolute hope in the all-sufficiency of God. It is a prayer of profound and permanent validity.

The introductory verses of St. Paul's first letter to the Corinthians transpose essentially the same point of view into a context no longer of petition, but of thanksgiving. Paul's gratitude is founded on his conviction that, as far as the Christians in Corinth are concerned, God can indeed demand what he wishes of them, because he has, in fact, given them what he demands. "God's gift *to* us of what God requires *of* us" is as good a way as any of describing what theologians mean by grace. And thus, although Paul begins by saying "I continually thank my God for you"—that is, for the Corinthian Christians themselves—he completes the statement in a way that makes its uniquely biblical point of view quite unmistakable. "I continually thank my God for you because of the favor he has bestowed on you in Christ Jesus, in whom you have been richly endowed." The word here translated as "favor" is the same Greek word which is more frequently rendered as "grace." Evidently, therefore, Paul's sense of gratitude for the Corinthians is not for what the Corinthians are in themselves, but for what they are in virtue of the grace of God. It is not anything they have made of themselves that matters to Paul; it is what God has made of them that evokes his prayer of thanksgiving. Humanity on its own arouses no more enthusiasm in Paul than it did in the composer of the Isaian psalm. The psalmist's prayer is a prayer of petition precisely because the people do seem to be on their own—and the condition is unendurable. Paul's prayer is a prayer of thanksgiving because his people are *not* on their own.

The story which we read in the parable from Mark's Gospel describes a universally familiar, usually unpleasant situation. The person in charge is away; his subordinates have been assigned their tasks; he may return at any time; it would be unfortunate to get caught slacking off. What does this parable mean? Scripture scholars warn us that this is a misleading question if it implies that every feature in the story has to stand for some element in a religious message. Commonly, the story content of a parable is mainly a device for directing attention to one basic point of teaching or exhortation.

In the case of the present parable, it is unmistakable what point is emphasized. It is stated at both the beginning and the end of the story. "Be constantly on the watch" is the introductory clause. And the concluding clause is an echo of it, "Be on guard." The early Church applied the parable to the readiness or unreadiness of Christians for the parousia, that final consummation of the divine plan which is the object of Christian hope. For, from a slightly different point of view, the final consummation is also the final judgment. The hope, therefore, carries with it an implicit warning, inasmuch as what Christians are most eager to possess they must also be most careful not to forfeit. Readiness for the parousia is another way, the eschatological way, of describing the state of grace. That state of grace, the state of secure dependence upon God, must not be allowed to give way to a state of sin, the fatal and fatuous pretense to be independent of God. That dismaying sense of what it means to be left to one's own devices by God is a dim foretaste of the ultimate danger which is the loss of the ultimate hope. Therefore, "Be on guard!"

FIRST SUNDAY OF ADVENT

Cycle "C" Readings: Jer. 33:14-16; 1 Thes. 3:12—4:2; Lk. 21:25-28, 34-36

The first reading appropriately exemplifies the attitude essential to Advent by its initial words, "The days are coming, says the Lord, when I will fulfill the promise." It is highly characteristic of Old Testament literature to portray the human situation as located in time between a divine promise, gratefully remembered from the past, and a divine fulfillment, eagerly expected in the future. This is one of the features of Old Testament religion that cause it to be, to a degree unmatched by other religions, fundamentally historical in outlook, greatly preoccupied with interpreting the present by reference both to the past and to the future. In Christian liturgical practice, Advent most consistently emphasizes this biblical attitude. And for the most part, the Old Testament texts chosen for this purpose have to do with the typically Israelite concept called messianism. Although messianism is not a simple and uniform notion throughout the Bible, it refers basically to belief in a divinely promised reign or Kingdom of God, which is usually associated with the coming of a divinely appointed leader who is to establish that reign as a kind of viceroy of God. The word "messiah" means anointed, and pertains to the fact that anointing was the ritual form of consecration for kings as well as for priests. In looking to their sacred record of the past for divine assurances of such a messiah, later biblical writers frequently focused upon an oracular pronouncement of the prophet Nathan, which appears in the second book of Samuel, the first book of Chronicles, and the eighty-ninth psalm. Here we read of a promise made to David of an eternal royal posterity, by means of which God would fulfill the destiny of Israel. It is to this prophecy that the book of Jeremiah refers in the first reading of today's liturgy, which represents God as saying, in a time of renewed national hope after the exile, "I will raise up for David a just shoot; he shall do what is right and just in the land."

The second reading is taken from St. Paul's first letter to the Thessalonians, probably the oldest document in Christian literature, written about two decades after the death of Jesus. The letter falls into two fairly distinct halves, and the passage read in today's liturgy begins near the end of the first half. The conclusion of the first half is given the form of a prayer. After praying that God might bring him to the Thessalonians in person, Paul prays also that God might increase mutual love among the Thessalonians and give them a firmness of mind that will enable them to meet God "blameless and holy" at the second coming of Jesus. This second coming of Jesus, apparently anticipated as quite near at hand, becomes the principal topic of the second half of the letter. But before introducing that topic, Paul sees fit to include a passage of concrete, practical moral instruction. It is noteworthy that, in doing so, Paul does not suggest that he is proposing, much less imposing, any ethical code of his own devising. On the contrary, he reminds his readers that they have definite traditions in the moral sphere which he has already imparted to them, and which he intends now simply to emphasize by reassertion. It is noteworthy that, less than a generation after Jesus' death, Christian morals already had, like Christian faith, a definite, articulate form that was inculcated upon new converts. The conception of Christian doctrine as comprising what Roman Catholic formulations call "faith and morals" has a very ancient and authoritative precedent.

The third reading in today's liturgy, from the Gospel according to Luke, resumes the theme introduced in last week's feast of Christ the King from the prophetic vision of Daniel about the coming of the Son of Man. Since this coming represents in Jewish thought the decisive judgment of God, anticipations of it express an atmosphere of combined fear and hope—fear of the terrible finality with which injustice will be destroyed, combined with hope for the absolute triumph and establishment of justice. Since in most honest consciences there must be some awareness of being both a perpetrator and a victim of injustice, most honest minds confront such finality with mixed emotions. To the extent, however, that the final judgment of God is felt to be intimidating, it is also, and more practically, felt to be an urgent summons to do whatever one can do toward reforming one's life.

In Luke's Gospel, as in the preceding reading from Paul's first letter to the Thessalonians, it is implied that the coming of the Son of Man, here identified with Jesus, is very near at hand. It is, in fact, closely associated with realistic anticipations of the imminent destruction of Jerusalem, which in fact took place in the year 70 A.D. Accordingly, the practical import of this passage is an urgent appeal for the strenuous renewal of religious fervor and the decisive rejection of worldly distractions, in readiness for what is to come. It is a reminder that the eschatological outlook of Christianity is essentially bound up with its moral outlook. Christian behavior is, in this respect, the behavior of those who are "getting ready" for a conclusive encounter with God.

SECOND SUNDAY OF ADVENT

Cycle "A" Readings: Is. 11:1-10; Rom. 15:4-9; Mt. 3:1-12

The first reading, from the book of Isaiah, must rank among the most familiar and impressive messianic passages of the entire Old Testament. Messianism, which took a variety of different forms, may be generally identified as anticipating a future Israel coextensive with the universal domain of Israel's God, Yahweh. After the time when Israel became a monarchy, this anticipation was associated with the prospect of an ideal king. The Hebrew word messiah, meaning anointed, like its Greek equivalent christos, designated a king who would be anointed, hence personally chosen and authorized, by Yahweh himself. It was further expected that this messiah would be a descendant of the last great royal family to reign over a united Israel, the house of David. Since David's father was named Jesse, a botanical metaphor identifies David as Jesse's "stump," and the metaphor is developed in order to suggest that, although the Davidic lineage might seem to have been cut off as abruptly as a severed stump, it had not lost its fertility, and its greatest royal progeny was still to come. In view of this king's messianic destiny, the vitality and power of Yahweh himself, the Spirit of the Lord, would be present to him in a unique way. This divine influence would be manifested in certain outstanding human characteristics. Six of these traits are named in the text, but in the Greek translation, their number is increased by one more, called piety, thus providing a biblical basis for Christianity's "seven gifts of the Holy Spirit." The messiah is here described, typically, as a perfect judge, who will restore justice to a world in which wickedness seems to gain all the advantages while victims of poverty and contempt find no vindication. Finally, a later messianic feature appears here in the anticipation that a primitive idyllic harmony of nature will be finally reestablished, making the messianic time a paradise repaired.

The second reading, from the letter to the Romans, begins with what was probably a familiar saying about the permanent relevance of biblical writings. As is well-known, Jewish interpreters tended to find in scriptural passages more meaning than the obvious ones. Christian interpreters did likewise, but in the interest of distinctively Christian beliefs. Paul cites the saying here apparently to justify the messianic interpretation he had just previously given of a verse from one of the psalms. Paul's use of this verse probably had no precedent among Jewish interpreters, and in fact it distorts the basic meaning of the text by forcing a Christian significance upon it. The far-ranging application attributed to scriptural passages generally included not only messianic forecasts of the future, but also moral exhortations, and Paul's interpretation includes both. He understands a reference to the suffering of the righteous as pertaining first to Christ and then, by way of example, to Christians generally, as a basis for hope and courage. These terms are then taken up in a prayer to the God of hope and courage, asking him for the blessing of social harmony and tranquility. Only at this point does Paul finally resume the main theme into which all these digressions have been inserted. That is the theme, begun in the previous chapter, of restoring mutual respect to two groups among the Roman Christians, one of whom attached great importance to Jewish external observances, and thereby came under the scorn of the other, more liberated group.

The reading from the Gospel according to Matthew is devoted to the figure, especially prominent in Advent liturgies, of John the Baptist. The whole presentation of John is so interwoven with messianic references that John is principally conceived as the herald of the messiah, soon to make his appearance. Thus John's message is expressed in Isaian terms of preparation for the Lord's return after the exile. John himself is described in terms that bring out his resemblance to Elijah, recalling a popular Jewish belief that Elijah would reappear at the dawn of the messianic age. The notion of the messiah as the just judge, and of his arrival as the occasion of judgment, underlies the urgency of John's personal mission. That is a mission of exhorting to repentance, understood as radical moral reform, so as to be ready for the judgment to come. The response of the general populace to this reform movement is made an occasion for criticizing the Jewish leadership, represented by its extreme opposite parties, the Pharisees and Sadducees. John is represented as using a ceremonial washing, called baptism, to symbolize repentance. This symbolic baptism, however, is contrasted with a coming baptism that will be carried out "with the Holy Spirit and fire." Fire is a traditional symbol of judgment, and it is here joined to another symbol of judgment, the harvest, when the good crops are preserved and the useless residue is burnt. The reference to the Holy Spirit anticipates the scene of Jesus' own baptism.

SECOND SUNDAY OF ADVENT

Cycle "B" Readings: Is. 40:1-5, 9-11; 2 Pet. 3:8-14; Mk. 1:1-8

The first reading of today's liturgy comprises the opening words of what is often called "The Book of Israel's Consolation." It is a part of the book of Isaiah which was composed at a time when the Israelites who had been deported to Babylon a generation earlier conceived for the first time a realistic hope that their exile would soon come to an end. Although the immediate basis for this hope was political, namely the threat posed to Babylon by Persian imperialism, such factors were, of course, interpreted by the prophets as part of a divine providential design. In the verses of Isaiah we hear the voice of God summoning the prophet to confirm his people's hope and to declare for them its religious significance. After the opening injunction to "give comfort to my people," the exile is interpreted as a heavy penalty which God imposed on the people for their sins and which they have now paid in full. The whole tone of the passage then takes up a triumphant motif. As the exile was a lesson which God taught to Israel, so the restoration will be a lesson he teaches the rest of the world, a demonstration of the glory of Israel's God, "and all mankind shall see it together." The prophet is called upon to interpret this universal lesson and instructed in the meaning of it. He is to declare the utter contrast which exists between ephemeral human achievements and the unshakable permanence of God's guarantees. Human enterprises rise and fall, not as humanity arranges but as God decides. And beneath all the vicissitudes of human history the only truly constant thing is what God determines, promises, and irresistibly accomplishes, at what he alone knows to be the proper time.

In the second letter of Peter, essentially the same religious conviction is expressed in a quite different context. Israel in Babylon was longing, waiting, and hoping for their return to the land God had given them. In the second century of the Christian era, when the second letter of Peter seems to have been written, Christians were likewise longing, waiting and hoping. The object of their hope was also the fulfillment of God's promise. But what they looked forward to specifically was, of course, the return of their Lord, when the reign of God would be fully and finally established among human beings. From the first, Jesus' departure from visible presence to his people was understood to be merely an interlude before he should come again and bring his work of salvation to completion. The first generation of Christians expected this interlude to be a very short one, as is clear in the early letters of Paul. They expected it to be shorter even than their own natural lives. But as time wore on, this interpretation of the interlude had to be modified if the whole object of Christian hope was not to be abandoned. The passage we have just read interprets the interlude in a new way by considering it from the point of view not of brief human lifetimes but of the vast temporal horizons of God himself. What to God is mere interlude may, by human standards, seem very protracted. But human standards are, in this matter, inappropriate standards. "In the Lord's eyes, one day is as a thousand years and a thousand years are as a day." Moreover, if God does indeed prolong the time before he brings human history to its unalterable climax, might we not suspect that the explanation is to be sought not in divine procrastination but rather in divine mercy? Is it not probable that God is giving humankind time to prepare for the coming crisis by sanctifying their lives? The final outcome is not in question. The point is not that we must be patient with God, but that God is being patient with us, because "he wants none to perish but all to come to repentance." From that point of view, the extended interlude does not imply frustration of humanity's hope, but encouragement for it.

Hope is the forward-looking component of a Christian life, and Advent is the forward-looking season of a Christian calendar. Accordingly, in today's Advent liturgy, hope, the forward-looking virtue, completely dominates every one of the readings. In the first, we saw Israel in exile looking forward to repatriation. In the second, we saw Christianity, as it emerged from infancy, looking forward to the parousia. And in the third, we see Judaism looking forward to its long-awaited Messiah. Judaism is here represented by the latest of its prophets, John the Baptist, and the Messiah whose coming John announces is, of course, Jesus of Nazareth. The announcement itself is a kind of medley of Old Testament verses, from Exodus, Malachi, and Isaiah, which originally pertained to the time of the exodus from Egypt, the time of the exile in Babylon, and the time of the return to Palestine. The very feasibility of combining verses from such a variety of historical contexts serves to remind us of how prevalent is the theme of hope throughout the entire Bible. John is here presented as a prophet sent by God to confirm the messianic expectation of the Jews and urge them to prepare themselves for its imminent realization. The preparation called for is basically a moral housecleaning. It is that thoroughgoing reform of life and attitude called in Greek *metanoia*, usually translated as repentance. To symbolize this process of ethical cleansing John uses the most appropriate of signs—baptism, a public washing. But we are reminded that this is only a prelude to another baptism, yet to come, when human beings will be washed in the very life-stream of divine grace, in the living water of the Spirit of God.

SECOND SUNDAY OF ADVENT

Cycle "C" Readings: Bar. 5:1-9; Phil. 1:4-6, 8-11; Lk. 3:1-6

The book of Baruch, from which the first reading is taken, is one of several works included in the Greek but not in the Hebrew Bible, and consequently included in Roman Catholic but not in Protestant versions of the Old Testament. Although Baruch was historically a companion of the prophet Jeremiah in the seventh century B.C., this book, which fictionally claims his authorship, comes from a period fully five centuries later and is the composite work of more than one writer. The verses read in today's liturgy are part of a concluding poem, which begins with the city of Jerusalem personified as speaking to its people still in exile. They are first reminded of their sins, for which the exile is a deserved punishment. They are then encouraged to believe that God intends to rescue them from their captors and restore them to the city to which they belong. In the final verses, which conclude the book and constitute the liturgical reading, the poet himself responds by addressing Jerusalem in words of reassurance. In anticipation of the longed-for deliverance, the city itself has been summoned to "take heart" and "look eastward and see the joy that is coming." Jerusalem is thus represented as one whose long period of mourning is at an end. Its garb of mourning is to be put off and replaced with the trappings of majesty. As the forsaken city, re-established in dignity and restored to gladness, gazes from its hilltop vantage, it sees the multitudes of its children, now fearless and joyous, returning home, so guided and protected by God that nature itself is imagined to assist their journey by transforming its rough, sun-drenched terrain into a level, tree-shaded highway.

The second reading is taken from the letter of Paul to the Philippians. Although there remain unsolved problems about where and when this letter was written, it contains repeated indications that Paul was in prison when he wrote it and by no means certain that imprisonment would not end with his death. The selection comprises all but one verse of that portion of the letter which immediately follows the salutation, and takes the form of an opening prayer. The prayer has two parts, the first of which is an expression of thanks to God for the part played by the Philippians in "the work of the Gospel." It is not altogether clear whether this refers to evangelization actually undertaken by the Christians of Philippi, or to support they gave Paul's own missionary endeavors, such as the gift referred to later in the same letter. It is typical of Paul's theology of grace that he attributes the good work of the Philippians not to their initiative but to God's. And as it is divinely initiated, Paul looks forward to the work's being brought to completion by the "day of Christ," that is, the day of Christ's second and final coming, which Paul probably did not suppose to be very far off from the time when he wrote his letter. This eschatological perspective is maintained in the second part of the prayer, which is a petition for the Philippians' continued spiritual growth. It is again typical of Paul's theology that he identifies the principle of spiritual development with love, and at the same time considers growth in love to entail a progressive deepening of religious awareness, the climax of which is called "the gift of true discrimination." Here we have an early Christian allusion to that "spiritual discernment" or "discernment of spirits" which was to play a permanently major part in Christian spirituality. For Paul, the deepening of Christian love and the sharpening of Christian vision go hand in hand. They are not alternative spiritualities, but correlative aspects of a developing spiritual life.

The third reading is from the Gospel according to Luke, who, like the other evangelists, opens his narration of Jesus' public ministry with an account of the preliminary mission of John the Baptist. Consistent with the historian's style that characterizes the third Gospel and Acts of the Apostles, Luke begins by giving a definite date for the beginning of the Baptist's ministry. He describes that ministry as one of proclaiming a baptism, that is, a ritual of washing or immersion already employed by certain Jewish sects, intended to signify repentance and to seek a forgiveness of sins. In order to relate this ministry to his conception of John as the forerunner of Jesus, Luke applies to John's preaching a passage from the prophecy of Isaiah, which is employed in a similar sense by all four evangelists. In its original context, it was a poem of consolation, lyrically envisioning Israel's repatriation after the exile, and it closely resembles the passage from Baruch cited in the first reading of today's liturgy. By the time of Jesus, these and other such passages had been invested with a more extensive messianic meaning of the final restoration to fellowship with God of a people who had been alienated from God by their sinfulness. Whereas the post-exilic prophets thought in terms of an exiled people's coming home to God as a return to their forsaken city of Jerusalem, their words are applied by New Testament writers to that transcendental coming home of all humankind to God made possible by Jesus Christ.

THIRD SUNDAY OF ADVENT

Cycle "A" Readings: Is. 35:1-6, 10; Jas. 5:7-10; Mt. 11:2-11

The verses from the book of Isaiah that constitute the first reading seem to have been displaced from the latter portion of that book, which dates from a time near the end of the exile, long after the lifetime of the prophet Isaiah. The passage's exuberantly hopeful tone suggests that circumstances had already inspired confidence that the exile was soon to end. The passage itself is an idealized, lyrical anticipation of the Israelites' long-awaited return to their homeland and its holy city, Jerusalem. The expectation of this all but miraculous outcome causes the whole description of the return to be expressed in a symbolism of miracle. Thus the long hard southward trek over great expanses of largely barren country is idealized into a triumphal procession through a land of terrestrial paradise. The very desert is imagined bursting into bloom at this joyous event which is the Lord's triumph. The exiles, weakened by their ordeal and disheartened by its long continuance, are conceived as suddenly restored to vigor and confidence. The arid wasteland is imagined flowing with life-giving water. The approach of the returning Israelites to Jerusalem or Mount Zion is described in terms suggestive of a devout pilgrimage, singing psalms as it draws near its sacred destination. The final verse anticipates the happiness of this momentous homecoming, and anticipates that its joy will be permanent. History was, of course, to contradict this expectation, and in after-years these verses tended to be applied in a more general way to the undying hope of divine salvation. In this sense, they were taken up by Christians as prophecies which found their fulfillment not in the political reestablishment of Israel, but in the mission of Jesus Christ.

The section from the letter of James which constitutes the second reading is one of many New Testament passages that deal with the interim period between the resurrection of Jesus Christ and his expected second coming, which was to bring the final judgment of God and the completion of the plan of redemption. It is clear that during the time when the New Testament was composed, it was widely supposed by Christians that this interval was to be quite brief, and even completed within the contemporary generation. As the years lengthened, this supposition became increasingly untenable, and the hope of Christians was threatened with perplexity and doubt. It is to this growing diffidence on the part of Christians that the passage is directed, and its basic message is that of the opening verse, "Be patient, my brothers, until the coming of the Lord." The final judgment is frequently represented by imagery of harvest time, and on the basis of that familiar imagery the readers of this letter are exhorted to emulate the patience of a farmer, whose crop has been sown but cannot be expected to appear until the proper time. The Palestinian rainy season is concentrated in two periods, that of the winter rains in October and November, and that of the spring rains in March and April. Until these rains occur, the farmer must wait patiently, however anxiously, for the result. Christians must do likewise, without belying their hope by discontented quarreling or succumbing to discouragement. Instead they must emulate the steadfast endurance of Job and the prophets.

In the Gospel according to Matthew, from which the final reading is taken, the arrest of John the Baptist is reported at the very beginning of Jesus' ministry, just after his temptation in the desert. John is not mentioned again until the present passage, which comes after a number of Jesus' discourses and miracles have been reported. John is represented as having been kept informed of these activities of Jesus, which prompted him to inquire at this point about Jesus' messianic claims. Jesus' reply is constructed out of familiar phrases from the book of Isaiah, including some which appear in the first reading. The collective import of these phrases depicts the Messiah, and Jesus himself, as an agent of compassion, bringing healing to the afflicted and good tidings of salvation to the poor. Some interpreters consider that John's inquiry was sceptical, deriving from a conviction that the Messiah should appear principally as a judge. In that case, Jesus' words would be intended to correct John's misapprehension about the messianic mission. The verses that follow, which give John the highest praise as a human being, and at the same time represent him as inferior to the least in the kingdom of heaven, may find explanation along the same lines. Thus John's greatness would be qualified by the fact that his outlook was limited by that very moral sense which he possessed in a high degree, but which failed to comprehend that the kingdom of God was based not on human conscientiousness, but on the saving power of God. Thus the contrast between John and Jesus would be brought into line with the contrast of Law and Gospel—a plausible but far from certain interpretation of verses that remain quite enigmatic.

THIRD SUNDAY OF ADVENT

Cycle "B" Readings: Is. 61:1-2, 10-11; 1 Thes. 5:16-24; Jn. 1:6-8, 19-28

The first reading joins together the opening and concluding verses of a poem contained in the book of Isaiah. The historical situation in which this poem took shape is strongly suggested by some of the intervening verses, such as, "They shall rebuild the ancient ruins, the former wastes they shall raise up, and restore the ruined cities." Reconstruction plans of this kind are very much in the spirit of that final period of Israel's exile in Babylon when the prospect of their restoration to their beloved homeland had become virtually certain. However others might view this development, for the Israelites it meant that God was satisfied that they had learned their bitter lesson, and that in his kindness and fidelity to ancient promises, he was calling them to the land he had destined for them. Accordingly, in the first part of the reading, we hear the prophet describing his mission as one of consoling, healing, and liberating a dejected, enfeebled, and enslaved people. The latter part of the reading expresses the people's intense reaction to God's message. It is a reaction of overwhelming gladness. The whole tone of these verses is filled with an atmosphere of celebration, accentuated by imagery of honor, fulfillment, and fertility. What the verses express is a kind of religious boast—a boast, inasmuch as the people delight in summoning all the world's attention to the good fortune which is theirs, but a religious boast, inasmuch as good fortune is ascribed wholly to God and not at all to merits of their own.

The second reading comprises the concluding passages of what appears to be the oldest document in all of Christian literature, Paul's first letter to the Thessalonians. Written probably no more than two decades after the crucifixion of Jesus, this letter expresses a belief generally shared during Christianity's first years that Jesus' promise to return and complete his work of salvation would be literally fulfilled in the very near future. "Be alert" and "Don't be caught napping" are refrains typical of this mood. The designation, probably borrowed from Jewish sources, of Christians as the children of light becomes in this context easily associated with the idea of daytime wakefulness as contrasted with nocturnal somnolence or stupor, for night is sleeping time for some people and drinking time for others, and in either case a time of minimal alertness. Having introduced the familiar motif in this rather homely fashion, Paul takes it as a point of departure for ending his letter, as he commonly does, with a series of practical moral injunctions. The theme common to them all is expressed by his opening phrase, which calls upon the Thessalonians to "upbuild one another." Alert, enlightened Christian living, in the proximate expectation of the parousia, is thus conceived in terms of responsibility on the part of each member of the community for every other member of the community. Alertness for the coming of Christ means, therefore, alertness for his coming not only to oneself, individually, but to the entire Christian community, and to each member of it in the particular circumstances in which people find themselves. What Christian hope demands is Christian charity.

The reading from John's Gospel puts together two passages dealing with the role of John the Baptist. The first is inserted within that hymn, usually called the prologue, with which John's Gospel so impressively opens. In the hymn, the incarnation, the Word's becoming flesh, is symbolically described as a coming of light into darkness. The inserted passage adopts the same symbolism in order to assert that John the Baptist was not himself the light, but only a witness to the real light. The point, of course, is to emphasize the subordination of John's mission to that of Jesus. This same idea is reaffirmed in the second passage within a narrative context. The underlying question is raised in traditional Jewish terms, by having Jewish religious leaders ask John directly if he is the Messiah, and, if not, if he is Elijah returned to earth, or a legendary figure likened to Moses, called simply "the Prophet." John's negative response is followed by a positive statement, expressed in words which originally, in the book of Isaiah, pertained to the Jews' preparation to return from their exile in Babylon. Here the same words are applied to preparation for the imminent coming of the Messiah. In answer to a final question, John asserts that the baptism he administers is nothing more than a symbolic washing, whereas one who far outranks John is already at hand, though not yet recognized. The purpose of these passages is clearly to emphasize the subordination of John's mission to that of Jesus. This insistence was presumably occasioned by a tendency on the part of some to regard John and Jesus as in some sense rivals. These passages firmly establish John's role as that of a forerunner to Jesus. It is in this role that John has special appropriateness to Advent, as one who heralds the coming of Jesus the Messiah.

THIRD SUNDAY OF ADVENT

Cycle "C" Readings: Zeph. 3:14-18; Phil. 4:4-7; Lk. 3:10-18

The book of Zephaniah as we now have it represents a later editorial compilation of material deriving from the third quarter of the seventh century B.C. Zephaniah lived in the reign of Josiah, a king who received from Old Testament writers high praise as a religious reformer. Zephaniah's prophecies, however, antedate the reform, and are full of denunciations directed against the superstitious and paganizing corruptions which were at that time prevalent and increasing. It is false worship rather than social vice that Zephaniah chiefly deplores, and he anticipates a day of doom when God will wreak terrible vengeance on his people. In the verses which immediately precede those read in today's first liturgical selection, Zephaniah foretells this fateful day for Jerusalem. What he anticipates, however, is not the indiscriminate infliction of punishment, but a process of purgation. He proclaims a message in which God tells the sinful city, not that he will ruthlessly destroy its whole population, but: "I will rid you of your proud and arrogant citizens" and at the same time "will leave in you a people afflicted and poor." It is to this humble remnant who survive the inexorable divine purge that today's reading refers in its opening verse, which introduces a message of hope and joy that is the concluding message of the book of Zephaniah. "The survivors in Israel shall find refuge in the name of the Lord." These survivors, who will be honest, unoffending people, can look forward to a future of peace and security, rejoicing in the knowledge that their corrupt element shall at last be eliminated, with the result that God himself can reign henceforth as the benevolent sovereign of his loyal subjects. In this and other Old Testament passages which envision the ultimate happiness of a faithful remnant of God-fearing sufferers, we find the background of that powerful New Testament theme most eloquently expressed in the Beatitudes.

The second liturgical reading, from Paul's letter to the Philippians, comes from a curiously parenthetical passage whose place in the original composition has been much debated by scholars. It begins with an appeal for two women to end their quarreling, and for some unnamed co-worker to help them patch up their differences. About these ladies we know only their names, Evodia and Syntyche (translatable respectively, and somewhat ironically, as "Good Progress" and "Joint Fortune"), and that formerly they had shared Paul's "struggles in the cause of the Gospel." Paul is evidently much distressed by the present mutual animosity of two old friends, and it is probably this that sets the tone for the following verses which comprise today's reading. Paul wishes joy to the Philippians, and he exhorts them to pray and exhibit a disposition of mind expressed by a Greek word for which, most unfortunately, we have no precise English equivalent. This virtue, *epieikeia*, possessed by truly great souls, includes such qualities as graciousness and forbearance. It characterizes the sort of person who is not such a stickler for his rights, however genuine, that he will insist upon them even at the cost of bitterness, hostility, and unavailing strife. The idea may be somewhat clarified by recalling that Greek philosophers aptly characterized the vice that is opposed to this virtue as the habit of being "sourly just." Given this attitude for which Paul appeals, and the prayer to which he exhorts, the result ought surely to be as he predicted: "God's own peace, which is beyond all understanding, will stand guard over your hearts and minds, in Christ Jesus." Since it was the wording of this passage that caused this Sunday of Advent to be distinguished as "Gaudete" or "Be Joyful" Sunday, it is a good occasion for recalling that Paul's wishes for joy accompanied wise and sober counsel concerning the moral prequisites for any lasting joy in human society.

John the Baptist, who figures prominently in Advent liturgies in his role of prophetic announcer of Christ's coming, is identified with a ministry of repentance. There is a recurrent human tendency to water down the meaning of repentance to a mere "feeling sorry" about one's past misdeeds. This trivial sentiment of deploring past delinquencies is morally valueless and receives no attention whatever from New Testament writers, for whom repentance means always a positive improvement of moral attitude manifested in a positive improvement of moral behavior. This is brought out admirably in today's reading from the Gospel according to Luke, which offers a few samples of the way John the Baptist bluntly responded to questions about what he meant by repentance. Of the well-dressed and well-fed, he demands that they share what they have with the ill-dressed and ill-fed. Of the notoriously fraudulent tax collectors he demands scrupulously fair accounting. Of the soldiers, Rome's military police force, he demands that they put an end to their brutality and graft. Such, plainly and practically, is the sort of thing preparing for the coming of Christ means. And the meaning of John's concluding metaphor about the harvesting of the wheat and the burning of the chaff is, quite simply, "Do it or else!"

FOURTH SUNDAY OF ADVENT

Cycle "A" Readings: Is. 7:10-14; Rom. 1:1-7; Mt. 1:18-24

The historical context of the first reading, from the book of Isaiah, is a political crisis in the history of Judah, during the time, in the eighth century, when that southern kingdom was ruled by Ahaz. The great problem of his reign was the formation of an alliance between Syria and the northern kingdom, Israel, to resist the imperial expansion of Assyria. This Syro-Israelite alliance attacked Judah, in the hope of replacing its king with a puppet ruler who would cooperate in the anti-Assyrian effort. In order to save his own position, Ahaz saw no recourse but to ally himself with Assyria. The great opponent of this plan was the prophet Isaiah, who appears to have been convinced that the Syro-Israelite alliance was doomed to failure in any case. Isaiah's advice, therefore, was that Ahaz should remain neutral. This advice was not, however, based on political foresight alone, but also on the religious conviction that the Lord was sovereign over the events of history, and that he would control those events for the ultimate benefit of his people. Ahaz rejected the prophet's advice, but Isaiah persisted in appealing for a policy based on faith in God, which called for a patient endurance of the political menace of the time, confident that events would have a providential outcome best for God's people. In order to intensify his prophetic message, Isaiah invited the king to ask for any sign he chose, as a symbolic confirmation that the message was divinely inspired. When Ahaz rejected this proposal, Isaiah proclaimed that there would be a sign in any case. It would consist in the fact that a young woman, already pregnant, would bear a son, to be designated "Immanuel," that is, "God with us," and that before this child had reached the age of discretion Judah would be in a state of grave austerity, but the Syro-Israelite alliance would be destroyed. Isaiah's prediction is of very imminent developments, and the concrete reference is rather to a young woman already pregnant than to a future "virgin" who would conceive and bear a son. The latter interpretation, however, encouraged by the Greek rendering of the Hebrew text, came to be adopted later in the biblical period and incorporated within messianic tradition, which identified the child Immanuel with a divinely-sent leader descended from David.

The second reading, which is the opening passage of the letter to the Romans, identifies the author as Paul, specially chosen by God to proclaim the gospel of Jesus Christ. Paul proceeds at once to remind his readers that this gospel is no innovation but was anticipated by the prophetic tradition of Israel. The reference is to the messianic expectations based on the Old Testament, and specifically associated with the descendant of David who would restore divine rule to his people. Paul identifies the Davidic Messiah as Jesus Christ, whom he characterizes as having been made "Son of God in power" in virtue of his resurrection from the dead. Thus, for Paul, the gospel, or good news, of Jesus Christ, is precisely the good news that messianic prophecy had anticipated and taught the Jews to pin their hopes upon. Paul's task, however, as he goes on to say, is not to convince the Jews that their good news was a reality, but rather to teach the Gentiles that the Jews' good news was theirs as well, and bring them to place their faith in the same person on whom the prophets had set their hope, Jesus Christ.

In the gospel according to Matthew, from which the third reading is taken, the birth of Jesus Christ is set within a narrative context designed to emphasize one of the principal themes of that gospel, the messianic identity of Jesus Christ. This narrative is immediately preceded by the genealogy with which this gospel begins, and in which the descendants of David are traced to "Joseph the husband of Mary" of whom "Jesus who is called the Messiah was born." Since lineage was traced through paternity, Jesus was thus of the Davidic line, even though, as the following narrative indicates, Joseph was not Jesus' natural parent, but his legal father. Whereas the genealogy is intended to confirm that Jesus was, as Jews expected the Messiah to be, a "son of David," the narrative of his birth expresses the Christian conviction that Jesus was Son of God. Joseph's perplexity at finding Mary already pregnant is related to his being "an upright man," that is, a man obedient to that Mosaic law which stigmatized union with an adulteress, and to his being also a compassionate man, unwilling to subject the woman to legal severities. The most conscientious course open to him appeared to be a private divorce, until his suspicions were dispelled by divine revelation. The miraculous birth is further linked with messianism, by its association with the Isaian text cited in the first reading. This text, for the Greek-reading evangelist, predicted precisely a virgin birth.

FOURTH SUNDAY OF ADVENT

Cycle "B" Readings: 2 Sam. 7:1-5, 8-11, 16; Rom. 16:25-27; Lk. 1:26-38

The first reading, taken from the second book of Samuel, refers to the time when, after all sorts of conflicts and predicaments, David was at last firmly established as king over Israel and Judah. The passage describes David as at last residing comfortably in his house in Jerusalem and, in this situation, suddenly recalling the ark of the covenant. This sacred object had, of course accompanied the people during their hard struggle for domination of the "promised land," and it represented for them that saving presence of God which assured their ultimate success. With that success now achieved, David recalls with embarrassed chagrin that, although he is royally housed, the ark itself is merely stored in a tent. The king confides to the prophet Nathan his concern about the ark and, apparently, his intention of constructing a temple to contain it in a more fitting manner. Nathan, however, is directed by God to communicate to David the essential pointlessness of such an enterprise. The idea of there being no good reason why David should build a house for God is then used to introduce a more important revelation, namely, that God will establish a house for David. The house of David was to be everlasting. Although the political continuity of kings directly descended from David was, of course, subsequently interrupted, the idea expressed in this divine promise took root in the messianic tradition which looked forward to a "son" of David who would preside over the definitive reign of God.

The second reading, a very brief one, is the conclusion of Paul's letter to the Romans. The passage is a doxology, a prayer of exalted praise or glorification of God. The fact that a passage of this nature does not correspond with Paul's habitual way of ending his other letters, together with certain peculiarities of style, strongly suggests that these verses were added to Paul's work by a later copyist. Whatever its source, the passage expresses an idea which is not featured in Romans, but which is prominent in certain later New Testament writings. It is the idea of a great "mystery" or hidden plan of God which was unfolded during the course of "salvation history" and expressed by the prophets, but which could not really be understood until it reached its climactic point with the coming of Jesus Christ. Implied in this concept is the conviction of the early Church that Christians, rather than Jews, were in a position rightly to interpret the Old Testament prophecies, because the ultimate meaning of these prophecies was what Christian faith alone apprehended. Consequently a whole new approach to reading the Old Testament developed among Christians and is frequently reflected in the New Testament. The New Testament revelation is the key to the Old Testament's deepest meaning, because the New Testament revelation is precisely the unveiling of the "mystery," the hidden plan of the God of salvation history. The understanding of the first reading, with its reference to an everlasting Davidic kingship, as pointing to "Jesus, Son of David" is an application of this kind of theology.

The third reading, from the beginning of Luke's Gospel, is an outstanding illustration of this Christian way of interpreting the Old Testament, and telling the story of Jesus, so as to emphasize the continuity between them and the light shed on Old Testament prophecy by Christian belief. The passage is the story of the annunciation. It first introduces Mary and Joseph, significantly pointing out that the latter, Mary's legal husband and therefore legal father of her offspring, was "of the house of David." Mary is then informed by the angel that she is to be mother of the "Son of the Most High," that is, the Messiah. And it is immediately added that "the Lord God will give him the throne of David his father. He will rule over the house of Jacob forever and his reign will be without end." These verses are clearly reminiscent of the ones in the first reading, from the second book of Samuel, promising an everlasting dynasty to David, and they vividly exemplify the way in which Christians reinterpreted the Old Testament in the light of their own New Testament faith. The latter portion of the annunciation narrative introduces the theme of the virgin birth of Jesus. Theologically, this theme serves to intensify the meaning of the messianic title "Son of the Most High" as applied to Jesus. Born of the Virgin Mary by the power of the Spirit of God, without human fatherhood, Jesus is considered to be the "Son of God" in a far more profound and literal sense than such messianic designations suggested among the Jews. Verses such as these mark a clear transition from Jewish hope for a Messiah to Christian belief in an incarnation.

FOURTH SUNDAY OF ADVENT

Cycle "C" Readings: Mic. 5:1-4; Heb. 10:5-10; Lk. 1:39-45

The first reading in today's liturgy is taken from the book of Micah, one of the so-called "minor prophets," a contemporary of Isaiah, whose preaching his own in most respects closely resembles. Like Isaiah, Micah vehemently denounced the social injustice that pervaded society in his native Judah. Anticipating divine vengeance in terms of current developments in international politics. Micah also foretold the destruction of Jerusalem, which was not in fact accomplished until more than a century later. (The verses concerning Assyria are believed by some scholars to have been inserted after the event.) Micah strongly echoed Isaiah in condemning the futility and impiety of external rituals, which seemed like hypocritical offerings to God in substitution for what God actually demanded—kindness and justice toward suffering humanity. Basic to the structure of Micah's book is an alternating pattern of threats and promises, denunciations and reassurances, the latter addressed to a faithful remnant whose fidelity to God would enable them to survive the coming vengeance. The liturgical selection comes from the more positive and encouraging side of Micah's message. The passage is messianic in character, and draws upon a venerable tradition which looked forward to the coming of a descendant of David who would exercise godly rule over a kingdom restored to righteousness and re-established in peace. It is his conception of the messiah as a new David which accounts for the prophet's reference to Bethlehem, David's birthplace, as the place of the messiah's origin. This detail, and the reference shortly after it to an interval of divine abandonment only "until she who is to give birth has borne," naturally caught the attention of Christian writers as anticipating the circumstances of Jesus' infancy. Micah's characterization of the messiah by the attribute of peace is likewise a theme that is prominent in New Testament messianic characterizations of Jesus.

The second liturgical reading is taken from the letter to the Hebrews which, here as elsewhere, pursues a favorite theme in a way that involves rather curious applications of Old Testament texts. In general, the author's intention is to demonstrate the validity of a thesis stated a few verses previous to the passage read in today's liturgy, namely that "the Law had only a shadow of the good things to come, and no real image of them." In keeping with this underlying conviction one finds that, throughout the entire document, various aspects of the Christian Gospel are compared with corresponding aspects of Old Testament religion in such a way as to emphasize the perfection and finality of the former in contrast to the inadequacy and impermanence of the latter. In the present passage, this line of argument is pursued in connection with the sacrificial worship that played a major part in the religious life of Judaism. It was often emphasized by the Old Testament prophets themselves that worship of this kind was totally worthless if it was unaccompanied by a moral integrity based on obedience to God's commandments. This criticism of a mere ritualism divorced from ethical responsibility finds expression in the fortieth psalm, where the psalmist addresses God with the words "Sacrifice and offering you did not desire" and then states implicitly what God does desire by his own claim of responding to that desire: "I have come to do your will, O God." The author of the letter to the Hebrews applies these words of the psalmist to Jesus Christ, thereby representing him as asserting the unacceptability to God of Jewish ritual sacrifices, and, the acceptability to God of his own offering of obedience. The writer's rather tendentious biblical argument thus enables him to conclude, concerning Jesus, that "he takes away the first covenant and establishes the second."

The third reading, from the Gospel according to Luke, is the familiar account of Mary's visit, immediately after the annunciation, to Elizabeth, identified simply as a relation and popularly assumed to be Mary's cousin. It is a conspicuous feature of Luke's early chapters that he interweaves the stories of the infancies of Jesus and John the Baptist by alternating episodes dealing with each of them. His purpose in this is to emphasize the connectedness of Jesus' and John's careers from the very start, probably in response to doubts among early Christians as to whether they were collaborators or competitors. Luke stresses the temporal priority of John's mission, and its essential subordination to the mission of Jesus, as integral components of the divine plan. This whole scheme is implied in the interview between the newly pregnant Mary, and Elizabeth, already six months pregnant, at which Elizabeth, under the influence of the Holy Spirit, articulates the symbolic reaction felt within her womb by greeting Mary as "the mother of my Lord."

CHRISTMAS SEASON

CHRISTMAS MASS AT MIDNIGHT

Cycles "A", "B", and "C" Readings: Is. 9:1-6; Tit. 2:11-14; Lk. 2:1-14

The first reading, from the book of Isaiah, is a poem celebrating the birth of a royal prince whose coming represents for his people both relief from present danger and suffering and the establishment of an ideal reign. The prince is thus represented as the Messiah. This title, whose literal meaning is anointed, was originally applied to kings and priests, but came to refer in a special sense to a future leader who would be sent by God as the savior of his people. In the eighth century, the popular conception of the Messiah was greatly influenced by the rise and spread of the Assyrian empire. On the one hand, the relentless progress of Assyrian imperialism was seen as a threat to the very existence of Israel, and the idea of a royal savior was identified with the acute need for a king who could resist this menace. It is probable that the Assyrian example of a potentially world-wide domain also served to foster an enlarged conception of the Messiah as one whose rule, representing the dominion of Israel's God, would be all-encompassing. Thus political circumstances made both the need for a Messiah more acute and the idea of a Messiah more expansive. The passage selected for the reading comes from this period, and it begins by envisaging an end to the prevailing national anxiety. This is expressed figuratively as the dispelling of darkness by the coming of a brilliant light. The atmosphere of the event is likened to the public joy of harvest time or of the sharing of spoils after a victory. The event's primary meaning is expressed in imagery implying the total destruction of a cruel oppressor. The famous concluding verses complete the picture by representing the messianic king as an ideal ruler, united with God, exercising a far-reaching dominion characterized by peace and founded upon justice, destined to endure forever. The final verse shows this idyllic picture to represent a still-future state, which the Lord of hosts is expected to bring about.

The second reading is from the letter to Titus, one of three short New Testament works that have come to be called the Pastoral Letters. This phrase expresses their common orientation, as directed to persons holding pastoral positions in local Christian churches. The traditional assumption that St. Paul wrote this material is no longer generally held by scholars, although Pauline influence is clearly present, and some think that portions of Paul's own writings are included. The characteristic tone of this literature is one of exhortation, commending the virtues appropriate for church leadership, and especially emphasizing firm orthodoxy in belief and doctrine. The passage cited in the reading has an unusually doctrinal character, but here too the doctrinal statements are made the basis of exhortation. Some of the language has a distinctly liturgical flavor, and may be borrowed from texts used in public worship. The passage begins by recalling the saving grace which has come to all mankind through Jesus Christ. It then reminds the reader that a proper response to this grace of salvation is the adoption of a virtuous manner of life "in this age." This age is conceived as an interim period, during which Christians live in a spirit of hope. The object of this hope is the "appearing of the glory of the great God and of our savior Christ Jesus" in which the work of salvation will have its ultimate completion. Meanwhile, the Christian is to express his freedom from wickedness, gained for him by Christ's sacrifice, by a life characteristic of one who is "eager to do what is right."

Most of the nativity story as narrated by the Gospel according to Luke constitutes the third reading. Typically Lucan is the dating of this event by use of historical references. The prophetic tradition of a messianic birth in the city of David, Bethlehem, is skillfully blended with secular history by means of the imperial census. Luke's account of why the newborn Jesus was placed in a manger anticipates his later emphasis on Jesus' homelessness, and his stress on an ideal of similar austerity for his disciples. It is in Luke's spirit that the first worshipers mentioned should be shepherds, whose nomadic occupation brought them into disrepute among Jews who insisted on a regularity of religious observance possible only in a more settled way of life. Luke's typical interest in Mary is exemplified by his reference to her continued pondering of the events surrounding Jesus' birth. The universal import of the occasion is expressed in the words spoken by the angels, the messengers of God himself, to the shepherds. The birth of the long-awaited Messiah is here proclaimed as joyous good news for all the people. The appropriate response is also exemplified by the angels in their hymn, which combines praise of God and blessings of peace for those whom God has favored. The whole passage is an extraordinary combination of literary skill and theological ingenuity, which works prophecy, history, and symbolism together into an exquisitely beautiful and richly meaningful narrative.

CHRISTMAS MASS DURING THE DAY

Cycles "A", "B", and "C" Readings: Is. 52:7-10; Heb. 1:1-6; Jn. 1:1-18

The first reading comes from a collection of later writings included within the book of Isaiah. Whereas the prophet for whom that book is named lived during the eighth century, this collection dates from around the middle of the sixth century. Between those times, Palestine had been devastated, conquered, and occupied by foreign enemies and much of its population had been exiled. The religious interpretation of this catastrophe regarded it as a salutary punishment for infidelity, and gave reason to hope that when the divine chastisement had accomplished its purpose, a new beginning might be made. In the middle of the sixth century, under the benevolent rule of a Persian empire that had supplanted Assyrian and Babylonian domination, political events indicated that the time of liberation was near at hand. The joyous atmosphere of the time is reflected in passages like the one read in today's liturgy, which is part of a longer poem that begins by recalling the divine purpose of the exile and announces that the cup of God's wrath has at last been drunk to the dregs. The section included in the reading dramatizes the joyful occasion by the imagery of a courier, carrying the news of liberation southward, over the mountains, to the forsaken city of Jerusalem, seemingly as abandoned by its God as by its people. The city's eager response is symbolized by watchmen, always the first to perceive a new arrival, who raise a shout of triumph at the great news. Their joyous cry expresses the religious import of the event. "Your God is King" proclaims the sovereign power and the constant providential care of the Lord of Israel, which had been the basis of the people's hope that is now to be realized. This climax of expectation forms an appropriate liturgical crescendo for the motif of hope and expectation that marks the whole spirit of Advent.

The second reading is the opening passage of the letter to the Hebrews. It introduces the main theme of that work, which declares Jesus Christ, the Son of God, to be the fulfillment of the religious expectations expressed throughout the Old Testament. In that perspective, the whole import of the Hebrew scriptures is reinterpreted as anticipating, however obscurely, the coming of Christ. Accordingly, Christianity is conceived as a new and climactic era of human history. The divine meaning of history is recorded in the inspired writings, but that meaning can attain full clarity only in the time of fulfillment. Thus the passage begins by contrasting God's revelation "in times past," when it was fragmentary and various, with the revelation in "this, the final age," when it is consistent and complete. And whereas formerly revelation was mediated by the prophets, God's spokesmen, now it is transmitted by God's own Son. The phrase, God's son, had been used in various senses, and this passage insists on its being given the richest meaning, as denoting the outward aspect of God's own glory, and the divine agency by which all things are created and preserved. The initial salvific effect of the coming of the Son of God is represented as already accomplished by his having "cleansed us from our sins." And the divine Son is now reunited with his divine Father in the exercise of a total sovereignty, incomparably superior to the power of even the highest celestial spirits.

Persons still alive can recall a time when the third reading of this Christmas liturgy, the prologue of the Gospel according to John, was for most Catholics the most familiar of all biblical passages, being read as the conclusion of virtually every Mass. Although this practice was changed for good reasons, this "last Gospel" did have a remarkable power to conclude worship on a note that was both solemn and joyous, and to impart in a highly concentrated way the essential meaning of the incarnation. The heart of the lesson is in what was then the concluding passage: "The Word was made flesh and made his dwelling among us, and we have seen his glory: the glory of an only Son coming from the Father, filled with enduring love." The preceding passages richly express the significance of this "Word" by declaring his union with God before the dawn of history, and his active presence in that whole work of creation on which history is founded. Thus the presence of the Word is conceived as the active presence of God himself, whereby all that is not God comes to be and continues to be. The presence of the divine Word is thus inseparable from creaturely existence, and to know that Word is to know the relationship of God to his creation. By the same token, not to know the Word is to fail to acknowledge that on which all creation totally depends, to miss the meaning of created reality, whereas to accept the Word is to accept creation's relationship to its very source and foundation, and thereby be united with God. Mankind's estrangement from God is thus interpreted as mankind's failure to recognize, in any practical sense, God's Word. In this perspective, the incarnation, whereby "the Word became flesh," is the divine means whereby the presence of the Word asserts itself with saving vividness.

SUNDAY IN THE OCTAVE OF CHRISTMAS: HOLY FAMILY

Cycle "A" Readings: Sir. 3:2-6, 12-14; Col. 3:12-21; Mt. 2:13-15, 19-23

The book of Sirach, sometimes called Ecclesiasticus, is a Jewish work that, although valued by the Jews, is excluded from the Jewish Bible. It gained much higher esteem among Christians, who made it part of their Old Testament and made more extensive liturgical use of it than of any other Old Testament book except for the Psalms. Protestant Bibles, following Jewish precedent, class it among the apocrypha. Much of the book is occupied with rather homely moralizing, which is presented as an application of divine wisdom to various human situations. The first reading in today's liturgy comes from a passage of this sort, concerning how children, regardless of their age, ought to behave with respect to their parents. In effect it is an exhortation based on the commandment to "honor your father and your mother." As often happens in this literature, the moral appeal takes the form of a recital of benefits, worldly as well as religious, that may be expected from the sort of behavior which is recommended. Thus, to honor one's parents is said to "pay off," so to speak, in atonement for sin, prosperity, enjoyment of one's own children, response to prayer, and length of life. The justification for promising these blessings is the belief that, in respecting parents, one is obeying God, who is the source both of blessings and of obligations. Similarly, disrespect for parents is equated with blasphemy, the dishonoring of God himself. The rather naive ethical outlook of this passage is typical of much of the Old Testament's wisdom literature: God's law obliges man's obedience, and man's obedience merits God's reward. As in the present passage, most of the behavior recommended, though on grounds that are seldom profound and sometimes not very convincing, corresponds practically to ordinary Christian morality.

The second reading is taken from the letter to the Colossians, traditionally attributed to Paul and certainly composed either by Paul himself or by someone thoroughly imbued with Paul's doctrine. The letter was occasioned by controversies, presumably introduced from non-Christian religious and philosophical movements, concerning the significance of certain spiritual beings, comparable to angels, and concerning the propriety of observing certain dietary and other ascetical restrictions. Concerning the spiritual beings, the author of this letter simply insists that, whatever these beings were or were thought to be, they are, like all other creatures, totally subordinate to the universal sovereignty of Christ. Concerning the dietary and other taboos, the author denies that such practices have any legitimate relevance to the lives of Christians. Having thus disposed rather summarily of these misconceptions, the letter proceeds in its second half to establish, on the basis of faith in Christ's resurrection, the outline of a Christian code of behavior. Having first listed a series of common vices to be avoided, the author develops, in the section read in today's liturgy, the more positive side of Christian ethics. To this end, he inculcates a series of virtues: mercy, kindness, humility, meekness, and patience. He applies these concretely by his insistence on forgiveness and the words "as the Lord has forgiven you." He asserts the primacy of love in the Christian scheme of virtues. Peace is conceived as the moral expression of Christians' having been called to be "members of the one body." He calls also for gratitude, and for an interior assimilation of "the word of Christ." This inner presence of Christ's word may be understood to be the source of that wise instruction and that worship expressed in song which are also demanded of Christians. After these more general norms, the exhortation addresses more particularly the relationships between spouses and between parents and children, insisting on respect for the authority of husband over wife and of parents over children, as well as on kindness and gentleness in using authority.

The third reading is composed of three well-known stories from Matthew's Gospel: the escape of Jesus, Mary, and Joseph into Egypt, the massacre of the children in and around Bethlehem by Herod, and the family's eventual return and establishment of a home in Nazareth. In reading the passage, one is struck by the fact that each of the three narratives is concluded in a very similar fashion. After each of the episodes is described, it is characterized as a fulfillment of something expressed by the prophets and followed by an appropriate quotation. The first two of these quotations come from the Old Testament, whereas the source of the third, "He shall be called a Nazorean," remains a matter of scholarly conjecture. But even the Old Testament citations can be rather puzzling, inasmuch as their original contexts are not conspicuously relevant to their New Testament use. "Out of Egypt I have called my son" refers in the book of Hosea to the exodus, God's calling of his "son," Israel, out of Egyptian servitude. The "voice in Rama" refers in the book of Jeremiah to the people's lamentation over those who suffered death or exile as a result of the Assyrian invasion of Palestine. Although the application of such passages to Jesus may seem far-fetched, it reminds us of how eagerly, and sometimes uncritically, early Christian writers sought foreshadowings of Jesus in the Old Testament. This tendency was, of course, motivated by the conviction of Jesus' messiahship, which implied that in his career Old Testament anticipations found their real fulfillment. Considered in detachment from these apologetic preoccupations, the stories about Jesus' childhood reflect the natural interest which developed in early Christian communities in whatever details they could recover about Jesus' human life. The stories characteristically combine the two perspectives in which Jesus' life was viewed, that of its immediate dependence on God's direction and control, and that of its deep immersion in ordinary circumstances of human experience. This double perspective is conspicuously present in the stories about Jesus' childhood, which present him as simultaneously the dependent child of his human family and the beloved son of his divine Father. It is this twofold aspect which Christian tradition epitomizes in the phrase Holy Family, where "holy" implies closeness to God while "family" implies closeness to human experience. That interpenetration of divine and human dimensions, which later theology expressed in philosophical terms of a "hypostatic union," is here expressed in more universally accessible terms of simple narratives in which the divine and human dimensions are seen to interact.

SUNDAY IN THE OCTAVE OF CHRISTMAS: HOLY FAMILY

Cycle "B" Readings: same as cycle "A" except Lk. 2:22-40

The third reading for cycle B describes an episode reported only in the Gospel according to Luke. Its background is the messianic legislation given in Leviticus, which regarded a woman who had given birth as subject to a kind of religious taboo for a stipulated period of time. If the child were a boy he was circumcised on the eighth day of this period, and after thirty-three days the mother brought an offering to the temple whereupon a priest ceremonially restored her to normal ritual status. Luke takes this occasion to emphasize Jesus' messianic character by introducing two persons otherwise unknown to us. Simeon, a man of great holiness, clearly represents, as one who "awaited the consolation of Israel," the Isaian tradition of messianic hope. His very Isaian words of gratification on finding Jesus anticipate a revelation of salvation to the Gentiles as well as to Israel, and his more ominous subsequent comments convey a foreboding of the tragic consequences of the Messiah's rejection by some of his own people. Simeon finds a female counterpart in the prophetess called Anna. This lady is identified in surprising detail, citing her parentage, her tribal affiliation, her exact age, and the duration and aftermath of her marriage. Her theological function in this episode simply reinforces that of Simeon, and her reaction, clearly corresponding to his, is reported in only general terms.

SUNDAY IN THE OCTAVE OF CHRISTMAS: HOLY FAMILY

Cycle "C" Readings: same as cycle "A" except Lk. 2:41-52

The third reading for cycle C on this feast of the Holy Family comprises an episode narrated by the Gospel according to Luke, whose evident theological purpose is embodied in a narrative having an extraordinary degree of what journalists call "human interest." Luke's touching account of Mary's and Joseph's discovery of Jesus' absence during their return from a Passover celebration in Jerusalem, of their anxious efforts to find out what had happened to him, and of their perplexity, and Mary's significant pensiveness, on being cooly received by their son when they found him among theologians in the temple, has contributed much toward making the Holy Family the familiarly real and human beings Christians have always found them to be. The main object of Luke's story, however, is to furnish an indication, from legends of Jesus' early life, of his precocious awareness of an intimate relationship with God and of a dedication to God's purposes that utterly transcended all other responsibilities and concerns. As Luke tells the story, the parents' mystification at Jesus' having apparently neglected them is translated by Jesus into terms of their strange failure to understand where his own priorities inevitably lay.

OCTAVE OF CHRISTMAS, SOLEMNITY OF MARY, MOTHER OF GOD

Cycles "A", "B", and "C" Readings: Num. 6:22-27; Gal. 4:4-7; Lk. 2:16-21

The book of Numbers, from which the first reading is taken is designated in Hebrew by the more attractive title, In the Wilderness, a phrase found in the opening verse. The events of the book take place between the sojourn at Sinai during the exodus and the westward advance from Transjordan that initiated the invasion of Canaanite territory designated as the "promised land." Numbers is not a very eventful book, and its narrative is closely interwoven with traditions of discipline and ceremonial. One such tradition accounts for the isolated passage that constitutes the reading. The passage consists mainly in a formula of blessing which is still in regular use at Jewish worship and often employed in Christian ceremonies as well. The formula is a very graceful one, which uses the typically Hebrew device of parallelism to express essentially the same basic prayer in three slightly different ways. The prayer calls upon God to be benevolent and beneficent, to think favorably of and deal favorably with his people. The imagery of a smiling God and a worshiper who enjoys that total well-being called, in biblical idiom, peace, beautifully expresses the prayer's intention. The prayer is said to have been given by God to Moses, who is instructed to transmit it to "Aaron and his sons," telling them that this is how they are to "bless the Israelites." The reference to Aaron and his sons is to the Aaronic priesthood, a hereditary clergy tracing its origin to the brother of Moses. The blessing is thus designated as a priestly blessing, and the passage is intended to indicate the divine institution of a form of blessing that had long been familiar to temple worshipers by the time the book of Numbers was written.

The second reading, from the letter to the Galatians, is closely connected with the main preoccupation of that letter, which is to contrast the situation of the Jews, subject to the Mosaic law, before the coming of Christ, with the new situation created by Christ's coming, of liberation from that law and establishment of its former subjects as the children of God. Paul expresses this contrast by using the metaphor of a child's coming to age, emerging from a minor's state of subjection, and attaining the liberated status of adulthood. Life under the law is presented by Paul as a kind of slavery, suitable to a preliminary stage in the history of God's people, but superseded after the coming of Christ. The new condition made possible through Christ is described by Paul as a condition of sonship. The phrase, "you are no longer a slave but a son" summarizes his basic message. The Spirit sent by God into the hearts of Christ's followers is said to cry out "Abba." In other words, Christ's followers are entitled and inspired to address God in the familiar manner of a child's speech to a loving parent. This way of addressing and regarding God recalls Christ's attitude toward his heavenly Father, and thus implies that it is union with Christ that establishes the new relationship with God. Thus the mission of Christ is seen as God's way of adopting as beloved children those who were previously in the position of legal subjects. Christ's heritage thus becomes the inheritance of those who believe in him. What makes this possible is the incarnation, whereby God's Son, "born of a woman, born under the law," assumed the servile status of humankind precisely in order to transform that status into a participation of his own divine sonship.

The reference in the previous reading to Jesus' having been "born of a woman, born under the law" links it with the third reading, from the Gospel according to Luke, which describes the nativity scene at Bethlehem from the viewpoint of the shepherds. The phrase "born of a woman" further points to the distinctive role of Mary in the incarnation, which is emphasized by the Lucan narrative and particularly appropriate to this Sunday, designated by the Church as the solemnity of Mary, mother of God. The phrase "born under the law" is recalled by the reference to Jesus' circumcision, a rite which entailed subjection to the Mosaic law. At the same time, we are also reminded that Jesus transcends that law by mention of the fact that the name he received at circumcision belonged to him already by a title altogether independent of Mosaic law, inasmuch as it had been bestowed on him by God himself, through his angelic messenger, even before Jesus was conceived.

SECOND SUNDAY AFTER CHRISTMAS

Cycles "A", "B", and "C" Readings: Sir. 24:1-4, 8-12; Eph. 1:3-6, 15-18; Jn. 1:1-18

The first reading is taken from a work of Jewish wisdom literature of the second century B.C., which is not a part of Hebrew or Protestant bibles but was very popular in the early Church and has been retained in the Roman Catholic canon of Scripture. The reading combines two passages from a section of the book in which wisdom is personified as making a speech in its own praise. The speech is represented as delivered in the heavenly court of God, but as addressed to "her own people," presumably the Jews. Thus from the start both the heavenly status and the human relevance of wisdom are established by the writer. Wisdom identifies herself as issuing from the mouth of God, and thus as embodying the invincible power of the divine creative Word. In the verses that the reading omits, wisdom is described as ranging through the entire cosmos, and exercising power over all creation. This cosmic journeying of wisdom is then used to introduce a quite different idea, by being described as a quest for some permanent dwelling place. The quest is ended by a divine decree which localizes wisdom in the territory of Israel, whose status as the homeland of God's chosen people is thus reaffirmed in sapiential terms instead of the more familiar terms of covenant. This aspect of the passage takes on a special force in view of the fact that in other wisdom writings wisdom is described as finding no suitable accommodations on earth and returning to its heavenly abode. In the final verses the two previous themes are combined. In the first place, wisdom is primordial, created by God before the very dawn of history. But in the second place, this timeless divine creation takes its place in the realm of time and space at the point which represents the heart of Jewish religion, Jerusalem.

The second reading combines two sections from the opening passage of the letter to the Ephesians. The first section takes the form of a prayerful exclamation in praise of God for what he has accomplished through Christ for the sake of his people. This divine accomplishment is regarded as by no means an historically contingent or temporally fortuitous event. Its source is to be looked for not in history but before history, in an eternal plan of God. The focus of this divine plan is Christ, and its significance for human beings is in virtue of their anticipated relationship with Christ. The human situation for which thanks are here given is a situation of divine election, expressed by the phrases "God chose us in" Christ and "likewise predestined us through" Christ. Christ is thus regarded as the medium of God's intervention to sanctify human beings and adopt them as his own children. In the verses omitted from the reading, the meaning of this divine intervention and its purpose are expressed more concretely and applied more specifically to the readers. In the final verses of the reading, use is again made of a prayer formula, calling upon God who has dealt so generously with his people to grant them sufficient wisdom to appreciate how great a thing has been done for them and how glorious a destiny it sets before them.

The third reading is the prologue to the Gospel according to John, the main theme of which is the incarnation of the divine Word. The terms in which the Word is described recall the description of divine wisdom in the first reading. Like wisdom, the Word is introduced as having been in the presence of God before the dawn of creation. The divinity of the Word is plainly stated, and its power is identified as the creative power itself. Like timeless wisdom, the timeless Word takes its place within time, in the midst of God's people. Distinctively, however, the temporal presence of the Word is expressed in terms of incarnation. "The Word became flesh and made his dwelling among us." The presence of the Word is thus visible, and those to whom this Gospel is addressed are those who have perceived it for what it is. Interwoven with these verses of highly abstract symbolism is a more concrete account, phrased much more prosaically. This latter account begins with John the Baptist and contrasts his role as witness with the role of "the real light" to whom he bears witness. This account indicates that it is by belief, or faith, that the divine adoption is accepted. And it ends by contrasting the law given through Moses with the love given through Jesus

Christ. The several motifs of this prologue all contribute to its suitability for introducing a Gospel whose central insistence is on faith in the incarnate Word of God identified with Jesus Christ, as the means to eternal life.

EPIPHANY

Cycles "A", "B", and "C" Readings: Is. 60:1-6; Eph. 3:2-3, 5-6; Mt. 2:1-12

Epiphany is the English form of a Greek word which means an appearing, and the root from which it derives refers especially to the appearing of light. Often, therefore, it is most accurately translated by words like shining or dawning. Among Jews and pagans, as well as Christians, epiphany was applied in religious contexts to the appearing of a god. This appearance was frequently described as light penetrating the darkness. In the Christian tradition, the idea of an invisible God becoming visible is mainly associated with the dawning of Jesus Christ, the world's light. Israel stressed the invisibility of God, and thus an epiphany was a revealing of God by a manifestation of his active presence in sensational historical events. Today's first liturgical reading draws upon this Israelite notion of epiphany and uses a series of jubilant phrases to express the idea that "the Lord shall shine upon you." Though included in the book of Isaiah it actually dates from long after Isaiah's time. All the evidence points to the poem's being written at a time when the Babylonian captivity of Israel was coming to an end. All loyal Jews looked forward to the restoration of Jerusalem, the "city of the Lord." They eagerly anticipated the time when the brilliant glory of the Lord would dispel the darkness and thick clouds under which they were living. The reconstruction of Jerusalem was a sign that God was once again present among his people. The Lord's brilliant light would shine upon his people and through them to all nations. All nations would then pay homage not just to Jerusalem but to the Lord. All nations would be drawn to the brilliant light of the Lord.

The writer of the verses from Ephesians which form today's second reading is convinced that in Jesus a measure of the vision of God has been revealed. Characteristically, this revelation is conceived in terms of a universal plan of salvation, hitherto concealed in the mind of God, which has been suddenly made public by the mission of Jesus Christ as preached by his apostles. Here the basic idea of epiphany, of God's sudden and brilliant appearing, is identified with the unveiling of the great "mystery" or hidden design: "unknown to people in former ages, but now revealed by the Spirit to the holy apostles and prophets."

Even in a specifically religious context the word epiphany does have a general meaning. However in Christian terminology it has taken on a very specific meaning and is used to refer to a particular story found only in Matthew's Gospel—the story of the magi coming to Bethlehem. In origin, the term magi comes from a Persian priestly caste. Later it became loosely used to describe magicians and sorcerers. In order to show God's universal plan of salvation, Matthew portrays the magi as Oriental astrologers who follow a star "from the East" which represents an area far beyond Jerusalem. In the context of Jesus' infancy the episode anticipates the worldwide appeal of Christian revelation and the positive response of the Gentiles to the preaching of the Gospel. Matthew contrasts the eager reverence of the magi with the hostility of Herod who saw in the child a threat to his kingly power. Matthew uses this tool to anticipate Jesus' rejection by many of those closest to him and his acceptance by people around the world. The writer deliberately echoes some of the passages from today's first reading in order to make the connection between the Oriental caravans paying homage to a restored Jerusalem and the Christian conviction that in Jesus God's glory has been revealed. Because the glory of the Lord has been revealed in Christ Jesus, all peoples will worship the Lord. In Christian culture the feast of the Epiphany has long been one of great celebration because it expands the notion of Israel's Messiah into a notion of the Savior of the world. The journey of the magi symbolizes the journey of all peoples who are seeking God.

SUNDAY AFTER JAN. 6: BAPTISM OF THE LORD

Cycle "A" Readings: Is. 42:1-4, 6-7; Acts 10:34-38; Mt. 3:13-17

Today's first reading comprises the initial verses of the first of four remarkable poems called "servant songs." In each of them we find reference to "the Lord's servant," who is understood to have been singled out and empowered by God to extend the light of revelation beyond Israel to the Gentile world. The servant's divinely appointed task is described in terms which associate its accomplishment with profound humiliation and extreme suffering, and entail striking similarities to the Gospel accounts of Jesus' passion and death. The servant songs are also prophecies of reassurance and hope. They date from the period of Israel's exile in Babylon, and contain God's promise of liberation. But what sets them apart is their linking of the destiny of Israel with the destiny of the whole world. The mysterious servant, almost certainly represents a personification of Israel itself, through whose faith, sustained through suffering, salvation would be made available to the Gentiles. The opening words of the first servant song are addressed by God to his servant, and express the servant's unique vocation.

He is one whom God especially loves and has especially chosen. He is the recipient of the very spirit of God. He is given the mission of making "justice shine on the nations." In a series of striking images the style of the servant's mission is characterized by modesty, simplicity, and gentleness, while the effect of his mission is described in terms of enlightenment and liberation. Nearly all of the first servant song reappears in the New Testament.

The second reading is the first part of a speech addressed by Peter to a Roman centurion named Cornelius and the relatives and friends he had assembled for religious instruction. Peter's words represent a concise statement of fundamental Christian belief. Several passages of this kind occur in Acts, and are commonly regarded as examples of the basic preaching of the early Church, the so-called *kerygma* or proclamation, comprising the nucleus of the Gospel message. Typically, such passages declare that God's plan of salvation, prophesied in Israel, is fulfilled in Jesus, whose ministry brought him to a cruel death, only to be raised by God and revealed to the apostles, who now preach salvation based on faith in Jesus Christ. In the speech attributed to Peter, the account of Jesus' ministry characteristically begins with reference to his baptism by John, whereupon "God anointed him with the Holy Spirit and with power," after which "he went about doing good." Jesus' baptism is thus conceived as the inauguration of his ministry, for which, like the servant in the Isaian passages, he is especially empowered by the gift of the Spirit.

Like the passage just read from Acts of the Apostles, our earliest Gospel, that according to Mark, makes it clear that for early Christians the active ministry of Jesus was considered to have begun with his baptism. This inaugural character of the baptism may be somewhat lost sight of as one reads the more expanded narratives according to Matthew and Luke, which precede this episode with considerable material concerning Jesus' birth, infancy, and childhood. In the case of Matthew's Gospel, the account of the baptism is itself somewhat expanded from the form which occurs almost identically in the other two synoptic accounts. What are added are two verses of dialogue between John and Jesus, in which the former protests his unworthiness to baptize a person who might more fittingly baptize him, and is reassured that, for all its seeming incongruity, the baptism is divinely intended. It would seem that, like many a Christian preacher after him, the author of this Gospel was concerned about a potential misunderstanding. Since baptism is a ritual normally applied to sinners, as a sign either of their repentance or of God's forgiveness, it might seem to follow that a baptized Jesus must be, or must have been, a sinful Jesus. John's words in this passage thus anticipate a difficulty, and Jesus' words declare the difficulty invalid. In his baptism as in so many other contexts, Jesus' mission requires him to be intimately associated with the sinfulness of mankind. The evangelist, however, wishes to remind us that the baptism no more implies Jesus' sinfulness than the crucifixion implies his criminality.

SUNDAY AFTER JAN. 6: BAPTISM OF THE LORD

Cycle "B" Readings: same as cycle "A" except Mk. 1:7-11

The earliest of the written Gospels, that which bears the name of Mark, opens with a quotation from Isaiah. It is used to introduce John the Baptist as one who prepares God's way by administering a baptism of repentance, while awaiting someone far greater than himself who "will baptize . . . with the Holy Spirit." Jesus makes his first appearance in the Gospel when he presents himself to John to be baptized. The moment of Jesus' baptism represents here, as in the preaching of Peter to Cornelius, the inauguration of his divine mission. The significance of this event is brought out vividly by the visionary symbolism which follows, when "he saw the heavens torn open and the Spirit, like a dove, descending upon him." The meaning of this vision is reinforced by words from heaven which are heard to say, "This is my Son, my beloved, on whom my favor rests." There is a basic similarity of meaning between this episode and the opening verses of the first servant song. In both we find God closely associating himself with a human being who is both the special object of his love and the special instrument of his work for the salvation of humankind. There are even good linguistic grounds for associating the Greek phrase rendered as "my Son" with the Hebrew phrase translated "my servant" in the passage from Isaiah. There can be little doubt that, for the Gospel writer, the episode of Jesus' baptism represents the fulfillment of what is prophesied in the servant song: God's sending of one who is filled with his own Spirit, sharing his divine life and divine power, to accomplish salvation for the world. As, in Catholic theology, baptism is conceived as a sacramental sign of the initiation of a new life in Christ, so the prototype of the sacrament, Jesus' own baptism, represents the initiation of that divine mission of Christ which brings new life to all humankind. The fact that early preaching, such as we find in Acts, as well as the earliest written Gospel, that of Mark, introduces the story of Jesus' career with the account of his baptism strongly suggests that the first Christians thought of this event as the initiation of his saving ministry.

SUNDAY AFTER JAN. 6: BAPTISM OF THE LORD

Cycle "C" Readings: same as cycle "A" except Lk. 3:15-16, 21-22

In the accounts we read in the New Testament, especially in the Acts of the Apostles, of the earliest form of basic Christian preaching, as also in our oldest written Gospel, that of Mark, we find that the story of Jesus' career typically begins with the account of his baptism. Apparently, therefore, the first Christians thought of this event as the initiation of Jesus' ministry. Later writings, such as the Gospel according to Luke from which the third reading is taken, precede this account with material pertaining to Jesus' birth, infancy, and childhood. This expansion of the narrative should not be allowed to obscure the fact that it is Jesus' baptism which, in Christian tradition, marks the outset of his distinctively messianic career. Today's reading calls attention to this fact by representing the people as "full of anticipation, wondering in their hearts whether John might be the Messiah." John, however, is presented as directing the people's messianic expectancy away from himself and toward another. This other is then immediately identified as Jesus when, at the moment of his baptism, a divine voice proclaims him to be God's "beloved Son" on whom God's "favor rests." These phrases of divine testimony bear significant resemblance to the language of the "servant "songs" in the book of Isaiah, and they are clearly to be understood as messianic designations of Jesus derived from God himself. The place of Jesus' baptism at the start of his ministry foreshadows the Christian understanding of baptism as a sacrament of initiation into a new life.

LENTEN SEASON

FIRST SUNDAY OF LENT

Cycle "A" Readings: Gen. 2:7-9; 3:1-7; Rom. 5:12-19; Mt. 4:1-11

The readings, as befits the first Sunday of Lent (and originally the beginning of Lent), all deal with man as sinner. But the emphasis is not exclusively on the negative aspect of his state. This aspect is indeed brought out in the first reading and the psalm, where the origin of sin is shown (it begins with the very first human beings), and the sinner, aware of his need, cries out to God for mercy. In the New Testament readings, however, the stress changes. Sin is indeed universal from Adam on, but the grace of Christ is equally universal and far more powerful. Finally, in the temptations of Christ, we are shown how to overcome our temptations and avoid sin.

The story in Genesis of man's creation, God's prohibition, and man's sin is told in poetic and not always clear detail, but the main point of the story is clear. From the beginning man has a special nature ("the breath of life") and destiny (as God's vice-gerent in the world). He is tempted to disobey on the ground that God's commands are an unwarranted restriction on his freedom and that God does not want man to become truly like him. The temptation is thus based on a distortion of the truth about man's relationship to God. He disobeys. The result is that he is cut off from God, the source of his true life and of the power to achieve his destiny, which is authentic assimilation to God.

The New Testament readings turn to Christ as the redeemer, the one who rescues man from his sorry state and enables him to reach his goal. Sin is evidently not played down. In fact, the Christian's sense of sin should not be less acute than that of Old Testament man; on the contrary, it should be more intense because of the Christian's greater understanding of the tender love God our Father has for us and of the proferred intimacy man rejects by sinning. At the same time, however, the Christian's sense of sin should not be tinged by the gloominess to which Old Testament man was liable, for the former knows that "grace more abounds."

In the letter to the Romans, St. Paul is telling us in this rather difficult passage that Christian man is a member of a race that has always been sinful. Each generation and individual has inherited (we are not told how) the alienation from God that was caused by the first man's sin and its effects. Each has, in addition, by its own acts deepened the enslavement to the flesh and to death which sin brings with it. But the coming of Christ means that however powerful and universal the grip of sin is upon individuals and societies, the power and love of God and the grace of Christ are still more powerful to convert, liberate, and remake man and society in the image of God and his Christ.

In the collect of the Mass we pray that our Lenten observance may help us understand the mystery of Christ and experience its effects in holiness of life. The Gospel gives us insight into that mystery insofar as the life of Christ—specifically his temptations—provides the key to the Christian's struggle against sin and the model of a life wholly directed to God.

The essence of the three temptations is the misuse of God-given powers for egotistic purposes. These powers in the case of Christ were messianic and miraculous; in the case of the Church (which the evangelist probably had in mind) they were special powers for carrying out her mission. As for the individual Christian, all the gifts of God can be used in ways that prevent them from serving the purpose God intended: our assimilation to Christ and our Father, and our more intimate union with each other and God.

Christ is urged to abuse his messianic powers and present himself as a false Messiah, that is, one who would deceive his followers about the true nature of God's rule over men and man's relationship to God. Every temptation we experience is based on the same kind of distortion. The answer, therefore, to all temptation and the way to guard against it is to reaffirm and deepen that dependence on God's will and that intimacy with him as sons and servants which Christ expresses in the three quotations from Deuteronomy.

FIRST SUNDAY OF LENT

Cycle "B" Readings: Gen. 9:8-15; 1 Pet. 3:18-22; Mk. 1:12-15

The first reading in today's liturgy is the concluding passage of the story told in Genesis of the great flood, inflicted by God on a sinful humankind, from which only the just man Noah and his family were spared. The deluge story appears to be an account fashioned by combining earlier narrative elements developed in Mesopotamian mythology with later theological elements developed in Israelite religion. Among the latter features, characteristic of Old Testament theology, most outstanding is the representation of God's transaction with Noah as the forming of a covenant. Thus, after predicting the intended destruction and describing the ark which is to be built, God concludes by telling Noah: "With you I will make a covenant, and you shall go into the ark, you and your sons." After Noah and his company have survived the flood, the promised covenant is made explicit in the form of a guarantee given to all of them and their descendants, of which the rainbow is to serve as a reminder that "never again shall the waters become a flood to destroy all living creatures." In the form in which the Old Testament was finally put together, this mythological narrative furnishes the first of many instances of God's covenant relationships with his people. The basic idea of covenant was undoubtedly transferred to theology from familiar social and political practices whereby important agreements provided stability for relationships between persons and groups. In the instances of divine covenants recorded in the Bible, one notices that invariably the covenant is initiated by God, who dictates the terms of it, a covenant by which he will abide and by which the human party is required to abide. The notion of abiding by such a covenant, adhering to the terms set by God, is basic to the biblical understanding of faith, which in later Christian theology came to be associated more with believing certain doctrines than with sticking by certain agreements, more with intellectual credence than with personal commitment. Similarly, the biblical understanding of hope is basically an acknowledgement of the absolute reliability of God's covenant promises.

Most Christians who habitually recite the Apostles' Creed would probably find considerable difficulty in explaining just what they are professing to believe when they assert that Jesus Christ "descended into hell." No doubt the most popular interpretation understands "hell" to mean a place or state of confinement occupied by those who had died before Jesus and which, after the crucifixion, he visited to give its occupants their freedom. This idea, which flourished in the Middle Ages as the "harrowing of hell," finds its most impressive scriptural support in the passage read in today's liturgy from the first letter of Peter. There we are told that Jesus, having been put to death "in the body" and restored to life "in the spirit," "in the spirit . . . went and made his proclamation to the imprisoned spirits." In the latter clause, the expression "in the spirit" encouraged a popular idea to the effect that Jesus emancipated the souls of the dead in a kind of ghostly existence, before his resurrection and after his crucifixion. This is a misunderstanding of a phrase which actually refers to the principle of Jesus' new, resurrected life, and not to a disembodied soul. The "imprisoned spirits" seem to be identified with, or at least intended to include, those whose infidelity was punished by the deluge from which Noah and his family were spared. By a strange pattern of thought, Noah's ark, as a means of salvation, then reminds the writer of the waters of baptism—a major theme of the first letter of Peter—by which Christians are saved through the resurrection of Christ. Apart from the basic insistence on the saving power of baptism, and the source of that power in the resurrection, very little in this passage can be interpreted very precisely or very confidently.

The third reading presents the account of Jesus' temptation in the wilderness as narrated in the Gospel according to Mark. In Matthew's and Luke's Gospels, this episode is recounted at considerable length as a series of temptations accompanied by a series of verbal exchanges between Jesus and Satan in which Satan is both morally and dialectically vanquished. By contrast, the account in Mark's Gospel is extremely brief and bare. It contains the familiar elements of Jesus' being led into the wilderness by the Spirit, implying that this ordeal is a part of his mission intended by God, of the forty-day duration, reminiscent of the forty years in the desert after the exodus, of the society of wild beasts, traditionally associated with the haunts of demons, and of the ministration of angels, implying the loving protection of God. On the generally accepted hypothesis that Mark's Gospel is older than the others, one can see in the different versions of this episode a tendency for which there is abundant evidence elsewhere in the Gospels, of early Christians increasingly to expand and elaborate their traditions concerning the earlier portions of Jesus' life and ministry.

FIRST SUNDAY OF LENT

Cycle "C" Readings: Deut. 26:4-10; Rom. 10:8-13; Lk. 4:1-13

The initial reading for this first Sunday of Lent, from the book of Deuteronomy, begins in a way that is somewhat puzzling until one discovers that "the priest shall then receive the basket from you" is part of a set of directions which began in a more intelligible way several verses earlier. They are directions for a liturgy, which is here described as being instituted by Moses as a ritual to be celebrated by his followers once they were settled in the promised land. The ritual was, in fact, used at a number of different Jewish feasts, and its principal element was an offering of first fruits to God by delivering them to his priests in the temple. Old Testament accounts of this liturgy show considerable variation, and the only indications of what motives were associated with it is provided by this passage. For in this account, the offering itself is immediately followed by the recitation of a kind of creed. The recitation has the form of an historical recapitulation, in which three events are typically singled out as decisive factors in Israel's providential development. First of these is the ancient migration from the north and establishment in the south of the ancestral founder, Abraham. Second is God's deliverance of his people from the servile condition in which they later found themselves in the land of Egypt. And third is God's guidance of his people to the new land of abundance which he destined to be their permanent homeland. This recital, followed by the words "Therefore, I have now brought you the first fruits," makes it clear that the ritual here described is understood by the biblical writer to be essentially a liturgy of thanksgiving, a periodic acknowledgment of lasting indebtedness to God for bestowing the land which made these first fruits possible.

The second reading, taken from the letter to the Romans, expresses one of the principal themes of St. Paul's teaching in that letter and elsewhere, which has also been one of the outstandingly controversial themes of Christian theology, the theme of justification by faith. As a former rabbi, Paul naturally understood terms like "justification" with reference to their Jewish usage. According to that usage, a "just" or "righteous" person was a person united to God by the fact that he obeyed the law which God imposed upon his people as the condition of their "covenant" or alliance with him. This was the law revealed by God through Moses, recorded in the Old

Testament, and interpreted and applied by generations of Jewish teachers. Justification, therefore, was achieved by doing the "works of the law." In this conception, the gift of God which made justification possible was the law itself, a divinely guaranteed guide to living as God intended his people to live. In assuming the role of Jesus Christ's apostle to the Gentiles, Paul was compelled, both by his understanding of the Gospel and by the situation of those to whom he preached it, to detach the idea of justification from its traditional dependence on fidelity to the Mosaic law. Paul was convinced that perfect fidelity to the Mosaic law was, in humankind's morally enfeebled condition, simply impossible. Paul was likewise convinced that the basic significance of Jesus Christ was that God's mercy intervened to save humankind despite its moral feebleness and chronic disobedience. As a result, Paul's teaching is characterized by an insistent contrast between justification by works, that is, by keeping the law, and justification by faith, that is, by relying on God's merciful intervention through Jesus Christ. Accordingly, in the present passage, a distinctively Christian creed is formulated precisely in terms of justification by faith, that is, by confidence that the Lordship of Jesus, manifested in his resurrection, assures the salvation of humankind regardless of their relationship to the Mosaic law. In this latter sense "there is no difference between Jew and Greek" and "all have the same Lord."

The Gospel reading for the first Sunday of Lent is invariably the account of Jesus' temptation by Satan in the desert, which is traditionally situated just after his baptism and just before the beginning of his public ministry. This year, the version used is that according to Luke, which, like that according to Matthew, considerably expands the brief statement in Mark. Apparently, therefore, we have here a very old tradition whose significance is clarified and somewhat modified by successive biblical writers. All the accounts mention Jesus' forty days in the wilderness, his guidance by the Spirit, his temptation by Satan, and his ultimate victory. Forty days in the wilderness would remind any Jewish reader of those forty years in the wilderness during which Israel after the exodus was both guided by God and tempted to reject God, and which ended with the arrival in the promised land. Along with this comparison, the longer accounts of Jesus' temptations emphasize his total fidelity to God, his absolute refusal to employ any means but those indicated by God, and his determination that his messianic mission should not be diverted from its course by self-interest or by suggestions whose plausibility and attractiveness derive from worldly standards and values. Luke's arrangement ends with an intimation that a further temptation is yet to be anticipated, and thereby points toward the final test on the eve of the passion.

SECOND SUNDAY OF LENT

Cycle "A" Readings: Gen. 12:1-4; 2 Tim. 1:8-10; Mt. 17:1-9

The theme of these readings is *calling*—more specifically, the call to faith which is a call from death to life. Abraham is presented as the human model of response to the call. The source of the call, however, and the basis for our faith and hope in answering is God. Finally, the saving power and fidelity of God are manifested in Christ who, even more than Abraham, is the prototype of all who are called.

The basic call given to every Christian is reflected in the words: "We have not here a lasting dwelling." The Christian is called to be a pilgrim and to move toward a goal which, though it may be in some measure possessed during his time on earth, lies, in its complete form, beyond the confines of this life and world.

The passage from Genesis shows us the first call by God after the fall of man and the first response by a man of faith. Both call and response are typical of all later calls and responses. God takes the initiative: his call comes suddenly, unexpectedly, without reference to previous merits or deeds of Abraham. The call can be explained only by the infinite love and goodness of God which are their own motive and seek to give men a share in God's happiness.

Abraham is asked to break with his past as an idolator (this means leaving his homeland and kinsfolk) and to go blindly on pilgrimage to an unknown country. His reward will be blessings for himself and his posterity. Here the pattern of that faith of which Abraham will be father and model is made clear: the acceptance of and trust in God's promises means a constant leaving behind and striving toward. It means for all others, as it meant for Abraham, a radical self-detachment and radical entrusting of oneself to the providence and care of God. Abraham's faith would be tested in many ways; he would be constantly breaking camp and pitching his tents in some new place, always a pilgrim on the earth.

In his exhortation to Timothy to be faithful to his calling, Paul repeats a constant theme: God has called us to holiness (union with him in and through Christ), and the call is a completely free gift on God's part, not due to any merits of ours. The personal call to each of us is part of a comprehensive plan which God conceived before creation and which he manifested to us when Christ came as redeemer. His intention is that we all form the one body of the risen Christ and share with him that life of union with God and immortality which he made possible for us by his death and resurrection and which we shall share fully only when we too have risen from the dead.

The Gospel according to Matthew in its account of the transfiguration shows us Christ as the prototypical "one called." It is "in him" and "for (the sake of) him," as Paul says, that the rest of us are called. He is "the beloved Son on whom God's favor rests." Because he is the beloved eternal Son, God has poured out on him in his resurrection the fullest possible measure of his gifts. In the transfiguration the disciples receive an anticipatory glimpse of the hidden splendor which belongs to Christ by birthright as the eternal Son made flesh and which he will also win for himself and all of us by his death and resurrection. To everyone who is called, God promises a share in this same splendor; it will be the outward manifestation of perfect inward possession by God's power, which is the Holy Spirit. To live by faith is to strive to become ever more like the God who manifests his true nature to us in the human life of Christ and calls us to be fully assimilated to him, at the resurrection, by that Spirit of holiness and love who even now urges us on.

SECOND SUNDAY OF LENT

Cycle "B" Readings: Gen. 22:1-2, 9, 10-13, 15-18; Rom. 8:31-34; Mk. 9:2-9

The story of Abraham's sacrifice of Isaac, is introduced by the words "God put Abraham to the test." The idea of testing is very prominent in the Bible and in religions derived from the Bible. What it means is very close to modern concepts of psychological experimentation. That is, conditions are set up in such a way that the behavior which is observed in those circumstances will confirm or refute some hypothesis. In the Bible, the hypotheses are typically moral and religious ones. The experimental conditions in which God places Abraham are of the "forced choice" type, in which he confronts an inescapable dilemma. That Abraham has strong motives for sparing the boy's life is clearly acknowledged by God's own description of Isaac as "your only son, whom you love." Abraham's motive for taking the boy's life is, of course, his religious conviction that his God must be obeyed at all costs. One may say that the experimental hypothesis tested here is that Abraham's devotion to God exceeds what was presumably otherwise his strongest devotion, to his beloved only son. The experiment, of course, confirms this hypothesis, enabling the divine experimenter to conclude, "Now I know that you are a God-fearing man." There is obviously a rather primitive anthropomorphism involved in supposing that God must perform experiments in order to evaluate people morally and religiously. However, events of this kind can preserve a theologically acceptable significance if they are thought to reveal the qualities of persons not to God, but to the persons themselves and to other human beings. On this basis, subsequent generations canonized Abraham, so to speak, on the grounds that this event, along with others, demonstrated his heroic submission to the will of

God. Abraham accordingly became Israel's legendary paragon of faith, understood as firm fidelity to God. Since, moreover, God's reward for Abraham's obedience was the promise of a vast and prosperous posterity, Israel attributed its fortunate history to the faith of its "father Abraham." It is probable that the original context of the story recalls existing practices of human sacrifice in the religions of Palestine, and that God's last-minute rescue of Isaac betokens the repudiation of such barbarity by Israel.

In attempting to explain the conviction shared by all Christians that salvation comes to humankind from God through the crucifixion of God's Son Jesus Christ, various theologians have concentrated on certain interpretations of that event, based on particular aspects of it. The various approaches have resulted in various "theories of the atonement," which are found, both in harmony and in conflict, throughout the history of speculative theology. There is, of course, no reason to presume that any single way of viewing and interpreting the crucifixion will prove so adequate as to exclude all others, and in the New Testament itself one finds that a number of later theological perspectives are anticipated. One such perspective regards the crucifixion as the supreme demonstration of God's love for his people, and therefore as the supreme basis for assurance of God's saving mercy. From this point of view the crucifixion, the cruel death endured by God incarnate, implies that if God would go to such lengths as this for love of sinful humanity, there are no imaginable lengths to which he would not go, and therefore no imaginable limits to our hope of salvation. It is essentially this point of view which Paul—who assumes different but not incompatible points of view in other passages—adopts in the passage from Romans read in today's liturgy. His message is: If God is on our side, we cannot lose. And how thoroughly God is on our side is made unmistakable by the crucifixion, in which—as in Abraham's demonstration of devotion—"he did not spare his own Son."

Attitudes toward Jesus Christ were, for his followers, utterly transformed by their belief that he had been raised from the dead. This transformation of attitudes touched nearly every aspect of Jesus' earthly career, but none more profoundly than his passion and death. Seen in pre-resurrection perspective, Jesus' passion and death meant his violent subjection to the will of his enemies. It meant therefore the ultimate defeat of the messianic hopes which had been placed in him. But seen in post-resurrection perspective, the same events meant rather the faithful submission of Jesus to the will of his Father. It meant therefore the ultimate triumph of messianic hopes, which were, by the very way in which they did triumph, purged of misunderstandings about what messiahship entailed. The transfiguration, narrated in today's reading from Mark's Gospel, is a symbolic vision anticipating the glorious view of Jesus formed by Christians after his resurrection. The final warning by Jesus not to talk about this vision until after the resurrection—another instance of Mark's notorious "messianic secret"—is a reminder of what had yet to take place before such a view of Jesus could be formed or even comprehended. Significantly, the verses which immediately follow this selection first describe the disciples as puzzling over "what this 'rising from the dead' could mean," and then proceed to a prediction of the passion as fulfilling the Scriptures.

SECOND SUNDAY OF LENT

Cycle "C" Readings: Gen. 15:5-12, 17-18; Phil. 3:17—4:1; Lk. 9:28-36

The first reading in today's liturgy is from the book of Genesis, and from that portion of the book devoted to the story of Abraham, with whom the religious history of God's chosen people was considered to begin. Previous chapters of Genesis deal rather with the remote beginnings of humanity in general in relationship to God, whereas from the first mention of Abraham the whole Old Testament narrative assumes a perspective focused upon the Israelite nation. Abraham was considered to be the ultimate ancestor of that nation. Consequently his story, fashioned as we now have it at a time when the Israelite nation was a reality, is filled with anticipations of his posterity's destiny. This characteristic of the narratives concerning Abraham is conspicuous in the present passage, which makes use of sacrificial symbolism in a visionary context to portend the nation which would come into being centuries later. Thus the passage begins with God's assuring Abraham, despite the apparent sterility of his marriage, that he will have abundant posterity. When Abraham accepts this assurance with the confidence of faith, God "credited it to him as an act of righteousness" and made him the further promise that his people would possess the land through which he had traveled as a stranger. A mysterious vision follows, which is based on an ancient ritual used for concluding treaties. According to this usage, parties who entered into covenants passed between portions of dismembered animals to signify their anticipation of a similarly bloody fate if they should be unfaithful to the agreement. Since, in the case of a covenant with God, there is no equality between the parties, in this case God alone, symbolized by the smoking brazier and flaming torch, guarantees the covenant. The meaning of the birds of prey which menace the dismembered animals, as brought out by verses which are omitted from the reading, is that Abraham's descendants must endure tribulations before finally possessing their promised land, which is geographically identified as the land between Egypt and Mesopotamia, that is, Palestine.

The second reading is taken from a part of St. Paul's letter to the Philippians, which many interpreters think originally belonged to a quite different letter. This part begins with a strong denunciation of certain adversaries, not clearly identifiable, who misled Christians by their advocacy of Jewish religious practices such as circumcision. After vindicating his right to pronounce on such matters by describing his own Jewish background, Paul insists on the absolute worthlessness of all former ritual practices in comparison with the value of knowing Christ and sharing in Christ's resurrection. Paul calls upon his readers to pattern themselves on his own example, presumably of fidelity to Christian teaching and practice. He then further denounces his adversaries—or possibly different adversaries from those previously denounced—as having an earthly rather than a heavenly orientation. The phrase "their god is their belly," commonly understood as a reference to gluttony, and presumably related to the "earthly" way of life, has no obvious connection with anything more definite Paul says about his opponents, and its meaning may be quite different from the most obvious interpretation. Finally, Paul reaffirms the Christian expectation of Christ's second coming and the transformation of human existence into a glorious condition corresponding to that of Christ himself. Although the positive elements of doctrine expressed in this passage are typically Pauline, they are all expressed more clearly and fully elsewhere, and the special circumstances which evoked them here remain largely a matter of scholarly conjecture.

The third reading is the account of the transfiguration as given in the Gospel according to Luke, which largely agrees with, but also somewhat expands, the corresponding passages of Matthew and Mark. In all three, Peter, James, and John are taken by Jesus to a hill where they behold him, transformed by an unearthly brilliance, in the company of Moses and Elijah, and hear a voice from heaven declare that Jesus is to be listened to as the Son of God. The appearance of Moses and Elijah may reflect a current Jewish belief that they had not, in the normal sense, died; they may also symbolize the law and the prophets. In any case they represent the Old Testament's anticipation of a fulfillment which comes only with Jesus. The force of the entire vision is clearly to establish the divinely appointed messianic character of Jesus. Luke is the only one of the evangelists to attribute words to Moses and Elijah, and it is significant that they are words which link Jesus' messianic glory to the anticipation of his passion and death by referring to what he was to "fulfill in Jerusalem." It is also a peculiarity of Luke's narrative that the transfiguration occurred at a time when Jesus and his companions went into the hills to pray. In all three accounts, it is noteworthy that Peter is the one who reacts verbally to the experience, a detail which suggests Peter's special status in the early Church.

THIRD SUNDAY OF LENT

Cycle "A" Readings: Ex. 17:3-7; Rom. 5:1-2, 5-8; Jn. 4:5-42

Of the dozen or so places where thirst is referred to in the New Testament, only three pertain literally to the biological need of bodily tissues for water. In the others, and invariably in the Johannine writings, thirst is obviously a metaphor which stands for an equally vital need of an even more serious kind. It stands, in fact, for precisely that need which it is the mission of Jesus Christ to satisfy. That its meaning is no less profound than that is made perfectly clear by the concluding words of the Christian Apocalypse (Rev. 22.17): "Let him who is thirsty come forward; let all who desire it accept the gift of life-giving water." The quenching of death-dealing thirst by life-giving water is, in other words, a primary biblical symbol for nothing less than the ultimate fulfillment of the whole divine plan for man's salvation. Consequently it is fair to say that, in biblical language, water and thirst stand respectively for the best and the worst prospects confronted by human existence, the worst of fears and the best of hopes—man's absence from God and God's presence to man.

There is, of course, no strict necessity for using thirst and water to symbolize man's ultimate spiritual need and its fulfillment, and the Bible does not, obviously, limit itself to those symbols. But there are excellent reasons why this particular imagery should have commended itself to the biblical writers, and the most conspicuous of these reasons is a combination of history and geography.

As nearly everybody knows, for the Israelites the basis of their extraordinary faith in a saving God was understood to be an historical event called the exodus, which is a Greek word meaning a "way out." What it refers to is Israel's way out of a situation which must have seemed utterly hopeless, a situation of oppressive servitude and progressive degradation in the land of Egypt. Religiously, the important thing is that the way out of that apparently desperate predicament was not discovered or contrived by Israel. It was revealed by God. And equally important, it was not revealed all at once but only gradually: not by God's telling Israel the way out, but by his showing it to them, as it were, step by step. And the way which God did show them was one which led into, of all places, a trackless desert.

The selection read in today's liturgy from the book of Exodus describes one episode in that desert trek which was the divinely appointed way to Israel's salvation, when their hope must have seemed the bitterest of mockeries. For their way out of slavery seemed to have led them to the only thing worse than slavery: a futile death, the death that awaits all who wander in deserts without guidance or provisions—death from thirst. And so they complained, with the impotent rage of betrayed, despairing men. But their angry, despairing cry was heard as a prayer and answered with a miracle of life-giving water. It was that water which enabled them not only to keep moving on the way to salvation, but also to keep believing that it really was the way to salvation.

It is this picture of a desert way to salvation, made both possible and credible by God's marvels of life-giving water, which should be in the back of our mind when we hear, as in today's reading from St. John's Gospel, Jesus speaking of one kind of water that will alleviate thirst only for a time, and of another, which he is to give, that will banish all thirst forever. For as Jesus conceives it, the great exodus has continued all through his people's history. It is still in progress. And God has never ceased to sustain his desert travelers with water. But the coming of Jesus means that the farther edge of that desert has come at last unmistakably into view, and it is he who shall bring his people—all people—into that longed-for land where thirst will be no more.

It is as an admirable summary of this theme, in more abstract and theological terms, that today's reading from St. Paul's letter to the Romans reminds us: "We have gained access by faith to the grace in which we now stand, and we boast of our hope for the glory of God." Here is Pauline eschatology at its hearty, exuberant best, full of the vigor of its hope! And what it calls for is precisely what today's lessons collectively invite us to do—"boast of our hope for the glory of God." It is a summons to that special Christian quality of celebration at confronting the future in Jesus Christ which is what one might expect of travelers whose way out of slavery has at last been clearly perceived as a way into freedom, "because the love of God has been poured out in our hearts through the Holy Spirit who has been given to us."

It is that outpouring of which Jesus speaks when he tells the Samaritan woman: "Whoever drinks the water I give him will never be thirsty; no, the water I give shall become a fountain within him, leaping up to provide eternal life."

THIRD SUNDAY OF LENT

Cycle "B" Readings: Ex. 20:1-17; 1 Cor. 1:22-25; Jn. 2:13-25

The first reading of today's liturgy cites from the book of Exodus one of the two passages in the Old Testament where the ten commandments are fully listed. The other formulation, different in some minor respects, appears in Deuteronomy 5:6-21. Modern studies of ancient Near Eastern political documents have demonstrated notable correspondences between these decalogues and a type of covenant called the suzerainty treaty, suggesting a possible origin for Israelite ideas of a covenant relationship with God, and a possible basis for conceiving the ten commandments analogously to the provisions or terms of a treaty. Although modern Jews and Christians are accustomed to rote learning of the decalogue as a kind of compendium of morals, it does not seem to have been used quite to formally in biblical times; even Jesus, in explaining what he means by "keep the commandments," does not quote the decalogue in full or in a familiar order. In reading either of the literary versions of the decalogue, one notices that whereas some of the commandments are brief, simple imperatives, others are more complicated, either listing specific applications, proposing motives, or supplying explanations. It is very likely that an original list of terse prohibitions was expanded over the course of time, resulting in the present unevenness. In addition to literary expansion, expanded interpretations have often occurred. For example, adultery, originally understood as the injustice done to a husband by his unfaithful wife and her accomplice, is commonly reinterpreted in accordance with ideas, not shared by biblical writers, of the equality of the sexes. Similarly, bearing false witness, which originally referred to a juridical abuse of testimony, is often applied to much broader categories of deception. Although such broadenings of application occurred within the biblical period, in Christian religious education they have been carried to an unfortunate extreme of making room within the decalogue for every moral conviction, to the almost total distortion of the meanings of the biblical words, and the false ascription of biblical sanction to moral opinions unknown to the Bible.

Paul begins his first letter to the Corinthians, from which the second reading is taken, by lamenting the factions which have developed in that community, with different groups professing competing allegiances to different Christian missionaries, of whom Paul himself is one. He reminds them that the only reason he ever came among them was to preach a Gospel not about himself nor in the interest of his own popularity, but about "the fact of Christ on his cross." He recalls that this singular message was equally, though differently distasteful to Jewish and to Gentile hearers. For the Jews, crucifixion had been stigmatized by the Old Testament as implying that its victim was cursed by God. Since the Messiah was one who enjoyed the unique favor of God, a crucified Messiah was tantamount to a contradiction in terms. For the Gentiles, on the other hand, neither Bible nor Messiah had any great significance. The Greek world did, however, entertain definite pre-conceptions about what sort of man might qualify to be considered a savior, and chief among those pre-conceptions was that he would be one who accomplished liberation of spirit by a lofty philosophical wisdom. To such pre-conceptions, the idea that Jesus accomplished salvation by getting himself nailed to a cross would be simply ridiculous; such a Gospel would be sheer folly. However, Paul insists, God is no respecter of either Jewish or Greek prejudices, and what is "a stumbling block to the Jews and folly to the Greeks" remains, notwithstanding, "the power of God and the wisdom of God."

The account of Jesus' vigorous action in the temple occurs in all four

Gospels. The kind of sensational behavior here attributed to Jesus is in the tradition of actions by which the prophets sometimes dramatized and advertised their messages. In this case, the action intimates Jesus' messiahship by recalling certain messianic prophecies of the Old Testament. One of these, from Malachi (3:1-4), announces: "Suddenly the Lord whom you seek will come to his temple. Who can endure the day of his coming? He is like a refiner's fire. He will purify the Levites and cleanse them." Another, from Zechariah (14:1, 21), proclaims: "A day is coming for the Lord to act. . . . When that time comes, no trader shall again be seen in the house of the Lord of Hosts." Verse 10 from Psalm 69 is cited with similar intent by the Gospel itself: "Zeal for thy house will destroy (or consumes) me." The whole episode has been characterized as an "enacted parable," that is, a dramatization which, like Jesus' parabolic narrations, vividly conveys a particular aspect of his message—in this case his own fulfillment of messianic anticipations.

THIRD SUNDAY OF LENT

Cycle "C" Readings: Ex. 3:1-8, 13-15; 1 Cor. 10:1-6, 10-12; Lk. 13:1-9

The first reading is taken from the familiar account in the book of Exodus of the vocation of Moses. The episode is situated at Mount Horeb, later called Sinai, the same place where the law was later to be given. The phenomenon of the burning bush is consistent with the frequent use of fire to symbolize the divine presence, and the demand that Moses remove his shoes reflects an ancient Oriental custom of religious respect which is still observed among Muslims. The fact that God appears only symbolically, as well as the fact that Moses covers his eyes, reflects Hebrew belief, corresponding to a strong sense of divine transcendence, that for a human being directly to behold God would actually be lethal. Continuity between the story, which begins here with Moses, and the previous legends of the patriarchs is established by God's identification of himself with the God of Abraham, Isaac, and Jacob. The subsequent development of the story is anticipated by God's declaration of his intention to set his people free from their Egyptian oppressors, and to lead them into a rich country then occupied by other peoples. Moses' inquiry as to what name he should apply to the God who is sending him to lead the people occasions a statement of the divine name. The name which is given was written in Hebrew without vowels as YHWH. It is generally thought to have been pronounced Yahweh, and to be derived from the verb "to be." The precise interpretation of this name is still disputed among scholars. Of ancient translations, the Greek rendered it as "he who is" and the Latin as "I am who am."

Some modern scholars interpret it as the beginning of a phrase which, in its entirety, would mean "he brings into being whatever comes into being," and thus as referring rather to God's creative action than to his existence. Other explanations are also plausibly defended by scholars. In any case, YHWH became the distinctive title of Israel's God, and the use of it in preference to El and Elohim characterizes a distinct tradition of Old Testament literature.

The second reading, taken from St. Paul's first letter to the Corinthians, is a warning against complacency and consequent backsliding. Apparently some of the Corinthian Christians, like some other Christians since their time, had allowed their faith in the efficacy of baptism to degenerate into an irresponsible presumption of more or less automatic salvation. For all his insistence on salvation by faith, Paul sternly denounces this perversion of his doctrine. In order to illustrate and intensify his warning, Paul recalls that the Israelites during the exodus had also been the recipients of many special and even miraculous helps from God that might be compared with baptism. Nevertheless, divine assistance did not in their case simply dispense with human cooperation, and the death of many of the Israelites in the desert was a sign of their repudiation by a God whom they had persistently dishonored and disobeyed. The passage contains a curious reference to "the spiritual rock that was following them," which finds its explanation not in the Old Testament narrative, but in a later Jewish legend to the effect that the rock from which Moses obtained water for his thirsty followers actually did follow them about thereafter as a kind of mobile fountain! In saying that this "rock was Christ" Paul is evidently thinking in terms of the eternal, divine Christ, "through whom," as he said earlier in the same letter, "all things came to be." The idea of Christ as the source of grace, combined with the common symbolism of grace by "living water," encourages the association of Christ with the legendary rock. But in making the association Paul is chiefly influenced by his desire to show that divine means of grace, like baptism, do not work automatically now any more than they did in the past.

The third reading, from the Gospel according to Luke, has no parallel elsewhere in the New Testament, and the two contemporary events it refers to are unknown from any other surviving record. Apparently Pontius Pilate, whose policy toward the Jews was characteristically severe, had caused some Galilean Jews to be put to death on an occasion of offering sacrifice. Jesus takes the mention of this event as an occasion for pointing out that the fate of those victims of brutality no more implied their outstanding sinfulness than did the accidental disaster in which a falling tower took the lives of eighteen persons at Siloam. Jesus' purpose, however, is not to defend the reputation of Pilate's victims or to deny the connection between sin and suffering, but to remind his hearers that their own survival is not to be taken as evidence of any special merit on their part, but rather as an opportunity to repent while it is still possible for them to do so.

FOURTH SUNDAY OF LENT

Cycle "A" Readings: 1 Sam. 16:1, 6-7, 10-13; Eph. 5:8-14; Jn. 9:1-41

It has often been observed that the religious experiences of individuals occupy a much smaller place in the Bible than they do in most other religious narratives we are familiar with. And, what is more significant, when the Bible does describe God taking some special interest in particular individuals, that interest nearly always has about it a curiously businesslike quality. As a matter of fact, it nearly always turns out that when in the Bible God singles somebody out for preferential treatment, it is in order to give him not some rapture of devotion to enjoy, but some job of work to perform.

Usually, moreover, the choices God makes of such individuals are not such as would commend themselves to the average personnel director. God shows a remarkably habitual predilection for incompetents and apparent misfits—a tongue-tied public leader like Moses, a diffident prophet like Amos, a guilt-laden reformer like Isaiah, or a jittery accuser like Jonah! David—that outstandingly glamorous combination of warrior, poet, ruler, lover, and man of God—might seem to be a notable exception to this rule. But today's reading from the first book of Samuel serves to remind us that even David was, when God singled him out, a nobody—the kid brother left at home to keep sheep from running away while his elders and betters engaged in nobler occupations. Nevertheless, "not as man sees does God see," and God's choice fell upon David, to everyone's surprise.

The most obvious lesson implied in this seemingly perverse pattern of divine election is that God is in no way compelled or confined by the intrinsic merits of his human instruments. He chooses them freely, requiring nothing of their special worldly qualifications, but simply deciding that his omnipotent will is to be done through the inauspicious human creatures he made out of nothing and can, therefore, make into anything. To be specially chosen by the sort of God our Bible portrays is reason for profound gratitude and abundant confidence. But it is certainly no reason for personal pride.

This pattern of God's summoning nobodies to be fashioned into somebodies is no less strongly present in the New Testament, and not only with respect to the vocations of individuals—like that marvelously ill-endowed assortment of Jesus' apostles—but still more with respect to the Church as a whole which is brought into being by the call of Christ. That Church which is called in the Gospel "the light of the world" certainly did not acquire its luminosity by the bringing together of distinct human brilliances. As the Ephesians are reminded in today's reading: "There was a time when you were darkness but now you are light in the Lord." Just as the raw material of the first creation is simply nothingness, so the raw material of that "new creation" called the "light of the world" is simply darkness. All the luminosity is God's. And if the Ephesians can indeed be called light "in the Lord," they must not be allowed to forget that apart from the Lord their condition was one of abysmal obscurity.

"I know this much: I was blind before; now I can see" is, in St. John's Gospel, the plain statement of a plain man's testimony to the truth of the most important and wonderful thing that had ever happened to him. It had happened to him without any action or asking of his own, simply because a man named Jesus had done to him something which was assumed to be humanly impossible. The whole episode is, of course, a symbolic story intended to reinforce with the vividness of a very touching drama a theological doctrine which precedes it in the fourth Gospel: "I am the light of the world. No follower of mine shall ever walk in darkness; no, he shall possess the light of life."

The blind man whose restored sight challenged a deeper spiritual blindness in those around him represents all those who, like the Ephesians, "were darkness but now . . . are light in the Lord." Their light is not self-generated. It is the reflected light of God's truth which, as the prologue to St. John's Gospel tells us, penetrates our darkness by the coming of the Word made flesh. And for that very reason it is a light which not only brings vision to those who welcome it, but also, as with the Pharisees in the story, confirms the blindness of those who refuse it. Faith is thus represented by St. John's Gospel as the acceptance of God's light by man's darkness. But there remain those tragic cases who judge even the light of God by the standard of their own darkness. And to them Jesus can only say: "If you were blind, there would be no sin in that. 'But we see,' you say, and your sin remains." Here, as always in St. John's Gospel, the word of salvation and the word of judgment, the light that illumines and the light that blinds, are one and the same.

FOURTH SUNDAY OF LENT

Cycle "B" Readings: 2 Chr. 36:14-16, 19-23; Eph. 2:4-10; Jn. 3:14-21

The title of the books called Chronicles comes from St. Jerome, who described their content as "a chronicle of the whole of divine history." Modern scholarship recognizes that these two works are continuous with the books of Ezra and Nehemiah. All four were apparently compiled, from earlier traditions, around the fourth century B.C. as a theological history extending from the origins of Israel to the rebuilding of Jerusalem after the exile. The passage read in today's liturgy from the second book of Chronicles refers to the exile itself and the restoration which followed it. The chronicler's account of the exile eschews all political explanations and concentrates on what for him was its real and ultimate cause. The exile was God's punishment of Israel for inveterate sinfulness which has persisted despite all the warnings of the prophets. Like the beginning, so also the end of the Babylonian captivity is explained not in political but exclusively in religious terms. When the Israelites had served their term of penal confinement, God prompted the Persian monarch, whose empire had by then gained control of Babylon, to fulfill the prophecy of Jeremiah. A religious paraphrase of the famous Edict of Cyrus, which made possible the reconstruction of Jerusalem, concludes the book and introduces that final period of Israel's history which is treated in Ezra and Nehemiah. The entire passage furnishes a striking illustration of the Old Testament's way of interpreting historical events as entirely manipulated by God with a view to the ultimate good of his people Israel. Historic disasters are his punishments, historic triumphs are his rewards, and history itself is the record of his providence.

The ups and downs of Israel's fortunes as presented in the Bible have been likened to a pattern of "divine pedagogy," in which God teaches his people as parents teach children, by chastising their misbehavior and rewarding their good conduct. At the same time that reformed behavior may be regarded in the Old Testament as prerequisite to receiving special favors from God after a period of punishment, it is consistently emphasized that God's saving acts are acts of generosity, of grace, and by no means the people's just deserts which God accords out of simple justice. In the New Testament, and especially in the Pauline writings, the idea of undeserved salvation is strongly emphasized, in accordance with the conviction that Christ is rather the savior of sinners than a rewarder of the sinless. It is this idea, basic to Christian theology, which finds repeated expression in today's liturgical selection from the letter to Ephesians. The point is made both positively and negatively. "For the great love he bore us" God restored us to life "even when we were dead in our sins." He did this to show "how immense are the resources of his grace, and how great his kindness to us." "It is by his grace you are saved." "It is not your own doing." "It is God's gift." "It is not a reward." "There is nothing for anyone to boast of." The final verse expresses the viewpoint of a genuinely Christian moral theology, in pointing out that, whereas God's grace is not a consequence of our "good deeds," our "good deeds" are the consequence of God's grace. Christian holiness of life is not the cause of salvation, but the effect of it.

The final reading, from the Gospel according to John complements the doctrine that is so emphatically reiterated in the preceding selection from Ephesians. Whereas that passage stresses that divine salvation is not earned by human beings but is given undeserved to them by God, the Johannine passage focuses on how human beings accept this gift from God. This acceptance or reception is identified with faith. By way of illustration, the saving cross of Christ is compared to the image of a serpent which, in the exodus narrative, brought a cure to the followers of Moses who had been bitten by snakes and who gazed upon it. The Gospel understands this gazing upon the curative image as a manifestation of trust or faith, comparable to Christian reliance on the power of the cross. Christ, the source of life, is the gift of God, but that gift must be embraced with the grateful confidence of faith. As Christ came to save, he did not, strictly speaking, come to judge. And yet there is in the very saving mission of Christ a kind of built-in judgment. For it is on the acceptance by faith or the rejection of what Christ brings that human fate ultimately hinges. Christ does not judge. He simply presents himself, the Savior. And yet to encounter Christ the Savior is to confront that fundamental choice between light and darkness in which judgment finally consists. This conception of Christ as one who, in bringing life, imposes a choice between life and death, and thereby accomplishes judgment by the very work of salvation, is one of the most characteristic themes of the Gospel according to John, and a profound development in the Christian theology of salvation.

FOURTH SUNDAY OF LENT

Cycle "C" Readings: Jos. 5:9-12; 2 Cor. 5:17-21; Lk. 15:1-3, 11-32

The first reading in today's liturgy is taken from the book of Joshua, which relates the events associated with the Hebrews' conquest of the promised land of Canaan, and their subsequent division of the conquered territory among their tribes. The present passage is from a section which describes an interlude before the siege of Jericho, at a place called Gilgal, where the rite of circumcision was renewed after having been neglected during the journey. During the rest period set aside for the recuperation of the newly circumcised, the time of Passover arrived, and the people celebrated this feast for the first time in their new land. This occasion marked the end of their miraculous feeding with the manna which had been provided by God for their desert journey. This provision was no longer required, since they had now entered the fertile country which was to be their homeland. The cessation of the manna thus represents their transition from a nomadic to a settled mode of existence. Hereafter, the promised land itself was to furnish their sustenance. The episode brings out clearly the basis of later Christian interpretation of the manna as foreshadowing the eucharistic bread which was to serve God's people as a "food of wayfarers" until they should finally arrive at their eternal homeland.

The second reading, from St. Paul's second letter to the Corinthians, is one of the principal passages in which Paul develops the theological conception that he characteristically associates with the term "reconciliation," a term not employed in this technical sense by other New Testament writers. The word itself, which is translated as "reconciliation," is based on a Greek word meaning, in general, "to change." As applied to social life it refers to a change in human relationships from hostility to peace, or, in other words, from being enemies to being friends. Since enmity normally results from an offense, reconciliation, as the abolition of enmity, depends on forgiveness, by one who has been offended, of one who has given offense. If this forgiveness is accepted and friendship is restored, reconciliation is accomplished. The reconciliation of which St. Paul speaks is mainly the restoration of friendship between humankind and God, based on the human acceptance of divine forgiveness. Thus in Paul's usage, to reconcile is always the action of God, whereas it is the part of the human being to be reconciled. This distinction is important for understanding the present passage, where Paul first declares that God "has reconciled us to himself through Christ," and then adds that he has also "given us the ministry of reconciliation." This "ministry of reconciliation" does not mean that man rather than God becomes henceforth the reconciler. Rather, as the subsequent verses indicate, to have the ministry of reconciliation means, for human beings, to bear the "message of reconciliation." This message of reconciliation is the good news, the Gospel, the announcement to humankind of God's forgiveness which, if accepted in a spirit of repentance and faith, re-establishes the friendship with God which is forfeited by that offending of God which is called sin. Thus the appeal of the "ambassadors for Christ" is precisely "be reconciled to God," based on the assurance that, through Christ, this reconciliation is available to all who will receive it.

The third reading, from the Gospel according to Luke, contains what is probably the New Testament's most eloquent and memorable expression of the doctrine of reconciliation, the parable of a forgiving father and his two sons, one of whom has offended him greatly and ultimately experiences the reconciling power of his forgiveness, while the other becomes estranged from both his father and his brother by his own unwillingness to enter into the spirit of forgiveness and the experience of reconciliation. The story has been well described as one of Jesus' "double-edged" parables. For the same story skillfully blends two episodes that convey respectively a message of warm reassurance and a message of solemn warning. The reassurance is addressed to those who are able to identify their own situation with that of the offending son, and to see in the forgiving father a portrayal of that God of mercy whose generous love preserves the hope of reconciliation despite the gravity of their offenses and the depth of their alienation from him. This deeply touching narrative of unqualified kindness and compassion toward the undeserving imparts a bitter irony to the episode that immediately follows it, in which the unoffending son is seen to be alienated from his father in an even deeper sense. For the very quality that chiefly characterizes the father and gives him that unique moral greatness which expresses the essence of God himself is neither shared nor even respected by the elder son, whose hard self-righteousness recalls the words of the Pharisees and scribes that introduced the parable in its Gospel setting: "This man welcomes sinners and eats with them."

FIFTH SUNDAY OF LENT

Cycle "A" Readings: Ez. 37:12-14; Rom. 8:8-11; Jn. 11:1-45

"While there is life there is hope" is a proverbial saying we generally interpret as highly optimistic. But an enormously higher optimism runs persistently through the Bible which might adopt as its proverb: "While there is death there is hope." Today's reading from the prophecy of Ezekiel is one of the Bible's most unforgettable expressions of that idea.

Ezekiel was a priest who shared Israel's captivity in Babylon after having prophesied for years previously that Jerusalem was doomed to a destruction which would be God's inexorable punishment for his people's sins. One of the most remarkable things about this extraordinary man, however, is the way in which, after the predicted devastation and exile had become realities, he transformed himself from a prophet of unmitigated doom into a preacher of the most dauntless and irrepressible hope. It is in this latter context that we read the famous visionary prophecy of today's liturgy.

The picture of a valley strewn with bleaching fragments of innumerable skeletons is a poignant image of that sense of futility and fatality with which the deported Israelites must have regarded their present and anticipated their future. And so Ezekiel's assurance that God could and ultimately would restore his chastened people is expressed in terms of that most impossible of revivals which made a purposeful multitude of living men out of material no more promising than desiccated, dislocated bones. For while there is death there is hope. Because while there is death there is still the source of life, the Spirit of God, the divine animating breath which brought life even out of nothingness "in the beginning . . . while a mighty wind swept over the waters" (Gen. 1:1).

In order to make sense out of today's fragmentary excerpt from St. Paul's letter to the Romans we must recall a few points about that writer's theological vocabulary, and in particular of the meaning he attaches to "flesh" and "spirit." By "flesh" he normally means the common natural component of humanity which, although in itself morally indifferent, had through man's disobedience become an instrument of sin. And, as Paul stated earlier, in one of his most quoted verses, "The wages of sin is death" (Rom. 6:23). Sin, in other words, earns death; to become a sinner is to contract for death; death is sin's pay-off. Consequently, three ideas get tied closely together in Paul's formula for man's fallen state: flesh, sin, and death.

However, it is essential to recall that Paul's statement, "the wages of sin is death," is only the first half of a famous sentence which concludes, "but the gift of God is eternal life in Christ Jesus our Lord." That second part of the sentence is the essence of "the Gospel according to Paul," his particular rendering of the good news of salvation. Death is the wages of sin, what sin earns, deserves. But Paul's apostolic message is that man does not get what he deserves or earns, does not get the wages he contracted for. Instead he gets a gift, God's gift, which is the gift of eternal life. God's offer of that gift is his revelation in Jesus Christ. Man's acceptance of the offer, what we call Christian faith, is his acceptance of that revelation. And finally man's reception of the gift is his receiving of the Spirit. For just as spirit, meaning breath, represents life, so the Spirit of God represents divine, eternal life.

Putting all this together we begin to understand why man, as Paul describes him, seems such a complicated, multi-layered being. For the basic stuff he is made of has first of all turned away from God by sin, and thus condemned itself to death. But Christian man has through Jesus Christ been offered, accepted, and received the gift of God which is life-giving Spirit. Hence in his present state man is a creature in whom death, the wages of sin, is replaced by life, the gift of God, and in whom a deserved mortality is replaced by an undeserved immortality. Paul's rather perplexing imagery seems to set us in the midst of this very process of replacement, in an attempt to express both the mortality man has earned and the vitality he has been given. Thus he can say, "The body is indeed dead because of sin, while the spirit lives because of justice" (meaning the justice that God's gift imparts to us). And, looking somewhat farther ahead, he can also say: "He who raised Christ from the dead will bring your mortal bodies to life also." It is, in other words, a picture of progressive revival, the gradual infusion of life into a moribund creature, a sort of artificial respiration of divine love applied with marvelous effect to the stupid, sordid suicide attempt of sinful man.

The account of the raising of Jesus' friend Lazarus in the Gospel according to John is a symbolic story which provides a fitting climax to the previous two readings and a no less fitting prelude to the imminent liturgical celebration of Christ's passion and resurrection. The basic meaning of the story is made explicit in Jesus' words: "I am the resurrection and the life; whoever believes in me, though he should die, will come to life; and whoever is alive and believes in me will never die." It is, in other words, a Johannine presentation of essentially the same message we have just discussed in Pauline terms. In this Gospel, as in our own liturgical sequence, the event in Bethany stands at the threshold of those developments which precipitate the events of Holy Week. It is a kind of enacted parable of resurrection which raises the curtain, so to speak, on the fourth Gospel's magnificent dramatic presentation of the paschal mystery.

FIFTH SUNDAY OF LENT

Cycle "B" Readings: Jer. 31:31-34; Heb. 5:7-9; Jn. 12:20-33

The verses cited in the first reading, from the prophecy of Jeremiah, furnish a conceptual bridge to the New Testament, or new covenant, which is the subject of this passage. The life of the prophet Jeremiah extended over the time when Israel finally succumbed to her northern enemies, with Jerusalem laid waste and the people driven into exile. Against the dreadful finality with which this event threatened the cherished hopes of Israel, Jeremiah's preaching declared that, even in the tragic end which had been put to Israel's kingdom, there was to be anticipated a new and glorious beginning. The old covenant, the bond of allegiance joining God to his chosen people, would be succeeded by a new covenant, similar in effect but quite different in character. The old covenant had been violated by the sinful infidelities of Israel. Jeremiah promises in God's name a new covenant, which will once again constitute a people of God. The bestowal of the new covenant is to be an act of sheer divine mercy, forgiving and forgetting the offenses of the past. Unlike the written Mosaic law with which the former covenant was identified, the new covenant would be expressed as a personal conviction, "written on their hearts." The new covenant, experienced interiorly as the mercy of a forgiving God, was naturally identified by Christians with the redemptive work of Christ, who, by shedding his "blood of the new covenant," accomplished release from sin and reunion with God.

The idea of Christ as minister of the new covenant, acting as God's agent in the forgiveness and reconciliation of humankind, is basic to the New Testament. The anonymous author of the letter to Hebrews expresses this by employing the concept of priesthood to convey the significance of Christ's role in the divine work of redemption. Describing priesthood as a service of mediation, whereby sacrifices are offered to invoke God's forgiveness of sin, Hebrews represents Christ as the consummation of all priesthood, for his sacrifice finally and fully achieves what all sacrifices have in view, the re-establishment of union between humanity which sins and God who forgives. Christ, the high-priestly mediator, represents both humankind, praying for forgiveness, and God, answering that prayer with forgiveness. Combining the prophetic imagery of Jeremiah with the priestly imagery of Hebrews, Christ is conceived as the priest "taken from among men," whose sacrificial submission to the will of God is the definitive sacrifice, whose definitive result is the new and everlasting covenant.

The death of Christ, which the letter to Hebrews present in retrospect, is presented in the Gospel according to John as eagerly anticipated by Jesus during the final days of his public life. The setting of the third reading is the very eve of the passion. The disciples tell Jesus that some persons of Gentile origin wish to see him. Instead of answering, Jesus announces that "the hour has come for the Son of Man to be glorified," and adds enigmatically that unless the grain of wheat "falls into the ground and dies," it cannot be fruitful. Then, addressing God as his Father, Jesus expresses simultaneously his repugnance for the terrible ordeal which lies before him, and his awareness that this ordeal represents the fulfillment of his mission. A voice from heaven then confirms the words of Jesus. To some of those present, the voice is clearly heavenly in origin, angelic. But others are quick to explain it away as merely a sound of thunder. As so often in John's Gospel, the evidence of Jesus' divine status proves to be equivocal, and leads persons of contrasting dispositions to draw significantly opposite conclusions. The encounter with Jesus in this Gospel is always a critical encounter, a test of where persons actually stand with respect to God. The episode ends without Jesus having made any response to the Gentile seekers. This is no accident or oversight, but almost certainly a conscious device on the writer's part. That the wishes of Gentiles to "see Jesus" would be satisfied, in the most significant sense, not before but after the crucifixion, was clearly understood in the post-resurrection Christian perspective in which the Fourth Gospel was written and read. The invitation to "see Jesus" is relevant only after the crucifixion, when it will have its full meaning and its full power. "I shall draw all men to myself, when I am lifted up from the earth"—"lifted up" in both senses, onto the cross, and into the eternal life of God in heaven.

FIFTH SUNDAY OF LENT

Cycle "C" Readings: Is. 43:16-21; Phil. 3:8-14; Jn. 8:1-11

The first reading of today's liturgy comes from a portion of the book of Isaiah which has been appropriately designated "The Book of Israel's Consolation." This writing cannot be attributed to the eighth-century prophet Isaiah despite its inclusion in the book which bears his name. Rather it is the work of an anonymous writer which dates from the time when Israel's period of exile was drawing to an end, and therefore from the latter part of the sixth century. This was a time when the long sadness of exile gave way to joyful anticipation of a return to Israel's homeland. Under the circumstances, it is natural that a parallel should have suggested itself between the Babylonian captivity and the former enslavement of the Hebrews in Egypt, and therefore between the anticipated return from exile and the famous exodus from Egypt. This parallel underlies the poem that is read in today's liturgy, and that views the longed-for restoration as a new exodus. Thus the passage begins by identifying God as the Lord of the exodus who opened a passage in the sea for his chosen people and destroyed the army that pursued them. It then calls upon the people to think of God no longer in terms of his great accomplishments in the past, but rather in terms of a great new deed that he is about to achieve. The exodus imagery is then resumed with a series of references to the provision of water in an arid wasteland to slake the thirst of God's people. At this point, however, the poet's thoughts dwell rather on the Syrian desert through which the exiles will travel southward to reclaim their promised land, than on the Egyptian desert through which their ancestors traveled originally to claim it as their gift from God.

The second reading, from St. Paul's letter to the Philippians, belongs to a part of that letter that does not fit together neatly with the rest of it, and is thought by some interpreters to have originated as part of a different document. It deals with an unidentified group of people whose influence on the Christians of Philippi Paul considered to be very dangerous. Whatever else they may have stood for, it is clear that what Paul most resented about them was their insistence on the importance of Jewish religious practices, such as circumcision. Thus Paul was once again confronted with the issue that had always been a source of great tension for his apostolate—the relevance of Jewish law in the light of Christian belief. Paul's view was that the whole significance of the Jewish law was to be found in its antecedence to the Christian Gospel, so that once that Gospel was embraced by faith, Jewish law was entirely superseded. It is this conviction which Paul expresses in the opening verse of today's reading: "I have come to rate all as loss in the light of the surpassing knowledge of my Lord Jesus Christ." The "all" that is here referred to, and is often interpreted in a very general sense, actually has a very specific sense: it means all the prescriptions of the Jewish law and all that results from obeying those prescriptions. The real force of this passage is, therefore, a radical cleavage between Jewish and Christian religion as Paul understands them. What Paul considers to be offered by Jewish religion, he emphatically rejects, namely "any justice of my own based on observance of the law." And what Paul considers to be offered by Christian religion, he no less emphatically accepts, namely "the justice which comes through faith in Christ." In the concluding verses of the passage, Paul reflects that what he possesses is not the end but the beginning of this salvation, that his present task is to be formed into the pattern of Christ's death, whereas his ultimate hope is to arrive where Christ's death brought him—at the resurrection. This conception of his present position as lying between the start and the finish of the process of salvation suggests Paul's final metaphor, of a runner who has left the starting line, but not yet crossed the finish line.

The third reading, from the Gospel according to John, is a famous narrative that most scholars consider to be an ancient element of Christian Scripture, but not originally a part of the Gospel according to John. It fits rather disjointedly into that Gospel in its present location, its style is unlike that of the rest of that Gospel, and the oldest manuscripts of that Gospel do not in fact contain it. Whatever its original context, the story presents a very recognizable portrayal of Jesus as he is known to us through the Synoptic Gospels, and it illustrates an attitude closely related to Jesus' basic message. Here, as so often, we find Jesus expressing in word and deed both an unqualified readiness to forgive and an intense disapproval of those who, forgetting their own need of forgiveness, are unready to forgive others. As in the petition, "forgive us our debts as we forgive our debtors," Jesus habitually links being forgiven with being forgiving, so in this episode his invitation to "be the first to cast a stone" is a reminder that only those who can afford to be unforgiven can afford to be unforgiving. Jesus' mysterious action of "tracing on the ground" may be a parody of the practice of Roman judges of writing down a judicial sentence before pronouncing it.

PASSION (PALM) SUNDAY

Cycle "A" Readings: Is. 50:4-7; Phil. 2:6-11; Mt. 26:14—27, 66

The initial reading in today's liturgy comprises the opening verses of the third of four Old Testament poems called "Servant songs." The poems originated during the time of the Babylonian captivity, and they convey a message of hope in the desperate circumstances of that time. Very likely in the original context the Servant represents, at least inclusively, Israel itself, God's suffering, humiliated people, who are to make an opportunity out of their misfortune by transmitting the saving revelation of their God to the rest of humankind. In Christian times, the applicability to Jesus of descriptions of this Servant gave these poems a special Christian significance, and there is good reason to believe that Jesus consciously applied them to himself. In the present passage, several outstanding characteristics of the Servant are clearly displayed. The Servant has a message to deliver or a lesson to impart, which will be a source of great comfort to those who receive it. Thus the Servant has "the tongue of a teacher and skill to console the weary." But the Servant's message is not his own invention, nor is his skill independently acquired; his effectiveness as a teacher depends entirely on his docility as a learner. The real source of his message is God, to whom therefore he must "listen like one who is taught." Nevertheless, the teaching mission which the Servant receives from God is not a matter of mere pedagogy, accurate learning and faithful rendering. Rather it is a harrowing ordeal, for the message has to be imparted under conditions of suffering so intense that only confidence of divine support can make them endurable.

Absolute docility to God, and courageous obedience to God are manifested in the Servant's resolute fidelity to the saving truth of God's message. The same pattern, as reproduced and magnified in the passion of Jesus Christ, remains for Christians the basic motive for their own courageous adherence to the Gospel. It is that motive which St. Paul presents to the church of Philippi. Today's text appears to be an early Christian liturgical hymn, presumably familiar to the Philippians, which Paul here quotes in a context of moral exhortation. The hymn summarizes the mission of Jesus Christ as a progressive descent from the transcendent heights of divinity to a servile status in the human condition and, in that status, to humiliation ending in the most ignominious kind of death, crucifixion. The hymn concludes with a triumphant acknowledgement that it is precisely what Jesus accomplished through this pattern of relentless degradation for which the whole universe now owes him the supreme honor of proclaiming his divine lordship. The early Church produced in this hymn a New Testament "Servant song," in which one of the most remarkable prophetic motifs of the Old Testament is effectively blended with the theology of the incarnation and resurrection.

The third reading in today's liturgy begins the account of Jesus' passion from the Gospel according to Matthew. This portion of the narrative, which concludes with the eucharistic words (Mt. 26:26ff), is dominated by Judas' betrayal of his master and Jesus' indication of his awareness of that betrayal. Here again, therefore, we are confronted with the same ironic pattern of God's salvific design which is poetically expressed in the other readings. The fulfillment of Christ's saving mission is accordingly introduced by an act not of loyalty but of treachery, and presented rather as a frustrating anticlimax than as a satisfying climax of his career. What by criteria of human reason can only amount to a guarantee of failure is, by the criterion of divine faith, an assurance of success. The two points of view appear juxtaposed in verses 23 and 24, where the startling announcement that one of Jesus' table companions will betray him is immediately followed by the firm assertion that the Son of Man proceeds unerringly along the way mapped out for him in the prophetic Scriptures. Isaiah's terrible figure of the Suffering Servant and Daniel's triumphant image of the apocalyptic Son of Man are here united in a seemingly impossible synthesis, identical with that interpenetration of cross and resurrection of which the Eucharist is Christianity's permanent reminder.

PASSION (PALM) SUNDAY

Cycle "B" Readings: same as cycle "A" except Mk. 14:1—15:47

The third reading is the entire passion narrative, from the Gospel according to Mark. Although Mark's Gospel, which is thought to be the oldest, is a much briefer and barer document than the others, the account which it contains of Jesus' passion and death is just about the same size and contains much the same material as the others. Since apart from the passion narrative Mark's material is mostly reproduced and extensively augmented by the other two Synoptic Gospels, Matthew and Luke, it appears that the others found little to add to the passion account. It seems, therefore, highly probable that the passion story was the earliest portion of our written Gospels to develop into a more or less definitive narration, which was afterwards reproduced with only minor variations. This literary comparison and the conclusions one seems justified in drawing from it, serve to remind us of how absolutely basic to the Gospel the passion narrative was understood to be. Without gross exaggeration one could go so far as to say that originally the Gospel story virtually consisted in the story of Jesus' passion and death which was afterwards supplemented by material about Jesus' public life as a teacher and miracle worker, and later by various reminiscences concerning his youth, birth, and ancestry. The notion that the basic story of Jesus Christ is that of an extraordinary teacher and social worker is totally irreconcilable with the literary data, quite apart from theological preferences. The development of the Gospels reflected a Christian conviction of the central and fundamental importance of Jesus' passion and death for the whole significance of his mission. The passion story is the very heart of the Gospel story.

PASSION (PALM) SUNDAY

Cycle "C" Readings: same as cycle "A" except Lk. 22:14—23:56

The third reading comprises the entire passion narrative of the Gospel according to Luke. In the account of the Last Supper, the lectionary includes verses (22, 19b, 20) which are omitted in many manuscripts, and consequently in many highly reputable translations, which regard them as later insertions aimed at making Luke's account more like Mark's and Paul's, in which case Luke may have had rather different notions of the event and of its relationship to eucharistic practice. Luke does show considerably individuality at other points in his passion narrative. He alone makes the Last Supper the occasion of the disciples' argument about their respective greatness, which is in turn the occasion for Jesus' last discourse. The account of Jesus' trials has a unique feature in Luke's telling inasmuch as he alone reports a trial before Herod. Luke is also our only source for the report that Pontius Pilate was personally convinced of Jesus' innocence. Again, in Luke's account, Matthew's and Mark's mere mention of the thieves crucified with Jesus has been expanded into the touching story of Jesus' forgiveness of the "good thief." Many other smaller but not insignificant points also have a specifically Lucan character. Although in comparing the different passion accounts one finds essentially the same story, testifying to a very ancient common tradition, it is worth noticing that the evangelists do introduce differences, both in material details and in their style of presentation. These differences have important scholarly implications, but they also enrich the experience of devotional reading.

EASTER SEASON

EASTER SUNDAY

Cycles "A", "B", and "C" Readings: Acts 10:34, 37-43; Col. 3:1-4, or 1 Cor. 5:6-8; Jn. 20:1-9

The first reading is a sermon which, according to Acts, was preached by Peter to a group of Gentiles in Caesarea. The occasion is led up to by a remarkable series of experiences the main effect of which was to convince Peter that the Gospel was intended no less for the Gentiles than for Jews. Peter acknowledges this at the start of his sermon, saying "God has no favorites" and "in every nation the person who is God-fearing and does what is right is acceptable to him." The sermon is immediately followed by a pentecostal experience, when "the Holy Spirit came upon all who were listening," thereby banishing any lingering doubts about the Gentiles' eligibility for baptism. Peter's sermon is, in effect, a pre-baptismal instruction, which takes the form of a concise proclamation of the essential ingredients of the Gospel. Similar sermons are recorded elsewhere in Acts, and are thought to represent the earliest form in which the essentials of Christian belief were presented. The sermon is, so to speak, a mini-Gospel. The pentecostal event, evidenced by the speaking in tongues, which follows, shows that the Gentile hearers have responded to the Gospel by putting their faith in Jesus and are immediately experiencing the consequences. Their baptism initiates them into the company of believers, conceived now as a truly universal fellowship, sharing "the life of the age to come."

It is to a realistic appreciation of this "life of the age to come" that we are summoned by the alternate reading taken from the letter to the Colossians. Being raised to life with Christ, a Christian's thoughts, aspirations, and undertakings are all meant to express this divine life. The direction given to Christian life by the resurrection, which is its source, is an onward and upward course. Retrogression or stagnation of moral attitudes and behavior is incompatible with such a life. What this means concretely is explained in thoroughly practical terms, first negatively and then positively, in the verses of exhortation which follow (3.5-17).

The second alternate reading is taken from a series of complaints by St. Paul about the moral behavior of Christians at Corinth. After deploring a particular scandal concerning incest, Paul sharply criticizes the community as a whole for its complacency. He quotes the proverb, "a little leaven leavens all the dough," equivalent to the saying that "one bad apple spoils the bushel," implying that one malignant member can corrupt a whole community. The proverb's reference to leaven then reminds him of the Jewish Passover, at which unleavened bread is consumed as a reminder of the hasty meal the Hebrews ate just before the exodus, and Paul exhorts the

Corinthians to become themselves like Passover bread by eliminating the "leaven" or moral corruption. By a further association of ideas, without much logical connection, reference to Passover carries Paul's thoughts to Jesus, symbolized for Christians by the Paschal lamb. The sacrificial death of Jesus makes of Christian life a kind of permanent Passover, a continuing celebration of deliverance, which must be as completely free of immorality as the paschal bread is of leaven. Easter, the Christian Passover, celebrates a new life, to be lived purely.

In the third reading, taken from the Gospel according to John, we view, as it were through a magnifying lens, that central element, the resurrection, which Peter's sermon in the first reading situated in its typical Gospel setting. The chapter just preceding this account, concluding the Passion narrative, had ended on a note of somber finality with the burial of Jesus on Saturday evening. The Easter narrative begins by specifying the time as early Sunday morning—a new week, a new day, a dawning after darkness—emphasizing from the outset that what had seemed the end of a life was really its beginning. Thus the stress of the whole passage is on "dawning": dispelling darkness, clearing up a sad misunderstanding with a joyous realization. The successive visitors to the tomb perceive with increasing vividness that the tomb and everything in it are totally forsaken by Jesus. The circumstances compel them to realize that Jesus is remote from the tomb, because tombs are for the dead and Jesus is vitally alive. Thus the empty sepulchre with its tidily discarded burial cloths proclaiming the definitive departure of its former occupant, represents the first effective revelation of the Good News. For "until then they had not understood the Scriptures which showed that he must rise from the dead." That new understanding of the Scriptures would thereafter be a constant motif of the Gospel message preached first to Jews and then, as in the first reading, to that vast Gentile world which, for Jews, represented the rest of the human race.

SECOND SUNDAY OF EASTER

Cycle "A" Readings: Acts 2:42-47; 1 Pet. 1:3-9; Jn. 20:19-31

The first reading, from Acts of the Apostles, is one, and probably the best known, of three passages in that book that seem to be inserted somewhat artificially into the narrative in order to give a summary description of typical daily life in the earliest Christian community. The Jerusalem Christians are represented as a very close-knit community. Among their distinctive activities are the receiving of instructions from the apostles, the "breaking of bread," which may be a form of the eucharist, and "prayers." Although the breaking of bread is said to have taken place in their homes, they are also reported as convening each day at the temple, implying the persistence among them of Jewish religious practices. Their sharing of meals suggests a family-like relationship. Much interest has been taken in what is sometimes called the "communism" of primitive Christianity, their system of something approaching common ownership. Individuals are said to have sold their property, presumably to facilitate the sharing of it, and to have distributed the proceeds on a basis of need. We learn from Paul that the Jerusalem Christians subsequently fell into such dire poverty that collections had to be taken up for them among churches of the Gentile world. Some commentators have attributed this to a lack of prudence in the economic policy alluded to here, but there are other, equally plausible explanations. The passage emphasizes the wholeheartedness of the first Christians, and suggests the power of that quality to attract new members to their community.

The second reading is taken from the first letter of Peter, of which it may be doubted both that it is a letter and that Peter wrote it. Most of the work has the character of a short treatise or sermon, and only the last portion is much like a genuine letter. The document begins with a greeting addressed to Christians in a number of Gentile locations, and then, in the section that comprises the reading, praises God for his gift of a new birth, the source of which is the resurrection of Jesus. The new life which is introduced by this new birth is characterized by a hope that is eternally imperishable. What the new birth looks forward to is a salvation that is still to be revealed, insured by a divine power predicated on faith. The importance of this faith is the basis of an exhortation to endure the sufferings caused by persecution, for these sufferings are to be understood in a positive way, as testing and purifying faith. The faith whose genuineness is thereby established will be the means of ultimate triumph when Jesus returns. The final verse of the reading is a succinct resume of Christian life, characterized by a love based upon belief, and manifested in a joyful sense of progressing toward the final goal called salvation. The basic elements of this description clearly correspond to what Christian tradition knows as the theological virtues of faith, hope, and love.

The third reading, from the Gospel according to John, begins with an account of Jesus' appearance to his disciples on Easter Sunday night, after their discovery that morning of the empty tomb, and his subsequent appearance to Mary Magdalen. This appearance to the disciples is a highly significant one, and it has often been thought of as a counterpart to the Pentecost account found in Acts. Jesus' greeting of peace is the conventional Jewish salutation, but under the circumstances its meaning implies much more than conventional good wishes. Jesus uses the greeting twice. The first time, it introduces his action of showing them the wounds which mark the continuity between his passion and death and the risen life he now possesses. His second use of the greeting of peace introduces the disciples to their own new life as his missionaries, sent by Jesus just as he had been sent by the Father. Their new life demands an interior transformation, represented by

Jesus' breathing upon them in token of bestowing upon them the divine Spirit, in virtue of which they are to exercise the divine function of bestowing or withholding forgiveness. The reading also includes the account of Jesus' third self-manifestation, this time to Thomas, who had remained skeptical about the previous appearance. The lesson of this episode is its insistence upon faith as the proper response to the mission of witness that had just previously been given to the disciples. Thus Thomas' personal lesson constitutes a kind of object lesson, directed to all those whom the disciples' mission would henceforth address, and thus to all those who should read this Gospel.

SECOND SUNDAY OF EASTER

Cycle "B" Readings: Acts 4:32-35; 1 Jn. 5:1-6; Jn. 20:19-31

The first reading begins with a general characterization of the attitude which prevailed in the earliest Christian community at Jerusalem, and then proceeds to describe a striking feature of that community's social organization which expressed their attitude. The opening verse observes that the large group of believers had what is very literally rendered as "one heart and one soul." The word translated "heart" denotes the center and source of life, whereas the word translated "soul" very frequently, and probably here, designates earthly life itself. The phrase, therefore, compares the life of this community of Christians to that of one living organism. One might translate it quite accurately by saying they all possessed "one single life and one single principle of life." Here we encounter the same direction of thought which, in the Pauline writings, leads to describing the Church as a "body with many members." The rest of the passage in Acts points out that this unity of inner vitality and outward life was exhibited by the Jerusalem Christians in the plainest of ways, namely, by sharing a common source of material sustenance. Concretely, the common sustenance of their common life was achieved through a pooling of economic resources. The result was that "they were all held in high esteem, for they had never a needy person among them." That is, the Christians earned the astonished admiration of others by effectively eliminating poverty from their midst. For the author of Acts, this was important less as an experiment in economic collectivism than as a vivid manifestation of the unity proper to Christian society. This needs to be borne in mind especially in view of the fact that St. Paul, in his letters to the Corinthians, refers to a collection taken up among Gentile churches for the church in Jerusalem, which seems to have experienced severe poverty by the middle of the first century. Some interpreters have conjectured that there may have been more enthusiastic generosity than long-range economic practicality in the system of sharing described in Acts.

The second reading, from the first letter of John, likewise pertains to the unity of Christian believers. Characteristically in this letter, however, unity is conceived here primarily under the aspect of love. The passage begins by observing that the result of believing in Jesus as Christ, that is, as Messiah, is being a child of God. This idea was formulated in Catholic dogma to the effect that justification, based on faith, makes us adopted children of God, deriving from him the new divine life of grace, sharing in the divine nature. From this starting point, an argument is developed, based on the ideas that, first, a child ought to love his father, and second, that love for a father cannot exclude his children. Consequently, our being children of God, which demands that we love God in the practical sense of obeying him, also involves our loving others who are likewise God's children. Just before this passage, it was stated that "he who loves God must also love his brother." By a rather intricate process of logic, the present passage leads to the complementary conclusion that he who loves God, and therefore obeys God, is thereby loving his brother. The argument then proceeds a further step by observing that it is even rather easy to obey God, because believing in Jesus as Son of God, which makes us God's children, also makes us victorious over the world, undaunted by the forces of sinfulness. To reduce the whole argument to maximum simplicity produces something like the following set of statements: Because we believe in Jesus, we are the children of God and victorious over the world. Because we are the children of God we love God. Because we love God we both obey God and love God's other children. Because we are victorious over the world we do not find it burdensome to obey God. The final verse of this reading, referring to the blood and water from the side of the crucified Jesus, and to the Holy Spirit's witness, actually introduces a new section of the letter and has no close connection to the rest of the reading.

The third reading, from the Gospel according to John, is an account peculiar to that Gospel of how Jesus appeared to his disciples on Easter Sunday night. The episode invites comparison with the account of Pentecost in Acts. It is apparent that this episode in the fourth Gospel, like the Pentecost story in Luke's writings, is intended chiefly to express how, after the resurrection, the divine life by which Jesus triumphed over death was transmitted to his followers. As spirit, a word whose literal meaning is breath, was understood as the principle of life, so the Holy Spirit represents the principle of divine life. Jesus' act of breathing on his disciples clearly signifies a transmission from him to them of the principle of that life which he then possessed. His accompanying words, "Receive the Holy Spirit," identify what kind of life is understood to be transmitted, the life of God himself. Since the Spirit of God is a Spirit of Love, and therefore of forgiveness, the reception of that Spirit appropriately entails the power to forgive. The further assertion of a power to refuse forgiveness implies a juridical function within the Christian community, concerned with discriminating between those who are and those who are not rightly disposed for divine forgiveness. That it is a question of divine forgiveness, rather than the individual forgiveness of personal offenses, is indicated by the fact that the power transmitted is not simply a power to forgive, but a power to forgive sins, offenses against God himself. It is entirely consistent with the implications of this text that it should have served as one of the main scriptural bases for the Church's later systematic development of a theology of the sacrament of penance.

SECOND SUNDAY OF EASTER

Cycle "C" Readings: Acts 5:12-16; Rev. 1:9-13, 17-19; Jn. 20:19-31

The first chapters of Acts of the Apostles, from which the first reading is taken, contain three summary passages which somewhat interrupt the narrative, and are apparently designed to typify the life of the first Christian community. This is represented as a very distinctive, closely-knit group, gathering for instruction, special meals (perhaps eucharistic), and prayers, going daily to the temple, and sharing economic resources, while they, and especially the preaching and wonder-working of the apostles, evoked great popular admiration (2:42-47; 4:32-35). In the last of these passages, which constitute today's first reading, it is indicated that although the number of converts continued to grow, new believers remained diffident about publicly joining the group which assembled in the temple area called Solomon's Portico. Apparently, therefore, a distinction must be made between those who accepted the Gospel teaching and those who took the further step of complete social immersion into the nuclear Christian community with its distinctive manner of life. The verses on which this observation is based rather curiously interrupt what appears to be the main theme of the passage, developing earlier references to the wonder-working activity of the apostles, and in particular of Peter. This activity is described as the working of miraculous cures, so spectacular that afflicted persons were brought even from outlying towns. In all of these passages, there is strong emphasis on the preeminence of the apostles and on their exercise of divine powers.

The second reading is from the book of Revelation, which is the New Testament's one full-scale example of a late form of Jewish religious literature called apocalyptic, examples of which are found both inside and outside the Bible. Apocalyptic represents a special development of prophetic literature, which is characterized by the unique role of the prophet, an individual to whom God directly communicates a divine message which the prophet in turn is required to transmit to others. God's ways of addressing his prophets are quite varied, as the Old Testament abundantly illustrates. A peculiar feature of apocalyptic is that the prophet receives his message from God through the medium of a vision, or series of visions, which are often of a highly sensational and rather fantastic character, and typically include a great many symbolic elements whose meaning may not be immediately apparent to the uninitiated. The book of Revelation is in a form quite typical of Jewish apocalyptic, but its message is distinctively Christian. The passage, of which parts have been put together to make the second reading, follows an opening address "to the seven churches of Asia," and introduces the visionary material which occupies the rest of the book. The initial vision is of a glorified Christ, likened to the "Son of Man" featured in an apocalyptic section of the book of Daniel, proclaiming Christ's resurrection and his sovereignty over death. The identity of the writer, who calls himself John, is unknown, although he has often been confused with the apostle of that name. He indicates that he is writing during troubled times, apparently during persecution, and this circumstance too is typical of apocalyptic literature.

The third reading, from the Gospel according to John, is an account peculiar to that Gospel of how Jesus appeared to his disciples on Easter Sunday night. The episode invites comparison with the account of Pentecost in Acts. It is apparent that both accounts are intended to express how, after the resurrection, the divine life by which Jesus triumphed over death was transmitted to his followers. As spirit, a word whose literal reference is to breath, was understood as the principle of life, so the Holy Spirit represents the principle of divine life. Jesus' act of breathing on his disciples clearly signifies a transmission from him to them of the principle of the divine life that he then possessed. His accompanying words, "Receive the Holy Spirit," identify explicitly what kind of life is understood to be transmitted, the life of God himself. Since the Spirit of God is a spirit of love, and therefore of forgiveness, the reception of that Spirit appropriately entails the power to forgive. The further assertion of a power to refuse forgiveness implies a juridical function within the Christian community, concerned with discriminating between those who are and those who are not rightly disposed for divine forgiveness. That it is a question of divine forgiveness, rather than individual forgiveness of personal offenses, is indicated by the fact that the power transmitted is not simply a power to forgive, but a power to forgive sins, offenses against God himself. It is consistent with the implications of this text that it should have served as one of the main scriptural bases for the Church's later systematic development of a theology of the sacrament of penance.

THIRD SUNDAY OF EASTER

Cycle "A" Readings: Acts 2:14, 22-28; 1 Pet. 1:17-21; Lk. 24:13-35

The first reading, from Acts of the Apostles, reproduces part of a sermon which, according to that book, was the first instance of Christian preaching, having been delivered to a cosmopolitan Jewish crowd in Jerusalem on Pentecost by Peter, just after the bestowal of the Spirit. Just as in the fourth Gospel Jesus' personal giving of the Spirit is linked with his making missionaries out of his disciples, so here, in a different narrative framework, reception of the Spirit finds immediate expression in missionary activity. Peter's sermon is one of several recorded in Acts, all of which have significant structural and verbal similarities. It has been plausibly argued that they all reflect a basic formula for the standard way in which the early Church presented its fundamental message to prospective converts. Major elements of this preaching appear in the reading. Jesus was sent by God and gave evidence of that fact by the marvelous and significant deeds of his public life. His betrayal was itself part of God's plan, but the Jews, who enlisted the Romans as accomplices, were nevertheless responsible for it. However, Jesus was raised by God from the dead. The final verses of the reading, cited from the 16th psalm, are taken as a prophecy of Jesus' resurrection, and they introduce the last part of the sermon which concentrates on establishing Jesus' messianic identity.

The second reading continues the series of reflections from the first letter of Peter which are read throughout this season. As in most of these passages, the tone is one of strong exhortation, addressed to Christians who are living through a time troubled by persecution. The passage begins by observing that Christians call upon God as their Father, probably referring to the formulation of the Lord's Prayer. In keeping with the tone of exhortation, however, the Christians are reminded that the God who is their Father is not for that reason any the less their judge. Quite differently from the Lord's Prayer, with its emphasis on a forgiving and saving God, this passage points rather to a demanding God, whose demands are not to be taken lightly. Salvation is here presented less as a basis for confidence than as a motive for virtuous behavior. Salvation itself is referred to in redemptive and sacrificial terms. It is conceived as a purchase of freedom, as in the manumission of a slave. But the purchase price is here extolled by being likened to the temple sacrifice of a flawless victim, identified with the blood of Christ. Christ's coming is conceived as part of a timeless divine plan, and the Christian response to his coming is linked specifically with the resurrection, as reliance upon the God who raised Jesus Christ from the dead.

The final reading, from the Gospel according to Luke, is a justly famous passage, rich in narrative quality as well as in theology. Like most of the readings of Easter season, this one points to the vital importance of Christ's resurrection for Christian faith. The episode is described as taking place on Easter Sunday, after the women, having found the tomb empty and been instructed by the angels are nevertheless unable to dispel the apostles' incredulity. The two despondent disciples walking from Jerusalem to a town, no longer identifiable, called Emmaus, are aware of these developments and share the general skepticism. In expressing their disappointment they make clear what their frustrated hope had been, namely that the prophet, Jesus of Nazareth, might have been Israel's liberator, that is, the Messiah. Jesus responds with a discourse which is only summarized, but clearly corresponds to a kind of exposition of which the New Testament contains a number of more detailed examples. It is a review of Old Testament material that can be read as anticipating a Messiah like Jesus, and especially one with whose mission suffering is by no means incongruous. Significantly, no immediate assent is expressed to this argument. Rather, during their breaking of bread with Jesus at the journey's end, they recognize him. It is only after that that they recall how strangely moving they had found his words, and hurry back to Jerusalem to share their newly kindled faith. The structure of the story gives clear expression to the idea that it is precisely acceptance of the resurrection that resolves all the ambiguities about Jesus and his mission. We also find a strong suggestion of the significance of the Christian meal that foreshadows our eucharist, as an occasion for acknowledging the living presence of that risen Christ from whose restored life Christian faith derives its spiritual vitality.

THIRD SUNDAY OF EASTER

Cycle "B" Readings: Acts 3:13-15; 1 Jn. 2:1-5; Lk. 24:35-48

The first reading comprises the opening statements of a sermon which, according to the Acts of the Apostles, St. Peter preached to a Jewish audience in Jerusalem. In Acts, this address is occasioned by the gathering of a throng of curious bystanders, astonished by the miraculous cure of a cripple at the temple gate. The words with which Peter, accompanied by John, accomplished this cure anticipate the theme of Peter's sermon. "I have no silver or gold; but what I have I give you: in the name of Jesus Christ of Nazareth, walk." Whereas it was the cure itself which attracted Peter's listeners, it was about the source of the cure that he was concerned to tell them. Peter's explanation of the cure, which immediately follows the verses of the liturgical reading, is simple and significant. "The name of Jesus, by awakening faith, has strengthened this man, whom you see and know, and this faith has made him completely well, as you can all see for yourselves."

In short, the cripple was saved by faith in Jesus. And salvation by faith in Jesus, the essential message of Christianity, is what Peter proceeds to preach. The miraculous cure serves in effect as an advertisement for the Gospel and a demonstration of its validity. What astonishes the onlookers is, from the viewpoint of Christian faith, precisely what ought to be expected. Peter uses the contrast between the Jews' amazement at divine intervention and Christian confidence in it to introduce his sermon. "Men of Israel, why be surprised at this?" The explanation, he observes, is really quite simple. It is that God—their own God, the God of Israel—has filled with divine power a man named Jesus, whom they, the Jews, despite even the reluctance of Pontius Pilate, succeeded in getting executed. "But," and here Peter enunciates the basic apostolic claim, "God raised him from the dead; of that we are witnesses."

The second reading, from the first letter of John, deals with an important issue which has arisen often and in many forms, the issue of whether or not Christianity and sin can co-exist. To some, the very concept of a Christian sinner is paradoxical, for a Christian is one who has been saved from sin. Indeed, not a few New Testament passages seem to suggest that after baptism a relapse into sin would be unthinkable and intolerable. Without dealing with the subtler implications of this issue, the first letter of John, in verses just preceding those of the liturgical reading, emphatically rejects the idea that Christians are, in the most obvious sense, sinless. "If we claim to be sinless, we are self-deceived." In the passage read in today's liturgy, the letter deals with two equally fallacious inferences from admitting the recurrence of sin in Christian lives. The first of these amounts to a kind of ethical apathy—if one is sure to sin, why bother with futile resistance? The author insists that his intention is the very opposite of encouraging moral indifference. "In writing thus to you my purpose is that you should not commit sin." However, it is equally his intention to assure those who do commit sin that salvation is not forfeited, that we can rely on Jesus Christ "to plead our cause," for he "is himself the remedy for the defilement of our sins." In the final verses of the reading, the author reasserts his insistence on active virtue by pointing out (probably against Gnostic tendencies) that the claim to "know" God is a claim which can and should be tested. The only valid test of it is whether or not one obeys God. Knowledge of God, conceived as that intimate familiarity which unites a human being to God, can only be real if it manifests itself in a godly manner of life.

The reading from the Gospel according to Luke begins with the return to Jerusalem of those two disciples who had met the risen Lord on their way to Emmaus, where, as they now report to the apostles and their companions, "he had been recognized by them at the breaking of the bread." At this strategic moment, Jesus appears among them and immediately sets about to convince them of his physical reality, first by inviting them to feel the unghostly solidity of his body, and finally by performing the unghostly action of eating a morsel of cooked fish. This, he assures them, is what the misunderstood messianic prophecies were really pointing to—the Messiah's suffering and death, followed by his resurrection into unequivocally real and bodily human life. This was the long-awaited work of salvation, and the present task of these witnesses is to make that work known by preaching everywhere a Gospel which calls for repentance and promises forgiveness. That preaching, the essential mission of the apostles and of the Church, "beginning in Jerusalem," was to be "proclaimed to all nations." The accomplishment of the mission of Jesus marks the beginning of the mission of his followers. As Luke's Gospel is devoted to the former theme, his book of the Acts of the Apostles takes up the latter one.

THIRD SUNDAY OF EASTER

Cycle "C" Readings: Acts 5:27-32, 40-41; Rev. 5:11-14; Jn. 21:1-19

The first reading, from Acts of the Apostles, narrates the first part of a juridical investigation of the apostles by the Sanhedrin, and then skips to the conclusion of the account, omitting a portion of it which is essential for its adequate understanding. Just before this episode, the apostles, who had been arrested at the temple, had miraculously escaped from prison and resumed teaching at the temple, only to be arrested again—gently, we are told, for fear of reprisals by a sympathetic populace. Questioning them before the Sanhedrin, the high priest forbade them to teach in Jesus' name, and complained that they were incriminating the Sanhedrin as Jesus' slayers. Peter flatly refused to obey the order, plainly contended that they were Jesus' crucifiers, and reasserted his message of salvation through Jesus now risen from the dead. In the portion omitted from the reading, we are told that a general clamor for the apostles' death was counteracted by a highly respected Pharisee, Gamaliel, who reminded the group privately that rebellious movements were nothing new and that in the past their activities had proved self-defeating. He urged that prudence favored a tolerant policy. Gamaliel showed himself to be a person who impressively combined open-mindedness with faith, by adding that evidence of the religious status of the apostles' teaching would be furnished by God, who would defend it against any odds if it came from him, but would otherwise let it go the way of other human ideologies. Although Gamaliel's wisdom spared the apostles' lives, they were again warned to be silent and the warning was reinforced by flogging—the "ill-treatment" referred to in the last verse of the reading.

The second reading comprises part of an elaborate vision recounted at some length in the book of Revelation. It is closely related to a vision described just previously, which presents, under symbolic imagery, God seated in glory on his throne in heaven, surrounded by a kind of spiritual court. The divine figure holds a scroll, which has the peculiarity of being sealed at seven successive [...] must be unrolled in seven distinct portions. As is made [...] tent of the scroll is a foretelling of the future course of [...] beholder of the vision, is at first grief-stricken because [...] ne is able to open the scroll, that is, to unveil the future [...] that "the Lion from the tribe of Judah, the root of David, has won the right to open the scroll." The reference is of course to the messiah, who is then beheld in the likeness of "a Lamb with the marks of slaughter upon him," evidently the paschal lamb taken as a symbol of Jesus. The Lamb, whose divine status is implied by his appearing at the very center of God's throne, thereupon takes the scroll. This action is accompanied by an outburst of song from the divine entourage, proclaiming the universally redemptive sacrifice which has consecrated mankind as a priesthood, and which entitles the Lamb to open the scroll. In the section which the reading reproduces, this song is taken up by a kind of second and third chorus, the first comprising innumerable angels, and the second including all of creation.

The twenty-first chapter of the Gospel according to John, most of which constitutes the third reading of today's liturgy, has long puzzled readers by the fact that it comes just after what certainly sounds like the conclusion of the Gospel according to John. Consequently, some have described this chapter (21) as an "appendix," and some have assumed that it derived from some other source and was tacked onto an otherwise complete work. Without taking sides in this debate, one is at least prompted by it to look for some special motive to account for this "extra" narrative of a post-resurrection appearance by Jesus. The most plausible indication of such a motive is furnished by the striking prominence of the part played by Peter in this final episode. Although it recounts an appearance to a whole group of disciples, it is Peter who first recognizes Jesus, it is Peter who responds to him most vigorously, and it is Peter whom Jesus singles out for a very special conversation. During that conversation, Peter is asked three times if he loves Jesus, and the correspondence of his three protestations of love to his earlier three denials of Jesus during the passion is eloquent. With each assertion of his love, Peter is told to nourish the flock of Jesus, to be their shepherd, their "pastor." Then Peter is promised an earthly destiny which is clearly to be understood as that of a martyr. And finally, he is simply commanded, "Follow me." Whatever literary history may underlie this passage, what we find in it is clearly a symbolic declaration of Peter's rehabilitated friendship with Jesus and his reestablished authority over Jesus' followers. In view of Peter's position in the early Church, and of his shameful behavior during the Passion, such a declaration would obviously seem fitting.

FOURTH SUNDAY OF EASTER

Cycle "A" Readings: Acts 2:14, 36-41; 1 Pet. 2:20-25; Jn. 10:1-10

The first reading, from Acts of the Apostles, begins with the final verse of Peter's Pentecost sermon in Jerusalem, the middle portion of which was read last Sunday. This final verse expresses the purpose of the entire sermon. It is an appeal to the Jews for acceptance, as the divinely sent Lord and Messiah, of Jesus, whom, Peter once again insists, they, the Jews, crucified. The sermon is represented as a thorough success. There is no suggestion of any resentment on the part of Peter's severely challenged hearers. On the contrary, they are represented as "deeply shaken," and as asking with almost pathetic docility what they are to do. They are, in other words, portrayed as ideally receptive to the newly launched program of evangelization. The instructions given to them are typically instructions for new converts who have been satisfactorily catechized. They are told what they are to do, and they are informed of what will follow. They are to repent, that is to adopt a totally reformed way of life, and they are to be baptized in Jesus' name for the forgiveness of their sins. Once this is done, they can expect to receive that same gift of the Holy Spirit which the apostles themselves had received earlier the same day. A final comment notes that the promise, whose fulfillment they are soon to experience, is one that has universal scope, including both future generations and distant peoples. Here there is a clear anticipation of the mission beyond the Jews to the Gentiles with which later portions of Acts are greatly occupied. What is not anticipated here is the resistance and unresponsiveness of the Jews which become increasingly prominent as the story proceeds.

The second reading is once again a selection from the first letter of Peter, and once again expresses the exhortation to persecuted Christians which characterizes that letter. The passage just preceding was addressed to slaves, reminding us that this bottom stratum of pagan society was well represented in Christian communities. The slaves were exhorted to be patient even under abusive treatment by cruel masters, and to adopt that attitude out of religious motivation, confident of pleasing God by their courageous endurance. The force of this exhortation, for Christians, is developed in the passage read in today's liturgy. What the slaves are asked to do is to be motivated not by prudent social calculations, but by a readiness to imitate Jesus Christ. The very means of their salvation, Jesus' passion, is precisely the sort of behavior that is now required of them. The unresisting submission of the innocent Jesus to the torments inflicted upon him by unjust accusers is to be the inspiration and model for these Christian victims of oppression. Implicit here is the familiar Gospel reminder that the servant is not greater than his master, that to follow Jesus entails carrying a cross of one's own, and that it is precisely in the similar endurance of comparable suffering that the Christian is united most intimately with his Savior. Ultimately, it is absolute confidence in a God "who judges justly," that enables the Christian as it enabled Christ, to endure affliction from human persecutors who do not judge justly.

The final reading, from the Gospel according to John, contains one of the only two passages in that Gospel that might be called parables, and even these are quite different from the parables found in the other Gospels. What we have in the reading is the figure itself, and the first of two interpretative applications that are given immediately after it. The figure contrasts two characters, an authentic shepherd, who enters the fold by the normal gate, recognizes and is recognized by the sheep, who therefore follow him, and a thief, who finds a stealthier way in, and is fled from as a stranger by the sheep. There can be little doubt that this figurative passage derives from a famous vision of Ezekiel, in which the rulers of Israel appear as false shepherds, and are deposed by God, who regains his lost sheep, and appoints a shepherd of his own choosing, the Davidic Messiah, to take proper care of his flock. Both the structure of the figurative passage in the Gospel and the meaning of its precedent in Ezekiel lead one to expect that the proper shepherd stands for Jesus as the true Messiah, while the thief symbolizes Christ's opponents and competitors. Surprisingly enough, the interpretation begins by identifying Jesus not with the honest shepherd, but with the gateway, representing him as the means of access to the fold rather than as the leader of the sheep. And the thief is likened not to Jesus' present and future opponents, but to "all who came before" him, presumably those whose misdirected leadership Jesus is at pains to counteract; more precise identification can only be conjectural. In the second interpretation, which the reading omits, Jesus does call himself "the good shepherd" and develops that idea.

FOURTH SUNDAY OF EASTER

Cycle "B" Readings: Acts 4:8-12; 1 Jn. 3:1-2; Jn. 10:11-18

The cure of the cripple at the temple gate, which in the Acts of the Apostles furnishes St. Peter with an audience of bystanders for one of his earliest efforts at preaching the Gospel, also attracted more hostile listeners, temple clergy and a group of the Sadducees. Outraged at the new teaching, and in particular at the doctrine of the resurrection, these opponents got Peter and his associates jailed for the night. In this episode, Luke's narrative is plainly pointing to the fulfillment of Jesus' warnings that his followers would "be brought before synagogues and put in prison" and of his promise to give them in such circumstances "power of utterance and a wisdom which no opponent will be able to resist or refute" (Luke 21:12, 15). The idea of their following in the footsteps of Jesus' passion is dramatically reinforced as the narrative continues by having the apostles haled before a tribunal of examiners comprising the whole high-priestly family, of whom the first named are Jesus' own legal persecutors, the infamous Annas and Caiaphas. To these official questioners, Peter's words reiterate, even more uncompromisingly, his earlier message to the random gathering of Jews. The miraculous cure which caused all the excitement was accomplished in the name of Jesus of Nazareth, whom they, the Jewish leaders, crucified, but whom God raised from the dead. Like Jesus himself in Luke's Gospel (20:17), Peter alludes in words from Psalm 118 to the stone rejected by the builders, that is, by the Jewish religious leaders, which is precisely the foundation stone on which all further construction depends. To build without it is to build on futility, for "there is no salvation in anyone else at all."

Here, as in earlier passages of Acts, Luke's insistence on the all-sufficiency of Jesus is closely linked to a severe condemnation of those who rejected Jesus. Analogy with Jesus' passion is further suggested in the aftermath by the inability of the apostles' examiners to find any effective way of condemning them, in view of the popular religious esteem they had gained by the miracle.

It is highly characteristic of the Johannine writings to describe the effects of Christ's atonement in terms of a new life received from God. This way of speaking and thinking is closely related to other characteristic motifs of this biblical literature, and in particular to the notion of Christian rebirth and, implicit in that notion, the idea of Christians as being in a new and special sense children of God. Since offspring of any kind naturally resemble their parentage, being children of God implies living a kind of life which expresses filial likeness to the divine Father. Translated into moral terms, this implication of being children of God demands behavior which imitates God, even as the earthly human behavior of the incarnate Son of God imitates the eternal Father. In keeping with this line of thought, the verse which immediately precedes today's liturgical reading from the first letter of John states, "If you know that he is righteous, you must recognize that every man who does right is his child." The two verses which comprise the liturgical reading itself apply this idea of the Christian's likeness to God in still other ways. For one thing, if human beings actually do imitate and manifest God to any significant degree, it is only to be expected that attitudes toward such human beings will correspond to attitudes toward God. Consequently, indifference to God or hostility to God should find expression in indifference or hostility to manifestations of godliness in human lives. "We were called God's children and such we are; and the reason why the godless world does not recognize us is that it has not known him." There is also in the idea of being God's children a further implication that children are destined to mature, and that a fully mature condition which lies in their future can scarcely be comprehended, no matter how eagerly it may be looked forward to, before it is actually achieved. "Here and now, dear friends, we are God's children; what we shall be has not yet been disclosed, but we know that when it is disclosed we shall be like him, because we shall see him as he is."

The third reading, from the Gospel according to John, is closely related to a short parable which precedes it. The parable contrasts people who enter a sheepfold through its door with those who enter by more devious ways. Shepherds do the former, whereas the latter behavior is typical of thieves. Even the sheep sense the difference. They recognize their shepherd and follow him, but they run away from strangers. Each of these two ideas is further developed. Related to the former (more by association of words than by logic) is Jesus' statement, "I am the door of the sheepfold." Related to the latter (in a more directly logical manner) is Jesus' further statement, "I am the good shepherd." Being the good shepherd means, in the first place, caring enough about the sheep to protect them from danger. In the second place it also means being recognized by the sheep as the one to whom they belong. Each of these implications is further developed in terms of the theology of Jesus' mission. As the one who cares for the sheep he is prepared to give his very life for their welfare. And as the one to whom the sheep belong—including sheep from other folds (a reference to the universal scope of Jesus' mission)—he will elicit from them a positive response.

FOURTH SUNDAY OF EASTER

Cycle "C" Readings: Acts 13:14, 43-52; Rev. 7:9, 14-17; Jn. 10:27-30

Whereas approximately the first half of Acts of the Apostles is dominated by Peter, the rest is mainly an account of Paul's activities. After the center of Christian influence moved from Jerusalem to Antioch in Syria, Paul and Barnabas were sent from there as missionaries. They sailed west to Cyprus, made a preaching tour across to the western end of that island, sailed north to what is now southern Turkey, and then continued northward overland to a different Antioch which is the scene of the first reading. Here as elsewhere they preached in the Jewish synagogue, being invited to do so as traveling Jewish teachers. Paul's sermon, omitted from the reading, traced the history of Israel up to God's promise that a savior would arise from David's posterity, and then introduced the Christian interpretation of Jesus as the fulfillment of that promise. The reading describes an enthusiastic reaction on the part of many hearers, which, however, prompted resentment and hostility among the local Jewish leadership. Acts of the Apostles treats this occasion as a major turning point in the history of the Church's expansion. The exasperation of Paul and Barnabas with their Jewish opponents is cited as the motive for a momentous decision expressed in the words "we now turn to the Gentiles." In justification of this reorientation of their mission, they appeal to a passage from one of the later portions of the book of Isaiah, which represents Israel as destined to transmit the light of God's saving revelation "to the nations." In Paul's view, this destiny is now to be fulfilled through his own mission, despite the Jews' widespread rejection of their own messiah, who is the whole world's savior.

Apocalyptic, represented in the New Testament mainly by the book of Revelation, is a type of religious literature that characteristically flourishes during times of anxiety and affliction, especially from persecution, and seeks to console believers with divine reassurances of their ultimate security. This typically apocalyptic motif is conspicuous in the second reading. It describes a vision of a great crowd of people whose ethnic diversity represents the catholicity of the Church, robed in white and holding palm branches such as were commonly waved like banners during celebrations. In verses that the reading leaves out, these people are represented as shouting in celebration of victory for God and for the Lamb, who symbolizes Christ, and their shouts are taken up by the attendants at God's throne in acclamations of gratitude and praise. The white-robed throng are then identified as "the ones who have survived the great period of trial," those, in other words, whose faith has stood firm under persecution. Just as in an earlier passage, sin is symbolized as "soiling garments," so here the white robes represent that sinlessness which has been gained for the faithful by "the blood of the Lamb," Christ's sacrifice. By keeping faith, the martyrs have reached the fullness of salvation, in which they are permanently united with Christ in the experience of eternal life, from which every trace of sorrow and suffering is excluded.

The third reading, from the Gospel according to John, is part of a reply which Jesus makes to unbelieving Jews who persist in asking him, apparently in the hope of an incriminating answer, to state unequivocally whether or not he is the Messiah. Significantly, in the preceding narrative of this Gospel Jesus had not made that claim in so many words, probably because the popular understanding of it was so different from his own, although the messianic import of his whole ministry must have been unmistakable to any well-disposed Jewish observer. In this instance, Jesus' reply hearkens back to his slightly earlier discourse beginning with the words, "I am the good shepherd." In that discourse, Jesus had compared the mutual understanding which created a bond of sympathy between himself and his "sheep" to the mutual understanding between himself and his Father. Those who recognize Jesus as sheep recognize their shepherd, as their loving protector and savior, show themselves spiritually attuned to him, just as he, by his whole ministry, shows himself spiritually attuned to the Father who sent him to exercise that ministry. This spiritual attunement is conceived as a disposition indispensable for faith. Jesus' reply to his hostile, skeptical questioners, "My sheep hear my voice," implicitly accuses them of lacking that essential disposition. His final words, which reassert his union with the Father in the unequivocal statement, "the Father and I are one," at last provide the self-incriminating declaration that is the only thing his opponents are spiritually attuned to hear. Accordingly we are told in the verse which immediately follows the reading, "they picked up stones."

FIFTH SUNDAY OF EASTER
Cycle "A" Readings: Acts 6:1-7; 1 Pet. 2:4-9; Jn. 14:1-12

In the first reading, from Acts of the Apostles, Luke's narrative of the early Christian community at Jerusalem introduces an early glimpse of how that community developed in complexity as well as in sheer size. The passage distinguishes two groups of Jewish Christians, whose different languages were tokens of much deeper cultural differences. "Those of them who spoke Greek" did so because they or their families had lived long outside the Jewish homeland. Their experience of life in Gentile centers would inevitably change much more than their language. In Jerusalem, their cosmopolitan ways must have contrasted not always pleasantly with more conservative local Jewish habits of life. The failure of the two groups to blend, even as fellow-Christians, into a harmonious community, is evident in this passage. Earlier in Acts it was enthusiastically reported that Jerusalem Christians maintained a system of economic sharing, whereby needier members could be provided for out of the pooled resources of those who were better off. Regardless of good will, this kind of arrangement always raises problems of kinds that demand organizational solutions. In the present instance, the problems found expression in charges of discrimination. The Greek-speaking faction charged their Aramaic-speaking brethren with neglecting their widows (a group outstandingly dependent on charity in the ancient world) in the daily dole. In response, the apostles called upon the whole community to choose some reputable men to deal fairly with the distribution, while the apostles would concentrate on more specifically religious and evangelical activities. It is notable in the list that all have Greek names, implying a deliberate effort to overcome, by the selection itself, any prejudice against the Greek-speaking portion of the community. Although chosen by the community, the new functionaries were presented to the apostles for official designation. The tradition of referring to the seven appointees as deacons is misleading if that term is understood anachronistically by reference to the later clerical orders. At the same time, the subsequent preaching and martyrdom of one of this group, Stephen, should deter us from thinking of them as merely a kind of ecclesiastical quartermaster corps.

The second reading, from the first letter of Peter, is a multiply-mixed metaphor whose common term is "stone." The readers, by way of being exhorted to adopt a wholeheartedly Christian way of life, are summoned to "Come to the Lord, a living stone," humanly rejected but divinely approved. The figure anticipates the passage from Isaiah cited below, in which the stone represents faith's firm foundation. The same image is further applied to the readers themselves, likened to building blocks. The building they are to constitute is conceived as a temple, thus introducing the idea of worship, and a further appeal for the readers to be united as a common priesthood offering spiritual sacrifices. The quotation from Isaiah identifies the stone once again with Jesus Christ as the foundation of faith. One final use is found for the metaphor in reflecting that to reject this stone is to make a foundation block into a stumbling block, the means of one's support into the cause of one's downfall. At this point references to stones give way to the theme they had earlier served to introduce, and the priestly aspect of the Christian community is further elaborated. The basic meaning of this tortured passage is simply an exhortation to the sharing of a firm common faith whereby Christians are joined in the new spiritual worship that has replaced the rituals of Jewish religion.

The final reading comes from the rich farewell discourses set on the eve of the Passion as given in the Gospel according to John. Jesus foretells his imminent departure with the reassurance that his followers will finally be brought with him. Thomas' puzzled questioning creates an opportunity for Jesus to declare himself the sole way of access to the Father. Philip is thereby prompted to express his longing to see the Father, and this introduces a final declaration by Jesus of his own unique relationship with the Father and the significance of that relationship for Christian faith. He presents himself as so closely united with the Father that their relationship is expressed as a kind of mutual interpenetration. For one who believes this, the visible deeds of Christ are the outward, visible manifestation of the Father's own divine activity. Thus the access to the Father through Jesus that was previously referred to in a context of the future when the disciples would be with Jesus in his Father's house, is applied also to the present, when faith so unites the disciple to Jesus that the disciple's own deeds will participate in the divine activity.

FIFTH SUNDAY OF EASTER

Cycle "B" Readings: Acts 9:26-31; 1 Jn. 3:18-24; Jn. 15:1-8

Today's reading from Acts tells of the Jerusalem disciples' skepticism about Paul's suspiciously abrupt conversion, and their corresponding fear of him. Barnabas, a Greek-speaking Jewish Christian, provided Paul with a favorable introduction to the apostles, after which Paul circulated freely, preaching to the Greek-speaking Jews of Jerusalem. These, however, reacted to Paul with the same hostility that had proved fatal to Stephen whom they stoned. In order to save Paul from a similar fate, the Christians who had learned of his danger escorted him to Caesarea on the way to his native city of Tarsus. The sequence of events reported in this passage differs significantly from the report given in the letter to the Galatians of the events following Paul's conversion, especially concerning his visit to Jerusalem. Since the latter account is in an older document, and one written by Paul himself, it is generally assumed to be more factually reliable. However, neither Galatians nor Acts is primarily interested in biographical exactitude, and whereas the account in Acts seeks to emphasize the expansion of the Christian mission, from Jerusalem where it began, to the Gentile world where it was destined to flourish, the account in Galatians is preoccupied with the conflict which developed between Paul's Gentile Christian communities and the Jewish Christian leadership in Jerusalem.

The second reading, taken from the first letter of John, addresses itself to a particular aspect of that new life which belongs to the children of God. That life had already been represented as irreconcilable with a life of sin, which is its very antithesis, belonging rather to the "children of the devil" than the "children of God." Positively considered, this life of the children of God, which is contrasted with a life of sin, is identified as a life of love. For love is God's gift to his children, and the outstanding attribute of those who are rightly called his children. But, as today's reading insists, "love must not be a matter of words or talk; it must be genuine, and show itself in action." Active manifestation of love is, for the author of this letter, the ultimately valid test of whether or not one really belongs to God, as one of his children, sharing his life. It is a test which takes precedence over all other indications, including even those which are furnished by one's own interior moral sentiments, called in this context "the heart" or "the conscience." By the evidence of active love it is possible, in the sight of God, to transcend the misgivings of moral subjectivity and "know that we belong to the realm of truth." Neither devout protestations on the one hand, nor guilty feelings on the other, are to be trusted when they conflict with the practical, visible reality of love. Just how practical and visible this reality is understood to be is made clear by the verse just preceding this passage: "If a man has enough to live on, and yet when he sees his brother in need shuts up his heart against him, how can it be said that the divine love dwells in him?" On the other hand, where this kind of love does exist, there is no reason for misgivings, but abundant reason for an utterly confident reliance upon God.

The characteristically Johannine motif of God "dwelling" in the Christian, and of how the inner presence of God is outwardly manifested, is further developed in the third reading, from the Gospel according to John. In this passage, emphasis is placed on the continuity which exists between the divine life of the Christian and that of Jesus himself. This continuity is brought out by the use of an extended metaphor involving a vine, its branches, and the person who tends the vine. In comparing himself to a vine and his disciples to the vine's branches, Jesus brings out several points of doctrine. First, a vine and its branches have a common organic vitality; in the same way, a single principle of life unites Jesus with his disciples. Second, whatever vitality there is in the branches comes to them from the vine from which they grow; in the same way, the disciple's life is derivative from that of Jesus. Third, a branch which does not draw its life from the vine is, by that very fact, dead, and must be cut away for the good of the living organism; in the same way, the disciple who ceases to live by Jesus' life must be repudiated by God, the giver of that life. In the verses which immediately follow this passage, this inner divine life, as in the previous reading, is identified with love. And the love with which it is identified is modeled on the self-sacrificing love of Jesus himself. Also as in the previous reading, the actuality of this love is established as the basis for confident reliance upon God.

FIFTH SUNDAY OF EASTER

Cycle "C" Readings: Acts 14:21-27; Rev. 21:1-5; Jn. 13:31-33, 34-35

The first reading of today's liturgy recounts the last stages of a missionary journey by Paul and Barnabas which began at Syrian Antioch (mentioned in the latter part of the reading, and not to be confused with another Antioch in Asia Minor, mentioned in the first part of the reading). They went first to Cyprus, and then to an area that is now southern Turkey, where they preached in a number of towns. The last town they visited was Derbe, after which they retraced their course, revisiting in reverse order many of the places where they had been already. Apparently there was a prudent technique in this itinerary, inasmuch as it enabled the missionaries to reinforce, after a short absence, the effect of their initial preaching, and to see how firmly their message had taken hold and what difficulties their converts encountered. The most recurrent difficulty was opposition, carried to the point of persecution, by Jewish leaders who interpreted the Christian movement not as a development of but as a threat to their own religious tradition. It was on this account that Paul and Barnabas "gave their disciples reassurances and encouraged them to persevere with this instruction: 'We must undergo many trials if we are to enter into the reign of God'." As part of this same effort to give stability to the new and threatened groups of Christian converts, "in each church they installed elders, and with prayer and fasting commended them to the Lord." Because the Greek word for elder is *presbuter*, from which our word priest derives, some have interpreted this appointment of local church leaders as foreshadowing clerical ordination, but it would be misleading to read the later theological meaning of priests into a word that has no priestly connotations and might better be rendered as "senior member," implying authority based on maturity.

The second reading, from the book of Revelation, is part of the concluding portion of that work, which ranks among the most movingly beautiful passages in all of religious literature. The type of visionary writing called apocalyptic typically offers an unveiling of the future, and while much of what is unveiled often has a terrifying character, because its principal message is one of hope, its climactic vision is normally a symbolic glimpse of the ultimate object of religious hope. Thus, after an account of the final judgment, Revelation begins, in the words of today's reading, its majestic finale which describes in dazzling imagery the final advent of the Kingdom of God. The old universe, with its sin-laden history of human grief, is simply brushed aside. Jerusalem, conceived in the Bible as the geographically central point of contact between God and his people, is totally renewed. God's contact with his finally perfected world is likened to a nuptial union of fidelity and love, an image used by the prophets to express the firm devotion of the covenant. And the ultimate purpose of the covenant, God's loving presence in the midst of his people, is now fully realized, with the result that there can be no more place in human life for that tragedy and sorrow which express humankind's alienation from the source and goal of their being.

The third reading is taken from that lengthy section of the Gospel according to John which is mainly occupied by what are often called Jesus' farewell discourses. The occasion is that of the Last Supper, which in this account takes place on the eve of Passover. The section begins with Jesus' washing his disciples' feet and exhorting them to the humble service this act exemplifies. after which he predicts that one of his table companions will betray him. Surreptitiously, Jesus intimates his knowledge to Judas, and sends him to "do quickly what you have to do." Thus the machinery of Jesus' passion and death is set in motion by his own bidding, and it is with a sense of this finality that he then speaks the words recorded in the reading. The opening words convey an irony that is deeply rooted in the spirit and style of the fourth Gospel. His reaction to what, humanly speaking, is the sealing of his doom in the gratified announcement that "now is the Son of Man glorified and God is glorified in him." The phrase recalls the similar irony of Jesus' earlier reference to his being "lifted up," implying a state of exaltation while referring concretely to his body's being raised upon the cross. The long-awaited "hour" of Jesus has now come, which is the consummation of his mission and the triumph of his love in the service of his Father's love. Thus, most appropriately, the discourse concludes as an exhortation to "love one another such as my love has been for you." The full meaning of this "new commandment" will only be revealed by the events of the following days, the historical reality of the Paschal mystery, in which the unique significance of Christian discipleship finds its basis.

SIXTH SUNDAY OF EASTER

Cycle "A" Readings: Acts 8:5-8, 14-17; 1 Pet. 3:15-18; Jn. 14:15-21

The first reading narrates an episode from Acts of the Apostles. It is reported just after the slaying of Stephen, as having taken place during a "time of violent persecution for the church in Jerusalem," when, for the first time, Saul makes his appearance as a persecutor. Under the circumstances it is understandable that Christian preachers should have directed their activities outside the city itself, and we are told that they were dispersed among the rural areas of Judea and Samaria. Even as refugees, however, they remained missionaries, and an unintended result of persecution was the actual spread of Christian evangelism. One of the itinerant preachers from Jerusalem was Philip, introduced earlier as one of the seven Greek-speaking Jewish Christians appointed to assist the apostles with their organized charity. Philip carried the message to Samaria, a territory inhabited by a people of Hebrew ancestry, who had long been socially alienated and religiously deviant from the main Jewish community. Since Samaritans formally rejected Jerusalem as a religious center, the previous Christian preaching within that city would be unlikely to influence them. Philip's Samaritan mission was a great success, accompanied by miracles. News of this success brought two of the apostles themselves to Samaria, where they prayed for the converts, who had already been baptized. At the imposition of the apostles' hands, the Samaritans received the Spirit. In this sequence of events one can easily see a foreshadowing of the later liturgical distinction between baptism and confirmation. Indeed, from the apostles' point of view, the bestowal of the Spirit on the Samaritans was precisely a divine confirmation of the authenticity of their conversion or, to speak in terms of a later theology, of the validity of their baptism. Clearly, the phrase "they received the Holy Spirit" refers, in this context, not simply to an invisible grace, but to perfectly observable phenomena, attributable to divine influence, such as occurred among the apostles themselves at Pentecost: what one might call charismatic evidence.

The second reading, from the first letter of Peter, again reminds us that the recipients of that letter were understood to be living under critical conditions, exposed to hostile attitudes and subject to violent persecution. Whereas Jewish opposition to Christianity was primarily based on religious differences, Roman persecutors characteristically leveled charges of immoral and antisocial behavior, attaching little importance to theological views that appeared rather foolish than dangerous. Thus the Christians are here exhorted to be tactful and judicious in responding to the inquiries, and even the jibes, of unsympathetic neighbors. In particular, they are urged to conduct themselves in such a way that their behavior can offer no handle to anti-Christian prejudices. If they must suffer, they are to suffer as Christ did, innocently. This prospect of the innocent suffering of Christians naturally recalls the innocent suffering of Christ, and its significance in the light of Christian faith. That significance is expressed by three distinct phrases in the final verse, which states that Christ died "for sins, once for all," "for the sake of the unjust," and "so that he could lead you to God." These phrases highlight different aspects or interpretations of the atonement. The emphasis of the first two is on expiation, and the language used is reminiscent of descriptions of the "sin offering" in Jewish ritual. The latter phrase may also reflect Jewish tradition, in the sense that ritual purification was considered prerequisite for approaching God's sanctuary, but in Christian understanding, this notion of access to God gained through Christ's sacrifice has more spiritual and transcendental connotations.

The third reading is again from the series of lessons presented by the Gospel according to John as Jesus' farewell discourses on the eve of his passion. After Judas' departure, Jesus' language with reference to his own situation assumes a tone of triumphant finality. At the same time, his attitude toward his disciples expresses the realization that he is soon to leave them. With this in view he delivers a concentrated series of what sound like final instructions for the new role they are to assume and the new circumstances they are to experience. Reassuringly, he announces his ultimate return, but more than that, he promises to have the Father send them "another Paraclete," or helper, of whose presence they will be aware even though others are not. The reading begins and ends with a characteristic appeal to have a love for Jesus that will find expression in obedience to him, and that constitutes the fundamental condition of closeness to God.

SIXTH SUNDAY OF EASTER

Cycle "B" Readings: Acts 10:25-26, 34-35, 44-48; 1 Jn. 4:7-10; Jn. 15:9-17

The first reading combines two disjointed statements addressed by St. Peter in the Acts of the Apostles to the Roman centurion Cornelius with an account of the coming of the Holy Spirit upon a group of Gentiles, comprising Cornelius and his family and friends, to whom Peter had just preached a very basic Christian sermon. Since, however, this sermon of Peter's is not included or even mentioned in today's reading, a completely false impression can easily be given that the experience of the Spirit was occasioned by the words spoken by Peter to Cornelius which are recorded in the liturgical reading. Since Peter's sermon itself is read in the liturgy of Easter Sunday, it might be advisable to refer to the commentary on that reading as a supplement to this one, for the sake of doing better justice to the biblical context. Of the two statements of Peter which have found their way into today's reading, the first records Peter's insistence, in reaction to Cornelius' exaggeratedly reverent reception of him, that he, Peter, was a mere human being, no more specially sacred than anyone else. The second statement follows Peter's account of how God had overcome his Jewish separatist attitude toward Gentiles, and states his newly acquired realization that "in every nation the man who is God-fearing and does what is right is acceptable to God." This conviction, more or less forced on Peter by special divine evidences, is in the same way more or less forced on his Jewish companions by the penetecostal manifestations of the Spirit's presence among the Gentile hearers of Peter's sermon. In the face of such dramatic evidence of God's acceptance of the Gentiles' faith, the Jews readily concede the Gentiles' eligibility for baptism. The episode strongly reinforces the universalist bearing of the words attributed to Peter, by providing the Gentile believers at Caesarea with a sort of Pentecost of their own, clearly modeled on that of the Jewish believers at Jerusalem: giving Jews and Gentiles as it were the same credentials within the Christian Church.

The tendency of the author of the first letter of John to extract the significance of an idea by approaching it successively from slightly different points of view is evident in the way the Christian idea of divine love is dealt with in the second reading. It begins with the familiar exhortation of Christians to love one another. And it explains why they should love one another, because love comes from God. The relationship of the idea of love's origin from God with the idea of its presence in Christians is then further indicated by stating that to love is to be a child of God and to know God. To be a child of God implies deriving life from God, and it is in this sense that the Christian derives from God that life which is love. Moreover, to know God implies an intimate familiarity with what is distinctively divine, and this again is love, as is made remarkably explicit in the statement which follows, asserting that "God is love." Consequently, not to love means to be unfamiliar with love and consequently unacquainted with God. What the love which is here referred to actually means is to be understood by reference to the incarnation, in which God's love for humankind is most fully expressed. It is, therefore, the love which originates in God, which emanates in the redemptive mission of Christ, and which finds expression in the love of Christians for one another which is said to be divine: not the love we have for God, but the love we have from God. This passage must rank among the most important in all of Christian literature for identifying a distinctively Christian conception of love.

The third reading, from the Gospel according to John, ends with the same imperative with which the second reading, from the first letter of John, begins: "Love one another." Here, the words are set among the farewell discourses addressed by Jesus to his followers on the eve of his passion. The doctrine which they express is essentially the same as that of the second reading. Here, once again, Christian love is traced to its source in God the Father, whence it is expressed in the redemptive mission of Jesus, and then in the further mission of Jesus' followers. Corresponding to the "downward" transmission of love, from the Father to Jesus, from Jesus to his followers, and among his followers themselves, this passage points to an "upward" direction of obedience. Thus, the Father's love for Jesus is matched by Jesus' obedience to the Father's commands. And by the same token, Jesus' love for his followers is to be matched by their obedience to his commands. And yet, the obedience which is called for by Jesus from those whom he loves is itself, in the final analysis, a matter of obeying his command to love. Ultimately, therefore, the response which divine love requires is love, the command is a summons to love, and the obedience is an act of love. And once again, the basic meaning of the love which God both bestows and requires is not left obscure. The nature of Christian love is made evident by the perfect exemplification of that love in the redemptive mission of Jesus. "Love one another as I have loved you" eliminates all the ambiguity for whoever appreciates the character of Jesus' mission. And, lest the practical significance of "as I have loved you" should still be missed, it is made humanly unmistakable by the statement which follows: "There is no greater love than this, that a man should lay down his life for his friends." Not the tenderness of sentiment but the generosity of self-sacrifice is the standard of perfection for that love which comes from God and makes human beings God-like.

SIXTH SUNDAY OF EASTER

Cycle "C" Readings: Acts 15:1-2, 22-29; Rev. 21:10-14, 22-23; Jn. 14:23-29

The portion of Acts of the Apostles from which the first reading is taken deals with an issue which was one of the primary sources of tension in the early development of Christianity, and on the resolution of which the Church's future was considerably dependent. Jesus had been a Jew, and so had all of his apostles. The very faith in Jesus which they preached was based on the uniquely Jewish religious concept of a messiah, and in support of their teaching they constantly appealed to the Jewish Bible. Clearly, neither Jesus nor his first followers understood their message as a repudiation of authentic Judaism. On the contrary, they presented Christian faith as a belief in the present fulfillment of ancient Jewish hope. Even the expansion of true religion to encompass the Gentile world was envisioned by later prophetic writings, and was by no means a Christian theological invention. However, to conceive of Christianity as a fulfillment rather than as an opponent of Judaism inevitably raised the question of whether or to what extent the ritual obligations of Mosaic law were incurred by those who became converts to Christianity. This problem especially affected Gentiles who, without any Jewish background or any special interest in Judaism, embraced the message of the Gospel, but remained understandably reluctant to submit to circumcision, dietary regulations, festival observances, and countless other Jewish requirements. Consequently, two factions emerged in the early Church, Judaizers, with headquarters in Jerusalem, and anti-Judaizers, based in Antioch. In the present reading we are told that the Jerusalem leadership were persuaded by Paul and Barnabas to make extensive concessions in favor of the opposing point of view.

The second reading, from the book of Revelation, contains portions of that book's final apocalyptic visions of the consummation of history, the final renovation of the world with the definitive coming of the Kingdom of God which constitutes the basic hope of Christianity and the ultimate goal of Christian life. The first part of the vision resumes the description of the New Jerusalem, symbolizing what Jerusalem had meant to the Jews, the central point of contact between God and his world. That this New Jerusalem is not man's construction but God's gift is symbolized by its coming down to earth from its place of origin in heaven. The symbolism is continued by a detailed description of the heavenly city. In the verses cited we observe that its gates face equally in all directions, representing its openness to all humankind, the universality or catholicity of the Church. On its gates are inscribed the names of the Israelite tribes, representing the Old Testament origins of Christianity, while its apostolic basis is symbolized by foundation stones on which are carved the names of the apostles. It is emphasized that the New Jerusalem, unlike its historical predecessor, contains no temple, as a reminder that the temple's sacrificial ritual was a mere anticipation of the definitive sacrifice by which Christ reunited humankind to God. The city is full of light, a traditional symbol of divine revelation, and the source of that light is God's own glory, transmitted by Christ as by a brilliant, unextinguishable lamp.

In the third reading, from the Gospel according to John, we have part of a passage from Jesus' farewell discourses at the Last Supper which is introduced by his promise to send "another to be your Advocate, who will be with you forever—the Spirit of truth." This promise declares that Jesus' personal guidance of his followers, which is soon to end, will not leave them directionless, but will be succeeded immediately by the guiding influence of the Holy Spirit. A life led in conformity with this influence is what Christians have traditionally understood as the spiritual life, a life in which one cultivates an habitual sensitivity to divine guidance together with an habitual promptness to follow that guidance in practice. In such a life, attention to God and obedience to God are the primary and inseparable aspects of what it means to love God. The same applies to loving Jesus, in whom God is made manifest to humanity by means of the incarnation. Jesus reassures his apostles that his own imminent departure will not cut them off from contact with God. His own function in their regard will be continued through a "Paraclete." This Greek word is usually translated advocate, meaning a person who takes one's part, who can be called upon and relied upon for needed help. With this assurance, the apostles have no reason to be "distressed or fearful." In this final gift they will find "peace," deep and permanent peace, "not as the world gives peace."

ASCENSION

Cycle "A" Readings: Acts 1:1-11; Eph. 1:17-23; Mt. 28:16-20

The first reading for the feast of the Ascension presents the opening paragraphs of Acts of the Apostles. We are reminded by the initial verse that this is the second part of Luke's two volume work, and that the dividing point between the two halves of his narrative is precisely the Ascension of Jesus. The significance attributed to the interval between Jesus' resurrection and his ascension is expressed by Luke's summary of what Jesus was doing during that time. "He showed them in many convincing ways that he was alive," and he also foretold that very shortly they would "be baptized with the Holy Spirit." It is from this pentecostal "baptism" that the whole narrative of Acts of the Apostles dramatically unfolds. It was to the risen life of Jesus that the whole narrative of the Gospel according to Luke had dramatically progressed. Thus we may think of the whole Lucan composition as a kind of diptych, and the episode of the Ascension as what the symmetrical panels of that diptych hinge upon. Apart from this structural significance, the theological significance of the Ascension as Luke describes it is evidently to represent the completion of Jesus' own glorification. It is the consummation of that divine action described, in a broad sense of the phrase, as the "raising up" of Jesus. Such clearly is the symbolism of what is described as Jesus' being "lifted up before their eyes," and naively literal speculation in astro-physical terms about just where Jesus was headed for when he "took off" is more distracting than helpful to the understanding of this passage. The two white-clad figures who remain to advise the disciples after Jesus' departure from the world are obviously counterparts of the similar figures who had remained to advise the women after Jesus' earlier departure from the tomb. Luke's arrangement for their reappearance at this point emphasizes the continuity of the resurrection and ascension as two partial aspects of the total "raising up" or glorification of Christ. Whereas on Easter, in affirming that Jesus was alive, the divine messengers proclaimed the basis of Christian faith, so also now, in predicting his return, they proclaim the basis of Christian hope.

The second reading, from the letter to the Ephesians, is part of a prayer for those to whom the letter is addressed. The prayer is immediately preceded by verses in praise of the readers' faith in Christ and love for one another. The spirit of the prayer is accordingly one of gratitude that these people have responded so well to the Gospel. What the writer prays for is a continuing and increasing appreciation of what their faith and hope are well grounded upon. He prays therefore for spiritual perception, for God to "enlighten" their "innermost vision" so that they can form some just estimate of "the scope of his power in us who believe." The measure of that power, of what God is capable of accomplishing in the transformation of human life, is what God has in fact accomplished in Jesus Christ, whom he raised from the dead and exalted to the plane of divinity, where he is endowed with the fullness of power over all creation, and at the same time linked to his Church as its directing principle so closely as to suggest the metaphor of union between head and body in a living organism. In the perspective of this prayer, the ascension of Jesus represents above all his assumption of full control over the destiny of the world he came to redeem.

The same idea of Jesus' assumption of sovereign authority, and in particular his directing influence on the subsequent life of his Church, is predominant in the final reading, from the Gospel according to Matthew. In contrast with Luke's location of Jesus' final communications in the neighborhood of Jerusalem, Matthew transfers his corresponding scene to Galilee, and to the physical setting that this Gospel so much favors for its more solemn occasions, a mountain. As with the Sermon on the Mount, so also here Jesus' ascent of the mountain, with its Mosaic overtones, symbolizes a nearer approach to the presence of God. Here, appropriately, Jesus declares that same fullness of power that was the theme of the second reading, and likewise affirms the permanent closeness of his relationship with his followers. Within this context of the assurance of Jesus' continued presence and power, this Gospel introduces the missionary directive that in the Lucan writings is concentrated on Pentecost.

ASCENSION

Cycle "B" Readings: same as cycle "A" except Mk. 16:15-20

There is considerable agreement among scholars that originally the Gospel according to Mark did not have the same kind of ending that is now attached to it, but there is little agreement as to how it did end originally. What we have in the third reading is the latter half of the ending that we find in most versions of this Gospel but which is omitted in important manuscripts. It seems likely enough that the original ending was for some reason lost and replaced by a kind of summary of what, from other sources, was judged to be appropriate material for the conclusion. The material does in fact correspond in part to elements found in the Gospels according to

Matthew, Luke, and John, but there are distinctive features as well. Most distinctive, perhaps, is the emphasis on the miraculous details that accompany Jesus' missionary injunctions. A very cryptic statement of the Ascension is included, and the emphasis of the passage is the extraordinary power possessed by the Christian missionaries in evidence of the fact that "the Lord continued to work with them throughout and confirm the message."

ASCENSION

Cycle "C" Readings: same as cycle "A" except Lk. 24:46-53

Luke describes the Ascension twice, in Acts of the Apostles, as already heard in the first reading, and also in the final verses of the third Gospel which comprise the final reading. The two accounts are compatible but not identical. Luke's Gospel narrative describes only two appearances of the risen Christ, one to the disciples journeying to Emmaus, and the other to the whole group of disciples at Jerusalem, who also allude to another, earlier appearance to Simon Peter. At the Jerusalem appearance, Jesus first gives evidence, by sharing a meal, that he is in the plainest sense alive. He then explains how his passion and death have fulfilled the Messianic prophecies, and how those prophecies also point to a worldwide missionary undertaking. This the disciples are to launch as soon as he sends them "the promise of my Father," that is, the pentecostal gift of the Spirit, described subsequently in Acts. Here the scene of the Ascension is given a definite location, at Bethany, a village near Jerusalem, where Jesus departs from his followers in the act of imparting to them a final blessing.

SEVENTH SUNDAY OF EASTER

Cycle "A" Readings: Acts 1:12-14; 1 Pet. 4:13-16; Jn. 17:1-11

The first reading is the part of the Acts of the Apostles that immediately follows the account of the Ascension. The passage is a thoroughly uneventful bit of narrative, but its emptiness of action is entirely appropriate to its function in the story. It represents an emphatic lull, which serves very effectively to mark the separation between the two successive movements of action in Luke's historical drama. The first movement is summarized retrospectively at the very beginning of Acts, as comprising "all that Jesus did and taught until the day he was taken up to heaven." On that day, the very last words attributed to Jesus summarize prospectively the second movement: "You will receive power when the Holy Spirit comes down on you; then you are to be my witnesses in Jerusalem, throughout Judea and Samaria, even to the ends of the earth." This prediction is in effect a *precis* of Acts of the Apostles. In between the two movements nothing, from an historical point of view, can really be said to happen. It is a kind of intermission in a two-act drama during which the characters remain onstage, simply waiting. Their waiting is a prayerful waiting, and it is typical of Luke to call attention to prayer before great happenings. This actionless occasion is also made use of for a kind of roll call, noting the presence of the apostles, of a group of women including Mary, and of Jesus' brothers. The number and identity of the latter are not stated, but it is noteworthy that at their earlier appearance, in the Gospel, they showed no understanding of or sympathy with Jesus' mission. It is often pointed out that the term translated as brothers is not applied exclusively to siblings, and that the tradition of supposing Jesus to have been Mary's only child is reconcilable with the text of the New Testament, though not directly supported by it.

The second reading, from the first letter of Peter, expresses once again the major preoccupation of that document with the sufferings, occasioned by persecution, to which its readers were exposed. Here, as previously, the sufferers are offered two kinds of consolation. In the first place, they are to see their own sufferings as intimately connected with the sufferings of their Lord, and therefore as participating in the positive significance that Christians attribute to Christ's passion and death. In the second place, and as a development of the same belief, they are to see their sufferings as a brief prelude to and preparation for a glorious destiny. No doubt, however, when a government is notoriously unjust and its victims are in many cases admirable, there is a tendency to glamorize the victims and opponents of government rather indiscriminately. There is evidence that in the early Church, idealization of the martyr's death became for some a quite fanatical compulsion. Thus the writer manifests understandable apprehension lest the positive interpretation of suffering and persecution should be misapplied so as to include penalties that were actually deserved. He accordingly insists that it is not being on the wrong side of the law that is commended, but being on Christ's side, the side of a just victim of an unjust judge.

The final reading, from the Gospel according to John, is taken from the last of Jesus' farewell discourses, as they are commonly called, which are immediately followed by the passion narrative. This particular discourse is not, like the others, directly addressed to the disciples. Instead, although it is clearly intended to serve a teaching function, it is directly addressed to God, whom Jesus regularly calls Father, as a prayer and a very solemn one. It has often been designated as Jesus' high-priestly prayer, and that designation is supported by a significant similarity of structure between Jesus' prayer and that which accompanies the atonement sacrifice as prescribed to the Jewish high priest, originally Aaron, in the book of Leviticus. As the high priest offers his expiatory rites "for himself, his household, and the whole assembly of Israel," so Jesus prays, successively, for himself ("give me glory"), for his intimate followers ("for these you have given me"), and finally by anticipation for the whole Church ("for those also who through their words put their faith in me"). The reading contains the whole first part of this prayer, the beginning of the second part, and none of the third part. The key word of Jesus' prayer for himself, repeated five times in as many verses, is glory. The prayer begins by declaring that "the hour has come," recalling earlier allusions that pointed to a still future "hour" which would be the consummation of Jesus' mission. The glorification is, of course, the passion itself, wherein the divine action exercised through Jesus reaches its maximum intensity and efficacy in those very events which, humanly interpreted, exhibit Jesus at his weakest and most ineffectual.

SEVENTH SUNDAY OF EASTER

Cycle "B" Readings: Acts 1:15-17, 20a, 20c-26; 1 Jn. 4:11-16; Jn. 17:11b-19

The Acts of the Apostles, from which the first reading is taken, continues the narrative begun in the Gospel according to Luke from the time just after the resurrection. Accordingly, Acts begins with Jesus' promise of the imminent coming of the Holy Spirit, by whose power the apostles would undertake a world mission of witness to Jesus. The ascension narrative then marks the termination of Jesus' earthly presence, and between that experience and Pentecost the apostles gather in Jerusalem to await the promised Spirit. During this prayerful interlude, St. Peter is represented as having called for a replacement of the defector, Judas. This concern and Peter's initiative reflect a sense of ecclesiastical structure and succession which became characteristic of early Christianity at a somewhat later date. It also reflects both an initial desire to retain the original number of apostles and a definite understanding of the qualifications for and the function of apostleship. Eligibility for apostleship depended on having been "one of those who was in our company all the while we had the Lord Jesus with us," from the time of John the Baptist until the ascension. And the purpose of apostleship was "to join us as a witness to his resurrection." It may be noted that St. Paul's later claim to be a true apostle, while retaining the idea of apostolic function as witness to the resurrection, dispensed with the qualification of having been associated with Jesus during his public ministry, as well as with the concern for a numerical complement of twelve apostles, implying a more flexible conception of apostleship than the present passage suggests. The application to Judas' defection of isolated verses from two different psalms reflects the tendency of early Christians to reinforce the notion of Jesus' messiahship by finding Old Testament foreshadowings in events in the story of Jesus no matter how farfetched and unrelated to their original context these Christian applications might be.

More than any other New Testament writing, the first letter of John adopts an experimental approach to the reality of Christian life. This brief document contains a remarkable number of hypothetical statements which could be compared with diagnostic tests. That is, the statements cite observable conditions from which conclusions may be drawn concerning whether or not, interiorly and spiritually, one is truly united to God. One such statement found in today's reading has more than a dozen equivalents in various other parts of the letter: "God himself dwells in us if we love one another." The verses immediately preceding this statement make it clear that our loving one another is understood to be an immediate consequence of God's loving us. By loving one another, Christians give the proper and effective response to God's love for them. Having established fraternal love as a visible criterion of the interior presence of God, however, the author proceeds at once to enunciate another "proof that we dwell in him and he dwells in us; he has imparted his Spirit to us." Since possession of the Spirit is hardly less mysterious than the indwelling of God, this may seem rather unsatisfactory as an experimental test. But that difficulty had arisen and been dealt with in an earlier passage: "This is how we may recognize the Spirit of God: every spirit which acknowledges that Jesus Christ has come in the flesh is from God." Just as right belief in the reality of the incarnation was there invoked to test the presence of God's Spirit, so here right belief in the divine source of the incarnation serves the same purpose: "If a man acknowledges that Jesus is the Son of God, God dwells in him." The two criteria of true interior Christianity which appear in this reading predominate throughout the entire letter—fraternal love and orthodox belief in the incarnation.

The third reading is taken from that section of the Gospel according to John which is often called the high-priestly prayer of Jesus. This prayer, whose setting is the eve of the passion, falls into three main divisions. In the first, Jesus prays for himself. In the third he prays for future believers. In the second, all but the beginning of which comprises the liturgical reading, he prays for his disciples, whom he sharply distinguishes from "the world" and characterizes as "those whom you (the Father) have given me." The prayer derives its orientation from the fact that whereas Jesus, having discharged the mission given him by the Father, is soon to leave the world, the disciples must soon take up in the world the mission given them by Jesus. As is customary in Johannine usage, the "world" is here understood as the domain of hostility to God, and therefore of hostility to all who represent and serve God, above all Jesus himself, but also those who will carry on his divine mission. Accordingly, Jesus prays for his protection, by the power of God, from the power of the "evil one." Finally, he prays for them to be "consecrated," in the sense of being equipped and sanctified, by the truth of that divine revelation which Jesus has transmitted to them. This portion of the prayer concludes with Jesus' statement that "I now consecrate myself," referring to the imminence of the passion and death whereby his own mission will be fully discharged, and that of his followers made efficacious.

SEVENTH SUNDAY OF EASTER

Cycle "C" Readings: Acts 7:55-60; Rev. 22:12-14, 16-17, 20; Jn. 17:20-26

The first reading of today's liturgy is the account given in Acts of the Apostles of the death of Stephen, venerated in the Church as the first Christian martyr. The Greek word martyr means witness, and in its full religious sense it refers to one who testifies publicly to his Christian faith even at the cost of his own life. Clearly, to assert one's belief under such circumstances manifests not only great courage, but also extraordinarily deep conviction, and has consequently a uniquely persuasive effect on others. The account of Stephen's death in Acts is preceded by a lengthy account of the testimony which cost him his life, a sermon before the Sanhedrin which he gave in response to charges of having made anti-Jewish statements. His sermon took the form of a recapitulation of biblical history up to the time of David, whereupon Stephen denounced the Jews of the past for persecuting the prophets "who foretold the coming of the Righteous One," and those of the present for having "betrayed him and murdered him," referring, of course, to Jesus. These last words gave ultimate offense to Stephen's hearers. And his claim, in face of their exasperation, to behold a vision of "Jesus standing at God's right hand" incited what seems to have been an outburst of mob violence, rather than an act of official retaliation. The episode is represented as beginning a major persecution of Christians in Jerusalem, and thus anticipates the transferral of Christian missionary efforts from Jerusalem to Antioch and thence to the Gentile world. It is also linked to later developments by the mention of "a young man named Saul" as the passive accomplice of Stephen's slayers.

The second reading, from the book of Revelation, has put together three separate passages from a collection of sayings which follow the book's long series of apocalyptic visions and bring it to a conclusion. Most of the sayings are represented as words spoken by Jesus to the author of the book. A common theme of the three selected passages is apparent when one observes that in the first Jesus says "I am coming soon." In the second a response, twice repeated, is "Come!" and in the third Jesus is again quoted as saying "I am coming soon," and the author himself responds, "Come, Lord Jesus!" In other words, the book of Revelation, mainly occupied with visions of the future, and mainly motivated by a desire to encourage Christians in a time of great stress, concludes by reiterating its essential message, the imminent return of Jesus Christ who will put an end to the tribulations of his followers. The second coming of Jesus is, of course, and was from the Church's earliest years, a basic article of the Christian creed, and one having intense motivational import. This doctrine in the book of Revelation is, however, complicated by the highly problematic word "soon." The word reminds us that among early Christians there was a widely shared assumption that worldly history would come to an end very soon, probably within the current generation. In the light of subsequent events, it became necessary either to reinterpret that word "soon" in some less than obvious sense, or else simply to put it down as a misconception on the part of the biblical writer.

The third reading, from the Gospel according to John, is taken from that final portion of Jesus' farewell discourses at the Last Supper which has traditionally been known as his High Priestly Prayer. Just as the Jewish high priest on the great annual festival of Atonement prayed, first for himself, then for the priests and levites, and finally for the whole people of Israel, so here Jesus prays, first for himself, then for his disciples, and finally for all future believers. It is the last of these three sections of the prayer that comprises the reading. Jesus' prayer for all the faithful is first of all a prayer for their unity, with the added reflection that their unity will itself elicit faith in the mission Jesus has from his Father. The unity for which Jesus prays is no mere social cohesion, but a profound spiritual interpenetration comparable to the bond by which Jesus and his Father are said to be not merely with one another but in one another. The second theme of Jesus' prayer for the faithful regards their ultimate destiny, asking that they should be where Jesus himself is, beholding his glory which issues from his Father's eternal love. The prayer concludes with two verses which summarize Jesus' ministry, of making the Father known to believers, in order that they might possess the Father's love and Jesus himself in whom that love is incarnate.

PENTECOST

PENTECOST

Cycles "A", "B", and "C" Readings: Acts 2:1-11; 1 Cor. 12:3-7, 12-13; Jn. 20:19-23

According to Acts, Jesus' last instruction to his disciples was to wait in Jerusalem until they should be "baptized with the Holy Spirit," and his last promise to them was, "You will receive power when the Holy Spirit comes upon you: and you will bear witness for me in Jerusalem, and all over Judea and Samaria, to the ends of the earth." The events which are described as having taken place among the apostles on the Jewish feast of Pentecost represent both their baptism with the Holy Spirit and the beginning of their world-wide bearing of witness. The roaring wind out of the sky and the tongues of fire clearly symbolize a spectacular divine intervention. In biblical language, the words for "wind" and "spirit" are closely related. The idea of "breath" brings out their conceptual relationship to one another, as well as to the idea of a principle of life. Coming from the sky, thought of as the abode of God, the mighty wind clearly suggests the application of an intense force of divine vitality. Fire, with its immense capacity both for destruction and for constructive use, was a familiar symbol of divine action, especially when conceived in terms either of punishment or of purification. In view of the earlier reference to being "baptized with the Holy Spirit," the symbolism of fire would seem in this instance mainly to suggest purification or refinement, implying divine cleansing and strengthening. The tongue-like form of the fire relates it to the phenomenon by which the apostles first show the effect of the Holy Spirit upon them. Some interpreters regard this as an instance of "glossolalia," that strange mode of verbalization, incomprehensible to ordinary understanding, associated with ecstasies. Other interpreters understand that the apostles were enabled to speak in a way that proved equally intelligible to members of different language groups, an idea that certainly seems to be implied by the text (2:6-11). Yet the other interpretation, which agrees with what "tongues" means elsewhere in the New Testament, would make it understandable why skeptical hearers thought the apostles' behavior was merely symptomatic of intoxication (2:13).

The second reading deals with spiritual gifts, or "charisms," here understood as extraordinary behavior manifesting the influence of the Holy Spirit. Before taking up specific problems raised by the occurrence of various ecstatic phenomena among the Corinthian Christians, Paul sets down fundamental principles which govern his approach to the whole matter. In the first place, the Holy Spirit's influence can be authenticated by its effectiveness in uniting persons to Jesus Christ. Just as Paul had previously pointed out that to say "a curse on Jesus" reflects a disposition irreconcilable with the Spirit's active presence, so here he observes that, on the contrary, to say "Jesus is Lord" represents the Spirit's proper effect. Second, Paul insists that diversity among spiritual gifts must be understood consistently with the unity of their giver. The gifts, for all their variety, are manifestations of the one Spirit of the one God. In developing this concept of many gifts from one Spirit, Paul adapted for Christian purposes a metaphor current in pagan philosophy, likening members of one society to organs of a living body. As different organs serve in distinctive ways the needs of one organism, so in Paul's view each Christian is intended to employ his own distinctive spiritual gifts for common Christian purposes. In these reflections we find the first ingredients of the later theology of the Church as the body of Christ.

The third reading for Pentecost, from the Gospel according to John, is an account of events represented as taking place on Easter Sunday night. We are thereby reminded of how closely the fourth Gospel associates Jesus' resurrection with the gift of the Spirit. Whether or not the account given in this Gospel can be reconciled in material detail with the account in Acts is questionable, and how much one cares about reconciling them depends on how factual one takes the accounts to be. In any case, both of them clearly understand that the gift of the Holy Spirit to the apostles is a consequence of Jesus' resurrection and a fulfillment of divine promises. In John's Gospel, it is noteworthy that all the main events of his narrative are anticipated by Jesus' predictions during the long discourse on Holy Thursday night, when he promised to return, and assured them of peace, joy, a mission like his own from God, and the sending of the Holy Spirit. The Johannine references to the Spirit as "sent" from God by Christ had profound influence on what, in subsequent theology, came to be known as the "processions" and "missions" of the three Persons of the Blessed Trinity.

TRINITY SUNDAY

Cycle "A" Readings: Ex. 34:4-6, 8-9; 2 Cor. 13:11-13; Jn. 3:16-18

The first reading, from the book of Exodus, is easily located in a familiar story by the fact that it begins with Moses ascending Mt. Sinai at the Lord's bidding, carrying the two stone tablets with him. The two tablets he carries up the mountain are different ones from the two he had previously brought down the mountain to show his followers the written law of their divine covenant. The first tablets were shattered when Moses flung them down in rage on seeing the crude idolatry that had developed among his people during his absence. After quelling this rebellion at the cost of considerable bloodshed, and reconciling the chastened people to the God who seemed on the point of abandoning them, Moses was directed to replace the broken tablets of the law and to reascend the mountain alone. This time the Lord declared his presence by pronouncing his sacred name, and identifying his characteristics of compassion, patience, fidelity, and readiness to forgive. Omitted by the liturgical reading is a verse containing the harsher reminder that the same Lord also punishes descendants to the third and fourth generation for the sins of their ancestors. Heartened by the divine words of reassurance, Moses implores the Lord to forgive his people, despite their recalcitrance, and to accept them as his own. In what follows, the Lord reaffirms his covenant, and furnishes instructions for the next major phase of the people's history, their penetration and conquest of Canaan.

The second reading comprises the concluding verses of the second letter to the Corinthians. The early years of the Christian community at Corinth were a stormy time, marked by numerous controversies which left considerable residue of bitterness. Paul's own relationship with the Corinthians was an uneasy one, with irritating misunderstandings occurring on both sides. The tension of the situation is frequently perceptible in both letters to the Corinthians, the second of which may embody contents of what originally was more than one letter. Under the circumstances it is not surprising that even the conclusion is not a mere conventional valediction, but contains heartfelt appeal. It appeals first of all for the reform of those who have allowed their behavior to degenerate to a level below the standards acceptable in a Christian. But since in Corinth even rigorist tendencies had fomented discord, Paul appeals particularly for social harmony and cooperation. His prayer for God to be with them reminds them explicitly that the God they pray to is a God of love and peace, whose presence is manifested where those qualities are found among human beings. Paul's final blessing suggests, in the light of later theology, the trinitarian conception of God, and is thus especially pertinent to this feast. Like the divinity of Father, Son, and Spirit, the blessings cited here as love, grace, and fellowship are ultimately the one reality of human participation in the life of God.

The third reading, from the Gospel according to John, is an excerpt from the concluding verses of a conversation reported as having taken place between Jesus and a Pharisaic sympathizer called Nicodemus. Nicodemus acknowledges from the outset that Jesus is a teacher sent from God, but remains understandably puzzled by Jesus' statement that to see the kingdom of God one must be "born again." The meaning of this phrase, now so familiar in the jargon of Christian conversion, remains obscure, although Jesus' words point to its symbolic force by their reference to water and the Spirit. The meaning of these words, as of Jesus' whole mission, depends for clarification on the completion of that mission when the "Son of Man" is "lifted up," that is, simultaneously crucified and glorified. This climax of Jesus' mission will be the object of faith and the basis of salvation through faith. The words quoted in the reading point to that faith and salvation, identifying the latter as "eternal life." They are an affirmation that the mission of Jesus is one of salvation, not condemnation. But the affirmation also implies that to reject Jesus' mission by a refusal of faith is itself tantamount to condemnation. The concepts of salvation and judgment are here closely linked as the conceptions respectively of belief and refusal to believe in a way that is highly characteristic of the fourth Gospel. As the reference to rebirth through "water" suggests, the considerations of faith and salvation in this passage are closely associated with baptismal practice in the early Church.

TRINITY SUNDAY

Cycle "B" Readings: Deut. 4:32-34; Rom. 8:14-17; Mt. 28:16-20

The book of Deuteronomy, from which the first reading is taken, forms a kind of theological introduction to a history which extends from Israel's occupation of Canaan to the Babylonian captivity. As a prelude to the exposition of the obligations of the covenant, Moses reviews events since the exodus from Egypt and points out the implications of those events. What they imply is, above all, the extraordinary divine favor of which the Israelites have been the always unworthy and often ungrateful recipients. In the perspective of Deuteronomy, the supreme manifestation of the favor shown by God to Israel is the law, the formal expression of the covenant, given to Moses in the great revelation on Mount Horeb, elsewhere called Mount Sinai. It is to the marvelous character of this event that reference is made at the beginning of today's liturgical reading, emphasizing the uniquely intimate and intense character of God's manifestation of himself to Israel. The same unique closeness of God's effective presence is further evidenced by the whole series of episodes in which Israel was divinely enabled to triumph over enemies. The final passage of the reading calls upon the Israelites to behave consistently with their appreciation of the favored status God has given them. They must allow nothing to conflict with the supremacy of God in their own lives. What this means in practice is fidelity to the law and the resolute determination to "keep his statutes and his commandments." If they prove faithful to this obligation, based on grateful appreciation, "all will be well with you and with your children after you, and you will live long in the land which the Lord your God is giving you for all time." Remembering the long history, ending with destruction and exile, which Deuteronomy introduces and interprets, one perceives an ironic ominousness underlying these words of reassurance, which are equivalently repeated many times as the book proceeds.

The second reading, from the letter of Paul to the Romans, is a passage which deals with certain fundamental aspects of the spiritual life, understanding that phrase in the Christian sense of a life whose basic principle is the gift of the Holy Spirit. Since the Holy Spirit is understood as the Spirit of God, and therefore the principle of divine life, what the effective presence of that Spirit entails in a human being is a human participation in divine life. And since the divine life in human beings is entirely derived from and conferred by God, the relationship it implies is analogous on the level of spiritual life, to the relationship of offspring to parent on the level of biological life. One is therefore led by analogy from the idea of having the Spirit of God to the idea of being the offspring of God. Paul then contrasts the attitude appropriate to consciousness of sonship with that characteristic of servile relationships. Whereas the latter is typically fear-ridden, the former is normally full of comfort and confidence. In illustration of the idea that the latter is the proper attitude for Christians, Paul recalls the practice, traceable to Jesus' own teaching, of addressing God in prayer as "Father," and even of using for this filial address the familiarly affectionate Aramaic word "Abba." In this way, Paul ties closely together his own teaching that a Christian is one who possesses the Spirit of God, with the already familiar Christian practice of addressing God as a trusting child addresses a loving father. He then pursues this line of reflection a step further by observing that one of the implications of sonship is inheritance. What the father has, his son is destined to possess. And in the same way Christians, as children of God, look forward in hope to their eventual full possession of all that God their Father has to give them. In the anticipation, they recapitulate the pattern of Christ's own life, by enduring like him an interval of suffering in the confidence of following him from suffering into glory.

The final reading in today's liturgy is the final passage of the Gospel according to Matthew. These climactic verses effectively transform this Gospel from a record of the past into a program for the future. Just as Jesus formed his disciples by the teaching of a new revelation, so they in turn, by transmitting the revelation they have received, are now required to make disciples of the Gentile peoples. In a sense, these few concluding verses do for Matthew's Gospel what Acts does for Luke's Gospel, that is, they carry the Christian story from its beginning and basis in the life of Jesus in Palestine to its continuation and development in the mission of the Church throughout the world. It is evident that the writer of these words lived at a time and place which enabled him to have a very definite conception of the Church as a missionary society commissioned by a master vested with divine authority to carry the message of that master to the Gentile world. Moreover, this missionary society is understood to possess an initiatory ritual of baptism and a trinitarian profession of faith by which its members are formally set apart from the unconverted. The permanence and the progress of the missionary society are understood to be guaranteed by the effective presence of its divinely empowered founder for as long as the world itself lasts. And it appears to be understood on the one hand that the world will not last forever, but also assumed on the other hand that it will have sufficient duration to make a worldwide missionary undertaking feasible and significant. The missionary and ecclesiastical point of view which appears so clearly in these final verses of Matthew's Gospel is present less obviously but no less significantly throughout that Gospel as a whole.

TRINITY SUNDAY

Cycle "C" Readings: Prov. 8:22-31; Rom. 5:1-5; Jn. 16:12-15

The first reading is from the book of Proverbs, a collection of what is called "wisdom literature" representing a wide variety of historical periods. Israel developed its wisdom literature long after and in dependence upon other Middle Eastern cultures. In its earliest form it represented a kind of instruction in morals and manners which might be likened to the books on "successful living" which have often thrived in our own culture. Thus, wisdom itself was initially conceived mainly as a kind of personal and social know-how, which enabled its possessors to enjoy life and get ahead. In Israel, religious presuppositions made it inevitable that pre-eminent wisdom should be attributed to God, and that any share of it by others should be considered not merely a product of training and experience but a blessed gift of God. As attention shifted from humankind's derivative wisdom to God's original wisdom, this divine quality or capacity was represented in certain writings more or less as a distinct entity. That is, although one may say synonymously either that God is wise or that he has wisdom, the latter formulation makes it relatively easy to think of God's wisdom not as a way that God is, but rather as an instrument that God employs. By an easy further step in this rather mythical way of thinking, the wisdom which belongs to God can be thought of less impersonally, and thus made to appear more like a divine assistant than a divine instrument. In the present passage this full development has taken place, and we find God's wisdom referred to as though it were an amiable offspring who is God's eternally inseparable companion and intimate collaborator. Such language and thought evidently prepare the way for later ideas of a divine son, and ultimately of a trinity of divine persons as in Christian theology.

The second reading, from Paul's letter to the Romans, is the beginning of the second major part of that work. The first part had been mainly concerned with justification, humankind's liberation from the bondage of sin by the grace of God. The human acceptance of this divine liberation, by humble reliance on God's merciful power exercised through Jesus Christ, is what Paul chiefly means by "faith." The second part of the letter, which presupposes that doctrine and proceeds to further developments, accordingly begins with the transitional phrase, "now that we have been justified by faith. . . ." Its theme, therefore, is the new condition in which humankind finds itself once divine liberation from sin has been appropriated through faith. This new condition is first characterized as one of "peace with God," replacing the previous state of hostility or alienation. The reference is not to a mere feeling of serenity, but to a profound harmony with God, and therefore with God's will and God's purposes. This harmony with divine purpose entails the next characteristic Paul attributes to the condition of humankind justified by faith, namely, "hope for the glory of God." This "glory of God" represents the full achievement, in all its splendor, of God's design for his creation. Being at "peace with God," humankind is enabled, as it were, to look forward to what God himself looks forward to, and to do so with an unshakable confidence that makes even affliction a source of strength.

The third reading, from the Gospel according to John, is taken from Jesus' farewell discourses at the Last Supper. This material can be divided into major sub-sections. The second sub-section, of which the reading is part, deals especially with future prospects for the life of the Church after the coming of the Holy Spirit. After likening the vital unity which links Christ with his followers to the organic unity of a vine and its branches, Jesus makes a sharp distinction between his followers and "the world." "The world" is here understood as human society alienated from God, and just as it opposed Jesus, it may be expected to continue exercising its opposition against those who are most closely united with Jesus. Suffering, therefore, must be frankly expected. But the world that inflicts this suffering already stands condemned, and its ultimate defeat is assured. Jesus' followers will need to be strengthened and guided to withstand the world's assaults. Jesus has already taught them much of what they shall need to understand, but he recognizes that they cannot at this point assimilate all the understanding they will eventually require to sustain them. Jesus gives them what might be called in military parlance a general preliminary briefing for their admittedly dangerous mission. But the lines of communication are to be kept open, so that they can receive the enlightenment they need at the times when they most need it. This will be the function of the "Spirit of truth," who "will guide you into all the truth," God's medium of communication, who "will tell only what he hears" in that divine realm where only truth is heard.

SEASON OF THE YEAR

SECOND SUNDAY OF THE YEAR

Cycle "A" Readings: Is. 49:3, 5-6; 1 Cor. 1:1-3; Jn. 1:29-34

The first reading is from the second of the "Servant Songs," a group of four hymns occurring in the second part of Isaiah and tied together by a common theme: the enigmatic figure of the "Suffering Servant of Yahweh" who by his sufferings wins justification for many. Here the role of the Father may be noted; it is he who says "You are my servant," who formed the Servant from his mother's womb, and who constitutes his strength. It is the Father, too, who is not satisfied with restoring the fortunes of Israel; he will make his Servant a "light to the nations," so that "salvation may reach to the ends of the earth." In the divine plan the initiative is always taken by the Father, "who administers everything according to his will and counsel," as Paul says (Eph. 1:11).

Only the greeting of the first letter to the Corinthians appears in the second reading, but it is enough to show that Paul writes from a vantage point where the new age has fully dawned. Jesus is no longer the humble Servant but the exalted Lord, ranged in conspicuous parallel with God the Father. Since the Spirit has been poured out, the converts whom Paul addresses are consecrated and "called to be a holy people."

In the loving initiative of the Father, the death and exaltation of the Son, and the outpouring of the Spirit, God's work is accomplished. In this age of the Spirit it goes on still, both within and without the Church.

In the Gospel according to John a sense of a time of transition between two eras is given almost palpably in a reading about John the Baptist. The last prophet of the age passing away is just now announcing the presence of the initiator of the new age, an event that John himself has only at this very moment come to realize: "I confess I did not recognize him, though the very reason I came . . . was that he might be revealed to Israel."

In indicating that Jesus is the one awaited, John the Baptist says: "Look! There is the lamb of God." Quite possibly the Evangelist has in mind here the paschal lamb, which is an important symbol in his Gospel, or perhaps the lamb "standing that had been slain" mentioned in Revelation (Rev. 5:6). But there is unquestionably also an allusion to the Suffering Servant; for he too is "like a lamb led to the slaughter" (Is. 53:7), and thereby takes away the sins of many (Is. 53:12). The Baptist's closing testimony, "This is God's chosen one," is likewise clearly a reference to the beginning of the Servant Songs (Is. 42:1). The evangelist must see in Jesus a fulfillment of the Isaian prophecy.

But to the Servant and Yahweh is added now a third figure: the Spirit. John the Baptist bears witness that the Spirit descended on Jesus; indeed, this was the very sign by which Jesus was to be recognized, for the inaugurator of the new age is one who baptizes not merely with water but with the Spirit. Thus the Spirit too plays his role in the transformation of human history.

SECOND SUNDAY OF THE YEAR

Cycle "B" Readings: 1 Sam. 3:3b-10, 19; 1 Cor. 6:13c-15a, 17-20; Jn. 1:35-42

The passage read in today's liturgy from the first book of Samuel has been cited countless times by religion teachers to illustrate the idea of divine calling, or vocation. This is a very prominent idea in much of the Old Testament, especially in connection with the prophets. A prophet is essentially one whom God designates to serve as his unfailing spokesman, and who is set apart by a total dedication to reverently hearing God's messages and faithfully transmitting them. Since God's messages must often be harsh ones, the task of a true prophet is often not only thankless and lonely, but decidedly dangerous. Among the rich variety of legends which became associated with the memory of Samuel, those concerning his early life strongly emphasize his having been set apart, by God and for God. This motif extends back even beyond his birth, for he is said to have been dedicated by his mother for the exclusive service of God, and raised in the temple under the tutelage of the priest Eli. It was during his childhood years in the temple that God called Samuel while he was sleeping. However we may conceive this experience, the boy recognized that he had been summoned, but, lacking the religious maturity to recognize the summons as coming from God, he reported to his custodian, God's priest. After initial puzzlement, Eli understood, explained the divine origin of his call, and told him to respond to it with the words, "Speak, Lord; your servant is listening." These words, which represent Samuel's perfect readiness to learn and do God's will, mark the beginning of his prophetic career.

Corinth, in St. Paul's time, enjoyed an international reputation for extraordinarily low standards of sexual morality. It was also a city which harbored a great variety of exotic and often bizarre religious philosophies. At certain points, religious novelty and sexual nonchalance seem to have joined forces. One school of thought which drew a very sharp contrast between the human body and the human spirit, and condemned the vile matter of bodies while glorifying the divine quality of spirit, appears to have drawn the startling conclusion that bodily activities simply did not matter to the spiritual life of people, so that just as there could be no real value in, say, married lovemaking, neither could there be any real disvalue in, say, adultery or fornication. The bodily realm, being a non-spiritual domain, was likewise a non-moral domain. It may be that some variant of this kind of thinking, which had infiltrated Christian ranks, provoked the response we read in today's selection from Paul's first letter to the Corinthians. He quotes what was no doubt a current saying, "I am free to do anything," and retorts, "Yes, but not everything is for my good." He then quotes another saying, "Food is for the belly and the belly for food," which, in its context, seems to imply the more general contention that all bodily appetites, including sexual ones, are mere animal cravings whose manner of gratification has no spiritual, and therefore no real moral significance—for, after all, bodies and bodily activities, not being destined for eternity but for destruction, are matters of indifference from a religious point of view. It is this whole way of thinking, and not merely the sexual promiscuity it fostered, which Paul rejects by insisting that the body, being integral to the person, is by no means irrelevant to Christian religion and morality. "It is not true that the body is for lust; it is for the Lord—and the Lord for the body." This statement, of profound significance in Paul's moral theology, is supported by the fact that the supreme redemptive event, the resurrection, witnesses to the fact that God's work of salvation embraces a person in his entirety, as a bodily and not only a spiritual self. It is on this basis that Paul condemns fornication. For the person who is redeemed by Christ belongs to God in his entirety. And whether a person turns away from God by the use of the body or by the use of the mind is equally to desecrate that union with God which Christ has made possible. Paul's rejection of licentiousness is not a matter of social ethics, but of religious ethics. For Christians, holiness and unholiness are conditions not of disembodied spirits, but of total, embodied personalities.

The Old Testament prophetic theme of being called by God and the New Testament redemptive theme of belonging to God through union with Christ come together in dramatic fashion where the Gospels represent Jesus as summoning individuals to join him as disciples in a way of life which will unite them to God and prepare them to bring others into that same union. The passage in today's reading from the Gospel according to John is a familiar illustration of this motif. Two of John's disciples, at John's prompting, go with Jesus. After a day spent in his company, they have seen and heard enough to make Jesus the object of their messianic hopes. One of them, Andrew, tells his brother Simon what they have found. Simon also joins them. The distinctive pattern of Christian discipleship, of Christian vocation, a discovery of Jesus Christ followed by a sharing of that discovery with others, is here clearly delineated.

SECOND SUNDAY OF THE YEAR

Cycle "C" Readings: Is. 62:1-5; 1 Cor. 12:4-11; Jn. 2:1-12

The first reading of today's liturgy is taken from a portion of the book of Isaiah which was composed, long after the lifetime of Isaiah himself, at a period when the Babylonian captivity had finally come to an end, and when the people of Israel were at last restored to their Palestinian homeland and its sacred city of Jerusalem. It was, therefore, a period of great national and religious rejoicing, and it is this joy which finds expression in the lyric poem that comprises the liturgical reading. The poem begins on a note of irrepressible celebration to develop its basic themes of Israel's vindication and of Israel's reconciliation. Israel's vindication means, in effect, the vindication of Israel's faith in God. For after years of national humiliation and contrary to all the expectations of her foreign enemies, Israel had at last repossessed her promised land and was currently in the process of making a great new national beginning. In the poet's declaration that "nations shall behold your vindication and all kings your glory" there is a somewhat typical smug suggestion that "he who laughs last laughs best." The closely related theme of Israel's reconciliation turns the poet's attention from Israel's relationship to other nations to her relationship to God. The imagery of this portion of the poem is drawn from a prophetic tradition which, from the eighth century onward, frequently represented the covenant bond between God and his chosen people as a marriage bond, offered in love by the divine bridegroom, and accepted in faith by the people as his bride. Given this imagery, it was natural that Israel's sins, being acts of infidelity to God and violation of the covenant, should be symbolized as adulterous behavior. When, therefore, the sinfulness of Israel was conceived to be the reason why God at last abandoned his people, leaving them to the mercy of their foreign invaders, the whole tragic period of the exile was thought of as God's divorcing of a spouse who had proved so callously unworthy of his constant love. Consequently, the atmosphere of Israel's restoration is that of a kind of symbolic "second honeymoon" of the people newly reconciled to the God whose love they had betrayed. "No more shall men call you 'Forsaken,' or your land 'Desolate,' but you shall be called 'My Delight' and your land 'Espoused.' "

The second reading, from Paul's first letter to the Corinthians, develops a theme that has been of great importance both for the guidance of Christian living and for the development of Christian theology. It is the theme of what has often been called the Church's "Pentecostal" character, or the "charismatic" dimension of life within the Church. Paul took it for granted that the behavior of Christians would be in many ways significantly different from that of non-Christians, and that the differences would be manifestations of that "new life" into which Christians believed themselves to have been "reborn." This new life was understood to be divine life, bestowed by

God's grace on those who accepted his gift with faith. And since "spirit" was a term applied to the principle of life in general, the principle of divine life was referred to as the divine Spirit, or Holy Spirit, or Spirit of God. The point which Paul wishes to stress in the passage read in today's liturgy is that although divine life may be manifested by different members of the Church in quite different ways, the principle of that divine life remains one and the same, the Spirit. Paul thus distinguishes between the unique Spirit and the many different "gifts" (or "charisms") by which the Spirit is variously manifested. Underlying Paul's thought in this matter is a concern to make clear to Christians that what really matters is whether or not one lives by the Spirit of God, and not how one happens to manifest the divine life. For just as in any organism many different vital activities are coordinated to serve one life, so the various charisms serve cooperatively the common life of the Church.

The third reading, from the Gospel according to John, recounts the narrative of Jesus' changing water into wine at the wedding feast of Cana. The significance of this episode in the structure of this Gospel is indicated by the concluding statement that "Jesus performed this first of his signs at Cana in Galilee. Thus did he reveal his glory, and his disciples believed in him." There are six more of these "signs" in John's Gospel. Each of them is a miraculous deed performed by Jesus, and each of the miracles has strongly symbolic implications. And what is said explicitly of this first sign may be applied to them all: they reveal Jesus' "glory," that is, the saving presence and power of God in his actions, and they are occasions for his disciples to believe in him. The symbolism of changing water into wine at a wedding feast can best be approached through recalling the established imagery of a messianic banquet representing the final salvation of God's people, and of marriage as representing the covenant union between God and his people. Wine, already in the Synoptic Gospels, represents the new order of things which Jesus' coming brings to the world. And the transforming impact of Jesus on the traditions of Judaism is further suggested by the fact that the new wine is made out of that very water which was "prescribed for Jewish ceremonial washings."

THIRD SUNDAY OF THE YEAR

Cycle "A" Readings: Is. 8:23—9:3; 1 Cor. 1:10-13, 17; Mt. 4:12-23

The destruction of the northern kingdom was a time of crisis for the Israelite nation, the first step in the dismantling of the nation as known to David and Solomon. Israel at such times tended to look to the future for a glorious restoration by Yahweh. In such a context the words of Isaiah prophesying glory to the humbled lands of Zebulun and Naphtali were probably written. "First he degraded the land of Zebulun and the land of Naphtali; but in the end he has glorified the seaward road, the land west of the Jordan, the district of the Gentiles." Once again the land of Galilee would be exalted. This work of God is presented under the symbols of darkness and light. "The people who walked in darkness have seen a great light; upon those who dwelt in the land of gloom a light has shone." This visitation of Yahweh will bring to his restored people an exuberant joy: "You have brought them abundant joy and great rejoicing; they rejoice before you as at the harvest."

Paul's brief moment of glory in the center of intellectual discussion at Athens makes a revealing story (Acts 17). The well-known insatiable curiosity of the Athenians for new ideas assured Paul a welcome to speak. He made all the right moves: complimenting the Athenians on their religiosity, referring to one of their shrines, even quoting a Greek poet. He took pains to confine his remarks to man's search for God in general, hardly even referring to Jesus. Alas, he made no headway. Some sneered while others genially put him off to another day, another discussion. Perhaps at this time Paul learned the painful lesson that recurs insistently in the first letter to the Corinthians. The wisdom of God is altogether different from the sophisticated wisdom of the world. Christ sent him to preach, Paul says, "not with worldly wisdom, however, lest the cross of Christ be rendered void of its meaning." In the Corinthians' disputes of "I belong to Paul," "I belong to Apollos," Paul very likely heard traces of that same worldly wisdom as he called them to a unity of mind and judgment in the one Christ.

The Gospel according to Matthew, with its predeliction for prophecy, never misses a chance to point up the fulfillment of an Old Testament text. Here Isaiah's text about the lands of Zebulun and Naphtali is seen brought to realization in Jesus' origins and early ministry in Galilee. The confident waiting of the psalmist is finally rewarded. In Jesus a great light appears, and the tension of an imminent event builds almost tangibly as Jesus announces: "Reform your lives! The kingdom of heaven is at hand."

For all that, the kingdom approaches quietly, no doubt in a way much different from that envisioned by those who for centuries had meditated on the prophecies. Jesus moves to Capernaum, hardly causing a ripple. There is no record that he was awarded a key to the city or that his new neighbors were aware of him at all. Little did they suspect that the nondescript carpenter from Nazareth was the light of the nations, that in him their land was being restored to its former greatness, and more. Jesus however contented himself with gathering together a few fishermen, walking about Galilee, teaching in the synagogues, proclaiming the good news of the kingdom, and healing the sick.

THIRD SUNDAY OF THE YEAR

Cycle "B" Readings: Jon. 3:1-5, 10; 1 Cor. 7:29-31; Mk. 1:14-20

The book of Jonah is a strikingly different sort of book from the other prophetic writings. In form it is a cleverly constructed short story, told with many traces of humor, but clearly intended for moral instruction. The name Jonah is borrowed from an Israelite prophet who lived at a much earlier date and in circumstances quite different from those of the story. Jonah is represented as a timid and temperamental prophet sent by God to the hostile Assyrian city of Nineveh to announce God's intention to destroy the city because of its prevailing sinfulness. After an unsuccessful attempt to escape this dismaying mission by a sea voyage ends with the famous incident of Jonah's being swallowed by a "great fish," the reluctant prophet finally does deliver his message of doom to Nineveh. But, much to his surprise, the Ninevites are sincerely moved to do penance and mend their ways. And to his intense annoyance, "God saw what they did, and how they abandoned their wicked ways, and he repented and did not bring upon them the disaster he had threatened." To Jonah, this is insult added to injury, and in the conclusion of the story his sulking reaction is contrasted with God's compassionate eagerness to forgive even the depraved Ninevites. The book of Jonah delivers a memorable reproach to the narrowness of mind and hardness of heart of which Jonah's words and behavior are a vivid caricature.

In Paul's first letter to the Corinthians, he responds to a variety of moral questions raised by the Corinthians. In the seventh chapter, these questions deal mainly with marriage and celibacy, and in responding to them Paul expresses several opinions which have often caused perplexity and controversy. One of them is the notion that Christians ought to rest content in whatever state of life—for example, married or unmarried, slave or free—they happened to be at the time of their conversion. Another much-debated idea is that celibacy is, in principle, preferable to marriage. And related to the latter opinion is Paul's bleak view of marriage as, although inferior to celibacy, justified by the difficulty experienced by some unmarried persons in maintaining sexual self-control. These and other somewhat extraordinary moral teachings of St. Paul undoubtedly owe an important part of their explanation to an idea which is expressed at the beginning and at the end of today's liturgical reading. The passage begins, "The time we live in will not last long." And it concludes, "The whole frame of this world is passing away." These statements express a belief which was shared by many, including Paul, during the earliest decades of Christianity. It is the belief that the second coming of Christ, bringing final judgment and a definitive end to the world as we know it, was to take place in the very near future, even during the lifetime of the contemporary adult generation. Christians of the time even worried about how those presumably few persons who died before this event would be provided for. Given such convictions, it would appear not at all unreasonable to discourage Christians from getting absorbed in such long-term undertakings as marriage and major social or occupational readjustment. It could be argued that the only wise attitude for Christians to adopt toward complicated worldly arrangements would be an attitude of extreme detachment, while preparing themselves spiritually for imminent judgment. Later portions of the New Testament show considerable modification in Christian thinking about the duration of the world's future, and the concrete applications of Paul's doctrine of detachment have also been modified during the subsequent history of Christianity.

For Mark, Jesus' preaching begins with the highly significant and concise expression: "The time has come; the Kingdom of God is upon you; repent and believe the Gospel." The words comprise both declarative and imperative elements. The declarative feature is the announcement of the Gospel itself, the "good news" that the long awaited salvation, the reign of God over human lives, has finally come. The imperative elements are a twofold demand, for repentance and for belief. Here there is nothing new or specifically Christian. Repentance was what John the Baptist had called for and what innumerable prophets before him had required, and what repentance meant was altogether familiar to Jews, whose people had devoted centuries of meditation and writing to determining how God intended humanity to behave in this world. The new imperative is belief in the Gospel, for which repentance is prerequisite. To believe in the Gospel meant to stake everything on a thorough acceptance of the "good news" of the Kingdom, committing oneself totally to everything this truth entailed. Repentance is preparation for the Gospel. Belief is response to the Gospel. Without the preparation there can be no response. Having sounded this vital opening note, Mark's Gospel proceeds at once to show the incipient building up of the Kingdom of God by describing Jesus' summoning of his disciples to be "fishers of men."

THIRD SUNDAY OF THE YEAR

Cycle "C" Readings: Neh. 8:1-4, 5-6, 8-10; 1 Cor. 12:12-30; Lk. 1:1-4; 4:14-21

The first reading in today's liturgy, taken from the book of Nehemiah, is part of the story of a fifth-century Jewish scribe named Ezra who had lived in Babylonia during the time when it was part of the Persian Empire, and who was sent by the Persian monarch to Jerusalem with authorization to engage in the reconstruction of his people's religion. Ezra brought with him to Jerusalem a special edition of the Mosaic law that may have been identical with what we now know as the first five books of the Old Testament, the Pentateuch or Torah. It was this document which furnished the foundation of Ezra's work as a religious reformer. Whereas formerly this body of sacred literature was regarded mainly as the historical revelation of God's covenant relationship with his people, under the influence of Ezra and his followers it came to be viewed rather as a body of detailed divine legislation. This development introduced the strongly legalistic orientation of Jewish religious thought that is so conspicuous in the New Testament. It also led to the increasing prestige of a group of scholars like Ezra himself whose expert knowledge of the Scriptures was necessary in order to apply them as complicated legal documents to the concrete circumstances of life. It is this phase of Israel's religious history that marks the beginning of what is called Judaism, considered by many scholars to represent so radical a transformation of the traditions of Israel as to constitute a truly new religion. Ezra has often been referred to as the "father of Judaism." The liturgical reading describes Ezra's reading of the Mosaic law to the people of Jerusalem and their enthusiastic reception of it after initial sadness. One notices also Ezra's scribal function in that, along with reading the law, he was "interpreting it so that all could understand what was read." The role of professional interpreters of Scripture was from this period onward a conspicuous feature of Judaism and afterward of the Christian and Moslem religions.

St. Paul's first letter to Corinthians, from which the second reading is taken, has been the Church's main biblical source for understanding what is called the charismatic element in Christianity. The Greek word *charisma* means gift and refers in religious usage to a variety of distinctive abilities manifested in religious communities and attributed by Christians to the influence of the Holy Spirit. In Corinth, such charisms flourished and caused a number of serious problems which Paul attempted to deal with in this letter. Underlying all of the problems was the basic issue of disunity. For one of the important things we learn from the letter is that, however holy the source of the charisms may be, no less than the more ordinary gifts of God, they can be put by human beings to decidedly unholy uses. In Corinth they were put to arrogant and invidious uses and generated a deplorable social atmosphere of boastful and derogatory behavior. It is against this background that Paul develops the metaphor, earlier employed by pagan philosophers, of society as analogous to a body and its members. The point of the metaphor is that, just as the total health of a physical organism depends on the complementary functioning of a great variety of organs, so too the vital integrity of the Christian community depends on the mutual cooperation of members endowed with very different spiritual gifts. There is, in this perspective, simply no sense in making favorable and unfavorable comparisons and cultivating preferences among charisms, for each of them possesses value only to the extent that it is coordinated with the others for their common advantage, as sharing in one life derived from the unique Spirit of God. This metaphor, although employed here for a specific pastoral purpose, represents an early stage in the development of the ecclesiological doctrine of the body of Christ.

The third reading, from the Gospel according to Luke, begins with the initial verses of that Gospel, which are similar to the introductory format of contemporary historical writers. It then skips over the subsequent material, devoted to the circumstances of Jesus' birth, the mission of John the Baptist, and the temptation of Jesus, which is more appropriate for Advent and Lenten liturgies. The account is resumed at the episode which in this Gospel introduces Jesus' active ministry, the public proclamation which he delivered at the synagogue of Nazareth. Apparently Jesus, as a visiting rabbi, was invited to read the second lesson, normally taken from the prophetic books of the Old Testament. The text which he read is very significantly selected from a well-known messianic passage in the book of Isaiah. The passage is expressed as a declaration by God that he is designating by anointing ("anointed" being the literal meaning of Messiah) one who, by the power of the Holy Spirit, brings good news (a rendering of the same word which is translated as "Gospel"). The nature of this good news is then represented as a ministry of liberation and of healing. This prophetic passage is a veritable synopsis of what all the Gospels describe as the main constituents of Jesus' public life.

FOURTH SUNDAY OF THE YEAR

Cycle "A" Readings: Zeph. 2:3, 3:12-13; 1 Cor. 1:26-31; Mt. 5:1-12

Zephaniah, from whose prophecy the first reading is taken, lived in the reign of Josiah, a seventh century king who is highly praised in the Bible for his major religious reform. The book of Zephaniah, however, appears to antedate that development, and reflects the deteriorated state of religion to which the reform was a later response. The prophecy opens with a horrendous prediction of what seems to be total destruction by an avenging God on the "day of the Lord," which is said to be near at hand. The passage given in the reading, however, injects a hopeful note. Here the threats and denunciations envisage an exception in favor of "the humble of the earth, who have observed his law." Thus Zephaniah takes up the Isaian motif of discriminating between the rich and powerful, whose irreligious ways condemn them to destruction, and the poor and weak, whose reliance upon God as their only support is destined to be rewarded. Thus in the passage from which the second part of the reading is taken, the prophet foretells not the destruction of Jerusalem, but its purgation. God will rid his city of its "proud and arrogant citizens," in order to leave it, not desolate, but populated by the only people worthy of its heritage. These are the famous "remnant," that is to say, the survivors, whom God's avenging wrath will leave undisturbed so that they can serve as the basis of a new and better people. Compelled by their very circumstances to place no hope in worldly power and influence, they have learned to trust exclusively in God, to "take refuge in the name of the Lord." It is by these honest, inoffensive sufferers that true religion has been preserved in a corrupt age. Therefore, in a new and better age the future lies with them.

The second reading, from the first letter to the Corinthians, is taken from a passage whose theme is one of contrast between two kinds, or conceptions, of wisdom. Paul's thesis is that "God has made the wisdom of this world look foolish." This world's wisdom does not, however, look foolish to its own adherents, but only to those who discern ultimate and divine wisdom in the cross of Christ. Thus the two kinds of wisdom represent two radically opposed viewpoints, from each of which what the other sees as wisdom is perceived as the very opposite of wisdom, folly. In the verses that appear in the reading, Paul applies the paradoxical sense of wisdom, which finds its ultimate realization in the cross, to his Christian readers in Corinth. He reminds them that God's choice of such people as them to constitute his Church is itself as foolish, by worldly standards, as is the cross in whose divine efficacy they believe. His words to them express a kind of congratulation that is the very opposite of flattery. Few of them are "wise, as men account wisdom," or "influential," or "well-born." Thus God's choice of them, like his choice of the means of atonement, is a mockery of what commonly passes for wisdom. For Paul, however, the history of worldly wisdom is a history of futility, depravity, and delusion. To consider that history candidly is either wholly to despair or to place one's hope wholly in God. Those who do place their hope in God find it fulfilled by the good news of the Gospel. They alone have something to boast about. But what they have to boast about is not self-sufficiency. It is the total sufficiency of God, available to those alone who have learned to acknowledge their insufficiency, to call their own wisdom folly, and God's folly wisdom.

The third reading is the beginning of the Sermon on the Mount in the Gospel according to Matthew. These famous opening verses are called the beatitudes from the fact that each begins with the Greek word translated into Latin as "beati," meaning blest, or, more precisely fortunate. The first eight of these are in the third person, and constitute the beatitudes proper, whereas the ninth is a direct address in the second person to the hearers, as an application of the general motif. The most striking feature is, of course, that the first four categories of the "fortunate" are precisely those whom one normally thinks of as most unfortunate. The designations are very similar in meaning, and refer to those who are most deprived of worldly means of support, dignity, or influence, and whose deepest craving is to have all their wrongs put right. They are, in other words, the same sort of people singled out by Isaiah, and by Zephaniah in the first reading, as those who have nothing but God to rely upon, and who do rely upon God, and whose reliance upon him will be rewarded. The second four categories, which are not, like the others, matched in the Gospel according to Luke, point rather to those who actively seek to make things right than to those who helplessly endure their wrongs. They too are fortunate in the richest sense, destined for the Kingdom of God.

FOURTH SUNDAY OF THE YEAR

Cycle "B" Readings: Deut. 18:15-20; 1 Cor. 7:32-35; Mk. 1:21-28

The first reading today comes from an Israelite collection of laws known as the Deuteronomic Code. The whole, rather uneven collection is formulated as a lengthy sermon spoken to the people of the exodus by the great lawgiver Moses, and is understood to be the gift and revelation of God, integral to the covenant. Actually compiled long after the time of Moses, it treats a wide variety of subjects, including various offices and institutional roles such as, in the present reading, the role of prophet. The passage represents Moses as the prototype of all prophets, conceived as divinely appointed spokesmen who transmit messages from God to his people. The value of having such mediators of divine revelation is here attributed to the fear and awe at the transcendent majesty of God which caused Israelites to believe that too familiar and immediate contact with him would be fatal. Since, moreover, the prophet is to speak not his own words but those of God, his authority commands unqualified respect, sanctioned by threat of divine punishment. On the other hand, for a prophet to exploit his position in society in order to pass off statements of his own as divinely guaranteed would obviously constitute a very dangerous kind of temptation. The penalty for such sacrilegious deception is death. Once a religion admits the essential validity of prophecy, in the sense of admitting certain human beings to be empowered to speak with God's own infallibility, potentialities for extreme abuse inevitably arise, and the problem of how to distinguish true from false prophets is one which recurs in various contexts in both the Old and the New Testaments, and is treated in other passages of the Deuteronomic Code itself.

The second reading, from the first letter to the Corinthians, is a passage of advice by St. Paul concerning the religious advantages of remaining unmarried and the corresponding disadvantages of getting married. In reading any of Paul's advice on this subject, it is good to bear in mind that he makes no claim to be imparting Christian revelation, for, as he states explicitly a few verses earlier, "On the question of celibacy I have no instructions from the Lord, but I give my judgment as one who by God's mercy is to be trusted." The key idea of the passage is expressed in the opening verse, "I want you to be free from anxious care." Paul then proceeds to argue that "anxious care" is something to which married persons are relatively vulnerable, and against which celibacy is therefore a safeguard. Paul is convinced that husbands and wives tend to be immoderately preoccupied, worried, anxious, about "pleasing" one another, or, as we might say, about keeping one another in "good humor" and out of "bad moods." The trouble he sees with this is not merely that it makes for a trivial, tiresome, nervous existence, but that it so dissipates the mind as to make it virtually impossible to attend, in a simple, serene, and habitual way, to discerning and doing the will of God. Although this passage occurs in a context which is strongly influenced by the belief that the end of the world was too near at hand for there to be much point in getting married, it is not at all clear that its validity as an argument for celibacy is in any way dependent on that belief.

In Mark's account of Jesus' public life, the calling of his first disciples is followed by their arrival at Capernaum, where Jesus profoundly impresses the people first by the quality of his teaching and then by his accomplishment of an exorcism. These two impressive features of Jesus' ministry are, however, for this evangelist, manifestations of the same decisive fact, the fact of Jesus' "authority." The Greek word here rendered as authority (*exousia*) suggests considerably more than a self-assured speaking style. A helpful clue to its deeper meaning is furnished a few verses later, where, after Jesus has driven out an "unclean spirit" by his mere verbal command, the people ask one another, "What is this? A new kind of teaching? He speaks with authority." In this context it becomes evident that the "authority" of Jesus' speech pertains not so much to its stylistic quality as to its effectiveness, its astonishing influence, its compelling power. The words of Jesus were words that made things happen to and in the people who heard them. The overt circumstances of exorcism provide a dramatic way of expressing what the words of Jesus were understood to be doing constantly in less spectacular ways—driving the unclean spirits, the interior forces of morbidity and malice, out of the bodies, the minds, and the lives of his hearers. Like the word of God, the words of Jesus Christ are words of salvation and words of power.

FOURTH SUNDAY OF THE YEAR

Cycle "C" Readings: Jer. 1:4-5, 17-19; 1 Cor. 12:31—13:13; Lk. 4:21-30

The first reading of today's liturgy combines two passages from the first chapter of the book of Jeremiah. The first passage, in referring to "the days of Josiah," specifies time and place as the second half of the seventh century in the kingdom of Judah. All the words that follow in this reading are intended to express two messages communicated by God to Jeremiah. The first of these messages constitutes God's designation of Jeremiah to be a prophet, that is, a person who, by God's choice rather than his own preference, serves as God's spokesman among human beings. The divine character of this prophetic calling is emphasized by pointing out that the appointment, although manifested to Jeremiah at a particular moment in his own life, is in fact an eternal decree whose validity is prior not only to Jeremiah's wishes but even to his very existence. The second message is a divine reassurance, corresponding to the fact, well documented in the Old Testament, that the kind of thing a prophet is required to say publicly is usually the kind of thing most of the public would rather not hear. Consequently, God, while leaving no false hope to Jeremiah that his reception would be otherwise than bitterly hostile, guarantees his ultimate safety by promising divine protection from the retaliation of his enemies. The divine words of reassurance echo the fundamental message that characterizes the God of Judaeo-Christian tradition: "I am with you to deliver you."

The second reading, from the first letter to the Corinthians, is perhaps the best known and most admired passage in all of St. Paul's writings, the passage in which he extols and characterizes Christian love. It is helpful to bear in mind that this passage immediately follows the one, read in last Sunday's liturgy, in which Paul insists that the variety of spiritual gifts or charisms is meant to serve rather than disrupt the organic integrity of the Christian community. It is by an extension of this thought that in the present passage he contrasts all of these individual charismatic endowments with "a way which surpasses all the others." This is the "way" of Christian love. And Christian love is not a gift that certain Christians are allotted individually but the essential gift of divine life that all Christians share in common. Indeed, whereas the charisms are particular manifestations of spiritual vitality, love is the principal aspect of that vitality itself. Consequently, apart from love, the exercise of any of the charisms, whether the gift of tongues, or prophecy, or sufficient confidence for miracles, or even heroic extremes of self-sacrifice, is simply pointless and absurd. This is, of course, Paul's basic indictment of the Corinthian charismatics, but it transcends this historical context and constitutes a fundamental declaration of Christian religious priorities. Paul is still thinking of the spiteful and pretentious uses to which the Corinthians put their spiritual gifts when he proceeds to characterize the love he is talking about as patient, kind, and constant, free from every trace of jealousy, ostentation, snobbery, rudeness, egotism, and animosity. Where vices of the latter sort flourish, love is absent, and although charismatic phenomena may still be present, they serve no good purpose. The passage concludes by observing that the other gifts, unlike love, are temporal rather than eternal attributes. They belong to the immature and incomplete phase of Christian life, whereas love is the outstanding feature of that life's eternal fulfillment.

The reading from the Gospel according to Luke narrates the aftermath of the event described in last Sunday's liturgy, when Jesus in the Nazareth synagogue publicly applied to his own mission a famous messianic prophecy from the book of Isaiah. Although only Luke's Gospel describes this episode, Matthew and Mark both refer to the skeptical reception Jesus was accorded by his townsfolk when, in the course of his active ministry, he returned to Nazareth. Although Luke situates the episode at the very beginning of Jesus's public life, his reference to the people's having "heard of all your doings at Capernaum" implies some confusion in the chronology. Apparently, it is best to understand this passage simply as recording what is generally agreed upon, that even when Jesus' popularity was at its greatest, the people of Nazareth remained unimpressed. Apparently their mentality was of the sort in which "familiarity breeds contempt," for to them the rhetorical question "Is not this Joseph's son?" was sufficient to settle the practical and religious question of whether any special deference or even attention should be paid to Jesus. Jesus himself retorts that this is the sort of narrowminded incredulity which had so often in the past alienated God's prophets from their own people. Luke's account of the people's murderous reaction seems better suited to the last than to the first phase of Jesus' public ministry, and again indicates some chronological displacement.

FIFTH SUNDAY OF THE YEAR

Cycle "A" Readings: Is. 58:7-10; 1 Cor. 2:1-7; Mt. 5:13-16

In the first reading, the Isaian passage speaks of fasting from the viewpoint of every believer, whatever be his further role in the work of salvation. The verses read convey the essential message of a longer passage: that the authentic "fasting" which alone gives meaning and value to bodily fasting is the conquest of egotism and its fruits in the form of such evils as oppression of others, false accusations and malicious speech. This kind of spiritual fasting will in turn produce a fasting or freedom from reliance on all false securities. But there is a further positive side to this conquest of egotism, since it is commended not simply for reasons of inner purity and freedom but also for the sake of the neighbor—the poor, the hungry, the oppressed, the outcasts of a self-centered society. It is only through this comprehensive "fasting"—which evidently is equivalent to authentic religion, that is, a valid relationship to God and neighbor, to God in and through the neighbor—that men, individually and as a community, will achieve wholeness or integrity and the lightsomeness which is a sharing in the purity and radiant holiness of God.

The relevance of these ideas is evident, and we find the early Christians applying them to all seasons of fasting. Bodily fasting was normally considered as part of a triad: prayer, fasting, almsgiving. Prayer in this context is chiefly petition for forgiveness, gratitude for mercy, and desire of deeper union with God, with man acting as a unique individual and as a member of the brotherhood of Christ's body. Such prayer overflows into and derives its power in part from bodily fasting which has the effect (among others) of liberating the spirit and making man more sensitive to the movements of the Spirit. But the whole complex of prayer and fasting receives an explicit social dimension through almsgiving. Prayer and fasting are legitimated through almsgiving, not as though they derived all their meaning and value from it but because they are thereby inserted into that larger human context in which they must bear one of their essential fruits: loving concern for the neighbor. "Almsgiving" includes the spiritual as well as the corporal works of mercy, for there are hungers and thirsts and captivities which no amount of bodily food and drink and liberation will necessarily cure. As understood by the Christian, then, the Isaian vision of true fasting and authentic religion becomes a vision of all God's people moving toward him as the body of Christ, with each member making up in himself the sufferings of Christ and also aiding the one same suffering Christ in his brothers.

In the second reading, from the first letter to the Corinthians, the idea of authentic religion and true fasting is expressed from the viewpoint of the apostles.

If the apostle is to succeed in his task, he must have the interior freedom to let God bear witness through him to Christ from whose death (and resurrection) all salvation comes. In so doing, the apostle must, however, achieve a rather delicate balance. He must not be misled by Paul's words into despising intelligence and eloquence, but must put the gifts and talents he has at God's service. The apostle must bear in mind (and here prayer and fasting perform an illuminative function) that faith is the gift of the Spirit who works in the hearts of men and that his own toil and example are but the occasion or human means which the Spirit uses to produce a result that far transcends them.

The reading from the Gospel according to Matthew speaks of a role shared by every disciple, but in doing so repeats in its own way the message of Paul. The Christian's life and example are intended to be like salt that seasons (that is, renders tasty and attractive) the Gospel as it is perceived by others who are thereby drawn to accept it. They are also like salt that acts as a preservative, for their example helps others to persevere in a life according to the Gospel. But the savor does not have its source in them; it is the work of the Spirit and must be retained through prayer and the kind of fasting that flowers into the authentic religion of which Isaiah speaks. The Christian is also to be a light by which others may walk; but the light is itself a reflected light, a gift of Christ, the light of the world.

FIFTH SUNDAY OF THE YEAR

Cycle "B" Readings: Job 7:1-4, 6-7; 1 Cor. 9:16-19, 22-23; Mk. 1:29-39

The first reading is a fragment of Job's part in a dialogue with one of three friends who come to talk with him about the terrible misfortunes which have suddenly and unaccountably fallen upon him. Readers of the story know, of course, that all this is no punishment, but rather a way of demonstrating the absolutely heroic character of Job's submissiveness to God. Both Job and his friends are equally unaware of this explanation. Job, for his part, knows only that he has been sincerely faithful to God, which makes his wretched condition very difficult to comprehend. His friends offer glib, doctrinaire explanations, and facile, pompous advice. These patronizing efforts increasingly exasperate a sufferer who is capable of perceiving the shallowness and inanity of their arguments. The first of the friends to speak is Eliphaz, who counsels Job to accept his suffering as a salutary corrective measure, understanding that, once he has "learned his lesson," Job can look forward to gentler treatment from God. But since Job's problem is precisely that he can find no "lesson" to be learned from his misery, this line of argument only deepens his feeling of senseless, pointless torment. At this point, Job associates his experience with the bitterness of the human condition, in which the struggles of people are like the toiling of slaves forbidden even to rest in the shade, or the occupation of menial laborers who cannot even hope to be paid on time. Viewed from the position in which Job finds himself, human life seems both fleeting and futile: it runs out quickly, and comes to nothing. Job's awareness that human suffering is a far deeper mystery than his friends are prepared to admit represents an important aspect of the wisdom this book seeks to impart.

In the ninth chapter of the first letter to the Corinthians, Paul writes rather defensively about his apostolic role and the distinctive manner in which he occupies it. He begins by insisting that he has as good a claim as anybody to be regarded as both a free individual and a Christian apostle. He then goes on to assert that, as a free man and an apostle, he has a perfect right to do two things which all the rest of the apostles do: first, live as a married man, and second, derive economic support from his apostolate. Nevertheless, although insisting on his right to have a wife and to receive ministerial wages, Paul makes it clear that he is resolved not to exercise either of these rights. He does not here explain why he alone among the apostles remains celibate. Paul does, however, shed some light on his unwillingness to accept pay for exercising an apostolic ministry. Basically, his argument is that his apostolic work is not an occupation which he has chosen and for which he has become personally qualified. On the contrary, he has been chosen for it by God, and in exercising his apostolate he is not employing his own special skills, but merely acting as God's instrument.

Not to do what God intends and directs him to do, namely preach the Gospel, would be unthinkable and utterly self-destructive, and at the same time he would find it repugnant to claim earnings for simply putting himself at the disposal of God. Paul's apostolate, as far as he is concerned, is its own reward.

Today's selection from Mark's Gospel illustrates two elements which figure prominently in the Markan account of Jesus' public career. The first is a presentation of Jesus' ministry as a combination of teaching and healing. This pattern closely reflects popular conceptions, based on the Old Testament, of how the Messiah might be expected to behave. The fact that Mark's Gospel, like the others, is full of accounts of words and deeds which proclaim Jesus' messiahship makes another, more distinctive feature of that Gospel difficult to explain. For, just as in today's reading, when the expelled demons correctly perceive Jesus to be the Messiah, Jesus commands them to keep their recognition a secret, so we find repeatedly that Jesus imposes silence on those who best appreciate his identity. This feature, called the "messianic secret," is highly paradoxical, inasmuch as Jesus seems to be simultaneously advertising his messiahship by his whole pattern of conduct and hushing it up as soon as it is recognized. It may be that this puzzling combination is related to the readiness of many of Jesus' contemporaries to accept him as a Messiah indeed, but a very different, more despotic and political sort of Messiah than the crucifixion and its sequel finally showed him to be.

FIFTH SUNDAY OF THE YEAR

Cycle "C" Readings: Is. 6:1-2, 3-8; 1 Cor. 15:1-11; Lk. 5:1-11

The first reading of today's, as of last Sunday's liturgy, describes the commissioning by God of one of the great prophets of the Old Testament. In the case of Isaiah, as in that of Jeremiah described last week, one notes that a prophetic career is wholly God-given, in the sense that its typical recipient neither desires it nor prepares for it, but finds it abruptly imposed upon him by a divine intervention. One notes also that both of these prophets had distinct misgivings about their fitness for the task assigned to them, and that both of them received needed reassurances from God. Isaiah and Jeremiah were, however, of quite different characters, and the difference is reflected in their respective apprehensions. Whereas for Jeremiah it was the danger of hostility and resistance that most threatened his prophetic commitment, for Isaiah it was rather a sense of his own sinfulness and profanity in contrast with the holiness and majesty of God. Consequently, whereas for Jeremiah it was God's promise of protection that brought reassurance, Isaiah's need was rather to be freed from a sense of sin and alienation from God. Therefore, the religious experience which accompanies Jeremiah's prophetic calling is an experience of divine forgiveness and purification. Isaiah's symbolic vision of God is one which emphasizes God's exalted holiness, and by the same token aggravates the prophet's consciousness of his personal unholiness. The image of the seraph who cleanses Isaiah's lips with an ember from the altar of God symbolizes a sense of spiritual purgation accomplished by the power and mercy of God—what in later Christian theology would be called the action of healing or "sanating" grace. It is after this experience that the prophet is able heartily to respond to God's summons: "Here I am . . . Send me!"

The second reading, from the first letter to the Corinthians, transposes the theme of divine vocation into a New Testament context. However, Paul's remarks in this passage are not primarily concerned with giving an account of his own vocation. Rather they are intended to introduce his teaching concerning the resurrection of the dead by establishing both that this teaching is part of the fundamental doctrinal heritage of Christians and that Paul himself possesses apostolic credentials for transmitting that doctrinal tradition authoritatively. Paul writes as a Christian missionary to those whom he himself converted, reminding them that the Gospel of salvation by which and to which they were converted has a definite and specifiable content. This content, in a bare outline which might be likened to an early Christian creed, states simply that in agreement with the Scriptures (that is, the Old Testament), Christ died for our sins, was buried, rose again, and was seen by many of his followers. Among these followers who saw the risen Christ Paul includes, last of all, himself, registering the proper embarrassment of a former persecutor who had been converted, practically despite himself, by rather sensational divine means. Paul typically qualifies his humility by taking a certain consolation in the claim, probably quite justified, that since his conversion he had toiled more energetically than any of the others. But the main point he wishes to make is that he is an authentic apostle and that what he preached to the Corinthians was the genuine Gospel. For it is on their acceptance of this Gospel that the rest of his argument, concerning resurrection, will depend.

The third reading is the account given by the Gospel according to Luke of Jesus' first encounter with Simon, later called Peter, and of his summoning of Simon to be his follower. There are interesting points both of similarity and of contrast between this account and the episode, clearly related to it, almost identically narrated in Matthew and Mark. In all three, the setting is the Galilean lake shore in the presence of fishermen and their boats. In Mark and Matthew, Jesus, while walking along the shore, first meets Simon and Andrew, who, at his bidding, follow him to become "fishers of men." Jesus then meets James and John, who also follow at his summons. In Luke's Gospel, however, Jesus, surrounded by eager listeners, chooses one of two available boats, the one manned by Simon, to serve as a kind of floating pulpit. Jesus then makes possible an enormous catch of fish where there had seemed to be no fish at all. The size of the catch brings assistance from the other boat. The fishermen are in awe at this marvel, but Simon alone is moved to protest his sinfulness. Jesus thereupon assures Simon that henceforth he "will be catching men." Only at this point are the names of James and John mentioned as Simon's partners. On landing the boats, "they" (presumably the three who have been named) "became his followers." Accepting the common view that Mark's is the oldest of our Gospels, it is natural to see in this Lucan narrative significant modifications of an older and simpler version of the event. And the outstanding characteristic of these modifications is the magnification of the role of Simon, and the subordinations to it of the roles of the other named disciples. It is very likely that this way of telling the story exhibits a perspective of the early Church in which Simon had assumed a very important position. This position of Simon is clearly brought out in Acts of the Apostles which, significantly, was also written by Luke.

SIXTH SUNDAY OF THE YEAR

Cycle "A" Readings: Sir. 15:15-20; 1 Cor. 2:6-10; Mt. 5:17-37

The first reading is taken from the book of Sirach, an example of second century wisdom literature, considerably influenced by Greek thought. Although not included in the Hebrew Bible, and accordingly regarded by Protestants as an apocryphal work, this book was very popular among early Christians and it remains a part of the Roman Catholic Bible. The book's philosophical interest, more typically Greek than Hebrew, is evident in the passage from which the reading is taken. That passage begins with the injunction, "Do not say 'The Lord is to blame for my failure.' " What follows is a vigorous affirmation of human moral responsibility, one implication of which is to exonerate God from any sort of complicity in wrongdoing. It is characteristic of the habitually religious outlook of the Jews that this declaration of human freedom should arise from a concern, not about human dignity as such, but about divine innocence. The writer's thought is dominated by two dogmatic convictions. First, "the Lord hates every kind of vice." And second, "he made man in the beginning." If one adds to these dogmas the simple observation that human beings do behave immorally, a problem inevitably arises. How can a God who "hates every kind of vice" have "made man" who seems to indulge in every kind of vice? The answer given here is that God "left him free to make his own decisions." No answer is given here to the further question, raised in later speculation, of why God left humanity free to do what God despises. In the concluding verses of the reading, however, another dogma is added to the previous ones, affirming

God's creativity and goodness. It is further insisted that "the eyes of God see all he has made." If, therefore, God leaves human beings free to choose good or evil, he remains fully aware of what they do choose; God's innocence does not imply any ignorance.

The second reading resumes the series of reflections on wisdom in the first letter to the Corinthians. Hitherto, Paul has insisted on the radical incompatibility between what believers and unbelievers value as wisdom. For believers, the only wisdom that really matters is the only wisdom that really works, God's wisdom. And that is exercised in the world with sublime indifference to human estimates about wisdom. Thus the only wisdom a Christian can really respect would seem to be a wisdom he cannot really possess, although he can, of course, greatly benefit from its use by God, who alone possesses it. Paul, however, has something more to say on this subject, as indicated by the opening verse: "There is, to be sure, a certain wisdom which we express among the spiritually mature." He proceeds to explain that the wisdom he now refers to is, indeed, God's, but it is a divine wisdom that human beings can in some sense share. As far as the reading takes us, this sharing of divine wisdom is conceived as knowledge of the "mystery," or hidden, eternal plan of God. It is the divine plan of salvation, which, from a biblical point of view, is the basic plan for all of history. The crucifixion of Jesus was part of that plan, but a part that could only be perpetrated by those who were ignorant of the plan. The wisdom here referred to is conveyed by revelation, the work of the divine Spirit, whose role in the transmission of wisdom is further explored in succeeding verses.

The third reading is part of a major section of the Sermon on the Mount from the Gospel according to Matthew. This section is introduced by Jesus' assertion that he did not come "to abolish the law and the prophets" but "to fulfill" them. The first part of the assertion is confirmed in the two verses that follow, which, despite efforts to interpret them differently, plainly affirm the continued validity of Mosaic law. What it means "to fulfill" the law, beyond merely not abolishing it, is suggested in the next verse, where Jesus calls upon his hearers to be "far better men than the Pharisees and doctors." It becomes clearer when Jesus then proceeds to cite a whole series of specific kinds of behavior for which the standards he sets are higher than those current or traditional. The condemnation of murder is extended over the entire domain of malevolence and maleficence. Litigants are told to settle their differences out of court. The value of sacrifice is subordinated to the pursuit of social tranquility. The evil of adultery is applied over the whole range of lustful attitudes. Divorce, except in cases of "lewd conduct" (the meaning of this is uncertain), is no more acceptable than adultery. The use of oaths, which had become sophistical, is simply rejected in favor of plain, honest speech. In these and other examples "to fulfill" the law seems to mean deepening and purifying motives, broadening applications, removing casuistic insincerities, and developing conditions favorable to faithful observants.

SIXTH SUNDAY OF THE YEAR

Cycle "B" Readings: Lev. 13:1-2, 45-46; 1 Cor. 10:31—11:1; Mk. 1:40-45

The thirteenth and fourteenth chapters of Leviticus comprise a set of priestly regulations for dealing with what in most English versions is translated as leprosy. It has been pointed out by qualified dermatologists, however, that what is described requires a much broader and looser designation than what is medically defined as leprosy. Even the non-expert is likely to infer as much when he notices that in these chapters what is called leprosy is sometimes applied to a discoloration which spreads not over living flesh but over cloth garments—suggesting something much more like a fungus than the bacterial infection of genuine leprosy. It was, of course, recognized that some skin afflictions were dangerous and highly contagious, and in the priestly directives, for identifying and treating "ritual uncleanness" in this connection, motives of preventive medicine are clearly discernible. The concept of ritual uncleanness is an alien and unattractive one for most of us. In Israel, the general idea of uncleanness had many applications, related not only to skin afflictions, but also to categories of food, to sexual functions, and to contact with dead bodies. In terms of later knowledge, some of the legislation concerning uncleanness is indefensible and even deplorable, but some of it was not lacking in practicality. Despite the seeming harshness of requiring a sufferer to "wear his clothes torn, leave his hair disheveled, cover his upper lip, and cry 'Unclean,'" some such system of mobile quarantine seems not unreasonable under the conditions of a society, economy, and technology which would have made clinical confinement a far more burdensome prescription for persons suspected of contagion.

The second reading comprises the final sentences of a prolonged discussion which brings out an interesting aspect of Paul's understanding of freedom of conscience. Among the Corinthian Christians, opposing moral attitudes had developed concerning the fact that in this largely pagan city much of the meat sold for table use was previously offered to false gods, that is, to idols. One group of Christians reasoned that, since the pagan gods were spurious, the fact that meat had been offered to them was insignificant, so that no one need hesitate to eat or serve it. The other group considered that meat offered to pagan deities was, so to speak, religiously tainted by idolatrous use, so that Christians could not in good conscience make use of it. In venturing to arbitrate this dispute, Paul first of all makes it quite clear that he agrees with the former group, that meat is simply food, and its having been involved in false worship should not deter Christians from using it. However, Paul is also highly sensitive to the fact that the second group, however ill-advised their scruples, were obliged to act consistently with their own consciences. Consequently, Paul's strongest appeal is to those who, having no moral reservations about their right to eat the controversial meat, might easily, by word and example, make it very awkward for the others to live peacefully according to the more stringent if less reasonable demands of their own consciences. Accordingly, Paul asks the more "liberated" Christians of Corinth to respect sincere consciences even though they disagreed with them. The willingness to forego legitimate pleasures or conveniences out of kindness to tender consciences is what, in this context, Paul means by trying "to meet everyone halfway, regarding not my own good but the good of the many, so that they may be saved." Eager as Paul was to rid Christians of scrupulous legalism, he would not do so at the expense of charity.

Leprosy in the New Testament has the same rather broad meaning that we have seen in the book of Leviticus. Attitudes toward its victims were, in Jesus' day, governed by the Old Testament legislation which, as indicated by the first reading, was directed not at curing lepers, but at protecting the rest of the community from dangerous exposure to them. Nothing in the law encouraged lepers to anticipate a cure. Consequently, when the episode narrated in the third reading, from Mark's Gospel, describes a leper as coming to Jesus convinced of his power to cure him, it shows Jesus to be the object of higher hopes than could be derived from the law. Jesus' response is a demonstration both of his mercy—he was "moved with pity"—and of his power—he said, "I do will it; be clean." Approaching the supposedly unapproachable, and curing the supposedly incurable, as in this episode, are recurrent characteristics of Jesus' public behavior, clearly regarded by the evangelists as manifestations of his messianic prerogatives. Here too, in Jesus' injunction to the leper not to discuss his cure, we have another instance of the curious "messianic secret" already discussed in connection with the exorcism in Mark 1:34. It is scarcely imaginable how a suddenly cured leper could avoid local publicity even if he wished to, and in fact the leper ignores Jesus' bidding completely. The artificiality of Mark's secrecy motif is made especially conspicuous here by a lack of verisimilitude.

SIXTH SUNDAY OF THE YEAR

Cycle "C" Readings: Jer. 17:5-8; 1 Cor. 15:12, 16-20; Lk. 6:17, 20-26

The first reading, from the book of Jeremiah, opens with the kind of cheerless sentiment that has become popularly associated with the name of this seventy-century prophet: "Cursed is the man who trusts in human beings." Although these bitter words are far indeed from any spirit of jovial humanism, they are not what, taken in isolation, they might seem to be, mere grumblings of cynical misanthropy. Their real point is brought out by the modifying phrase, "whose heart turns away from the Lord." What

Jeremiah deplores is not mutual confidence among human beings, but replacement of ultimate faith in God by ultimate faith in human resources. And when Jeremiah describes the attitude of what might nowadays be called atheistic humanism as "accursed," he means to express not a feeling but a fact. The trouble with ultimate reliance upon human resources is, in his view, that it doesn't work, that it is in the final analysis as fruitless as "a barren bush in the desert." To appreciate Jeremiah's conviction on this score, it is important to bear in mind not only his religious faith but his historical milieu. The days of his adult life were the days of the final decline and fall of Judah. Those were days when both the ruthlessness of the powerful and the desperation of the weak made humankind's capacity for duplicity, inconstancy, treachery, and violence painfully visible. It was therefore under circumstances which vividly displayed the folly of ultimate reliance upon human plans and promises that the prophet proclaimed the only true blessedness to be that of "the one who trusts in the Lord." Grim as his message may seem, its intention is the wholly constructive one of deriving God's lesson of hope from history's lesson of hopelessness.

The second reading, from the first letter to the Corinthians, continues Paul's effort to correct the distortions of Christian belief which were making alarming headway among members of the church at Corinth. Most disastrous of all these departures from orthodoxy was, in Paul's view, abandonment of belief in resurrection. That even before Jesus' time there had been heated controversy over this matter is clear from the Gospels, where the Sadducees in particular represent a partisan disbelief in any resurrection of the dead. It is not clear on what grounds such skepticism developed among the Corinthians, nor whether they may have adhered to the idea, more acceptable to Greek philosophy, that at death an inherently immortal soul was released from confinement in an inherently corruptible body. In any case, Paul appears to have interpreted their position as a denial of the very possibility of resurrection. He accordingly argues that to hold such a view is radically incompatible with the very heart of the Gospel message. For in his view the central belief of Christians is the resurrection of Christ, which is certainly not to be conceived merely as a survival of Christ's soul at the dissolution of his body. Hence, Paul concludes, if resurrection is deemed impossible for a human being as such, it must be considered impossible for Christ. But if it is impossible for Christ, the Gospel is illusory and in the final analysis Christianity is pointless. In view of the numerous contemporary efforts by liberal theologians to determine, usually optimistically, what Christianity would be if relieved of such "mythical" embarrassments as belief in bodily resurrection, it is useful to recall that Paul explicitly anticipated this question. His own plainly stated answer to it is that Christianity would, if disburdened of the doctrine of resurrection, be a commitment to something totally absurd.

The reading from the Gospel according to Luke is a passage which immediately suggests, by a number of striking similarities, the beginning of the famous Sermon on the Mount in the Gospel according to Matthew. The common feature of both is found in both the structure and the content of a series of verses, each beginning "Blest are . . ." and therefore called Beatitudes. Matthew's hilltop setting, suggesting comparison of Jesus with Moses on Sinai, contrasts, however, with Luke's explicit location of the discourse on low ground. And whereas Matthew lists eight Beatitudes, of which the first four are addressed to sufferers and the remainder to benefactors, Luke gives only four and all of them are in the former category. Moreover, the exclusive concentration of Luke's Beatitudes on those who suffer is further emphasized by the fact that these are followed by a set of four symmetrically antithetical declarations called, from their opening words, Woes. Thus four declarations of the ultimate blessedness, or good fortune, of those who endure suffering are intensified by four matching declarations of the final misery destined for those who do not suffer. Luke likens the condition of the sufferers to the immemorial tribulations of God's prophets, whereas the comfortable lives of the others are significantly compared to those of false prophets. Although the theme of suffering is prominent throughout the New Testament, it is Luke who most unqualifiedly links suffering to fidelity and ease to godlessness.

SEVENTH SUNDAY OF THE YEAR

Cycle "A" Readings: Lev. 19:1-2, 17-18; 1 Cor. 3:16-23; Mt. 5:38-48

The first reading is taken from a large collection of Israelite laws which occupies nearly half of the book of Leviticus, and is commonly referred to as the Holiness Code. It is not a law code in any strict sense of that phrase, but a rather loose compilation of ancient regulations, some of which we would classify as moral principles, but many of which could be more accurately described as ceremonial conventions and simple taboos. In this compilation, probably made in the sixth century under priestly auspices, the material is distributed among largely unrelated groupings of related norms. The reading includes a portion of one of these groupings, devoted to matters of social justice and mercy. The preceding verses express prohibitions of such things as theft, deceit, oppression, postponement of wages, cruelty to the incapacitated, biased judgment, prejudicial witness, holding of grudges, and seeking of revenge. This catalogue of forbidden social offenses ends with the summary injunction, "You shall love your neighbor as yourself." It is evident from the context that what loving means here is not a mood of affection but a policy of beneficence. To love others as oneself implies exercising beneficence in a fair, impartial way that acknowledges the basic equality of others with oneself. The context also indicates that neighbor is here a limited category of persons, for in the particular injunctions the expressions which are used in parallel with neighbor are such terms as fellow-countryman and kinsman. The idea of neighbor thus appears to be defined by familial and political ties.

The second reading, from the first letter to the Corinthians, comes from a longer passage in which Paul makes rather elaborate use of a favorite metaphor. The Christian community is compared to a building in the process of being constructed. Paul likens himself to a master builder, who laid the foundation of the building. Subsequent influence on the community by others corresponds to the work of those who build upon an existing foundation. They may build well or ill, strongly or flimsily, and they will be judged by the quality of their building. As for the foundation itself, which Paul laid, that is Jesus Christ, to whom Paul's apostolic preaching is entirely devoted. The metaphor of building suggests to Paul two other ideas. One is the idea of the final judgment, often described in imagery of fire and conceived in terms of testing. By this association of ideas, Paul is reminded that buildings, and the durability of the materials used by their builders, are tested by fire. Still another line of association leads Paul to identify his metaphorical building with a particular kind of building, namely a temple, a dwelling place for the Spirit of God, and a place, therefore, to be regarded as holy. At this point, with characteristic abruptness, Paul abandons the building metaphor and returns to his previous theme of the contrast between divine and human wisdom. His concern about the kind of construction that other builders are carrying out on his foundation is mainly a fear lest the reputed wisdom of individual leaders should generate a kind of rivalry and factiousness that would divide the community. Thus he concludes by reminding the community that these leaders are indeed at their disposal, but only with a view to making them as perfectly subordinate to Christ as Christ himself is to God.

The third reading, from the Gospel according to Matthew, is another selection from the Sermon on the Mount. It comprises two passages in which traditional interpretations of divine law are declared to be inadequate to the standards implicit in the Gospel. Jesus first recalls a passage from Exodus in which the phrase "an eye for an eye and a tooth for a tooth" expresses the idea that fair retaliation should not inflict punishment greater than the injury it is intended to avenge. Rather than requiring moderation in vengeance, Jesus opposes vindictiveness altogether, and by a series of deliberately shocking examples calls upon his followers to endure injuries without avenging or even resisting them. This hard lesson is followed by the broad principle on which it is based. "You shall love your countryman but hate your enemy" is not a quotation from the Old Testament, but an expression of how the Mosaic injunction to love one's neighbor had in fact been understood. Jesus insists that there is nothing very admirable, much less divine, about merely being friendly toward one's friends. What is distinctively divine, as Jesus so often taught, is readiness to forgive. And it is this characteristic of the Father that is to characterize his children.

SEVENTH SUNDAY OF THE YEAR

Cycle "B" Readings: Is. 43:18-19, 21-22, 24b-25; 2 Cor. 1:18-22; Mk. 2:1-12

It has often been observed that Israel's religion was, to a remarkable degree, fashioned by Israel's history. That history was viewed in retrospect, and presented by the biblical writers, as a long experience of being saved by God. And among the events of that history which most vividly expressed Israel's experience of being saved by God, the outstanding one was, of course, the exodus. Emphatic in all biblical reflections is the recognition that God's favor to the Israelites was not something they had earned from him, but an act of sheer divine generosity—what later theology called "grace." When in the sixth century Israelites found themselves once more enslaved in a foreign land, this time in Babylon after the Assyrian conquest and deportation, their hopes for eventual liberation were naturally patterned on the classic events of the exodus, and therefore they envisioned a dramatic liberation, not achieved by their own efforts or deserved by their own merits, but done for them, out of sheer kindness, by their saving God. It is this hope, conceived in this fashion, which finds expression in today's reading from a section added to Isaiah, and known as the Book of Israel's Consolation. Expressing the mood of hope which prevailed at a time when events indicated that the Babylonian exile might soon be at an end, the verses proclaim in God's name a new exodus, a new divine rescue of this people whom God persists in loving and preserving, not because of their virtues but in spite of their vices. God provides for them, not because of what they are, but because of what he is.

Paul's relationship with the church of Corinth, which he himself founded, seems to have been a consistently stormy one, marked by many mutual misunderstandings. The selection in today's liturgy from the second letter to the Corinthians is part of a passage of self-justification which is developed into a general theological reflection. Apparently the source of friction intimated by this part of the letter was a change of itinerary which involved Paul's postponing a visit to Corinth which he had intended to make on his way to Macedonia. His decision not to visit Corinth at that time was occasioned by a grave offense committed by a member of that church. The Corinthians complained that Paul had not kept his promise to them. Paul's argument is that he cannot be fairly charged with insincerity because his decision to postpone the visit was not made lightly and was made in their own best interests. It is in this context that Paul evinces a positive horror at the thought that he, like "worldly" people, might break promises so casually that "yes" from him might just as well be a "no," and a "no" a "yes." Paul's acute distress at suspicions of disingenuousness is not, however, based on pride in his honor as a gentleman or anything of that sort, but derives from a distinctively Christian point of view. Ultimately, it is based on the conviction that insincerity on his part would be radically inconsistent with the following of Jesus Christ. For to Paul, as to other Christians, the very meaning of Jesus Christ is the fulfillment of God's Word. By sending Jesus Christ, the promised Messiah, God kept his promises. Jesus Christ, who confirms the unimpeachable sincerity of God, is the foundation of Christian prayer, and Paul recalls that Christian prayers typically conclude: "through Christ our Lord, Amen," where the latter word, a borrowing from Hebrew, is precisely a protestation of sincerity, a formula of guarantee that one really means what one is saying.

The account of Jesus' public ministry in the Gospel according to Mark gives greater attention to his works than to his words, although it does refer to Jesus' preaching and cites examples of it. The account begins by remarking on how greatly moved people were by Jesus' teaching, but then, without saying just what it was that he taught, it proceeds to describe, with a terse vividness characteristic of this Gospel, a series of extraordinary actions: first an exorcism, then the cure of Simon's mother-in-law, then a whole array of cures and exorcisms, then the healing of a leper. Finally, in the passage read in today's liturgy, a new element is introduced. A paralytic is presented to Jesus by the strenuous means of lowering him through an opening in the roof, in order to make sure Jesus did not miss him in the surrounding crowd which jammed the place where he was. Consistently with the preceding narratives, one naturally expects Jesus immediately to cure the sufferer of his paralysis. But instead, we are told, Jesus perceived the faith of the four men who had carried the paralytic and said to the paralytic, "Your sins are forgiven." In response to the unspoken criticism of some lawyers who regard these words as blasphemy, Jesus then cures the paralytic, in order to show that "the Son of Man has the power on earth to forgive sins." A number of interesting features make their initial appearance in this episode. It is explicitly noted that Jesus' benevolent action is occasioned by faith—and not even the faith of the person he cures, but of the friends who presented him. Second, we are alerted for the first time to the existence of enemies of Jesus, represented by the Jewish lawyers. Third, for the first time we hear Jesus appropriate the title, used only by him in the Gospels, "Son of Man," which has highly distinctive messianic connotations, and which there is good reason to believe Jesus deliberately adopted in place of more popular messianic titles which had unacceptable overtones. Finally, with the demonstration of a power interchangeably applicable to paralysis and to sin, we are made aware of the broad scope of Jesus' work of salvation, an assault upon evil in all its forms, an attack on everything that mars the goodness of God's creation.

SEVENTH SUNDAY OF THE YEAR

Cycle "C" Readings: 1 Sam. 26:2, 7-9, 12-13, 22-23; 1 Cor. 15:45-49; Lk. 6:27-38

The first reading, from the first book of Samuel, recounts a famous episode from one of the most fascinating biographical narratives in all of literature, the story of David. The episode belongs to a period in David's life when his fortunes had taken an ironic turn. Raised from obscurity into the favor of King Saul in virtue of outstanding talents, David found at a certain point that royal admiration soured into royal envy. Henceforth, the king's affection for his remarkable protege gave way to an insane hatred which alternately smoldered in moroseness and flared into violence. When the situation became intolerable, David fled from Jerusalem to the wilderness, where his skills continued to serve him well and won him the leadership of a formidable contingent of bandits and guerrilla fighters. Saul, meanwhile, pursued a relentless manhunt, and his wrath fell murderously on those who offered David assistance. It was during this time when David was a fugitive outlaw that he happened to find Saul and his men helplessly asleep and entirely at his mercy. Despite the understandable urging of his companion to seize the opportunity for putting an end to his royal enemy, David spared Saul's life. His alleged reason for doing so was neither chivalry nor sentimentality. Rather it was a religious conviction that the anointed king of Israel, however mad his behavior, retained the prerogatives of an appointment that was not human but divine, and that God could not be expected to leave his murderer unpunished. David's attempt, by drawing attention to his act of mercy, to effect some change of heart in the king had no success in bringing about a reconciliation. (The very similar episode recounted only two chapters earlier in the same book, of David's finding Saul at his mercy and sparing him, is presumably a variant account of the same tradition.)

The second reading is a fragment taken from a rather complicated section of the discussion of resurrection in St. Paul's first letter to the Corinthians. In meeting actual or anticipated objections to belief in resurrection, Paul confronts the question of what kind of body one might suppose to exist in a risen life. Paul's attempt to deal with this question involves a distinction between what he calls a "natural" and a "spiritual" body, meaning by the former our normal earthly condition and by the latter the condition of those who have been raised from the dead. Paul suggests that these two conditions, while radically different, have a continuity analogous to that of a seed with the full-grown plant which proceeds from it without having any observable resemblance to it. Whereas for Paul the "natural" body of a human being expresses his natural ancestry traceable to Adam, there is also a spiritual parentage which is manifested in the "spiritual" body of those who have been raised from the dead. This spiritual parentage corresponds to the life-giving power of Christ, who is thus conceived as a second Adam, not of earthly but of heavenly origin. Paul thus appears to relate the controversy over a person's risen body to the more general Christian idea of rebirth into a newness of life. For Paul, the post-resurrection condition stands in the same relation to the pre-resurrection condition, as the once-born heritage of Adam to the twice-born heritage of Christ. It can hardly be maintained that Paul actually explains what a risen body is or even that such a thing is intelligible. What he does do is to situate the whole topic within a more familiar framework of experience and doctrine, and in this way makes the problem seem to be not so much a new difficulty as another aspect of the already accepted mystery of Christian regeneration. The whole discussion may be seen as foreshadowing later speculation about the "natural" and "supernatural."

The reading from the Gospel according to Luke is part of that Lucan counterpart of Matthew's Sermon on the Mount which is sometimes distinguished as the Sermon on the Plain. The passage cited is one of the New Testament's most important statements on Christian love, and the gist of that statement is effectively summarized by the very first words: "To you who hear me I say: 'Love your enemies.'" The verses which follow simply illustrate what is enjoined by these words by means of examples clear enough and extreme enough to make their practical import unmistakable. The passage then proceeds to remind us of something that is lost sight of remarkably often in Christian ethical discourse, namely that Jesus Christ had no particular interest in commending or extolling what might be called well-deserved benevolence. To reciprocate generous favors, to respond affectionately to affectionate treatment by others, to give kindness for kindness—these are splendid things, but to identify behavior of this kind with Christian virtue betrays a total misunderstanding. For such behavior is mere decency and normality, and to fall short of it is not sub-Christian but sub-human. The Christian virtue of love is not identified with decent, normal reciprocity, but with that divine love of which Christ is himself the revelation, a love gracious and unearned, which is brought into play not by the goodness of its recipient but by the goodness of its giver.

EIGHTH SUNDAY OF THE YEAR

Cycle "A" Readings: Is. 49:14-15; 1 Cor. 4:1-5; Mt. 6:24-34

The first reading is from what is called Second Isaiah, a portion of the book of Isaiah composed nearly two centuries after that prophet's lifetime. Its contents therefore took shape close to the time when the Persian emperor Cyrus made it possible for the Israelites to repossess and reconstruct their homeland after their long exile. The significance of this momentous event, and the mood of hope and exhilaration occasioned by its prospect are very evident in Second Isaiah. The transition to this new frame of mind is well expressed in the reading, which presents a kind of oblique dialogue between Jerusalem and God himself. Expressing the sense of desolation following the exile, the devastated, depopulated city is imagined to lament that it has been forsaken and forgotten by God. To this plaintive cry God delivers a long reply, full of reassurance, of which the reading includes only the touching introductory verse. For God to forget his beloved city, he himself declares, is more unthinkable than that a loving mother should forget her own baby. The passage goes on to anticipate the rebuilding of the ruined city, and its reoccupation by hordes of returning exiles. The imagery throughout the entire passage is warm and intimate, implying that the events which are about to take place are no mere accidents of history, but the very personal interventions of a tenderly loving God.

The second reading, from the first letter to the Corinthians, is the beginning of a passage that Paul devotes to his own role as an apostle, evidently in reaction to criticism on the part of the Corinthian Christians. Those who function in Paul's capacity are, he says, subordinates of Christ. The implication would seem to be that Christ should be the one to direct and criticize his subordinate. Along with the idea of being Christ's subordinate, however, Paul introduces the further assertion that the apostles are administrators, or as it is sometimes translated, stewards, of the mysteries of God. What are here called God's mysteries or secrets might, to clarify the metaphor, be translated by some such phrase as "God's private plans." The idea is that God is in the position of the head of a household, who decides privately what he wants done and how he wants it done, and discloses his plans not to the general public but to a subordinate administrator, or steward, who is appointed to carry them out. The steward is not responsible for the plans, but he is responsible for carrying them out reliably in the ways indicated. In refutation of whatever criticism had been raised by the Corinthians, Paul appeals to his steward-like role. He is not answerable to the Corinthians, but to God. If they object to something, let them bear in mind that what is demanded by his position is not adaptability to their preferences, but fidelity to God's intentions. In a sense, therefore, Paul dismisses criticism with a bureaucrat's shrug, implying that he is merely carrying out orders. By the same token, he observes that the self-criticism of his own conscience is, in the last analysis, no more definitive than the criticisms raised by others. The only criticism that matters ultimately is God's, and the practical concern of Paul, as God's steward, is simply to prove faithful to God in the carrying out of his plans.

The third reading contains two passages, very closely related in their present context, from the Sermon on the Mount in the Gospel according to Matthew. The first passage gives striking expression to the idea that among one's competing values there has to be an order of priority, that different allegiances lead to conflicts that must be resolved and can only be resolved by choosing one over the other. This general idea is given very specific application by the well-known saying, "You cannot give yourself to God and money." It is the notion of giving oneself to money, with all that implies, that provides a natural transition to the second passage, which combines a condemnation of anxious preoccupation with material security and an exhortation to peaceful reliance on the providence of God. Readers have often felt that this passage comes dangerously close to encouraging a kind of shiftless improvidence, and it is important to note just what is being denounced. The prohibition is "Do not worry about your livelihood," which is quite a different thing from not providing for one's livelihood. It is not the virtue of prudence but the vice of anxiety that comes under attack. For whereas prudence is precisely characterized by moderation, anxiety is essentially immoderate and ultimately imprudent. The rhetorical questions, "Is not life more than food" and "Is not the body more valuable than clothes" point to the hierarchy of values that anxiety invariably distorts.

EIGHTH SUNDAY OF THE YEAR

Cycle "B" Readings: Hos. 2:14b, 15b, 19-20; 2 Cor. 3:1b-6; Mk. 2:18-22

In the prophecy of Hosea it is notoriously difficult to distinguish between realism and symbolism, and in particular between biographical references to the prophet's own marriage to an unfaithful woman, and his metaphorical references to the infidelity of Israel as a people bound by covenant, and in that sense "wedded" to God. It seems likely enough that Hosea actually was the devoted husband of a promiscuous woman, and that in experiencing the bitterness of her habitual betrayal of his love, he came to realize with a kind of personal sympathy how tragic and vicious a thing was Israel's infidelity to God. The time in which Hosea lived was not long before northern Israel collapsed before the Assyrian invasion. The Bible consistently describes that time as a period characterized by extreme social injustice and by the corrupting influence of pagan practices on Israelite religion. Under the circumstances, faithful Israelites like Hosea regarded the dark days that had come upon them as divine retribution. In Hosea's prophecy, however, along with warnings of divine punishment, there are frequent reassurances that divine chastisement does not mean divine rejection. This is brought out by the parallel case of Hosea's faithless spouse who, having deserted him for random lovers, finds herself at last a miserable outcast, abandoned by them all, only to be lovingly sought, reclaimed, and reinstated by her husband. Even so, the prophecy suggests, God, the victim, so to speak, of Israel's infidelity, will not himself be unfaithful. Israel must learn the painful lesson of what it means to neglect God, but once that lesson is learned, the relationship with God will be re-established. Here, in keeping with the prevailing conjugal imagery, the covenant assurance is expressed in terms of a marriage promise made by God to Israel: "I will betroth you to myself forever, betroth you in lawful wedlock with unfailing devotion and love; I will betroth you to myself to have and to hold, and you shall know the Lord."

In the third chapter of his second letter to the Corinthians, Paul reflects on the words of self-justification with which that letter begins, and cuts them off rather abruptly. The relationship between him and them is not, he insists, so distant or insecure that they must approach one another with letters of reference, like those brought by certain strangers. This allusion to introductory letters generates an extremely mixed metaphor which accompanies Paul's thought through a variety of subjects. First, the Corinthians themselves are said to be the only letter Paul needs, meaning apparently that the church which he founded testifies to his apostleship far more significantly than any written commendation could do. They are also said to be a letter written on Paul's own heart, a basis not only for his public credibility but also for his personal reassurance. Pushing the metaphor farther, Paul says that they are a letter from Christ, given to Paul to deliver, implying that the Corinthians' conversion was the accomplishment of Christ, in which Paul merely assisted as an instrument. The letter which the Corinthians are is written not with ink but with the Spirit, the divine principle of that new life in which their essential Christianity consists. This last turn in Paul's remarkably long and twisted metaphor brings it into line with a famous saying in the book of Jeremiah (31:33), promising a new covenant which will be written not on stone tablets, but on the people's very hearts. The contrast between the old and new covenants, between the Mosaic law and the Christian Gospel, is one of Paul's favorite theological topics, and the passage concludes with a highly typical Pauline reflection.

The third reading, from Mark's Gospel, contains two parables which have little connection either with one another or with the surrounding text. The first is occasioned by a question about why Jesus' followers, unlike those of the Pharisees and those of John the Baptist, are not fasting on some occasion which is not identified in the text. Jesus' answer, to the effect that wedding guests do not fast while the groom is still with them, is widely interpreted as an oblique reference to his messianic character. It is true that the comparison of God as faithful lover of his people to a devoted bridegroom, first elaborated in the prophecy of Hosea, was in later times, and certainly among Christians, transferred to the Messiah. It may be, however, that the imagery refers in a more general way to the joyous atmosphere of the coming of the Kingdom, in which fasting would be as incongruous as it would be at a wedding party. The subsequent reference to the bridegroom's being "taken away" probably refers to the time after Jesus' death and possibly refers to the acceptance of fasting as a religious practice among early Christians. Although there is no really logical transition from this passage to the following one, about not putting new cloth on old garments or new wine in old wineskins, there is probably a real similarity of viewpoint.

For, supposing that the new cloth and the new wine stand for the new age that the Messiah's coming inaugurates—a supposition well-supported by biblical imagery—we have here another reference to behavior that is inappropriate to existing circumstances and implies a total misunderstanding of the radically transformed situation of humankind. Both passages seem mainly intended to criticize, as foolish and pointless, the continuance of old pre-messianic ways in the new messianic age.

EIGHTH SUNDAY OF THE YEAR

Cycle "C" Readings: Sir. 27:4-7; 1 Cor. 15:54-58; Lk. 6:39-45

The second century wisdom book of Sirach, from which the first reading is taken, although excluded from Jewish and Protestant Bibles, is accorded full canical status by Roman Catholics. Its contents are extremely various and of very uneven quality. Much of its teaching has little or no religious or theological significance, and pertains rather to popular, practical psychology or social savoir-faire. The passage given in the reading is of the latter sort, and its lesson is one that has been taught and put into practice by people of common sense and mature experience in every culture. The importance attached in our own society to the personal interview and to oral testimony is a reflection of the same idea. It is the idea that our estimate of any person must remain very tentative until we have an opportunity to hear that person talk, and not talk simply at random or at whim. Seriously to address some serious topic or issue reveals qualities of mind and disposition that may be otherwise entirely overlooked or misconceived. Human character is complicated and subtle, and its countless ingredients are hard to sort out under uncontrolled circumstances. Serious discussion thus acts as does a sieve with some unanalyzed mixture. It serves as a screening device, revealing the relative proportion of coarseness and fineness. The effectiveness of unrehearsed debate for dispelling illusions and unmasking pretensions of knowledge, intelligence, and sensitivity has always been appreciated by persons of experience and discrimination, especially in such departments of life as politics, where impressions formed on other bases can be so disastrously deceived.

The second reading, from the first letter to the Corinthians, is the conclusion of Paul's lengthy discourse on life after death. For Paul the reality of such life is not a philosophical conclusion but an implication of faith in Christ's resurrection, which he calls "the first-fruits of the harvest of the dead." But firm belief that there is life after death does not answer, and may riase with special urgency, the question of what sort of life it is. Paul addresses this matter in the last part of his discourse, especially in connection with the question of what sort of body is vivified in the resurrection. Neither Paul nor his readers envisage a disembodied life after death, since the mere survival of a bodiless spirit would not be a true resurrection at all. Despite Paul's initial impatience with this question, he does try to answer it. In doing so he proposes that a very different sort of body, which he rather mysteriously calls a "spiritual body," is possessed in the risen life. It is to this transformed bodily condition that the reading refers as the corruptible frame's taking on of incorruptibility. In the concluding verses these not very enlightening speculations give way to the real point, which is that, however it may happen, death loses all power and all real significance. Paul's theology had already established a close relationship between death and sin, and between sin and the law. All three of these are to be eliminated together by the victory gained by Christ.

The third reading is taken from what is sometimes called the sermon on the plain, designating it as a Lucan counterpart to the Sermon on the Mount, with which it has much in common. The verses that comprise the reading belong to a collection of originally independent passages applicable to different aspects of discipleship. The first passage identifies the essence of discipleship as the faithful following of a master, and points out that only on this basis can the disciple himself exercise any useful leadership of others. A second passage takes up the idea of a disciple's initial responsibility for his own character and conduct, and satirizes the common tendency to neglect fundamental self-criticism, while indulging in relatively trivial criticism of others. The third passage expresses metaphorically a basic principle to be applied in all criticizing of human character. It is the simple idea that all we can know about what a person interiorly is depends completely on our observation and assessment of what he or she exteriorly does. Just as the quality of a fruit tree is inferred from the kind of fruit it bears, so the moral quality of a human being is manifested by actions. The context does not make it clear what application of this general principle Luke has in mind. It may refer either to a disciple's assessment of Jesus himself, or to the basis on which a disciple is to be assessed by others.

NINTH SUNDAY OF THE YEAR

Cycle "A" Readings: Deut. 11:18, 26-28; Rom. 3:21-25, 28; Mt. 7:21-27

The book of Deuteronomy, from which the first reading is taken, is widely regarded as a kind of introductory volume to a series of historical works recounting developments in Israel down to the time of the exile, and organizing and interpreting the historical material in accordance with theological principles formally expressed in Deuteronomy itself. That book is presented, fictitiously, as the very words of Moses, and its principal contents are statements of the Mosaic law, on the observance of which Israel's future was believed to depend. The passage from which the reading is taken is the conclusion of one of two introductory discourses that precede the lengthy declaration of the law often called the Deuteronomic Code. The verses selected from that passage express the importance of remembering and obeying the law. As a token of mindfulness of the law, Jews adopted the custom, here alluded to, of wearing on their head and arm small capsules containing representative texts. For Deuteronomy and the narrative books that follow it, the law furnished the basic key for understanding the vicissitudes of Israel's history. Bad times resulted from neglecting the law, and good times depended on fidelity to the law. In this sense, the giving of the law entailed "a blessing and a curse," "a blessing for obeying" and "a curse if you do not obey." Underlying this idea is the conviction that Israel's well-being and its very being depended on the covenant. The stability of the covenant depended on both the fidelity of God, which could not fail, and the fidelity of the people, which could fail. The Deuteronomic history is in large measure an account of that failure, and of its grievous consequences.

The second reading is a passage that immediately introduces the main argument of the letter to the Romans. It follows a preliminary argument in which Paul contends that not only the Gentile world, instructed by the law of nature, but also his own Jewish world, endowed with the precious divine law of Moses, have failed to achieve that justice or righteousness for which genuine law exists. On the contrary, the past history and present experience of Jew and Gentile alike is a tale of sin and the consequences of sin, of God's wrath rather than God's justice. Paul concludes that introductory section with his cheerless answer to the question of what the law has actually conferred upon mankind: "Law brings only the consciousness of sin." The passage taken for the reading immediately follows this somber reflection, and begins with a resounding "but," which the reading, presumably to avoid such an odd way of beginning, does not translate. "But now the justice of God has been manifested apart from the law." What is here translated as justice is rather different from what that word generally means in English; it is, broadly speaking, the triumph in the world of the goodness of the world's creator, whereby sin and its consequences are overcome, and human life is, in the deepest and fullest sense, put right. This, says Paul, has now been accomplished through Jesus Christ, and it is made effectual by faith in Jesus Christ, rather than by observance of the law which sinful humanity has shown itself unable to observe.

The third reading is the ending of the Sermon on the Mount in the Gospel according to Matthew. The very situation of that discourse on a mountain is but one of many indications that the evangelist here intends to present Jesus as a second Moses, a divine lawgiver, and the sermon itself as the divine law corresponding to a new covenant. It is in keeping with this theme that, just as in the Mosaic literature exemplified by the first reading, so also here, the divine law is delivered with emphasis on the critically opposite consequences of keeping it or failing to keep it. Just as Deuteronomy insists that it is not the mere acknowledgment of God but the observance of his law that is the way of life for Israel, so here Jesus declares that the Kingdom of God belongs not to those who merely cry out, "Lord, Lord," but to the "one who does the will of my Father." The same lesson is reinforced by the parable with which the discourse is concluded. Merely to hear what Jesus says is as useless as a foundation of sand to the builder of a house. To do what Jesus says is the only stable foundation on which the new divinely instituted construction can be built. The sharp difference between this theme and the one expressed by Paul in the previous reading exemplifies a tension between "faith" and "works" that has provoked so much Christian perplexity and controversy. This tension is clearly recognized in the New Testament writings themselves, which also point toward solutions elaborated by later theologians. Nowhere, however, are the polarities of thought more immediately apparent than in the juxtaposition, as in this liturgy, of the letter to the Romans and the Gospel according to Matthew.

NINTH SUNDAY OF THE YEAR

Cycle "B" Readings: Deut. 5:12-15; 2 Cor. 4:6-11; Mk.2:23—3:6

The first reading is taken from the Ten Commandments as given in the book of Deuteronomy. The Decalogue is also listed in the book of Exodus and, despite basic similarity, there are significant differences between the two formulations. One example of this is the third commandment, which the reading reproduces in full and which, in the Deuteronomic list, is the longest of all the commandments. The basic statement of the commandment is identical in both lists: "Six days you may labor . . . but the seventh day is the Sabbath. . . . No work may be done then." Both lists then proceed to specify, very inclusively, who are not to work on the Sabbath: the domestic circle of family, slaves, and work animals and, in addition, resident aliens. It is at this point that the two formulations diverge, each seeming to give a completely different rationale for the same commandment. Exodus refers it to the creation mythology of Genesis, according to which God, having fashioned the universe in six days and rested on the seventh, blessed and sanctified that day. In Deuteronomy, however, the rationale is introduced by an association of ideas with the previous reference to slaves. The passage repeats that slaves are to share in the general rest. It then reminds the people of their own former days as slaves in Egypt, from which they were rescued by God, and concludes that "that is why" God prescribed the

Sabbath observance. Although it is commonly assumed that what is implied here is that the experience of slavery should make one compassionately ready to give slaves a weekly day of rest, this humanitarian interpretation would not account for the commandment as a whole. It may be that the real point is not the remembrance of slavery as grounds for compassion, but the remembrance of God's rescue as grounds for the gratitude that underlies all observance of the commandments. The latter interpretation would regard the Sabbath rest as a "eucharistic" interlude, an occasion for grateful remembrance.

The second reading is taken from a section of the second letter to the Corinthians in which Paul, partly from motives of self-justification, develops his ideas about several aspects of apostleship. The first person plural, used throughout the reading, does not refer to Paul and his readers, but to Paul and his apostolic counterparts. Reading the passage out of context makes it important to note that "we" does not mean you (Corinthians) and I (Paul), but rather they (the other apostles) and I (Paul). This explains the opening metaphor, wherein Paul likens the apostles to sources of light, whose light of revelation is transmissable to others only because it is first derived from another source. Ultimately that source is God; proximately it is God's manifestation, or "glory," in the visible person, or "face," of Jesus Christ. After summarizing the function of apostleship, Paul turns to the conditions under which that function is carried out. The derivative nature of apostolic function is taken up by a transitional metaphor, which likens the divine message carried by its all-too-human messengers to a precious treasure carried in a cheap earthenware pot. An apostle is weak and vulnerable, and suffers both from his own weakness and from the abuses of others. Nevertheless, by their sufferings no less than by their words, the apostles continue to convey their message of the life-giving death of Jesus Christ.

The third reading, from the Gospel according to Mark, contains two episodes of Jesus' Galilean ministry in which that Gospel develops the theme of conflict between Jesus and influential Jewish leaders, described as "lawyers," that is, interpreters of Mosaic law, and in particular Pharisees, a highly respected group of lay theologians. In both of the episodes narrated in the reading the same accusation is brought against Jesus, namely violation of that Sabbath obligation whose basic statement, in the Decalogue, was discussed in connection with the first reading. In the course of time, questions inevitably arose about precisely what should be included in the "work" that was not allowed on the Sabbath, and it came to be understood that such things as the harvesting of grain by farm-hands and the treatment of patients by physicians ought to be suspended on the day of rest. To include in these categories such actions as Jesus' verbal curing of a paralytic and his disciples' casual plucking of some wheat to ease their hunger as they walked seems, and is, fantastic. Thus, in the second episode, it is parenthetically explained that the Pharisees were "hoping to be able to bring an accusation against" Jesus. Both episodes serve not only to demonstrate that

Jesus had, from early in his career, powerful enemies, but also to exemplify his own hierarchy of values with respect to legal obligations. These are not repudiated, but are rather subordinated to an overriding concern for mercy, expressed in both of Jesus' references to the Old Testament and in his counter-question about rescuing a sheep from a ditch on the Sabbath.

NINTH SUNDAY OF THE YEAR

Cycle "C" Readings: 1 Kgs. 8:41-43; Gal. 1:1-2, 6-10; Lk. 7:1-10

The first reading is taken from the chapter of the first book of Kings that describes King Solomon's dedication of the great temple in Jerusalem of which he had completed construction during the previous year, postponing the celebration until a suitably impressive feast day. The fact that the designers and builders of this immense project were not Israelites but the much better qualified Phoenicians, imported for the purpose by royal commission, is a reminder of the international outlook which characterized Israel's foreign policy under Solomon. This international breadth of vision, combined with a new kind of national pride, is conspicuous in the reading. This is part of a prayer which, although attributed to Solomon on this occasion, is actually a combination of two much later compositions, fashioned at a time when the national glories here referred to had been followed by a long history of national humiliations. The passage is made somewhat complicated by its concern, on the one hand, to exclude any idea that God in a crudely physical sense actually inhabits the temple and, on the other hand, to stress the merit and propriety of making the temple a focus of worship. The latter concern predominates, and leads to an emphasis on the efficacy of praying in the direction of the temple. In the reading, Solomon is represented as praying that this efficacy might be experienced not only by the Israelites themselves, but also by well-disposed (and suitably impressed) foreign visitors.

The second reading is taken from the first part of Paul's letter to the Galatians. It begins with the writer identifying himself as an apostle, whose commission is from Jesus and from God, not from human beings. The greeting that follows is cooler and more formal than is usual with Paul, anticipating the censorious tone of the sequel. After a blessing, which the reading omits, the writer comes directly to the point, which is an accusation that the Galatians are turning away from Christ and adopting an alien gospel. He then refers to what is the main cause of his distress, namely that certain unnamed persons are influencing the Galatians to misconstrue the very meaning of the Gospel. The nature of this unwelcome influence, actually a campaign to reinstate Jewish ritual obligations among Christian converts, is indicated only later in the letter. At this point what Paul insists upon is that the Gospel he himself preached to these people is their standard of orthodoxy, and that any teaching contradicting it cannot be tolerated. The last part of the passage indicates a further problem for Paul. In stressing the normative authority of his own teaching, and denouncing other teachers who disagreed with him, Paul left himself open to criticism of a less theological and more personal kind. Those who insisted on the importance of observances that Paul repudiated could, and apparently did, charge him with watering down divine revelation so as to make it more palatable to potential converts. Paul angrily denies that in his capacity as an apostle he consults the preferences or interests of any but the Lord who made him an apostle.

The third reading, from the Gospel according to Luke, tells the story of a miracle that is also reported, with some discrepancies, in the Gospels according to Matthew and John. In all three accounts the beneficiary is a Roman officer, but Luke represents him as also a generous benefactor of the Jews, who is actually brought to Jesus' attention through the commendation of Jewish elders. Both of the Synoptic evangelists describe the man's behavior as profoundly respectful of Jesus. His respect is manifested first in humility, declaring himself unworthy to have Jesus actually visit his home, and then in faith, professing his confidence that Jesus acts with decisive authority. His words imply that he supposes Jesus to command forces of life and death as peremptorily as he himself might issue orders to a military subordinate. It is this striking declaration of confidence in Jesus' power that prompts Jesus to declare that he has found greater faith in this foreigner than among his own people. And as so often in the Gospel stories, this acknowledgment of faith is followed immediately by a miracle of mercy, in this case the complete and instantaneous cure of the officer's servant who had been declared mortally ill. There can be little doubt that, especially for Luke with his deep interest in the early flourishing of Christianity in Gentile lands, this narrative is more than an illustration of humble faith and merciful power. The whole episode expresses both Gentile receptivity to the Gospel, and the intermediary role of the Jews in bringing the Gentile world into effective contact with the saving power of Jesus Christ.

TENTH SUNDAY OF THE YEAR

Cycle "A" Readings: Hos. 6:3-6; Rom. 4:18-25; Mt. 9:9-13

The initial verses of today's selection from the prophecy of Hosea (and those which immediately precede them—3:1-2) probably impress the average person who hears them in the liturgy as beautiful and consoling words, constituting a prayer which any Christian might readily make his own. They seem in fact to express precisely that kind of humble confidence in the mercy of a forgiving God to which Christians, following the teaching and example of Jesus, attribute the highest religious value. Consequently it comes as rather a surprise that the words ascribed to God himself, which follow this prayer, far from expressing satisfaction or even compassion, are saturated with an unmistakable tone of ironic exasperation. With this as a clue, further examination of the context leads to the conclusion that what may have seemed at first an exemplary prayer is in fact a sarcastic parody of what in the prophet's judgment is despicable lip-service paid to God as a shameless substitute for authentic devotion. Very likely, those words which Hosea's God so pointedly ignores were a liturgical recitation accompanying an expiatory rite. In any case, what they stand for is words instead of deeds, tokens instead of efforts, ritual piety as a pretext for moral apathy. And so God rejects them, with the grim reminder that what he wants from man is not ceremonies, but personal fidelity to himself.

It is possible to interpret the second reading, from the letter to the Romans, as conveying a message which flatly contradicts the one we have just drawn from the prophecy of Hosea. Hosea is unequivocally calling for moral reform, for what might well be described as practical obedience to God's law, and insisting that so long as that is lacking, the people's liturgical assurances of divine mercy merely add insult to injury. In Romans, on the other hand, the extolling of Abraham's faith is part of a larger context whose central motif is the famous Pauline contrast between the inadequacy of the law and the adequacy of faith for man's justification. One might therefore be understandably tempted to suppose that Paul is simply reversing Hosea's insistence on moral earnestness and replacing it with that smug reliance on God's mercy which the prophet excoriates. Paul has often been interpreted in this sense, probably even in his own time, and it would be a betrayal of him to pretend that personal moral reform has in his theology the same priority as in the preaching of the prophets. And Paul's rejection of reliance upon the law does seem to include a firm disbelief in man's capacity to rid his life of immorality. But at the same time, the faith which Paul so characteristically emphasizes is not a morally empty confidence in God, but a confidence in God which is precisely manifested in obedience to him. Hence the appropriateness of Paul's example, Abraham, whose life was a tale of courageous obedience issuing from faith in the promises of God. If Abraham was justified by faith, it was certainly not a faith devoid of moral striving. And if Abraham was justified without the law, he was surely not justified without both knowing and doing the will of God.

In the final reading, from the Gospel according to Matthew, we hear Jesus cite the concluding words of our first reading from the prophet Hosea. However, they are cited in a context strikingly different from the one in which Hosea delivered his denunciation of morally ineffectual religion. The main thing to keep in mind in interpreting this New Testament adaptation of a thousand-year-old prophetic text is that Jesus is speaking defensively, and that what he is defending is his own conduct. If he speaks also accusingly, his accusation is of a kind of religious blindness on the part of his adversaries which had moved them to accuse him of improper behavior. Jesus is not speaking here on behalf of sinners, much less of their sins. In fact he is not speaking for man at all; he is speaking for God, and for his own mission as the faithful instrument of God. God, he insists here as so often in the Gospels, does not passively await the sinner's conversion. Rather he actively seeks, assists, and precipitates it. God is not a dispassionate critic of man's moral life, but the active inspirer and reformer of it: a healer, not a connoisseur of health.

TENTH SUNDAY OF THE YEAR

Cycle "B" Readings: Gen. 3:9-15; 2 Cor. 4:13—5:1; Mk. 3:20-35

The first reading, from the book of Genesis, is part of the story of what is generally called the Fall, the account of the first human experience of sinning and its consequences. In the section contained in the reading, the sin has already been perpetrated and consequences have already begun to appear, inasmuch as the human pair find themselves embarrassed by their nudity, which they hide with makeshift clothing, and frightened by their God from whom they hide among the trees. In the ensuing dialogue, God makes it clear that this is guilty behavior, and accuses them of having committed what, as the myth is constructed, was the only sin available to them, disobedience of God's one prohibition. Their response to the incontestable charge is also symptomatic of the transformation sinning has wrought in their personalities: each attempts to shift the blame to another, the man to the woman, and the woman in turn to the serpent. The final words of the reading, spoken by God to the serpent, are in the myth itself immediately followed in turn by God's words to the woman and his words to the man. Each of these addresses has a distinctly judicial tone, and is equivalent to the imposing of sentences on three convicted criminals. In the myth, these divine sentences are ingeniously used to associate the primordial sin with explanations of certain perplexing and distressing features of ordinary human experience. The sentence passed on the serpent represents a mythological explanation both of the odd posture and locomotion characteristic of snakes, and of the mutual fear between snakes who are vulnerable to being trampled, and people who are vulnerable to being bitten. Christianity later made a new myth out of this story, by associating the woman with Mary and the offspring with Jesus, and misreading the text to mean that the woman would trample the serpent, as represented in a great many statues and paintings.

In the second reading, from the second letter to the Corinthians, Paul's account of what it means to be an apostle is concluded in a way that introduces his next theme, that of the destiny that Christians believe awaits them after death. Paul has emphasized that the work of an apostle is both hard and hazardous. Although he has also emphasized that an apostle's success depends not on his own skills but on the power of God, the question may still be raised of why anyone should undertake, or how anyone could persevere, in so arduous a mission. For Paul, what he preaches contains the obvious explanation of why he preaches. His message is the Gospel, the good news, and what makes it good news is what makes the rigors of apostleship endurable, and even negligible. Paul here uses a rather distorted quotation from one of the psalms (116.10) to say "I believed, therefore I spoke out," and proceeds to explain that what he believed and spoke out about is the prospect of being raised to life by God just as Jesus was raised to life in his resurrection. With such a prospect in view, inevitable bodily deterioration is constantly offset by spiritual revival, and temporary sufferings pale into insignificance before what the believer understands to be their eternal outcome, "a dwelling provided for us by God."

The third reading continues the account in the Gospel according to Mark of the buildup of opposition to Jesus' Galilean ministry. The episodes immediately follow the selection of the twelve disciples. The first scene exhibits the great public interest in Jesus by describing a crowd so pressing as to make ordinary dining impossible. A new and well-intentioned opposition to Jesus comes now from his own family, who fear for his sanity and try to take control of him. A different kind of opposition is represented by scribes, from Jerusalem itself, who accuse Jesus of using diabolical means. Jesus' famous refutation of their charge points to the inconsistency between what he has been doing, overcoming those very evils with which demons were popularly credited, and what the scribes were claiming, that he was allied with demonic powers. The parable embodies this refutation and also serves to introduce Jesus' solemn warning to the effect that the only strictly unforgivable sin would be to set oneself in opposition to the very source of divine forgiveness, the Spirit of God. Although the scribes are not directly accused of this sin against the Spirit, the implication is clear and ominous. A final feature of this intense and crowded episode reintroduces the theme of well-intentioned opposition with which it began, announcing the arrival of Jesus' mother and "brothers." The Greek of this last term is masculine, but could be applied to both sexes. Later in this Gospel four brothers of Jesus are named and sisters are alluded to. Belief in Mary's perpetual virginity has dissuaded Catholics from supposing that true siblings are meant. The point of the episode is Jesus' insistence on subordinating family ties to the deeper bonds of common obedience to God.

TENTH SUNDAY OF THE YEAR

Cycle "C" Readings: 1 Kgs. 17:17-24; Gal. 1:11-19; Lk. 7:11-17

The first reading, from the first book of Kings, narrates part of an episode in the career of the famous ninth-century prophet, Elijah. Much of that career was taken up in bitter conflict with the notoriously despicable royal couple, King Ahab and his pagan queen, Jezebel. At the very beginning of that conflict, Elijah prophesied that until he declared otherwise the land would suffer a total drought. The point of this was to demonstrate the powerlessness of pagan deities to bring the life-giving rain that only the Lord could control. Elijah was forced to flee from the royal anger aroused by the fulfillment of this prophecy. He took refuge with a widow, and it is this woman and her son to whom the reading refers. Elijah's presence had already brought sustenance to this woman by miraculous means during the drought and the famine which resulted from the drought. But the widow also attributed to the prophet the subsequent death of her son. Apparently she interpreted this tragedy as punishment for her own sins, supposing that the presence of God's holy prophet had the effect of activating divine vengeance. Elijah's prayer for the stricken boy protests the irony of allowing this loss to be suffered by the widow who had shown her true quality by giving him shelter despite her own poverty and the danger of incurring the king's wrath by assisting his enemy. Elijah's prayer is granted, confirming the widow's conviction that he is "a man of God" but at the same time deepening her understanding of what that meant.

The second reading, from the letter to the Galatians, continues Paul's argument that his readers are being deceived into adopting false doctrine. He has contended that it should be recognizable as such by its inconsistency with what he himself originally preached to them. In taking this line, Paul is obliged to defend the normative authority he claims for his own teaching. He therefore interrupts his denunciation of his adversaries in order to clarify his own position. He is determined to establish that he and his opponents are not simply theological disputants. Paul insists that his doctrine, unlike theirs, is not a humanly contrived philosophy or theology, but a divinely conferred revelation. In claiming this dogmatic status for his teaching, Paul puts himself in an altogether different category from that to which he assigns his opponents. He accordingly reminds his readers of the unique personal history of his apostolic vocation. Initially, he observes, he was a devout and studious Jew, and is therefore no stranger to the Jewish traditions that his adversaries are urging upon the Galatians. However, it was not his Jewish religious and theological formation that made Paul an apostle, but the direct intervention of God himself, revealing the truth of his Gospel, and commissioning him to preach it to the Gentiles. After that, he insists, he did not adopt any merely human counsel. Indeed it was only years later that he even met any of the other apostles in Jerusalem. This account of Paul's activities right after his conversion seems to disagree somewhat with Luke's account in Acts of the Apostles, and, as an earlier and first-hand statement, it is presumably more accurate. At the same time, it must be recalled that what we are reading here is not autobiography, but heated argument.

The third reading is a story recorded only in the Gospel according to Luke. It is one of the three occasions on which Jesus is described as raising the dead to life: the restoration of Jairus' daughter being reported by all three Synoptics, and the raising of Lazarus only by the fourth Gospel. The location of this story is a Galilean town, and the miracle is described as an entirely spontaneous act of compassion on Jesus' part, without even the usual mention of faith on the part of his beneficiary. The episode of restoring to life the only son of a widow inevitably recalls the similar story about Elijah which is presented in the first reading. Since the resemblances extend even to several points of phraseology, it is highly probable that Luke's narration of this episode is directly influenced by the Old Testament precedent. Even the people's response, in acknowledging Jesus to be "a great prophet" is significantly like the other widow's reaction to Elijah in declaring that "the word of the Lord comes truly from your mouth."

ELEVENTH SUNDAY OF THE YEAR

Cycle "A" Readings: Ex. 19:2-6; Rom. 5:6-11; Mt.9:36—10:8

The first reading of today's liturgy introduces the account of the covenant given by God through Moses to his chosen people, Israel. This covenant was absolutely basic to Israel's historical and theological self-knowledge, and was later to enter deeply into the theology of the Christian Church. Today's reading tells how the Israelites, three months after their escape from Egypt, came to Sinai, where Moses ascended the mountain and received from God a series of instructions which he transmitted to his followers. In the present literary structure of the Pentateuch, the account of this period of communication with God extends all the way from the verses we just read from Exodus to the 10th chapter of Numbers. As a result, the account is enabled to contain a large mass of religious legislation, some of it broadly general like the decalogue, but with innumerable distracting minutiae. For the average reader, therefore, it is important to concentrate on those passages which bring out the most basic aspects of the covenant and the Mosaic law.

Such a passage is the one in today's liturgy, where God's words to Moses bring out two characteristic features. First, the people of Israel are reminded of the salvation they have received from God, their rescue from slavery, which is the historical basis for their confidence in God. And second, they are told that if they respect the covenant which God is about to give them they will enjoy a uniquely favored and intimate relationship with God. It is in this latter sense that we should understand the concluding reference to a kingdom of priests and a holy nation. The idea is not that Israel was to be some kind of clerical hierarchy. Rather, the reference to priesthood, like the equivalent one to holiness, indicates that special closeness and ease of access to the divine, and consequent elevation above the profane, which were commonly associated with the sanctuary and its ministers. The emphasis, therefore, is on Israel's status as God's chosen people, hallowed by that unique familiarity with God which later prophets would describe in even marital terms.

Israel's understanding of itself as God's chosen people has inevitably appeared to some critics as extremely arrogant and a virtual canonization of chauvinism. It should, however, be borne in mind that Israel did not consider God's special favor to be a sign of his admiration for Israel. Quite the contrary, it is made very clear that Israel did not by any means deserve to be God's chosen people. In fact, the impression one gets from the account of the exodus is of a singularly recalcitrant and ungrateful people, saved and sanctified practically despite themselves. This understanding of salvation as undeserved grace is preserved, with perhaps even greater emphasis, in the New Testament. It is brought out vividly in today's reading from the letter to the Romans, where what is elsewhere described as the new covenant in Christ's blood is shown to be the result of a self-sacrifice undertaken not for good men but for bad men, not for God's friends but for his enemies. In the New Testament as in the Old, man's salvation is God's achievement and the consequence of God's loving initiative. The saving grace of God is not divine flattery.

It is this same characteristic of divine grace that is constantly represented by Jesus' own ministry and by the ministry he enjoined on his disciples. Typically it is a ministry of mercy and healing, and to be singled out by Jesus for special attention is invariably a sign not of one's merit but of one's need. Jesus' work is not one of decoration but of repair. Thus in today's fragmentary selections from the Gospel according to Matthew, we find that Jesus' consideration of the people moved him not to admiration but to pity. And accordingly, his missionaries' proclamation of the kingdom of heaven is to be accompanied by a vast campaign of physical and spiritual healing.

ELEVENTH SUNDAY OF THE YEAR

Cycle "B" Readings: Ezek. 17:22-24; 2 Cor. 5:6-10; Mk. 4:26-34

The three verses from the book of Ezekiel that comprise the first reading are generally thought not to have originated in their present context. The whole section of the book in which these verses occur is characterized by ominous discourses by the prophet in evident anticipation of the fall of Jerusalem, which occurred during his lifetime, when he himself was among those deported into the Babylonian exile. The reading, however, has an auspicious rather than an ominous tone, and is ordinarily classed among those prophecies of hope and reassurance that are called messianic. It is in keeping with Ezekiel's highly figurative style that the prophecy is expressed entirely in metaphor. God is represented as saying that he plans to snip off one of the topmost sprigs of a great cedar tree, and to transplant it on a mountain in Israel, where it is to grow to enormous size and offer shelter to all sorts of creatures. The reference is clearly to restoring on Mt. Zion, or Jerusalem, from the northern habitat of the mighty cedars, a newly thriving kingdom, founded on the people of the exile, which would offer security to all who allied themselves with Israel's God. The last part of the metaphor describes all the trees as marveling at the Lord's ability to reverse the conditions of nature, and stands for the international respect that might be expected to result from Israel's emergence from political insignificance and subservience.

The passage from which the second reading is taken is a discussion in the second letter to the Corinthians, of the relationship between the present, earthly, embodied existence of Christians, and the future, heavenly, existence in which they believe and for which they hope. It is an unusually speculative passage, which seems to be in response to concern about what happens during the period after death but before the return of Christ and the ensuing general resurrection. Earlier Pauline writings imply an assumption that Christ would return very soon, making such concerns of little practical relevance. The main anxiety Paul seems to have in view is fear of a disembodied condition that would leave the deceased without any real individual identity or personality, and without any means of communion with others: a state of bare existence, alienated from both society and personal history. Although there are many ambiguities in Paul's treatment of this problem, his practical conclusions are plain enough. The first of these introduces the reading: "We continue to be confident." There is nothing to worry about, as we are assured by our faith, even if our theological explanations may not be entirely satisfactory. The other practical conclusion is that with which the reading ends: each one's destiny, at Christ's return, will be "according to his life in the body." Our concern, therefore, should be to live worthily of Christ during our embodied, earthly phase of existence, rather than to know in advance precisely what happens once that phase is completed. Paul's more speculative comments, developed more fully in the verses that precede the reading, emphasize that the end of our bodily life brings us closer to Christ, and that death, far from threatening us with an isolated, alienated condition, has the very opposite effect. To be "at home" in our present bodily state means being "away from home" in terms of our final dwelling with Christ. Paul's play on the Greek words meaning at and away from home is rather obscured by most English versions.

The final reading, from the Gospel according to Mark, comprises two parables, of which the first is peculiar to this Gospel. Both are figures of botanical imagery. In the first, what is emphasized is the invisible germination of a seed that is finally manifested when a shoot emerges from the ground and then grows till it is big enough for harvest. In the second, what is emphasized is the contrast between the smallness of the mustard seed and the bigness of the plant it produces, with the added notion that this big resultant shrub offers a home to nesting birds. Both parables share a common pattern in the sequence of seed, sprouting, and full growth. The first, however, emphasizes the invisibility of germination whereas the second emphasizes the smallness of the seed, and the first has its climax in the harvest whereas the second has its climax in the provision of nesting places. Both parables pertain explicitly to the reign of God which is the constant theme of Jesus' preaching. One of them is a reminder of the long inscrutable preparation in the history of God's dealings with his people for what has now, with Christ's coming, become a visible and thriving reality. The other focuses on the continuity between the first manifestations of the reign of God in Jesus' initial ministry and the final scope and magnitude by which it was destined to embrace all peoples.

ELEVENTH SUNDAY OF THE YEAR

Cycle "C" Readings: 2 Sam. 12:7-10, 13; Gal. 2:16, 19-21; Lk.7:36—8:3

The first reading, from the second book of Samuel, is taken from the story of King David and his eventual Queen Bathsheba, one of the great narrative masterpieces of biblical literature. It tells of how David, best-remembered of all Israel's kings, despite the many virtues that immortalized him as a hero, succumbed to his own selfishness and became responsible for a whole concatenation of the most grievous sins. With terrible inevitability, David's behavior, at first arrogant and then anxious, carried him from neglect of duty to lust, to adultery, to deceit, to treachery, to conspiracy, and finally to murder. Having concealed his crimes from all but God, David is finally accosted by God's prophet, Nathan. The prophet's ingeniously ironic presentation of a fictional case leads David to condemn behavior which is only a mild allegorization of his own vicious deeds. Made aware that he is condemned out of his own mouth, David is convicted and sentenced in the words of the prophet with which the reading begins. By the law that Israel understood to be God's law, David's conduct had merited the death penalty on more than one count, and it is implied that the prophet's coming will actuate a sentence of doom. David, however, as the reading indicates, humbly and unprotestingly confesses his guilt and, as appears subsequently, is profoundly repentant. The result is that the Lord forgives his sinfulness, and remits the worst, though not the whole of his punishment. The entire story, in its moralizing function, comprises both a severe warning to human pride and, at the same time, a gracious assurance of the availability of divine mercy to repentant sinners.

The second reading is a selection from the letter to the Galatians which epitomizes a fundamental and extremely influential aspect of Paul's theology. Its context here is the argument in which Paul maintains that certain teachers are winning members of the community away from the authentic Gospel he himself had preached to them. After reviewing some of the outstanding features of his vocation and missionary career, and emphasizing their basis in divine revelation, Paul returns here to the doctrinal issue. The issue is clearly between those who do and those who do not consider Christians as subject to the obligations of Mosaic law. Paul's adversaries have evidently been trying to impose such obligations, and Paul's opposition to them is absolute. Paul's thesis is plainly stated in the first verse of the reading: "a man is not justified by legal observances but by faith in Jesus Christ." According to Paul, in other words, a right relationship with God simply cannot be had by trying to conform one's life to the Mosaic law. It can only be had through a wholehearted acceptance of and reliance upon Jesus Christ. Given such faith, the life of Christ himself becomes operative in the life of the believer, who is saved in virtue of that divine power, and not in virtue of his own always imperfect efforts at legal obedience. This decisive alternative to the Mosaic law is for Paul absolutely basic to the Gospel, the condition of the very meaningfulness of Christ's death.

The episode and parable reported in the third reading are peculiar to the Gospel according to Luke. The episode forms the context of the parable, and the parable is Jesus' comment on the episode. Jesus is the guest of a rudely inhospitable Pharisee who is shocked by Jesus' ready acceptance of kind and familiar attentions from a woman known to be a sinner. Jesus responds to the unspoken criticism by telling a simple story of two debtors, of whom one was forgiven a very small debt and the other a very large one. Jesus' concluding question as to which of these two debtors would prove more grateful receives the only plausible answer. The point of the parable, therefore, is that forgiveness elicits the loving response we call gratitude, and that the more generous the forgiveness is the more intense the response is likely to be. Jesus then applies this lesson to the case of the woman whose conspicuously loving behavior had earned the Pharisee's disapproval because she was a sinner. Just as the love of the debtor was a response to the forgiveness he had received, so, Jesus suggests, is the love shown by this woman. His remark that "her many sins are forgiven for she has loved much" is verbally ambiguous, and is often misinterpreted or mistranslated as though it meant that she had, as it were, earned her forgiveness by her loving. What it means rather is that her loving is a response to, and therefore a sign of, her being already forgiven. We have here the typical insistence of Jesus on divine initiative in forgiving sinners, an insistence expressed as much in his behavior as in his words.

TWELFTH SUNDAY OF THE YEAR

Cycle "A" Readings: Jer. 20:10-13; Rom. 5:12-15; Mt. 10:26-33

The English word "jeremiad," meaning a doleful complaint, is a fair enough reminder of the kind of message which characterized the prophet from whose name the word is derived. Jeremiah, whose personality emerges from the pages of the Old Testament with remarkable vividness, appears to have been a decidedly shy and timid man. But despite his timidity, he found himself undeniably singled out by God for a career of prophetic preaching which for such a man must have been sheer torture. His divinely enjoined task was to denounce rampant moral and religious corruption and to call for the most strenuous repentance. And such a message, scarcely ingratiating under the best of circumstances, had to be delivered at a time when many other religious leaders were gaining favor and prosperity by flattering the people's presumption and conceit. From time to time in the book of Jeremiah, the prophet's exasperation is given full vent, and the reader cannot but feel his deep frustration at being committed to a message nobody wanted to hear, and his gnawing fear of ever more bitter and ever more numerous enemies. Yet invariably these outbursts of eminently understandable desolation give way at last to restored courage and renewed determination, based on the prophet's ultimately indestructible faith in God. This is well exemplified in today's first reading, which begins on the concluding verses of one of Jeremiah's most resounding complaints, only to continue on a note of rising hope and confidence in the ultimate justice of God.

The passage from the letter to the Romans which constitutes the second reading of today's liturgy is one which has exerted enormous influence on the development of Christian theology, especially with regard to original sin, and which has been endlessly cited on opposite sides of vehement theological controversies. If we prescind from this stormy theological history and concentrate on the plainest (if not necessarily deepest) meaning of the verses, we find Paul asserting that sin, ever since the beginning of man's history, has pervaded the human family and carried death (physical and spiritual) with it as its inevitable consequence. This somber view of the human condition is one which Paul has already vigorously propounded, in both Jewish and Gentile terms, in earlier chapters of the same letter. In a sense, therefore, Paul's teaching might seem to be itself a jeremiad, for basic to it there certainly is an inflexible and universal accusation of sin which Paul will not allow to be overlooked or attenuated. However, Paul's ultimate message is quite different from Jeremiah's. For the prophet denounced human wickedness and impiety and declared what the people should do about it, namely repent and reform their ways. But Paul's no less severe denunciation of human wickedness leads him instead to a declaration of what God has done about it—namely, he sent his Son Jesus Christ, whose grace of forgiveness immeasurably exceeds man's worst capacity for wrongdoing. Paul, like Jeremiah, had a harsh divine verdict to pass on human society, and one which aroused resentment and required courage. But Paul's faith in the Gospel gives to his confidence in God a dimension of universal encouragement, even for the morally weakest of men, which we find only vaguely and remotely foreshadowed in the Old Testament prophets.

The requirement of courage on the part of those who are entrusted with divine messages to deliver is a recurrent motif in today's reading from the Gospel according to Matthew. In these eight verses we find three times repeated an explicit injunction not to be afraid. The significance of this refrain in Matthew depends on the circumstance that the author has incorporated these verses (which occupy a rather different context in Luke) within that instruction by Jesus to his missionary disciples which occupies the whole 10th chapter. This preoccupation with the problems of missionary preaching reflects the situation of the early Christian Church in its initial phase of expansion, when, in obedience to the mandate of the risen Christ and the impulse of the Holy Spirit, Christian evangelists strove to carry the Gospel to every attainable part of the civilized world. Matthew, in other words, presents Jesus' teaching in a form which maximizes its relevance to a Church of missionaries who not infrequently turned out to be martyrs. To that end, Jesus' injunctions not to fear are presented as a threefold exhortation addressed to missionaries. They are not to fear because that revelation which remained hidden before the Church's post-resurrection enlightenment must now be proclaimed openly to all. They are not to fear because the worst they have to fear, physical death, is insignificant compared to the life of the spirit. And they are not to fear, finally, because God, whose providence is coextensive with his creation, takes care of his own.

TWELFTH SUNDAY OF THE YEAR

Cycle "B" Readings: Job 38:1, 8-11; 2 Cor. 5:14-17; Mk. 4:35-41

The first reading, from the book of Job, comprises some of the early verses of the final answer given by God to the questions and complaints that Job expresses during a long series of increasingly bitter conversations with the friends who so greatly misunderstand him. The detached fragment of this divine response given by the reading fails to convey the immense power and sublime majesty that characterize the whole passage in its proper context. It begins, like the reading, with the voice of God issuing forth from a storm, but unlike the reading it does not proceed immediately to specific questions. Instead, it opens with a series of mocking taunts, inviting and compelling Job to take on divinity itself as an adversary in debate, and to experience in so doing the feebleness of his own mental resources, the narrowness and shallowness of his own experience, and the absurd arrogance of his demands that God's ways should be justified to his satisfaction. Job's is the problem of reconciling belief in a just God with his own experience of extreme suffering despite perfect innocence. His friends have been worse than useless, for their theology implies that Job's situation is simply impossible, and, fanatically, they deny the facts they are unable to explain. Tormented by his afflictions and exasperated by his counselors, Job cries out plaintive challenges to God. When at last God answers, it is to vindicate Job's innocence and to denounce his friends' dogmatism. But first, Job must be made fully aware of the immense difference and distance between his own petty reasonings and the mind of the God who created and sustains the countless inexplicable marvels of the material universe.

The second reading, from the second letter to the Corinthians, is part of a passage that resumes Paul's discussion of his apostolic role, which he had interrupted to deal with the problem of life after death. In this passage, Paul focuses on the idea that in the behavior of apostles such as himself there is an extravagance that seems, in itself, scarcely rational. However, Paul argues, it is quite rational if one believes what an apostle believes about the meaning of Christ's death. Christ's death, he asserts, entailed a kind of universal death. Part of what he means by this is brought out in the following verse, which states that "Christ died for all so that those who live might live no longer for themselves but for him who for their sake died." In other words, Christ's death, as Paul understands it, marks an end and a beginning. It marks an end to the self-seeking that is otherwise the basic motif of human living. And it marks the beginning of a radically new kind of life, closely linked with and stringently modeled upon that of Christ himself. "In terms of mere human judgment" to live such a life is nothing short of fanatical. But for Paul, such terms are no longer relevant. Paul's life, therefore, is as radical as his message, and it is radical precisely because of his message. To live such a life can only seem irrational to one who is not convinced of the truth of the message or aware of its implications. To one who is convinced and aware as an apostle must be, the opposite is true.

The third reading is the account from the Gospel according to Mark of the storm on the lake of Galilee. The same story is told, but less vividly and more briefly, in the other Synoptic Gospels. It is a miracle story, in which all the circumstances lead up to a miracle, and the miracle has didactic implications. The kind of sudden storm described is a familiar phenomenon of the place, which often proves alarming and dangerous even to experienced boatmen. The disciples' words to Jesus are softened by the other evangelists into more tactful but less realistic versions. What they express here is terror at their plight and resentment of Jesus' inactivity. There is no reason to imagine they are explicitly inviting a miracle. Indeed, expectation of a miracle would seem to imply that they had that very faith which Jesus chides them for lacking. By the same token, it is faith in God, rather than in special powers of his own, that Jesus finds irreconcilable with their panicky and desperate behavior. It is consistent with this interpretation that when Jesus does manifest his miraculous power, what the disciples express is not satisfaction and relief, but awe. A more literal rendering of the words that describe their reaction would be "they feared with a great fear." It is this sense of fear or awe, a sense of the inexplicable or uncanny, that prompts their concluding question. It is the basically thematic question underlying the writings of all the evangelists: "Who can this be?"

TWELFTH SUNDAY OF THE YEAR

Cycle "C" Readings: Zech. 12:10-11; Gal. 3:26-29; Lk. 9:18-24

The first reading consists of two verses from the book of Zechariah, which, as it now stands, contains material not only from the lifetime of Zechariah in the sixth century, but also from a source some two centuries later. The two verses which comprise the reading belong to the later material. This material is messianic in character, but its anticipation of the messianic triumph is here, as in apocalyptic literature, projected beyond Israel's political horizons to the very end of time. Moreover, the messiah is no longer conceived in terms of conventional royalty, as a powerful king who would establish political ascendancy for Israel. On the contrary, we find a conception of the messiah which is especially congenial to Christian perspective. The latter portion of the book of Zechariah describes a messiah of Davidic origin, whose dominion is to be world-wide, but whose character is by no means that of a typical world-conqueror. We read instead, in words familiar from the New Testament, of one who comes, "humble and mounted on an ass." The word here translated "humble" refers to that quality which became idealized as characterizing the "poor," who, relying in their defenselessness solely upon God, were to be the chief beneficiaries of messianic salvation. This is in fact the only kind of messianic outlook that Jesus seems to have adopted or encouraged, and the phrase which appears in the reading, "they shall look on him whom they have thrust through," was, of course, applied to Jesus in the Gospel according to John.

The second reading, from Paul's letter to the Galatians, is part of that letter's long and vehement discussion of the relationship between Mosaic law and Christian faith. The letter indicates that during Paul's absence from Galatia, the Christian community there had come under the influence of zealous agitators who contended that, just as historically Christianity presupposed Judaism, so being a faithful Christian morally and religiously presupposed being a conscientious Jew. However acceptable this might be for Jewish Christians, it was inevitably offensive to Gentiles, whose conversion was in response to the Christian Gospel, and who were neither attracted by nor interested in Judaism. In this letter as elsewhere, Paul argues vigorously against the "Judaizing" point of view in early Christianity. The passage cited in the reading represents the conclusion of his argument. He has maintained that the Mosaic law was, by God's providence, a preliminary stage in a process of maturation which culminates in the Gospel. With faith in the Gospel, Jewish law becomes as irrelevant as childhood discipline would be to a mature adult. There is, therefore, among Christians no significant distinction between Jewish converts, for whom the Mosaic law is superseded, and Gentile converts, in whose lives that law continues to have no part. In this sense Paul says to Christians that "there does not exist among you Jew or Greek." Faith suffices for salvation as indiscriminately for those of Jewish and Gentile background, as it does for slaves and masters or men and women. However, to apply this text as is often done, to the elimination of social distinctions between the sexes, or to the abolition of slavery, is to exceed Paul's meaning.

The third reading, from the Gospel according to Luke, recounts that episode which, in the Synoptic Gospels, confronts most directly the question of Jesus' messiahship. In response to Jesus' question about how people interpret his identity, he is told that some suppose that he is a prophet come back to life—a reflection of certain beliefs then current about how the messianic age would be introduced. To Peter's emphatic assertion that Jesus is himself the messiah, Jesus responds by imposing silence. Part of the significance of this somewhat surprising response is probably to be sought in the fact that currently popular conceptions of the messiah as a gloriously triumphant political leader were totally incongruous with Jesus' own style of messiahship. Accordingly, Jesus goes on to declare that "the son of man" is destined for suffering, death, and resurrection. In the book of Daniel the "son of man" is a mysterious figure of apocalyptic imagery, symbolizing Israel, and likewise committed to suffering. Luke, unlike the other Synoptic evangelists, does not report that at this point the disciples protested against

Jesus' prediction of suffering. Instead, in this account Jesus proceeds without interruption to declare that suffering is a condition imposed not only on him, but also on his followers, who must in this respect assume the attitude characteristic of the Passion. The reference to taking up one's cross is not a conventional expression, and is clearly based on knowledge of how Jesus met his death.

THIRTEENTH SUNDAY OF THE YEAR

Cycle "A" Readings: 2 Kgs. 4:8-11, 14-16; Rom. 6:3-4, 8-11; Mt. 10:37-42

The first reading, from the second book of Kings, is an episode contained in a series of miracle stories glorifying the prophet Elisha, who, earlier in the same book, is represented as having been designated by the prophet Elijah to act as his successor. Elisha is portrayed in a less humanly attractive way than his illustrious predecessor, and some of the behavior attributed to him appears harsh and unscrupulous. Elisha seems to have been esteemed less for his prophetic words than for his wonder-working activities. He is also presented as closely associated in a kind of fraternal league with other prophets, and a certain religious professionalism seems to characterize his ministry. The reading recounts the first miracle that Elijah performed for a wealthy Shunnamite woman, whose hospitality to the prophet went so far as to provide him with special quarters in her own house to use at his convenience. The miracle corresponds to a classic type of which the Bible offers several well-known examples, namely, the conferral of motherhood on a woman for whom there seemed to be no longer any hope of fertility. It is characteristic of Elisha's close political associations that his first offer to the woman was to put in a good word for her with the king or military commander. When she declined this offer it was Elisha's servant, Gehazi, who suggested the more welcome favor. Subsequently, Elisha's second miracle in the same woman's behalf was to be the restoration to life of the child whose birth was made possible by this first miracle.

The second reading, from the letter to the Romans, contains Paul's only explicit references in that letter to baptism. The passage belongs to a new phase of Paul's argument, which up to this point had dealt with salvation through faith in Christ rather than through observance of the law, and had explained that doctrine by presenting Christ as a second Adam, to whom redeemed humanity is mysteriously, but intimately and effectively related. Having thus affirmed a profound solidarity between Christians and Christ, Paul goes on to draw out some of the implications of this idea. Baptism is for Paul the rite of initiation whereby those who profess faith in Christ are made visibly part of what Paul calls elsewhere "Christ's body." The union with Christ that is thus initiated entails a kind of participation in the death and resurrection whereby Christ's redemptive mission was accomplished. Paul sees this participation as symbolized in the baptismal action itself, wherein the sequence of immersion in and emergence from the water suggests the sequence of burial and resurrection. Like the life of Christ after his resurrection, the life of a Christian after his baptism is not the resumption of his former life but the commencement of a new life. The new life of Christ himself is no longer subject to the influence of sin, of which death is the outstanding manifestation. So too, Paul declares, the Christian in his new life is, at least incipiently, brought into that new condition of existence which Christ now totally experiences. Thus the sincerely baptized Christian is said to be "dead to sin but alive for God in Christ Jesus." What this means is further explored and more concretely declared as the letter proceeds. For Paul it is a basic formulation of the essential meaning of Christian existence.

The third reading, from the Gospel according to Matthew, is part of a collection of sayings about what it means to be a disciple. That the notion of discipleship is of cardinal importance in this Gospel we are reminded by the fact that it ends with Jesus' climactic words of appeal to "make disciples of all nations." The material found in the reading concerns first of all the proper attitude of a disciple, and second, the proper attitude toward a disciple. Though distinct, both of these teachings have a common basis in the identification or solidarity of Christ's disciples with Christ himself. With respect to the proper attitude of a disciple, this means that the disciple's first priority must be his fidelity to Christ, and that this fidelity will be manifested in a basic resemblance at crucial points between his own life and his master's. With respect to the proper attitude toward a disciple what is here maintained is that one's treatment of a disciple is to be regarded as the practical equivalent of one's treatment of Christ himself. Moreover, in view of Jesus' messianic relationship to the Father, it is further maintained that one's response to a disciple is the practical expression of one's response to God himself. There is therefore, an important difference of implication between the kindness and respect which acknowledge someone to be a "holy man" or even a "prophet," and the acknowledgment of a disciple as representing the Messiah sent by God.

THIRTEENTH SUNDAY OF THE YEAR

Cycle "B" Readings: Wis. 1:13-15; 2:23-25; 2 Cor. 8:7, 9, 13-15; Mk. 5:21-43

The book of Wisdom, from which the first reading is taken, is one of those writings, retained in the Roman Catholic Bible, which Jews and most other Christians relegate to the category of "Apocrypha," because they were not part of the Hebrew scriptures. Whatever opinions they may hold concerning the canonical status of a book like Wisdom, all Christians should be aware of its very extensive use in the liturgy until very recent times, and of its very strong influence on many aspects of Christian thought, including thought contained in the New Testament itself. Artificially attributed to King Solomon, Wisdom was written in Greek by a Jew of Alexandria nearly a thousand years after Solomon and scarcely a century before Christianity came into being. As a result, Wisdom exhibits many characteristically Greek forms of thought and expression which are much more familiar to our own theological traditions than to those of Israel. Today's reading exemplifies this in its emphasis on the idea of personal, individual immortality and its implications for both speculative and practical ethics. The basic premise of the author in the passages cited is that God neither wants nor causes death, the explanation of which must be looked for elsewhere. In general, that explanation is to be found in moral evil, which is as alien to the actions and intentions of God as death itself. This moral evil is ascribed in the first instance to wicked human beings, who "by their words and deeds have asked death for his company." But the author also looks to diabolical wickedness as responsible for death, on the grounds that "it was the devil's spite that brought death into the world, and the experience of it is reserved for those who take his side." This understanding of death as resulting from the combined evil of men and of the devil is closely related in this book to an understanding of immortality as the consequence, and therefore the sanction, of moral goodness. The arrogance of sinners is thus attributed to their ignoring of the momentous fact that "God created man for immortality" with its momentous implication that "holiness of life would have its recompense."

The second liturgical reading, from the second letter to the Corinthians, refers to a collection which, according to an earlier passage in Galatians, St. Paul organized in fulfillment of a promise he had made in Jerusalem to contribute to the support of poor Christians in that city. This collection, taken up among the Gentile churches Paul had founded, is mentioned in several of his letters, and in the second letter to the Corinthians Paul praises the Christians of Corinth for responding to his appeal with particular enthusiasm. He tells the Corinthians that he has sent them some friends of his to arrange for the collection before his own arrival, and he takes the occasion to exhort them once more to give generously. In the liturgical reading, which connects several separated verses Paul first insists that the contributions be made freely, and not grudgingly conceded, citing in this sense the Greek version of an Old Testament proverb, "God loves a cheerful giver." He also insists that God will reward the generous by providing them with enough both for their own needs and for their charity. He observes that the kind of generosity he anticipates will kindle in others gratitude and praise for the God who inspires it. And, finally, he regards this generosity as itself a grateful response to God for "his gift beyond words." The reference here is, of course, to the ultimate motivation of all Christian charity, that "good news" which is the basis of Christianity itself, the unmerited grace of God bestowed on sinful mankind in Jesus Christ. Paul's whole discussion of this collection for the poor of Jerusalem furnishes a set of Christian reflections whose relevance to ecclesiastical "money-raising" deserves more attention that it often receives, and offers useful correctives to uncritically commercial attitudes and procedures.

The third reading, from the Gospel according to Mark, comprises a story within a story. Both the way the stories are combined and the way they are narrated have persuaded a number of critical scholars that these accounts are unusually close to the actual events they are reporting. Both stories deal with miraculous cures. One of them takes place while Jesus is on his way to the scene of the other one in response to an explicit appeal. The intervening episode is peculiar, in that the woman's hemorrhage is cured without any deliberate intention or action on the part of Jesus. No doubt the woman's reliance on merely touching Jesus' garment could in itself be interpreted in sheerly superstitious or magical terms. But such an interpretation is opposed by Jesus' own explanation that "your faith has saved you," where "faith" must be assumed to retain its usual meaning in the Synoptics of reliance upon the power and mercy of God. That such faith in God should be elicited and found effective in particular material circumstances closely associated with Jesus is both intelligible in itself and helpful for an understanding of Christian sacramental practice. For, like the woman's behavior, any Christian's recourse to sacraments can represent an act either of superstition or of faith, and to determine objectively which of the two it does represent requires divine, not human powers of discernment. The far more spectacular miracle of raising the dead daughter of Jairus is likewise attributed to faith, only in this case it is the faith not of the subject of the cure but of another who loves and intercedes for her. Here again, the relationship suggested between human faith and divine grace calls to mind sacramental parallels, and in particular the significance attributed to the community's faith in relation to the individual's grace. If miracle stories of this kind serve to illustrate and emphasize the Christian conviction of salvation by faith, they should also serve to discourage over-simplified interpretations of that conviction.

THIRTEENTH SUNDAY OF THE YEAR

Cycle "C" Readings: 1 Kgs. 19:16, 19-21; Gal. 5:1, 13-18; Lk. 9:51-62

The first reading taken from the first book of Kings, describes the process by which the prophet Elijah was provided with a successor in the person of Elisha. The story of Elijah is recounted in five distinguishable sections of the two books of Kings, and this episode is narrated in the second of them. Its background is the flight of Elijah to escape the mortal vengeance sworn by Jezebel, pagan wife of Ahab, a ninth-century king of Israel. Elijah had resolutely opposed the queen's efforts to paganize Israel, and finally carried his resistance to the point of massacring four-hundred-and-fifty prophets of the Canaanite deity, Baal. While fugitive in the wilderness across the border in Judah, Elijah was summoned by God to Mt. Horeb, the place of Moses' reception of the covenant, where God spoke to him. Elijah was told to anoint Hazael king of Damascus, a future enemy of Israel, to anoint Jehu king of Israel, who later succeeded Ahab, and to anoint Elisha his own prophetic successor. It is only the last of these commissions that Elijah is said to have carried out personally. Elijah's throwing of his cloak over Elisha symbolized the adoption and empowerment of the one who would succeed him. Elisha's assumption of his new role is dramatized by destroying the plow and oxen that had been the means of his former livelihood, and making them the materials of a sacrifice.

The second reading, from Paul's letter to the Galatians, must be read in the context of that letter's main purpose, which is to refute the contention, vigorously upheld by Paul's adversaries, that to be a Christian made it necessary for one to assume the obligations of the Mosaic law. Paul has repeatedly asserted that the Gospel, far from binding its adherents to Jewish law, freed them from enslavement to that law. Thus he contended that faith, rather than the "works" of the law, was the key to salvation. This contention, however, raised another issue that has never ceased to be a focus of dispute. For Paul's vigorous rejection of the law in favor of the Gospel, or of "works" in favor of faith, can easily be interpreted to mean that morality itself, with which the law was greatly concerned, is irrelevant to Christianity and even to salvation. Martin Luther's notoriously paradoxical injunction to "sin strongly, but believe more strongly still" illustrates the problem with rhetorical vividness. Paul's recognition of the difficulty, and the gist of his answer to it, are expressed in the reading, which begins, "do not take on yourselves the yoke of slavery" (meaning the Jewish law), but immediately adds the warning that this is "not a freedom which gives free rein to the flesh." And Paul continues by asserting that Christians are indeed subject to obligation, but the basis of their obligation is no longer the law, but rather "love" which is "in accord with the Spirit." Paul, therefore, in opposing "faith" to "works" is not opposing himself to morality. He is rather transposing morality from a legal to a spiritual basis, and envisioning it not as preliminary to, but as consequent upon God's gift of justification. For Paul, morality is a vital manifestation of the new life of the "new man."

The reading from the Gospel according to Luke contains material that is partly shared by the other Synoptic Gospels and in part peculiar to Luke. It begins with a clear statement that the consummation of Jesus' mission is not far off, and the suffering which leads to that consummation is clearly implied in the phrase that Jesus "firmly resolved" to go to Jerusalem. The whole tone of the passage is meant to suggest that the journey is, as it were, the beginning of the end. Ironically, the fact that Jesus is on his way to

Jerusalem excludes him from the hospitality of the Samaritans, who had long since established their own religious center in opposition to the holy city of their persecutors. The irony of this episode is intensified by the fact that the Gospel which alone narrates it is also the only Gospel to record, in the very next chapter, the parable of the Good Samaritan. Bearing in mind that Jesus' traveling is, from this point on, a journey to his passion and death, one detects the special significance of those who, in the following verses, offer themselves or are summoned to follow Jesus. To follow him, at this point, can be no casual accompaniment of a wandering preacher. It can only be a matter of going where Jesus is unswervingly headed. Consequently, in this context, the following of Jesus takes on its full meaning, and implies the full "cost of discipleship." The three nameless characters who are represented as potential followers of Jesus are all, in one way or another, unprepared to assume the "cost of discipleship," and Jesus' words are designed to exclude all possibility of their supposing that cost to be less than it is.

FOURTEENTH SUNDAY OF THE YEAR

Cycle "A" Readings: Zech. 9:9-10; Rom. 8:9, 11-13; Mt. 11:25-30

The first reading is from the book of Zechariah. Zechariah was a prophet active in the latter part of the sixth century. A large part of the book that bears his name, however, including the reading, appears to have been added more than two centuries later. The content of this later material is strongly messianic, but it shows striking differences from messianic material found in older parts of the Bible. Rather than a new phase in the national history of Israel, what the Messiah's coming is here associated with is the final phase of the history of the world. More like apocalyptic than traditional prophetic literature, the last part of the book of Zechariah envisages a final battle, situated at Jerusalem, the outcome of which is tantamount to final judgment. Following the victory of the Lord's forces in the ultimate struggle, the Lord's reign will be permanent and unopposed. The Messiah himself whom this part of the book describes is also significantly different from earlier versions. Although royalty of Davidic origin is ascribed to him, his character is such as the reading describes. He is poor and humble, and the dominion he introduces is not one of military and national supremacy, but a reign of universal peace in which the instruments and activities of war have no part. The agreement of this messianic conception with that of the New Testament is striking. And the influence of this book on the New Testament is evident even in details, such as the description here, applied to the appearance of Jesus on Palm Sunday.

The second reading comprises four verses from the letter to the Romans. The fact that the word spirit occurs six times in those four verses is a clear enough indication of the main subject of the passage from which they are taken. It belongs to a part of the letter that comes just after Paul's account of the human predicament resulting from reliance on obedience to the law as the means to achieving a right relationship with God. Paul contends that complete obedience to the law is simply beyond human moral strength, with the result that human ideals and human conduct tend in opposite directions. The predicament finds its solution through faith in Christ as the means to salvation. Through union with Christ, the external standard of the law is replaced by the internal dynamism of the Spirit, that divine principle of vitality by which Jesus was raised from the dead. For Paul and his contemporary Christians, this dynamism was considered to be manifested in a great many extraordinary phenomena. The most fundamentally important of these phenomena are those that make a Christian's life most like Christ's own life, and earlier in this same letter Paul had characterized the presence of the Spirit as "God's love flooding our hearts." To be "in the Spirit" means for one's life to be dominated by the power of divine love. Not to be dominated by that power, but to be controlled instead by natural human cravings is what Paul understands as being "in the flesh." He is here reminding his readers of the tremendous difference between these two principles of life, and of the difference this should make in the way they live their lives.

The third reading contains two passages which the Gospel according to Matthew presents as having been spoken by Jesus during his ministry in Galilee. Both of them, like so much of what this Gospel contains, are mainly concerned with discipleship. The first is about the kind of people who do, and the kind of people who do not become disciples of Jesus, and it is expressed in a prayer of thanksgiving to the Father. The second is an invitation and encouragement to become Jesus' disciples, addressed to those who find their situation in life burdensome. Jesus' contrast between the "learned and clever" from whom God's revelation is hidden, and the "merest children" to whom it is made manifest, is in keeping with this Gospel's relentless indictment of the religious leaders of the Jews. The reference to the "learned and clever" resembles a similarly critical verse of Isaiah, which is also taken up by Paul, who severely berates conventional religious wisdom for its insensitivity to revelation. The kind of people who typically do follow Jesus in this Gospel account are at best socially undistinguished and at worst socially disreputable. The references to them as "children" or "little ones" connotes primarily their human inadequacy and social insignificance rather than any romantic idealization of childhood. The reference in the second passage to Jesus' easy yoke and light burden recalls similar language in a chapter of Sirach which also contains verses very similar to the opening words of each of these passages. Jesus appears to be presented here as the source of a higher wisdom, just as he is presented elsewhere as the source of a higher law.

FOURTEENTH SUNDAY OF THE YEAR

Cycle "B" Readings: Ezek. 2:2-5; 2 Cor. 12:7-10; Mk. 6:1-6

The first reading is a passage which, in the book of Ezekiel, immediately follows a description of this prophet's most famous vision. This strange vision, which was profoundly to influence imaginations in succeeding ages, is highly elaborate. Its basic constituents, however, are a representation of divine glory enthroned upon a wheeled vehicle, and four monsters of combined human and animal appearance, borrowed from Assyrian mythology, that move the vehicle's wheels. Whatever else this bizarre picture may imply, it appears to signify at least that Israel's God is, so to speak, mobile, and that the terrifying forces of paganism are as humbly at the disposal of Israel's God as the merest draft animals. The relevance of such symbolism becomes apparent when we recall that Ezekiel was a temple priest who experienced the fall of Jerusalem and who shared the Babylonian captivity of his people. Ezekiel interpreted these events as acts of divine justice, fulfilling rather than frustrating God's plan. Ezekiel's first prophetic mission, given to him shortly before these catastrophic events, requires him to proclaim God's word to Israel with every reason to expect that Israel will disregard or disobey God's word. Ezekiel's prophecy is not to soften Israel's heart, but rather to demonstrate its obdurate hardness and thereby demonstrate the abundant justice of the punishing events which are soon to follow. The unenviable task of transmitting divine messages to people who more than likely will resent and reject them is characteristic of the great prophets of the Old Testament. As God says to Ezekiel: "When you say to them, 'These are the words of the Lord God,' they will know that they have a prophet among them, whether they listen or whether they refuse to listen, because they are rebels. But you, man, must not be afraid of them."

The visionary experience of a prophet like Ezekiel finds a certain parallel in Paul's declaration, in his second letter to the Corinthians, that he has been no stranger to "visions and revelations granted by the Lord." This is not, however, a matter which Paul refers to frequently, or even comfortably. He seems to mention it at all only in order to make the point that his own religious experience is quite as rich as any that other preachers may choose to boast about, and that even in this respect their credentials are in no way superior to his own. But Paul was also keenly aware that extraordinary religious experiences can easily become an end in themselves and an occasion of conceited self-esteem. Paul did not consider himself exempt from this kind of temptation, and he considered that God had given him, as a safeguard against it, a severe affliction, which he does not identify in any more specific terms than as a "sharp pain in my body." Although innumerable efforts have been made to identify this affliction of which Paul speaks, there is little or no evidence to support any of the resultant conjectures. Whatever Paul's trouble may have been, there are only two things he wished to make public about it. In the first place, it was a source of grave suffering, from which he begged God to release him. And in the second place, the result of his prayers was not to rid him of this suffering but to convince him of its value as a preservative against pride by reminding him of his own weakness, which derived all its real effectiveness from the grace of God that "comes to its full strength in weakness."

Insofar as we understand by a prophet a human being who acts as God's chosen spokesman in transmitting divine revelation, Jesus Christ was undoubtedly, among other things, a prophet. This was probably one of the principal ways in which his mission was interpreted by his contemporaries, just as it is the basis on which Moslems continue to honor Jesus without regarding him as literally divine. And as with the Old Testament prophets, the prophetic role of Jesus both demanded and suffered from the human ordinariness of the prophet himself. Jesus' social origins were familiar and humble. He did not appear on the scene of his ministry suddenly and mysteriously or with any awe-inspiring accompaniment. His ministry never took him very far from his home town and it sometimes brought him very close to it. And when it did, as we are reminded by today's third reading, from the Gospel according to Mark, he experienced that kind of familiarity which is said proverbially to breed contempt. "Who does he think he is?" is the kind of public reaction reflected in this episode as characterizing those who knew his family and remembered the ordinariness of his upbringing. This disdain, perhaps not unmixed with a certain envy, prevented these people from taking Jesus seriously. And in refusing to take Jesus seriously, they prevented themselves from taking seriously what came to them through Jesus—the power and wisdom of God. Consequently, their negative attitude toward Jesus meant, in the last analysis, a refusal of faith. And by refusing faith they cut themselves off from the effective influence of God's power and wisdom. Hence, "he could work no miracle there, except that he put his hands on a few sick people and healed them; and he was taken aback by their want of faith."

FOURTEENTH SUNDAY OF THE YEAR

Cycle "C" Readings: Is. 66:10-14; Gal. 6:14-18; Lk. 10:1-12, 17-20

The first reading of today's liturgy comes from that final portion of the book of Isaiah which is sometimes called Third Isaiah to signify that its contents are of much later origin than those of previous chapters. It belongs to the period after the Babylonian exile had ended and the restoration of Jerusalem had begun, and it reflects the attitudes and issues of that time.

The liturgical passage is part of an apocalyptic poem. Its tone is one of warm consolation and exalted hope, based on assurance that Jerusalem, having survived humiliation at the hands of her enemies, is now destined to enjoy the abundant blessings of God. In keeping with the idea that Jerusalem's fate is the fate of her people, the imagery of this consoling poem likens the city to a mother and the people to the infant children who rely on her for nourishment and comfort. The experience of the city's restoration is thus likened to the happiness of babies nursing at full breasts and reveling in maternal caresses. These metaphorical delights are still in prospect, for the era of restoration has only just begun. The message, therefore, is one of promise for the future, intended to overcome any popular misgivings and to bolster national morale. The image of the full-breasted mother is thus a forecast of the city's anticipated restoration, by the power of God, to wealth, power, and prestige.

The second reading, from Paul's letter to the Galatians, comprises the concluding verses of that letter. They are introduced by a final denunciation of the adversaries whom Paul assails throughout the entire letter, those who would impose upon Christians the whole burden of Mosaic Law, with its array of ritual observances. Paul's concluding assault on these people is the frankly cynical contention that their motivation is basically self-serving. He accuses them of advocating Jewish observances simply to escape persecution by the Jews. He even charges them with the hypocrisy of insisting on circumcision merely to keep on the right side of the Jews, without actually observing the rigorous legal demands to which that ritual makes them subject. Thus Paul contrasts the behavior of those whose "only purpose is to evade persecution for the cross of Christ" with his own resolution never to "boast of anything but the cross of our Lord Jesus Christ."

Paul goes on to declare what does matter and what does not matter, thereby emphasizing the fundamental difference between himself and his adversaries. What does not matter in the least, according to Paul, is "whether one is circumcised or not." What alone does matter supremely for Paul is "that one is created anew." Since this new creation is achieved through the cross, it is only the cross that is suitable matter for "boasting."

The third reading, from the Gospel according to Luke, is one of a number of passages dealing with discipleship, which this Gospel places at the beginning of Jesus' final journey toward Jerusalem. The occasion is Jesus' dispatching of a group of disciples, whose number, seventy-two, is a traditional symbolic enumeration of all the nations of the world. The occasion, therefore, suggests a universal mission entrusted to the emissaries of Jesus. The mission is likened to the work of harvesting a ripe crop, which because of its ripeness cannot be delayed, even though few workers be available for the vast undertaking. This note of urgency pervades the whole passage, and what may seem rather eccentric or pointless instructions may be understood as ways of emphasizing that no time can be spared, even for passing pleasantries, and that nothing resembling excess baggage is tolerable under the circumstances.

All this emphasis on haste and immediacy pertains to a sense of the imminence of that Kingdom of God which Jesus is understood to be bringing upon humankind. As the Kingdom is the whole point of Jesus' mission, to which everything else in his life must be subordinated and may be sacrificed, so too is it the whole point of his disciples' mission, to which they also must expect to sacrifice all other concerns. In the subsequent passage, which recounts the return of the disciples to Jesus after their mission, it is made clear that what the disciples are engaged in is the redemptive mission of Jesus himself, the overthrowing of satanic power, the vanquishing of evil. The whole episode is undoubtedly best understood as an anticipation of the missionary effort of the early Church, which brought the saving Gospel of the Kingdom to all nations.

FIFTEENTH SUNDAY OF THE YEAR

Cycle "A" Readings: Is. 55:10-11; Rom. 8:18-23; Mt. 13:1-23

The first reading is taken from what is often called Second Isaiah, a part of the book of Isaiah that was evidently composed long after the lifetime of the prophet for whom the book is named. The time of its composition was one of renewed hope for Israel, with the imminent prospect that release from exile would make possible the reoccupation and reconstruction of the divinely given homeland. The verses selected for the reading are part of a poem that celebrates the generosity and faithfulness of God to his people. Its words are presented as spoken by God himself, who begins by issuing an invitation for the hungry poor to come and enjoy a banquet he has prepared for them. What this represents is the institution of a new covenant, replacing the covenant forfeited by sinfulness, and destined this time to last forever. This new covenant, moreover, is not exclusively for the people of Israel, but through them it extends its summons to the Gentile world as well. In preparation for this new covenant the people are called to repentance and reform. The promise itself is represented as a triumph of divine graciousness, far exceeding the reach of merely human expectations. The accomplishment of the promised marvel is guaranteed by the invincible power of God's word. In the verses given in the reading, the life-giving efficacy of that word is likened to that of the snow and rain that irrigate the earth and restore it to fertility. The poem concludes with a lyric description of luxuriant new growth bursting forth from a desert landscape.

The second reading, from the letter to the Romans, comes just after Paul, having developed the idea that to be guided by the Spirit of God is to be one of the children of God, carries this metaphor a step further by observing that to be a child is also to be an heir. God's children, therefore, are like Christ himself God's heirs. By thus introducing the idea of a divine heritage, Paul turns his perspective from the present to the future, in which the full richness of salvation is to be experienced. But the way to that future heritage, for the Christian as for Christ himself, lies through suffering. This reflection provides Paul's point of departure for the passage presented in the reading, in which "the sufferings of the present" are said to be "as nothing compared with the glory to be revealed in us." Thus for Paul a Christian attitude toward suffering comprises both fortitude and longing. The Christian can endure his afflictions bravely because he knows not merely that they will end, but that what they will end with is something incomparably good. Moreover, the tremendous disproportion between the suffering he endures and the glory he anticipates gives the Christian a predominantly forward-looking orientation. As in the biblical account of creation the material world is conceived as intimately related and essentially subordinated to human existence, so here Paul regards the present plight and future prospect of the material world as inseparable from the human condition and destiny. He accordingly represents the whole of created nature as sharing in humanity's eager, confident longing.

The third reading comprises three distinct elements which are joined together in all three Synoptic Gospels as here in the Gospel according to Matthew, but which seem to have originated quite separately. The first element is Jesus' parable about a farmer's seed which fell on various kinds of terrain and only flourished where it found good soil, but there produced an abundant harvest. Jesus seems to have used this simple story to express his conviction that the preaching of the Kingdom of God, despite the ambiguous response it initially received, was sure of ultimate success. The plainness of the parable is somewhat obscured by the fact that the evangelist has placed right after it an account, clearly taken from a different source, of a conversation in which Jesus' disciples ask about his use of parables and are told in answer that the parables are designed not for comprehension but for incomprehension, so as to fulfill a saying of Isaiah about the hardening of the people's hearts and their deafness to prophecy. It is evident that we have here an interpretation of parable which is entirely foreign to Jesus' use of parables, and the use made of them by Jewish teachers generally, which was as a teaching device, designed to simplify, clarify, and intensify a message, not to conceal it. On the basis of this notion that parables are difficult to understand, a detailed interpretation is then attributed to Jesus as a kind of private lesson given to his disciples. This too is a later addition, more characteristic of Greek than of Jewish literary usage, and apparently used to give the parable a new application suitable to Gentile Christian churches.

FIFTEENTH SUNDAY OF THE YEAR

Cycle "B" Readings: Amos 7:12-15; Eph. 1:3-14; Mk. 6:7-13

Amos, from whose prophecy the first reading is taken, is the earliest of the Old Testament prophets whose messages have come down to us in the form of written books. Amos was a Judean who delivered his prophecies at Bethel, a place in the northern kingdom which served as a royal sanctuary and attracted much unfavorable attention from prophets like Amos, who denounced current modes of worship as hollow religiosity which coexisted easily with flagrant injustice. In the episode from which the reading is taken, Amaziah, the priest of Bethel, has denounced Amos to the king, Jeroboam, as a conspirator who has come from the southern kingdom announcing that Jeroboam will die by the sword. Having thus kindled royal anger against the prophet, Amaziah warns Amos that he must return to his own country and never again venture to prophesy at Bethel. In the course of delivering this warning, Amaziah refers to Amos as one who earns his living by prophesying, thus categorizing him as one of a rather disreputable group of mercenary or professional prophets for whom prophecy was a means of livelihood, a kind of business, controlled more by laws of supply and demand than by divine inspiration. Amos protests angrily against being classified with those prophets who say what it pays them to say when it pays them to say it. His words "I am no prophet . . . nor a prophet's son" are a denial that he belongs to the kind of prophetic fraternity in which such abuses were common. Amos' livelihood is not that of a prophet but that of "a herdsman and a dresser of sycamore-figs." In prophesying he is not plying a trade, but responding to the quite unsolicited invitation of God, who "took me as I followed the flock and said to me: 'Go and prophesy to my people Israel.' " Like all the great prophets of Israel, Amos' status in the service of God is not that of a volunteer or professional careerist, but that of a draftee. His role is not one that he chose but one that he was assigned. And so he may be expected to say what God wants him to say, wherever and whenever God wants him to say it. Prophets of this kind are always dangerous. And prophets of this kind are always in danger.

The letter to the Ephesians, written either by or in close dependence on St. Paul, begins on a very lofty note of praise to "the God and Father of our Lord Jesus Christ who has bestowed on us in Christ every spiritual blessing." The passage chosen for the second reading of today's liturgy develops this theme of praise by focusing on six principal aspects of what is meant by these "spiritual blessings" which come to us from God through Christ. First is God's decision, antecedent to the creation of the world, to consecrate us to himself in holiness and love. Second, this was to be achieved by making us, through Jesus, God's own sons. Third, the means to this end was the forgiveness made possible in virtue of Jesus' sacrifice. Fourth, God made known the full scope of his eternal plan to unify all things in Christ. Fifth, the realization of this plan was based on the fulfillment of Israel's messianic hope. And sixth, the good news of salvation was carried beyond Israel to the Gentiles, who are being addressed in this letter. What is most striking to the Christian reader of this passage is that it presents, and appears to take for granted, an extraordinarily expansive understanding of Jesus Christ. In the pattern of most Christian thinking, even today, Christ is introduced first, both logically and chronologically, at a point which comes after the creation, the fall, and the religious history of Israel. And Christ is introduced at that point exclusively as a kind of emergency measure by which God rescued humankind from the consequences of sin which would otherwise have thwarted God's creative purpose. In Ephesians, on the other hand, while nothing of this conception is contradicted, we find a pattern of thought which situates Christ at the very fountainhead of creation, as the divine means ordained from all eternity and applied through all of history to unite humankind in the closest intimacy with God.

The third reading, from the Gospel according to Mark, narrates an episode from Jesus' lifetime that clearly anticipates the missionary character of that Church which came into being only after Jesus' resurrection. Whereas the proper function of an apostle is normally identified as preaching the Gospel, the activity of those whom Jesus sends at this point is described in more restricted terms as calling for repentance, driving out devils, and healing the sick. But although this kind of activity is not a preaching of the Gospel in that full Christian sense which depends upon the significance of Christ's resurrection, it clearly does, like Jesus' own public ministry, proclaim the good news of the Kingdom of God, a fulfillment of messianic hopes manifested in moral, spiritual, and physical healing. This ministry, inaugurated by Jesus and carried on by those whom he sends, represents that aspect of the unfolding mystery of God's eternal purpose which, in the previous reading from Ephesians, was identified with God's will "that we (namely the Jews), who were the first to set our hope on Christ (that is, the Messiah), should cause his glory to be praised." The next aspect of that unfolding mystery would be the worldwide apostolate of the Church—what for Christians is understood to be the present phase of the eternal plan of God to unite us with himself.

FIFTEENTH SUNDAY OF THE YEAR

Cycle "C" Readings: Deut. 30:10-14; Col. 1:15-20; Lk. 10:25-37

The Book of Deuteronomy, from which the first reading is taken, was traditionally regarded by Jews and Christians as the work of Moses himself, and the last of the "books of Moses" which are the first five books in our Bible. Critical scholarship has long demonstrated that the book is of much more recent composition, and that its ascription to Moses of speeches like the one in today's reading is a device of literary fiction. These speeches are represented as having been addressed by Moses to his people on the west side of the river Jordan, shortly before Moses' death and their own entry into the promised land. The outstanding purpose of the speeches is to insist on the people's fidelity to the Law of God (identified, of course, with the "Law of Moses") and on the close, inseparable connection between their obedience to God's law and their enjoyment of God's blessings.

The biblical writers of Deuteronomy, and of the series of historical books that Deuteronomy introduces, are constantly concerned to emphasize that, as far as Israel is concerned, divine law is the key to human success. In accordance with this theme, the historical books following Deuteronomy interpret major events, like the establishment in Palestine of an Israelite kingdom, and the later political devastations of that kingdom, as rewards and punishments bestowed by God according to his people's observance or neglect of his law. The present passage accordingly exhorts the people to keep in mind that the law which Israel had, so to speak, learned by heart was the indispensable condition of personal and national well-being.

The letter to the Colossians, from which the second reading is taken, although traditionally ascribed to St. Paul, is thought by many scholars to be the work of another writer. One reason for this opinion is that the letter contains material that seems in many ways much more highly developed theologically than comparable material elsewhere in the Pauline literature. This point is abundantly illustrated by the reading, where we are presented with a remarkably broad and exalted conception of Jesus Christ. This is most evident in the way this passage carries its account of Jesus far beyond not only the chronological boundaries of his earthly life, but also beyond the usual interpretation of his redemptive death and resurrection. The Christ of this passage is not simply God's obedient servant and emissary, but the visible manifestation of divinity. He is not simply the Messiah who comes at the appointed time in Israel's history, but the timeless principle and prototype of all creation. He is Lord not only of humankind, but also of the loftiest unseen realms of spiritual being. The scope of his sacrificial mission is here seen as nothing less than the total reconciliation to God of the whole created universe.

Closely related to this greatly expanded theology of Christ is the conception of the Church, not simply as a body in the sense of an organic unity, but as a body of which Christ is the head, or controlling principle. Here, and in the somewhat similar letter to the Ephesians, the doctrine of the body of Christ, as applied to the Church, reaches its fullest biblical development.

The parable of the good Samaritan is found only in the Gospel according to Luke. In that document it is attached to the teaching which is several times attributed to Jesus in the New Testament, that the Law of God is reducible to two basic commandments, bidding us to love God unreservedly and to love our neighbor as ourselves. As centuries of Christianity have sadly demonstrated, these Christian commandments are admired more universally than they are obeyed and more uniformly than they are interpreted. Indeed, they are often interpreted in such a way as to leave intact the very prejudices they most oppose. Most of the interpretations which do the gravest violence to their meaning involve greatly constricted meanings of both love and neighbor.

The parable of the good Samaritan is calculated to resist this tendency to narrow the meaning of neighbor. Thus it is introduced by the question "Who is my neighbor?" The question is answered by telling a story about three men who discover in turn the plight of a wretched victim, and only one of whom behaves toward the sufferer in a way that expresses the mentality of a genuine neighbor. Thus the structure of the story draws the hearer away from the discriminatory implications of the question "Who is my neighbor?" while directing his or her attention instead to what being a neighbor means in terms of active benevolence. The fact that in the story it is one of the despised social group called Samaritans who alone behaves like a neighbor further intensifies the parable's anti-discriminatory force.

SIXTEENTH SUNDAY OF THE YEAR

Cycle "A" Readings: Wis. 12:13, 16-19; Rom. 8:26-27; Mt. 13:24-43

The first reading is from what is called the Wisdom of Solomon, although actually written some eight centuries after Solomon's own lifetime. Although included in Roman Catholic bibles it is not considered a canonical scripture by Jews or Protestants. The part of the book from which the reading is taken presents a very brief recapitulation of the ancient history recounted in the first four books of the Bible, interwoven with theological commentary by the author. He is chiefly interested in what the events of this period reveal about the character of divine Wisdom, which is understood here as more or less equivalent to what is generally called divine providence. The whole series of events is thus interpreted as the object of God's very special interest and very active control. All of his intervention is understood to be irresistibly powerful, and much of it is perceived to be severely punishing, mainly toward the enemies of God's people. But it is benevolence and mercy rather than punitive force that these passages mainly wish to establish as divine attributes attested by history. Thus even the Egyptians of the Exodus and the Canaanites of the conquest are represented (not always quite convincingly) as having been treated more leniently than they had any right to expect. The first verse of the reading develops the idea that, in acting mercifully, God does so entirely on his own, for there is no higher standard than God to which God might defer. Divine responses are ultimate and autonomous. If, as the author contends, divine responses are also characteristically benevolent and merciful, that is because God is himself benevolent and merciful.

The second reading, from the letter to the Romans, is a passage that comes just after Paul has described the world as a suffering world, in which not only humankind, but the whole cosmic environment, are united in a kind of universal dynamic tension. Implicit in this condition is the suffering of an intense longing or striving for an ultimately satisfying destiny. Christian faith imparts the assurance that such a destiny is real and attainable. But, however buoyed up they may be by the confident expectation of a glorious outcome, human beings, in their still unfulfilled condition, remain very weak creatures. Since, moreover, the consummation they wait and hope for is entirely beyond their present power to envisage, human beings cannot articulate their longing, cannot express, even as the object of their deepest prayer, what it is they ultimately seek. It seems very likely that these are the kinds of considerations that lead Paul to his next theme, the one expressed in the reading. Since the human mind as such has no competence to conceive and express what it most profoundly longs for, "we do not know how to pray as we ought." And yet the Spirit of God, being the source no less of this human longing than of its divine fulfillment, forms a vital link between the one and the other. The Spirit may thus be said to "make intercession for us with groanings which cannot be expressed in speech." In other words, the ultimate aspiration of human life, however mysterious and inexpressible for human beings themselves, is full of meaning for God because it is from God's own inspiration that it originates. It is by God's prompting that, however uncomprehendingly we seek God, and all the validity there is to prayer depends on that ultimate, interior plea that issues rather from our being than from our wishes and thoughts.

The third reading comprises two parables of Jesus and an explanation of the first which was probably added by the writer of the Gospel according to Matthew. As often happens with later interpretations, the relatively simple point of the original story is somewhat obscured by the tendency, more Greek than Hebrew, to attach distinct meanings to a lot of details in the narrative. In this case, the point of the original story is concentrated in the harvester's question and the owner's answer to it. Since a good crop is mixed up with weeds, the question is raised whether or not to separate out the weeds during the growing season. The answer is negative, in the first place because such a procedure risks losing some of the good growth along with the bad, and in the second place because a much better opportunity will be provided by harvest time. The story plainly points toward the final judgment, preceding that ultimate arrival of the Kingdom of God which is often likened figuratively to a harvest. At the same time it warns against any human efforts to anticipate a kind of discrimination for which God alone is competent. In the interpretation of the evangelist, this warning note is lost in the process of allegorizing a parable that originally called for patience in leaving judgment to God. The short parable of the leaven is one of several that contrast insignificant beginnings with great eventual developments. They reassure the hearers that the unimpressive initial response to Jesus' preaching of the kingdom neither frustrates nor invalidates the Gospel.

SIXTEENTH SUNDAY OF THE YEAR
Cycle "B" Readings: Jer. 23:1-6; Eph. 2:13-18; Mk. 6:30-34

Both in the pagan religions of lands bordering Palestine and in the religion of Israel itself, "shepherd" was used as a divine title suggesting the divine "pastoral" functions of providing guidance, sustenance, and protection. Both in and around Israel, "shepherd" was also a title applied to kings, in view of the analogous functions they were expected to perform in political society. As is well known, it was strongly insisted upon in Israel that God alone was to be regarded as king in any absolute and ultimate sense of the word. By the same token, that "shepherding" which was done by human kings and to a lesser degree by other human authorities was considered entirely subordinate to the divine "shepherding." In the passage read in today's liturgy from the prophecy of Jeremiah, the prophet reproaches in God's name those who have abused the function of shepherds in Israel, and declares God's determination to dispense with these shepherds and to do his own shepherding directly and immediately. The failure of the shepherds, that is, of the kings and leaders of Israel, is described, consistently with the metaphor, as that gravest failure of any shepherd, failure to keep the flock together. For a scattered flock is a flock that can no longer be guided, protected, or maintained. There can be no doubt about the appropriateness of describing as a scattered flock the "people of God" in the time of Jeremiah. The once united kingdom had long since been split in half. One of those halves had already collapsed before its enemies and its people were driven into exile. And the other half was soon to suffer a similar fate. Religious, moral, social, and political disintegration were rampant and made the failure of the shepherds undisguisable. Against this background, Jeremiah offers his prophecy of hope, based on God's promise to reassemble his scattered flock and to give them a new shepherd, a descendant of David under whose rule Israel had been consolidated as a unified "people of God."

The second reading, from the letter to the Ephesians, like the concluding verses of the first reading, deals with the initiative of God in reassembling his scattered people. In this case, however, the message is addressed to Gentile Christians, and it does not anticipate a future intervention by God to restore unity, but proclaims that this divine intervention is already accomplished. The disunity which the passage has in view is the separation and hostility of Jews and Gentiles. And the divine intervention to which it refers is the sacrificial atonement accomplished by Jesus Christ. The atonement principally wrought by this sacrifice is, of course, the reuniting of humankind to God by overcoming the alienating force of sin. Nevertheless, in this passage Paul suggests an intrinsic connection between the reconciliation of humankind to God and the integration of humankind itself. He thus conceives Christ's overcoming of humankind's alienation from God as essentially entailing the repair of humankind's internal disunity. And the most basic and significant of humankind's divisions, from the viewpoint of Pauline theology, is that between God's people, Israel, and the Gentiles, the godless people who have now found God through Jesus Christ whom his own people rejected. In this passage Christ is said to be "our peace," in the sense that he is the basis of our reconciliation, both to God and to one another.

The third reading, from the Gospel according to Mark, is a very simple narrative which, in this Gospel, serves mainly to introduce the account which follows of Jesus' miraculous feeding of the five thousand. The account opens with the return of Jesus' apostles, whose commission to undertake a missionary tour had been described earlier in the same chapter. The apostles are represented as so overwhelmed by throngs of people that they have not even the opportunity to take a meal. Out of consideration for them, Jesus invites them to accompany him by boat to an uninhabited place where they may be able to relax. It is both ironic and touching that they should be met at their supposedly secluded destination by the very crowds they meant to escape from. And the character of Jesus is strikingly conveyed by the description of his reaction to this disappointing turn of events: "His heart went out to them, because they were like sheep without a shepherd; and he had much to teach them." The last phrase introduces the following episode, when Jesus' protracted lesson detains his hearers until late in the day, by which time they are hungry, far from home, and without provisions. The preceding phrase reintroduces the theme, found in the first reading, of the uncared-for flock and its need for shepherding, and is almost identical in wording with several passages in the Old Testament. These Old Testament parallels all refer to a need for leadership, but are not invariably messianic, and it does not seem necessary to interpret Jesus' words as intended to carry messianic overtones.

SIXTEENTH SUNDAY OF THE YEAR

Cycle "C" Readings: Gen. 18:1-10; Col. 1:24-28; Lk. 10:38-42

The first reading is taken from the account in Genesis of the patriarch Abraham, with whom, according to the Old Testament, biblical revelation had its real beginning. Abraham, who migrated from a Mesopotamian region called Ur, is represented as worshipping a family deity called El Shaddai. Later, when the main lines of Hebrew religion had been developed, this God of Abraham came to be identified with the unique God of Israel, Yahweh. This identification is taken for granted in the Bible, as in the present episode which begins by stating that "Yahweh (translated as 'the Lord') appeared to Abraham."

The story introduced in this way is about a strange visit paid to Abraham by three men. The details of this story seem to have become somewhat confused and inconsistent before it found its way into writing, and resulting obscurities can no longer be resolved with any conviction. At all events, it is evident that the visit of the three men was a divine visitation, and that the way Abraham received his visitors won him divine favor. His manner of receiving them was, in fact, an exemplary instance of a kind of behavior which has always ranked very high in the moral estimation of Middle Eastern peoples, namely, hospitality to friendly strangers.

The reward of Abraham's hospitality was the fulfillment of the greatest of his hopes, which the passage of time had placed beyond the reach of normal expectations, the hope of having a child by his aged wife Sarah. It is consistent with Abraham's reputation as an exemplar of faith that he believed unhesitatingly in the promise of parenthood. And it is consistent with the biblical evaluation of faith that this trusting attitude should have been rewarded by the birth in the following year of Isaac. Here, as in other stories, Abraham is presented as both the natural ancestor of God's chosen people and as the prototype of that virtue of faith, or confidence in the promises of God, which was all-important to the religious ethics of Israel.

The second reading, from the letter to the Colossians, represents St. Paul as writing from prison to a church which he had not personally founded or visited but about which he was deeply concerned. It cannot be determined with certainty just where this imprisonment of Paul is understood to be taking place, but it provides an occasion for the emphasis found in this reading on the suffering he undergoes in carrying out the ministry entrusted to him by God, an emphasis which may be intended to overcome a certain distance or impersonality in the author's relationship with this church.

The ministry is described here, in language characteristic of this letter, as the preaching of a "mystery hidden from ages and generations past but now revealed." The Gospel is thus conceived as manifesting to the Gentiles the accomplishment of a divine plan, of which they are the beneficiaries, brought to fulfillment in Jesus Christ. As subsequent passages make evident, Paul's account of this Christian "mystery" is meant to counteract erroneous teachings promulgated by representatives of one of the mystery religions that were winning adherents to a curious blend of pagan and Jewish religious ingredients.

The little story of Mary and Martha that constitutes the final reading is peculiar to the Gospel according to Luke, although in the Gospel according to John these two sisters are again encountered at their own home in connection with the death and restoration of their brother Lazarus. Here the two women appear as characters in a kind of living parable which, like so many parables, leads up to a decisive saying by Jesus. It is noteworthy, and usually unnoted, that Jesus is the guest specifically of one of the sisters, Martha: "A woman named *Martha* welcomed him to *her* home." It is not, therefore, surprising that the tasks of hospitality should have been mainly assumed by the hostess. There is no indication that Jesus was in any special sense the guest of the other sister, who, as far as we can see, just happened to be there.

However understandable it may be, under the circumstances, that Martha should find herself with the whole burden of domestic work, it is equally understandable that she should have resented her sister's leisurely enjoyment of the conversation of Jesus who was, after all, Martha's guest. Her protest, however much one may sympathize with it, enabled Jesus to make the essential point of the story: that the best thing one can do in the presence of Jesus is to hear what he has to say to us. Thus the part chosen by Mary, however insensitively under the circumstances, is in fact "the better portion." The frequent use of this text in the early and medieval Church to prove the superiority of the contemplative life is somewhat misleading.

SEVENTEENTH SUNDAY OF THE YEAR

Cycle "A" Readings: 1 Kgs. 3:5, 7-12; Rom. 8:28-30; Mt. 13:44-52

The first reading, from the first book of Kings, recounts a popular legend that expresses both a typical idealization of Israel's third monarch and a significant development in Israel's understanding of wisdom. Put in the simplest terms, Solomon, during the centuries after his own death and after the collapse of what had been his kingdom, was remembered as a kind of "patron sage," as that person in Israel's history who chiefly represented the quest for and attainment of wisdom. Thus even wisdom literature composed many centuries after Solomon's time was often fictitiously attributed to him. In addition to this traditional conception of Solomon, which had some basis in historical reality, the passage also exemplifies a traditional conception of wisdom itself. Although much of what we read in the wisdom literature may seem to us no more than the expression of ordinary human reflection on experience, for the Israelites all true wisdom was believed to depend in a special sense on God. From an early date this is expressed by such sayings as "the fear of the Lord is the beginning of wisdom," meaning that without reverent submission to God, no real wisdom is attainable. A later development of the same basic conviction is the idea that wisdom comes from God in somewhat the same way that prophecy comes from God, as a gift or charism directly bestowed by God. The story about Solomon's dream is based on this understanding of God's relationship to human wisdom, while Solomon is extolled for being, so to speak, antecedently wise enough to prefer wisdom to God's lesser gifts. The fact that the secondary gifts were added as a kind of complimentary premium serves as a reminder of Solomon's reputation as not only a wise king, but also a rich and honored one.

The second reading, from the letter to the Romans, continues Paul's reflections on the relationship between the present condition of Christians and their ultimate destiny. The first verse, somewhat ambiguous in Greek, has become proverbial in the translation "All things work together for good to them that love God," but is probably better, and is now more usually rendered, "God works all things together. . . ." "Those who love him" are further identified as those "who have been called according to his decree." It is thus emphasized that the source and instigator of our loving God is God himself, who invites and enables us to do so, that this divine initiative is part of a divine plan, and that the purpose of the plan is to unite human destiny with the destiny of Christ himself. Paul then develops this idea by use of a series of terms expressing a logical sequence of aspects in the carrying out of this divine plan. Thus God is said to have foreknown, predestined, called, justified, and glorified, where each term presupposes the one before it. For Paul, the Christians he addresses have been "called," and through the faith whereby they responded to the call they have been "justified" and furnished with the hope in which they now live, their expectation of being "glorified." But, to locate this present calling and justification, and the future glorification, in the eternal plan of God, Paul goes on to say that God knew "in advance," and decided "in advance" whom he would call, justify, and glorify. To deny this would seem to Paul an implicit denial of his basic conviction that an eternal divine plan of salvation encompassed the whole span of history. But to press these phrases into the systematic predestinarianism of an Augustine or a Calvin ascribes to them a technical theological rigidity which their context in no way implies.

The third reading includes three short parables peculiar to the Gospel according to Matthew. The first two are very similar in structure and significance. Both describe the finding of something immensely valuable, which the finder takes possession of at the expense of everything else he had previously possessed. What is called the "reign of God" in introducing the first parable is identical with what is called the "kingdom of heaven" in introducing the second parable, but the latter usage reflects a Hebrew source, characteristically reluctant to express the divine name. The coming of the kingdom or reign of God is what Jesus' preaching and the Christian Gospel are basically about, and the point of both parables is that no cost could possibly be too great to bear for the possession of the kingdom, whose worth transcends all price. Like the first two parables, which exemplify a common type and convey the same meaning, the third also conforms to a type, another example of which was read last Sunday in the parable of the weeds and wheat. In this parable of the net we find again the situation in which valuable and worthless elements are randomly mixed together. And the mixed catch is dealt with just like the mixed crop: everything is left together till the end of the whole operation when the sorting out is done once and for all. The reference once again is clearly to a divine judgment that is truly final, and not to be anticipated.

SEVENTEENTH SUNDAY OF THE YEAR

Cycle "B" Readings: 2 Kgs. 4:42-44; Eph. 4:1-6; Jn. 6:1-15

The mysterious and not altogether amiable figure of Elisha, the ninth-century successor of the prophet Elijah, is known to us mainly through a series of loosely connected episodes recounted in the second book of Kings. Whatever the real Elisha may have been like, the legends preserved in the Old Testament curiously combine the characteristics of an Israelite prophet with those of a wonder-worker who, were it not for his reliance upon God, might be described as a magician. Most of the miraculous deeds of Elisha have a benevolent purpose, as in the episode narrated in the first reading of today's liturgy, which has striking parallels in the Gospel accounts of miracles performed by Jesus. According to this story, which is one in a series of miraculous events, a man brought Elisha some new bread and fresh grain which the prophet directed him to distribute among a large group of people. In answer to the objection that so little food could scarcely be offered to so large a company, Elisha declared God's assurance that they would eat the food and even have some of it left over. It turned out as the prophet had foretold. Christian readers of this passage have naturally associated it with Jesus' multiplication of the loaves, and on that basis it has sometimes been interpreted as distantly prefiguring the sacrament of the Eucharist.

The second reading is taken from the letter to the Ephesians. Like much of the Pauline literature, this document, after expounding various matters of doctrine, concludes with a section of exhortation concerned with fostering Christian attitudes and encouraging Christian behavior. In Ephesians, the first part of this exhortation is devoted to the theme of Christian unity. The opening verses of this part comprise the liturgical reading. The fundamental note of exhortation is struck in the initial verse: "As God has called you, live up to your calling." This general appeal to live in a manner consistent with the divine calling is immediately translated into very specific terms. Translated by such words as "humble," "gentle," and "patient," what these terms collectively demand is a quality of social behavior that excludes, as far as possible, the development of hostility and strife. In what follows it is made clear that this appeal is based on the conviction that social unity is so indispensable and essential a feature of Christianity that no efforts of self-control and no sacrifices of self-esteem are too great to demand for the preservation of unity. This unity is understood not as an achievement of human social initiative, but as the gift of the Spirit. Christian unity is characterized with respect to a number of aspects in the famous verses which conclude the reading. Here the Church is conceived as one body animated by one Spirit and tending toward one goal. It is one also in its dependence on Jesus Christ, to whom its members are united by faith and baptism. And the ultimate principle of unity is the unique supremacy of God, who is the source and the sustenance of all else.

The central portion of the Gospel according to John has been called by some modern scholars the "book of signs," in view of the careful way its content has been arranged around the accounts of seven miracles which this Gospel calls "signs." Each of these signs is closely related both to certain Jewish festivals and to certain discourses of Jesus that express verbally the same theological themes that the signs and the festivals represent symbolically. The fourth of these so-called signs is the miraculous feeding of the multitude, which is reported by the other Gospels also, but in different contexts. In the Johannine account of it, which constitutes the third reading of today's liturgy, this event is related to the Jewish festival of Passover, and the theological theme it represents is developed later in the same chapter by the discourse in which Jesus identifies himself as the "bread of life." This "bread of life" motif, in connection both with the feeding of the hungry crowd and with the Passover feast, looks both backward to the exodus of Israel and forward to the Christian Eucharist. Underlying the symbolism of the miracle one can discern the episode in which the Israelites of the exodus were sustained during their journey to freedom by the God-given bread from heaven called manna, which represents the life-giving power of God. It is with this life-giving power of God that Jesus identifies himself, both by the miracle and by the words which follow and interpret it, wherein Jesus describes himself as the bread of life. The bread which Jesus gives, like the bread which Jesus is, represents the very purpose of the incarnation—"that they might have life."

SEVENTEENTH SUNDAY OF THE YEAR

Cycle "C" Readings: Gen. 18:20-32; Col. 2:12-14; Lk. 11:1-13

The first reading continues the narrative of Abraham's visitation by the Lord and his two mysterious companions. After the promise that Sarah would bear Abraham a child, the heavenly visitors turn their attention to the region where Abraham's brother Lot had settled after they agreed to go separate ways. This was the area near the Dead Sea whose principal towns, Sodom and Gomorrah had so bad a reputation as to become traditional symbols of moral depravity. In this account, Abraham is represented as interceding with the Lord in behalf of his brother's homeland. The form that his intercession takes is a fascinating combination of nervous diplomacy and ethical insight.

Abraham's appeal is based on his recognition that, no matter how just it may be to punish the guilty, it is nonetheless unjust to punish the innocent, and when punishment of the guilty entails punishment of the innocent, justice is compromised. Abraham is represented as endeavoring to remind the Lord of this moral principle, and of its application to the prospect of levying wholesale destruction on two cities in which it is hardly imaginable that at least a few people should not deserve a better fate. Thus, with whimsical rhetoric, Abraham asks if the Lord would not spare the place for the sake of fifty, forty-five, forty, thirty, twenty, or even ten innocent persons. The progressive reduction of the number has, of course, no logical reason for stopping short of one single innocent individual. Abraham leaves the Lord to draw that conclusion for himself, as the ultimate implication of his thesis: "Far be it from you to . . . make the innocent die with the guilty, so that the innocent and the guilty would be treated alike!"

The second reading, from the letter to the Colossians, is part of an argument against those who were teaching the Christians at Colossae a curious doctrine, involving some kind of superhuman spiritual beings whose supposed authority apparently threatened the supremacy of Christ, and imposing the obligation of circumcision as well as other ritual and ascetical practices. The passage selected for the reading is concerned with asserting the total sufficiency of Jesus Christ and, in consequence, the total dispensability of such practices as circumcision. In the verses just preceding these, Christ is said to possess "the fullness of deity," and to be "the head" of any and all spiritual beings. Baptism is here conceived as a rite which expresses one's effective participation in the death and resurrection of Jesus, in virtue of one's faith in the saving power of that God who raised Jesus from death into new life.

The passage is thus a part of the relentless Pauline polemic of "faith" against the "works" of religious ritual, as well as a part of the Pauline insistence on the divine status and redemptive power of Jesus Christ. As the final words of the reading insist, the work of atonement is, in principle, already accomplished, and its effectiveness, which prevails over sin and death, is certainly not to be thought of as contingent on such practices as circumcision or on such influences as those of real or imaginary spiritual beings.

The third reading is a portion of the Gospel according to Luke which brings together several originally separate passages, apparently because all of them are applicable to the general topic of prayer. A dramatic setting is provided by having the disciples observe Jesus himself at prayer and ask him for a lesson on this subject. The lesson is introduced by what is probably the most original version we have of the Lord's Prayer, shorter than the one generally adopted from the Gospel according to Matthew. The prayer is basically a declaration of eschatological hope and longing for the final coming of the Kingdom of God.

This prayer is followed by a little parable, intended to urge persistence in prayer even when it seems to remain unanswered. The rather comic description of a disgruntled man who is effectively nagged out of laziness into hospitality is a typically parabolic way of drawing attention to a simple general lesson—in this case, that persistence is rewarded. Our cultural unfamiliarity with the parable form may betray itself in a feeling that the story suggests, rather unfittingly, that God responds to persevering prayer out of a kind of exasperation, merely to rid himself of a nuisance. Such misunderstandings arise from the error of attaching symbolic meaning to all the elements of a parable, as one might do with the quite different literary form called allegory.

An isolated saying, attached to this parable, amounts to an assurance that prayers are in fact answered, and thereby raises the inevitable objection that people simply do not always get what they pray for, no matter how persistently. Thus a final passage deals with this objection by pointing out that we sometimes pray for things that are, unknown to us, harmful to us.

EIGHTEENTH SUNDAY OF THE YEAR

Cycle "A" Readings: Is. 55:1-3; Rom. 8:35, 37-39; Mt. 14:13-21

The first reading comes from a portion of the book of Isaiah which was added long after Isaiah's own lifetime. It strongly expresses that atmosphere of renewed hope and rekindled enthusiasm which characterize the period when the exile was ending and a new national beginning lay in view. This document sometimes, and very appropriately, called the book of Israel's Consolation, ends with a poem of which the reading comprises the first three verses. The verses take the form of an invitation issued by God to his exiled people, to come and eat their fill and drink to their satisfaction. A rich and lavish menu is set before the hungry, thirsting people, and they are assured that everything is free, provided without any expense or labor on their part, out of sheer generosity. It is easy to perceive in this figurative language a reference to the contrast between the hard-earned preservation of life in a foreign, hostile land, and the lavishness of the land which the Lord had made their own and was now about to restore to them. The basis of their title to that "promised land" had been their covenant with God. Their loss of that land had been caused by their breaking of that covenant. Consequently, a restoration of that land must entail a re-establishment of the covenant. In the final verse of the reading, therefore, the promised blessings are given their theological foundation by the promise of a new covenant, founded like the old one on divine fidelity, but destined this time to last forever.

The second reading is part of a section of the letter to the Romans in which Paul considers on how firm a basis the ultimate hope of Christians is established. He had previously argued that divine calling and justification are a prelude to final glory, and that the expectation of glory is what makes life's troubles endurable. But at that point a further question seems to have occurred to him, the question of just how confident that expectation of glory can really be. For Paul had also previously emphasized human weakness, and it might seem that weak human beings, subjected to suffering, could easily forfeit their title to so exalted a destiny. Paul accordingly takes up the question of whether or not Christians might justifiably feel some anxiety on this score. The most obvious and serious threat is posed by sin itself, and Paul certainly had no illusions about the sinlessness of the Christians he knew. He therefore begins his discussion of the matter by arguing that if God justifies us, we would seem to be singularly well-insured against the worst that sin can do. It is at this point that the reading begins, with the result that it omits Paul's main argument and includes what is really a secondary reflection and summary. For if sin is not likely to deprive Christians of the ultimate effects of Christ's love, it is hardly imaginable that anything else could do so. Paul's formidable list of physical dangers can, therefore, be dismissed almost breezily in a rhetorical question. And so he sums up with a sweeping catalogue of the main sources from which danger might come, only to proclaim, in one of his most memorable sentences, the Christian's basic safety from them all.

The third reading is the account in the Gospel according to Matthew of an episode that is described, with some differences of situation, in all four Gospels, and seems even to be repeated in two of them. It is said to have taken place not long after the execution by Herod Antipas of John the Baptist. This was an ominous as well as a tragic event, and it is readily understandable why on hearing of it Jesus should have sought to withdraw temporarily from public activities. However, the public he was trying to avoid came after him, and his reaction was altogether typical: "his heart was moved with pity and he cured their sick." The presence of this crowd and their distance from any town sets the scene for what follows, Jesus' miraculous multiplication of the scanty provisions to feed the entire multitude. One is inevitably reminded of the many Old Testament passages in which God's care for his people is demonstrated or symbolized by the providing of nourishment. It is a motif not only of the exodus narrative, but also of the restoration from exile, as in the first reading, and of later messianic passages. Here too, we find that the people are not merely tided over with emergency rations, but fed to satiety and with plenty to spare. The messianic import of the episode is evident, and, especially through the way it is presented in the fourth Gospel, it became closely associated with the Eucharist.

EIGHTEENTH SUNDAY OF THE YEAR

Cycle "B" Readings: Ex. 16:2-4, 12-15; Eph. 4:17, 20-24; Jn. 6:24-35

Exodus is a Greek word meaning "a way out," and the Old Testament book called by that title is a narrative of how the Hebrews found their way out of the land of Egypt and out of the servile condition of their life in that land. The story begins with the account of God's selection of Moses to lead the people, and of his victory over the resistance of Pharaoh, and it continues with the narrative of their trek across the desert and the establishment at Sinai of the covenant on which Israel's life was thereafter to be based. Throughout the account of their journey through the desert, two contrasting themes are prominently combined. One of these is the theme of God's unfailing reliability, rescuing his people from every predicament that befalls them. The other theme is that of the habitual unreliability of the people themselves, whose recurrent distrustfulness and persistent complaining are so often recalled in the literature of the Old Testament. This twofold theme of the providence of God and the plaintiveness of his people is illustrated by the first reading of today's liturgy, which significantly opens with the phrase "The Israelites complained . . ." What they were complaining about this time was the danger of starvation with which the desert seemed to threaten them. God's patient reply to Moses was his promise to "rain down bread from heaven." Plausible explanations of this substance as a natural secretion of a desert shrub have been advanced by naturalists familiar with the region. But the origin of the story is less important for students of the Bible than its significance within the Bible itself, where it is clearly understood as a dramatic expression of God's power and will to provide for his people regardless of their circumstances.

The second reading in today's liturgy, taken from that section of the letter to the Ephesians which deals with the "new life" which is to characterize the followers of Jesus Christ, represents a very basic statement of what might be called from one point of view Christian morality, and from another point of view Christian holiness. It can be called Christian morality insofar as it represents the manner of life which the mere fact of being a Christian obliges one to cherish and cultivate. On the other hand, it is not understood to be, like secular ethics, a set of moral principles which are discovered by human ingenuity, determined by human experience, and implemented by human effort. On the contrary, both the understanding of this way of life and the capacity to live according to it have their origin not with human beings but with God. Thus, after warning Christians against the insensitivity of conscience and degeneracy of behavior commonly found in pagan society, the letter reminds its Christian readers that "that is not how you learned Christ." What "learning Christ" means in this context is in part realizing that pagan standards of behavior belong to a life which Christianity altogether supersedes. For just as becoming a Christian is described as a "new birth," so being a Christian is understood as a radically new life which develops from this new birth. Like the new birth, so the new life is a divine, not a human accomplishment. It is thus called a "new creation," as though brought from nothingness into being by the sheer omnipotence of God. And yet, that the human recipient of this new life is not an entirely passive recipient is implied in the imperative phrase, "put on the new nature of God's creating."

The themes of the two previous readings, that of the manna in Exodus and that of the "new life" in Ephesians, are brought together in the third reading, from the gospel according to John. In this episode, Jesus and his disciples are overtaken by the crowds of people who had been fed by the miraculous multiplication of bread. Jesus tells them they have come after him because their hunger was satisfied and not because they "saw signs." In other words, their response has been to the material effect of Jesus' action rather than to its spiritual significance. Accordingly, Jesus develops this spiritual significance in a lengthy discourse the opening verses of which are given in today's reading. These verses contrast the perishable bread with another, permanent food, which nourishes eternal life. It is this latter kind of food which Jesus has come to give them. And what they must do about it is believe in the one whom God has sent. When the disciples, desiring a sign, in the sense of a miracle, to support their belief, recall the manna of Exodus, Jesus contrasts that miraculous food also with the life-giving bread which God is now bestowing. In language which is strongly suggestive of the Eucharist, Jesus identifies this life-giving bread with himself, as "the bread of life." Throughout this passage, with its typically Johannine play on multiple meanings, one discerns a basic statement concerning God's gift of eternal life and humankind's acceptance of that gift. God bestows the gift by sending Jesus Christ. Humankind receives the gift by believing in Jesus Christ.

EIGHTEENTH SUNDAY OF THE YEAR

Cycle "C" Readings: Eccl. 1:2; 2:21-23; Col. 3:1-5, 9-11; Lk. 12:13-21

The first reading, taken from the Book of Ecclesiastes, opens with the second verse of that book, which sounds a topical refrain that re-echoes gloomily throughout the entire work. "Vanity of vanities" is a Hebraic form of superlative, where the term vanity has its original meaning of emptiness. The phrase means, therefore, something like "utter emptiness," and in answer to the reader's natural question "*What* is utter emptiness?" the verse concludes by applying this phrase universally: "All things are vanity." Throughout the pages that follow this somber introduction, both the personal experience of the writer and the records of history are invoked to confirm the opinion that, when all is said and done, the whole of life is utter emptiness, absurdity, futility.

After the opening verse, the liturgical reading skips to a passage toward the end of the second chapter which contains one of the writer's many observations on the inanity of human experience. What he reflects upon is the familiar situation of an ambitious, hardworking man who devotes most of his life's time, toil, and worry to the building up of some substantial property, only to die and leave it to an heir who has done nothing to deserve it or contribute to it. Here, as often in Ecclesiastes, we find a deep sense of the injustice of a world where there is little relationship between what one does and what one gets, between merit and acquisition. Later interpreters of Ecclesiastes, who have left their mark in places on the text itself, understood passages like this as motives for turning from materialistic and secular concerns to spiritual and religious ones, but for the original writer the outlook appears to have been one of unrelieved bleakness.

The second reading from the letter to the Colossians, turns from warning against the ascetical and ritual demands of false teachers to exhorting the Christians of Colossae to live up to the standards of a genuinely Christian life. So much of the Pauline writings is taken up with denouncing the insistence of Jewish teachers on "doing the works of the law" that there is a danger of interpreting these writings as advocating a kind of religion in which self-discipline and moral striving have no place. It is important therefore to notice how frequent are passages like the present one that set a high standard of aspiration and behavior for the life of a Christian.

It is also important to note that in the Pauline writings the high quality of a Christian life is conceived not as a means to salvation but as a consequence of salvation. Thus the present passage of spiritual and moral exhortation is introduced by the words, "Since you have been raised up in company with Christ, set your heart on what pertains to the higher realms where Christ is seated at God's right hand." Thus, the virtues for which the writer goes on to appeal are considered by him not as means to being "raised up" but as expressions of the fact of being already "raised up in company with Christ." Christian virtue, accordingly, is here as elsewhere conceived as manifesting the new, eternal life gained for us, not by our deeds but by Christ's great deed of redemption.

The third reading is a parable, preserved only in the Gospel according to Luke, which focuses on one aspect of the Christian evaluation of material wealth. It is occasioned by a request for Jesus to act as arbitrator in a legacy dispute between two brothers. As usual on occasions of secular contention, Jesus refuses absolutely to intervene and shows no real interest in the matter of who is technically, legally, or even morally, in the right. He makes his refusal an occasion for pointing out that the values here involved are entirely remote from the values that alone concern his mission. That mission is devoted exclusively to bringing what is called both "the Kingdom of God" and "eternal life." And the kind of gain represented by material inheritance has simply nothing to do with the gaining of that Kingdom and that life. The parable sets the two realms of incommensurable value in the sharpest possible contrast, by representing them as they must appear at the moment of the death of one who has devoted his life to accumulating a kind of gain from which death separates him completely and forever.

The verdict Jesus passes on such a life is perfectly expressed in the words he places on the lips of God himself: "You fool!" It is not malice but folly that most adequately characterizes the life of one who has invested all his personal resources in acquiring something he cannot retain, and can scarcely even enjoy. The judgment passed by the Gospel on such a life is the same as Ecclesiastes' judgment of life in general—vanity, emptiness, absurdity.

NINETEENTH SUNDAY OF THE YEAR

Cycle "A" Readings: 1 Kgs. 19:9, 11-13; Rom. 9:1-5; Mt. 14:22-33

The first reading, from the first book of Kings, is part of the account of the prophet Elijah's visit to Mount Horeb. This is the same mountain, sometimes called Horeb and sometimes Sinai, on which Moses received from God the covenant that was to bind Israel to God as his own specially chosen people. For Elijah as for Moses, the mountain is the site of an extraordinary experience of the powerful and majestic presence of God. But whereas Moses was brought to this mountain to receive the covenant from God and transmit it to his people, Elijah came to the mountain to declare to God that the covenant had been shamefully violated by a people who had desecrated the Lord's altars and slain his prophets. The reference is to the bloody and sacrilegious activities of King Ahab and his pagan queen Jezebel in the northern kingdom. Elijah himself, as their sworn enemy, was among their intended victims, and he came to Horeb as a fugitive from their vengeance. The cyclone, earthquake, and fire recall the tremendous storm during Moses' visit to Horeb, and Elijah's cave recalls the cleft in the rock where Moses took shelter. However, whereas God spoke to Moses against a background of thunderings and trumpetings, Elijah's divine message came to him only after the tumultuous phenomena had faded away, and made itself heard through a "tiny whispering sound." This striking circumstance has been variously interpreted. It may reflect the idea that whereas God's words to Moses were his revelation intended for the hearing of all the people, those people were in Elijah's day deaf to his words. What God delivers to Elijah is a quite private inspiration to undertake what might be fairly described as a secret mission.

The second reading is the introductory passage of a major section of the letter to the Romans, which occupies three full chapters. In earlier parts of the letter Paul has alluded to a comprehensive divine plan of salvation, encompassing the whole of human history, which he considers to be decisively illuminated by the Christian understanding of Jesus. In Paul's view, Jesus' death and resurrection introduce the climax of God's salutary direction of human history. But one implication of this view is, for Paul, distressingly ironic. For Paul is a Jew, Jesus himself was a Jew, and Paul's understanding of Jesus is as the Messiah whom the Jews awaited as their deliverer. At the same time, Paul is aware that the messianic claims of Jesus are generally disregarded and resented by the Jews, whom Paul considers to have been chiefly responsible for Jesus' death. For Paul, therefore, the divine plan takes a strange and lamentable turn when the Messiah, whom the Jews alone consciously expected, finds acclamation as savior mainly among the Gentiles. Paul expresses profound personal grief over this development. He expresses his compassion for his fellow Jews in the strongest possible terms, declaring that for their sake he could wish to forfeit his own Christianity. He wonderingly reviews the outstanding historical manifestations of Israel's unique status as God's chosen people, concluding with the fact that from this people the Messiah did in fact come. He ends the passage with a blessing, but the underlying problem remains unsolved, to be dealt with through the succeeding chapters.

The third reading comprises two episodes which, in the Gospel according to Matthew, occur successively right after Jesus' miraculous feeding of the crowd who had followed him to a remote part of the lakeshore. The episodes occur while the disciples are returning by boat, having left Jesus to pray in solitude. During a storm the disciples are frightened by a spectral appearance of Jesus walking to them over the sea. Although his reassuring words might conclude a complete episode which is narrated also in the Gospel according to Mark, this Gospel records a further development. Peter's audacious proposal that Jesus invite him to walk on the water proves humiliating when Peter's fear overwhelms his former confidence. He does call on Jesus for help and is promptly rescued, but is also admonished for his diffidence. With Jesus on board the storm is abated and the disciples worship Jesus as Son of God. The reference to this title and worship, as well as the whole story about Peter, is omitted in the Gospel according to Mark. Thus we have from one evangelist a story which contrasts the fear and danger when Jesus is absent with the calm and security when he is present. But the other evangelist has made this story the setting for another story, about the development of Peter's faith, a matter in which the Gospel according to Matthew takes characteristically strong interest.

NINETEENTH SUNDAY OF THE YEAR

Cycle "B" Readings: 1 Kgs. 19:4-8; Eph. 4:30—5:2; Jn. 6:41-51

The first reading of today's liturgy, taken from the first book of Kings, records an episode from the life of the prophet Elijah which was occasioned by Jezebel's murderous hatred of him. Elijah, as the prophet of God, was inevitably in conflict with Jezebel and her husband Ahab, whose scandalous lapses into pagan idolatry owed much to the influence of his queen. Jezebel, herself a pagan princess from Phoenicia, or what is now Lebanon, spared no pains to establish her native cult of Baal in the territory of Israel. As part of this paganizing campaign, she succeeded in banishing the Israelite prophets and replacing them with prophets of Baal. Elijah, by a miraculous demonstration of the power of his God, incited a popular uprising which led to the slaying of hundreds of these pagan prophets. Enraged by this slaughter, Jezebel swore that she would avenge it by the death of Elijah. It was fear at this threat that caused Elijah to flee from Israel to the southern kingdom of Judah, where he finally collapsed in the wilderness outside Beersheba and prayed for death. It was at this point that an angel provided him with the food and drink that enabled him to undertake a journey of forty days and forty nights to Mount Horeb. This was the mountain, called Sinai in a different tradition, where Moses had his decisive encounter with God, and Elijah's sojourn there is clearly intended to bring his own mission into close contact with the roots of Israelite religion in the Mosaic covenant.

The second reading of today's liturgy comes from that final section of the letter to the Ephesians which is primarily concerned with moral exhortation. The exhortation begins with an appeal to preserve the unity of the Christian community, a unity which is likened to that of a living body and which is attributed to the Holy Spirit. The exhortation then proceeds to develop the idea of that new life which Christ makes available to humankind and the appropriate living of which constitutes genuinely Christian morality. Within this context, the letter specifies several kinds of behavior which are disruptive of unity and incompatible with the new life. Such kinds of behavior are deceit, anger, theft, and abusive language. It is as a kind of summation of these admonitions that the letter continues with the words, "do not grieve the Holy Spirit of God." This grieving of the Spirit is, of course, a metaphor, implying that all conduct of the kind which has just been denounced offends against that Christian unity and Christian newness of life of which the Spirit is the principle. By another turn of metaphor, the Spirit is likened to a seal, by which Christians are said to have been "sealed for the day of redemption." The Spirit is thus conceived not only as the principle of the new life of Christians, but also as the confirmation of the destiny in which that new life finds its ultimate fulfillment. In the ancient world, seals functioned very much as signatures do in our own culture, to make agreements and commitments matters of record. Thus to be "sealed" by the Spirit is to bear as it were the divine signature, attesting to the divine redemptive purpose in the process of its actual accomplishment in human life. The reading concludes with a further exhortation to avoid contentious and provocative behavior, and to cultivate compassion and kindliness. The kind of behavior that is called for is meant to express the resemblance of God's children to God their Father. That resemblance is realized above all in the kind of divine love which finds expression in the redemptive sacrifice of Christ.

The third reading, from the gospel according to John, continues Jesus' discourse on the "bread of life" which was begun in the liturgy of the previous week. Here we find the idea, which appears in a different context in the Synoptic Gospels, that the familiar and unpretentious social background of Jesus caused some of his countrymen to regard his authoritative claims as presumptuous. The fact that some reject Jesus suggests first of all that to accept him depends on divine influence, and not simply on human judgment and decision: "No one can come to me unless drawn by the Father who sent me." But on the other hand, the readiness of human beings to accept Jesus is understood to depend on their more general readiness to attend and respond to God: "Everyone who has listened to the Father and learned from him comes to me." These two ideas strongly suggest the divine status of Jesus, inasmuch as they point out that human reactions to Jesus are virtually identical with human reactions to God himself. The same interpretation is prompted by the statement of Jesus which follows, that "he who has come from God has seen the Father, and he alone." Against this background, the theme of Jesus as the bread of life is resumed with deeper implications than before. Like the manna, Jesus comes from God, a source of life for humankind. And here again, the sacrament of the Eucharist is both implied in the final verse and linked by that verse with the sacrifice of Jesus: "The bread which I will give is my own flesh: I give it for the life of the world."

NINETEENTH SUNDAY OF THE YEAR

Cycle "C" Readings: Wis. 18:6-9; Heb. 11:1-2, 8-19; Lk. 12:32-48

The book from which the first reading is taken, called the Wisdom of Solomon, actually came into being nearly a thousand years after Solomon's time. It is not included in the Hebrew Bible, and is regarded by Protestants as an apocryphal rather than a canonical work of Scripture. Its thought, like its language, is in form much more Greek than Hebrew, but its purpose was to reinforce the biblical faith of Jews at a time when the prestige of Greek culture was threatening to undermine the influence of Jewish tradition.

Part of the work from which the reading is taken comprises a religious philosophy, or theology of history, based on the conviction of a special, preferential providence, exercised by divine wisdom, in behalf of the Jews. This thesis is illustrated at length by reference to the circumstances of the Exodus, when events were consistently managed by God in such a way as to ensure the Hebrews' liberation and the defeat of the Egyptians who sought to detain them. Today's reading categorically contrasts God's just people with those who are neither God's nor just. The work is a profession of religious faith and a rather unqualified assertion of ethnic pride.

The second reading is a passage from the letter to the Hebrews which begins with a famous description of faith that many theologians of the early and medieval Church understood as a kind of technical definition and made the basis of their theological analyses of faith. It is a notion of faith based on the combination of three ideas: confidence, anticipation, and invisibility. This faith is regarded as a state of mental assurance concerning something not present to our experience but eagerly expected in the future. Thus understood, faith is very similar to what most of us ordinarily mean by hope, when the hope is not a mere wistfulness but full of eagerness and free of doubt. Probably the most ordinary circumstance in which we experience such a state of mind is when someone whom we completely trust makes an important promise to us.

The examples of Abraham and Sarah make clear the faith that is understood as a confident anticipation based on promises made by God himself. Moreover, the unique importance of what God alone can promise arouses an intensity of expectation that makes the present seem, in contrast with the future, dull and insignificant. Just as the wandering patriarchs were more intensely aware of the homeland they were seeking than of the wastelands through which they passed, the Christian is here conceived to be one whose interest in a present temporary dwelling place is altogether overshadowed by a longing for the eternal home promised by Christ.

The third reading, from the Gospel according to Luke, begins with a passage that draws a practical conclusion from the idea of a Christian as one whose heart is set rather on an eternal future than on an ephemeral present.

Given such a state of mind, there could be no strong motive for acquisitiveness or tenacity with respect to temporal possessions. And at the same time, there would, in the light of Christian values, be every reason for exercising generosity with whatever temporal goods one happened to possess. For whereas one cannot bring one's temporal possessions into the eternal life promised by Christ, one can, and indeed must, bring one's charity.

The parable which occupies most of the reading is one of several parables that urge their hearers to hold themselves in readiness for the final destiny that has been promised to them. Since that destiny is associated specifically with the second coming of Jesus Christ, a parable about servants waiting for their absent master to return has very pointed applicability. In the discussion that follows the parable, the appeal for constant readiness takes on a certain ominousness by emphasizing the dreadful possibility of being in fact unready for the return of that master who here clearly symbolizes Christ. The two passages taken together show the logical relationship of hope and fear in Christian motivation. The confidence of hope is rooted in the perfect reliability of God, whereas the basis of fear is human unreliability. There is no question about the master's coming, but only about the servants' readiness.

TWENTIETH SUNDAY OF THE YEAR

Cycle "A" Readings: Is. 56:1, 6-7; Rom. 11:13-15, 29-32; Mt. 15:21-28

The first reading is the beginning of a long final section of the book of Isaiah which appears to come from a later period than any of the material that precedes it in the same book. Apparently it is the work of more than one writer, produced during the time after the restoration from exile, when the repatriated Jews were striving to make a vigorous new beginning in their homeland. The initial verse of this section introduces an exhortation to obey the law of God, confident that he will make his justice felt in vindicating those who are faithful to his commandments, the conditions of fidelity to his covenant and membership in the covenant community. Significantly, this appeal to abide by the terms of God's covenant is addressed not only to the natural descendants of the Israelites, but also extended to foreigners who wish to be part of the community. In verses omitted from the reading, a similarly hospitable attitude offers welcome also to eunuchs, a class of persons whose infertility had caused them to be excluded by the earlier Deuteronomic formulation of covenant law. The last verses of the reading resume the address to foreign converts, who are expected to assume the religious as well as the moral obligations of Israel. If they do so, they are to regard the temple itself, newly reconstructed on Zion, God's "holy mountain" in Jerusalem, as their own place of worship, where their sacrifices will be fully welcome. The last verse epitomizes this newly broadened conception of Israel's mission, in designating the Jerusalem temple as "a house of prayer for all peoples."

The second reading is taken from the letter to the Romans. It comprises two fragmentary excerpts from Paul's long, rather complicated discussion of the place of Israel in the plan of salvation envisaged by Christianity. It is probably impossible to harmonize all that Paul says on this subject, but it is clear that he cannot simply accept the idea that Israel has permanently forfeited salvation by rejecting the Messiah. He takes it as evident that, at least for the present, the Jews have lost what the Gentiles have gained, and he attributes this to the Jews' insistence on pursuing a justification based on the law rather than on faith. He refuses to concede that their disregard of the Gospel can be ascribed to ignorance of its message. And even more emphatically he refuses to concede that God can in any sense be blamed for the way things have turned out for Israel. But when he asks himself if, in the last analysis, "God rejected his people," he is compelled to reply, "I cannot believe it." Granted that the Jews' loss has been the Gentiles' gain, he does not regard the Jews' own loss as final, but expresses a hope in terms of strong conviction: "If their falling off means the enrichment of the Gentiles, how much more their coming to full strength?" The same conviction is expressed in the reading, where Paul conceives his own mission to the Gentiles as calculated to arouse in the Jews a kind of salutary envy. Here again he anticipates an ultimate conversion of the Jews and sees that eventuality as significant for the resurrection itself. He develops this idea in a metaphorical passage which the reading omits, concluding that God, who does not break promises, will ultimately fulfill his promises to Israel.

The third reading recounts an episode that is described, with some differences, in the Gospels according to Matthew and Mark. Like so many of the episodes in Jesus' public ministry, it is a miracle story, and the miracle is one of healing. What makes the story remarkable, however, is that the girl whom Jesus heals and her mother who solicits his help, using a Messianic title, son of David, are not Jews but pagans. The place where the event is situated represents the northernmost point that Jesus is said to have reached, a region of what is now southern Lebanon and was then Phoenicia. The woman who petitions Jesus to help her daughter is described here as a Canaanite, associating her with a pagan culture whose relations with Israel had been close and tense since the time of the exodus. The disciples' ungracious reaction to the woman expresses a conventional Jewish attitude toward pagans, and Jesus' own distinction between "children" and "dogs" reflects a conventional anti-pagan vocabulary. Jesus' final action, in acceding to the woman's request and praising her faith is, therefore, contrary to all expectations. The episode is undoubtedly seen by the evangelist as an anticipation of the later controversy between Jewish and Gentile Christians, and the resolution of that controversy in favor of the Gentiles.

TWENTIETH SUNDAY OF THE YEAR

Cycle "B" Readings: Prov. 9:1-6; Eph. 5:15-20; Jn. 6:51-58

The first reading is a passage from the book of Proverbs that, in its literary context, is clearly intended to be read in close conjunction with another passage, closely similar in form, but diametrically opposite in significance. Both of the passages are extended metaphors or allegories, and both of them are based on personifications around which simple realistic scenes are constructed. In the first passage, given in its entirety by the reading, Wisdom is personified as a lady who has just completed the building of a new house and made careful preparations for a housewarming party to which she is currently in the process of issuing invitations. In the second passage, entirely omitted from the reading, Folly is personified as a woman of conspicuously meretricious demeanor, who sits beside her doorway, soliciting passersby to come in and enjoy the forbidden pleasures she can make available to them. Thus both Wisdom and Folly are represented as extending invitations and as having, both of them, definite appeal. But the kinds of appeal they have are totally different, as different as a formal invitation from a lady and a sly solicitation from a whore. And as different as the invitations are the occasions they make available, in the one case likened to a well-arranged dinner party and in the other case compared to a stealthy indulgence in stolen provisions. The final point of comparison brings out the full seriousness of what these two passages are intended to represent. For the final results of responding to Wisdom's invitation or to Folly's solicitation are, respectively, life and death. Thus wisdom and folly here correspond to the radical alternatives described elsewhere in the Bible as obedience or disobedience to God, the way of life or the way of death.

The second reading continues the exhortation of the letter to the Ephesians to live in a manner worthy of Christ because modeled upon and actually derived from Christ's own life. In this passage the alternative ways of life, previously described in terms of contrast between light and darkness, are further contrasted as respectively wisdom and folly. Expressed in this perspective, the exhortation to live a good life is led to take account of the fact that the intellect no less than the will has to be involved in responding to such an appeal. For wanting and trying to do the right thing are clearly futile unless one first arrives at some knowledge of what the right thing is. Accordingly, the readers are here exhorted to "not continue in ignorance, but try to discern the will of the Lord." It is probably this insistence on mental discernment that calls up in the following verse a condemnation of drunkenness, in view of the effect of drunkenness on mental efficiency. And by a further association of ideas it is undoubtedly the reference to drunkenness that introduces the final exhortation to "let the Holy Spirit fill you." For wine is a common symbol of the Spirit, and there are frequent suggestions in the New Testament that the effects of the Spirit can be likened to a kind of divine intoxication, such as caused the bystanders on Pentecost to mistake the apostles themselves for a group of unruly drunkards.

The third reading, from the Gospel according to John, is part of Jesus' lengthy discourse on the bread of life. Throughout this Gospel, Jesus' principal statements and his principal actions are closely related, and their relationship is discernible in common patterns of symbolism. Thus, the chapter that includes this discourse on the bread of life begins with the account of Jesus' feeding a large crowd of followers by the miraculous multiplication of loaves and fishes. We are told that the occasion of this miracle was near the time of Passover, and are thereby reminded that it is also characteristic of the fourth Gospel to relate its presentation of Jesus' symbolic words and deeds to appropriate feasts in the Jewish liturgical calendar. The Passover motif is recalled once again when Jesus' hearers refer to the manna which God provided for the followers of Moses during the exodus. Jesus contrasts this bread from heaven with himself, describing himself as "the bread that came down from heaven". His statement that "if anyone eats this bread he shall live forever," and his description of the bread he gives as his "own flesh" are understandably bewildering to his Jewish hearers, who take the words literally. To the Christian readers of the Gospel, however, the reference is clearly to Jesus' life-giving passion and death, and to the eucharistic liturgy which sacramentalizes that event.

TWENTIETH SUNDAY OF THE YEAR

Cycle "C" Readings: Jer. 38:4-6, 8-10; Heb. 12:1-4; Lk. 12:49-53

The first reading, from the Book of Jeremiah, narrates part of the long-continued strife between the famous prophet and the last of the kings of Judah, Zedekiah. This weak and inconsistent monarch was appointed to his kingship as a vassal of the king of Babylonia, to which Judah had become subject after Babylonia's victory over Assyria, Judah's former master. Zedekiah was persuaded by a powerful faction in Jerusalem to revolt against his feudal lord. The king of Babylonia promptly responded by laying siege to Jerusalem. Jeremiah, who had from the start advised strongly against what seemed to him a suicidal rebellion, continued throughout the siege to urge surrender. To the Palestinian nobility who influenced Zedekiah, Jeremiah was little better than a traitor, and was a gravely demoralizing influence. They accordingly recommended to the king that the prophet be put to death, and Zedekiah delivered him into their power. Apparently out of reluctance actually to shed the prophet's blood, it was decided that he should be left in the muddy bottom of one of the many deep cisterns used in that part of the world for storing water. An Ethiopian eunuch named Ebed-Melek, serving in Zedekiah's court, took pity on Jeremiah and persuaded the king to release him from his fatal imprisonment. Subsequently, Jerusalem fell within a year to the Babylonian siege. Jeremiah was well treated and left in a position of influence. Zedekiah was made to witness the execution of his sons before being himself blinded and sent to perpetual exile.

The passage from the letter to the Hebrews read in today's liturgy immediately follows a long section, introduced by a classic description of faith, which presents a sort of literary pageant of the Old Testament's illustrious examples of great faith, beginning with the patriarch Abraham and continuing up through the prophets. The point to which all this is leading is introduced by the rhetorical question, "And what about us?" The passage then adopts a metaphor in which all the past paragons of faith are imagined as spectators at a great public spectacle in which Christians race toward the goal that faith has presented to them through Jesus Christ. This athletic metaphor makes it possible to liken ridding oneself of sin to a runner's stripping himself of all encumbrances that might slow his progress.

Jesus is presented as not only the goal of faith, but its perfect model, who allowed nothing, not even the prospect of the cross, to interfere with his unswerving course toward "the joy which lay before him." Jesus' example of being undeterred by the most fearsome obstacles placed in his way by sinful people is a permanent encouragement for Christians who are disheartened to the point of abandoning the goal of their faith.

The third reading, taken from the Gospel according to Luke, is introduced by two metaphors peculiar to that Gospel. Each of them is presented in the form of an intense wish on the part of Jesus that something were already taking place which still lies in the future. One of the metaphors refers to something Jesus is to do, the lighting of a fire on the earth, and the other refers to something that is to be done to Jesus, his receiving of a baptism.

The former metaphor, of fire, has considerable precedent in Old Testament usage. Typically, in contexts like the present one, fire refers to divine judgment, in which the quality of human lives is tested as relentlessly as the purity of metal is tested by fire. Indeed, the word pure is derived, almost unchanged, from the Greek word for fire. Jesus sees his own mission as one that brings upon humankind the purifying, discriminating power of divine judgment. This notion of separating purity from impurities is made more concrete in the subsequent tests that develop the idea that Jesus has come to bring, not peace, but division. This division, which is to sever even the closest family ties, depends on the inescapable challenge to either accept or reject Jesus and his message. Since Jesus comes as the image and emissary of God, humankind's response to him represents their response to God himself.

The metaphor of baptism is one that takes on a special significance in the New Testament. The word had not yet, of course, taken on its technical meaning as the name of a religious rite, and it still meant simply a dipping or bathing, which might be adapted to religious purposes as it was by John the Baptist, who used the ceremonial bathing to symbolize a reform of life. Jesus used the term baptism as a metaphor referring to his passion and death, as in the present text. Apparently, the conception that underlies this metaphor is that of a critical transformation into a new way of life or state of being, as in the penitential symbolism of John the Baptist. Thus both the fire and the baptism symbolize the imminent crisis of divine judgment, brought about by the consummation of Jesus' mission whereby, through his death, new life is offered to the world.

TWENTY-FIRST SUNDAY OF THE YEAR

Cycle "A" Readings: Is. 22:15, 19-23; Rom. 11:33-36; Mt. 16:13-20

The first reading, from the book of Isaiah, is an isolated and, in the context of our present Bible, relatively insignificant episode. A man named Shebna is identified as master of the palace, indicating that he held a high position at the court of Hezekiah, who was king, and a religious reformer, of the southern kingdom toward the end of the eighth century. The prophet Isaiah expresses divinely inspired indignation over the fact, mention of which is omitted from the reading, that this man had had a richly ostentatious tomb constructed for himself. The prophet, therefore, predicts Shebna's deposition, and his replacement by Eliakim, an official who is subsequently highly praised by Isaiah. The latter part of the reading alludes to the official dress worn by, and the authority wielded by, the master of the palace, who appears to have exercised many of the functions of a prime minister. The key which is referred to symbolizes this official's unique prerogative of granting or preventing access to the royal palace in Jerusalem belonging to the dynasty of David. The kind of key used by such a functionary was in fact a much larger implement than the keys we are normally familiar with. Thus the description of Eliakim as carrying the key on his shoulder refers to a procedure that was not merely symbolic, but practical as well.

The second reading, from the letter to the Romans, is entirely composed of exclamations and rhetorical questions. Both the style and the content are strongly reminiscent of Old Testament wisdom literature, which contains many passages expressing admiration and awe at the creative and directive power of God, and the profound divine wisdom implied in the combination of complexity and order found in both nature and history. In discerning this complexity and order, human beings are reminded of how immensely the workings of their own minds are exceeded by the mind of God. In their recurrent experience of seemingly chaotic circumstances leading, unpredictably, to coherent and significant outcomes, the sages learned to rely upon the wisdom of God even when they were least able to perceive it or anticipate its operations. It is this attitude of mind that Paul brings to what may well have been the most disconcerting of all his Christian convictions. For he had been compelled to conclude that the messiah promised to his own people, the Jews, prepared for by the whole history of that people, and come at last out of the very midst of that people, was by that same people generally unacknowledged and even repudiated. Paul is sure that this seeming perversity of history is part of a flawless and indefectible divine plan. He has already offered his readers his own expectation of how that plan is to achieve a happy outcome in the reunion of Jews with their Messiah in company with the Gentile believers. In this spirit of confidence, he concludes his discussion of this difficult subject on a note not of argument but of prayer. His prayer takes the very appropriate form of a doxology, or glorification of God, who gives initial origin, continuing direction, and ultimate purpose to everything.

The third reading, from the Gospel according to Matthew, is typical of that Gospel's great interest in the role of the apostle called Simon and re-named Peter. There can be little doubt that this concentration on episodes in which Peter figures prominently reflects, and is motivated by, a unique importance attributed to Peter in the early Church. Peter's distinctive leadership and prestige during the first Christian generation is abundantly indicated by Luke in Acts of the Apostles, and it is understandable that an evangelist should have wished to show the roots of Peter's subsequent authority in the context of Jesus' own lifetime. Thus in the present passage, Jesus is represented as asking the whole group of his disciples what they understand his identity to be, but as receiving an answer from Simon Peter alone. Peter's answer, acknowledging the messianic character of his master, prompts a response which expresses basic beliefs among the early Christians. There is implied first their belief that the builder of their "assembly," to translate more literally what is also rendered as "church," was Jesus Christ himself. And there is further implied their belief that Jesus had given Peter a relationship to that construction which was uniquely fundamental. Peter's role is represented as that of a bearer of the keys, like Eliakim in the first reading, a holder of authority from the highest source to admit or exclude. Likewise indicative of authority are the references to binding and loosing, rabbinical terms denoting legitimate powers of prohibition and permission. Only in Peter's case, the sphere of authority is not a human realm of government and law, but the transcendent scope of the Kingdom of Heaven.

TWENTY-FIRST SUNDAY OF THE YEAR

Cycle "B" Readings: Jos. 24:1-2a, 15-17, 18b;
Eph. 5:21-32; Jn. 6:59-69

The first reading in today's liturgy is taken from the account in the book of Joshua of the great assembly held at the ancient city of Shechem of all the tribes of Israel. Joshua, presiding over this assembly, is described as delivering an address having three main parts: first, a summation of the history of God's guidance of Israel up to that time; second, a summons for the people to choose between this God called Yahweh and other gods; and third, the confirmation by covenant of the Israelites' allegiance to their own God, Yahweh. The liturgical reading comprises the opening of this address and the second part of it, in which first Joshua and then all the people declare their deliberate choice of Yahweh as the God whom they acknowledge and serve. A passage of this kind serves to remind us that for ancient Israel, religious diversity was conceived as a matter not so much of different ways of worshiping God as of different gods competing for worship. By the same token, early monotheism was not a systematic denial of the philosophical possibility of multiple deities, but rather an unqualified commitment to one god exclusively. Monotheism was not a metaphysical conclusion but a moral decision. Israel's fundamental religious assertion is not that "there are no other gods," but that "there are no other gods for us." This passage also reminds us that Israel's exclusive worship of Yahweh was moral not only in its form, but also in its motivation. Israel chose Yahweh over all other gods for the plain and excellent reason that Yahweh was understood to have chosen Israel over all other peoples. The first part of Joshua's address calls attention to the belief that the Israelites' preservation and progress, under very unpromising historical conditions, was owing to the constant concern and intervention of Yahweh. And given such a belief, for Israel to opt for Yahweh as its sole deity was a matter of elementary gratitude or even of elementary self-interest.

The second reading, from the letter to the Ephesians, is one of two well-known passages in the Pauline literature that are based on the idea that "the man is the head of the woman." This idea makes its first appearance in St. Paul's first letter to the Corinthians, where he objects to women's uncovering their heads in religious assemblies as a failure to acknowledge the social subordination and intrinsic inferiority which Paul, like his Jewish contemporaries, attributed to women as a fact established and intended by God. Without in any way relinquishing the assumption of male superiority represented by man's "headship" or softening the demand for wifely submissiveness, Ephesians also applies the idea of male headship in a new way. The new application rests on an analogy between the husband as head of his wife and Christ as head of his Church. The force of this analogy is to emphasize that the husband ought to love his wife as Christ loves his

Church, with tender solicitude and self-sacrificing devotion. In this context, the words of the creation account in Genesis concerning the conjugal union of man and woman is viewed as a symbolic foreshadowing of the relationship of Christ to his Church. This latter idea has furnished Roman Catholic theology with its favorite argument for regarding marriage as a Christian sacrament. Whatever the merits of this argument, which has found little acceptance among other than Roman Catholic theologians, there can be little doubt that it received strong but illegitimate support in the past from the fact that in the Latin translation of the New Testament, Ephesians 5:32 is rendered by the words *Sacramentum hoc magnum est*. These words were not infrequently interpreted as a plain Scriptural assertion that marriage is, in the technical theological sense, a sacrament. Whereas, of course, that technical theological vocabulary was unknown to the writers of Scripture, and *sacramentum* merely translates the Greek word *mysterion*, meaning in this context something like "hidden symbolism."

The last reading in today's liturgy is an account which, in the Gospel according to John, is presented as the final scene of Jesus' Galilean ministry before his journey to Jerusalem. The occasion immediately follows the discourse in which Jesus identified his flesh as "bread for the life of the world." These words are said to have proved intolerable to many of Jesus' disciples. The whole episode registers an atmosphere of dissolution, of declining confidence in Jesus and weakening adherence to him. At the same time, Jesus himself is represented as unsurprised and undismayed, fully anticipating the defection of his followers in general and the treason of Judas in particular. Although the disaffection of Jesus' disciples has often been attributed to their sense of scandal or incredulity at an announcement of the Holy Eucharist, there is good reason to doubt that a proclamation of the Eucharist originally preceded the present passage. There is likewise good reason to believe that the present passage originally referred to an earlier context, in which Jesus called himself the "bread of life" not in the Eucharistic sense, but rather according to Jewish imagery which equated "bread" with divine revelation. On this understanding, what Jesus' disciples are rejecting is not simply sacramental doctrine, but the whole idea of Jesus as God's Word.

TWENTY-FIRST SUNDAY OF THE YEAR

Cycle "C" Readings: Is. 66:18-21; Heb. 12:5-7, 11-13; Lk. 13:22-30

It is the opinion of many biblical scholars that our present Book of Isaiah combines three distinct works, issued at different times from different writers. According to this view, the last ten chapters constitute a relatively late work, perhaps of a number of writers, called for convenience "Third Isaiah." The material contained in this work comes from the time after Israel's exile in Babylonia, and it has in many places a rather triumphal air, reflecting a spirit of relief, vindication, and restoration. In the present reading, this atmosphere is conspicuous. The vindication of Israel is understood to be the accomplishment, not of Israel's people, but of Israel's God.

The renewed glory of Israel, restored after such inglorious years, is identified with the divine glory. This idea of divine glory is an important one in the Old Testament, signifying an outward derivative brilliance manifesting the greatness of a God whose intrinsic brilliance exceeds the power of human contemplation to behold. The restored Jerusalem is here regarded as the focal point of God's glory, and as a kind of beacon drawing together a gathering of the nations, that is, of the non-Jewish world, to experience the greatness of Israel's God and declare that greatness to the farthest extremities of the known world, represented by the series of exotic place-names. With this image of a kind of worldwide publicity for the glory of Yahweh, the author combines the Zionist motif of bringing the far-flung Jewish exiles back to their ancestral homeland.

The second reading, from the letter to the Hebrews, follows that letter's long catalogue of the Old Testament's heroes of faith, which concludes with an exhortation to Christians to see themselves as the heirs of that tradition, striving under the gaze of their illustrious predecessors to achieve the goal offered to them through Jesus Christ. Against this background, the writer then confronts the painful realities of what this striving actually entails for dedicated Christians in the way of suffering. To the endurance of this suffering he offers consolation in the form of a traditional interpretation of suffering as divine discipline.

The author cites a passage from the Book of Proverbs which represents the hardships of the God-fearing as God's rigorous training of them to become what he means them to be. Understood in this way, suffering is indeed attributed to God as its source, but as a source motivated by love. The author reminds Christians that fatherly love, responsibly exercised, inevitably inflicts pain, but does so in an effort not to torment but to improve, not to frustrate but to develop. The writer thus characterizes the exasperation of Christians whose lives are fraught with suffering as similar to the typical resentment by children of a severe parental discipline which is inflicted entirely for their own good. They are thus exhorted to consider their suffering from a more enlightened viewpoint, as part of the process of their formation as mature Christians.

The third reading, from the Gospel according to Luke, is a passage situated in the account of Jesus' final journey to Jerusalem. Inasmuch as this is the journey that ends with Jesus' passion and resurrection, it takes on in this Gospel a symbolic character, and serves as a constant reminder that Jesus is not a wandering teacher but a resolute messiah intent on the destiny appointed for him by God. A sense of the universal import of that destiny is reflected in some of the episodes of the journey, such as the present one, which is introduced by someone asking whether there are only a "few in number who are to be saved." This is a kind of question that Jesus seems to have avoided answering in plain, direct terms. Here the answer he gives is certainly compatible with the idea that only a few are to be saved, inasmuch as he appears to assert that many, in fact, will not be saved.

Jesus sounds a warning which seems to be intended explicitly for the Jews, whose privileged status as the messiah's own people might lend support to a tragic presumption of immunity from divine judgment. There can be little doubt that this passage has been influenced by subsequent developments such as those narrated in the Acts of the Apostles, involving the ultimate breach between Christianity and its Jewish origins, and the receptivity of the Gentile world to the message of the Gospel. Thus the force of the passage is not so much a statistical anticipation of the relative proportion of the elect and the reprobate at the last judgment, as an historical retrospect.

TWENTY-SECOND SUNDAY OF THE YEAR

Cycle "A" Readings: Jer. 20:7-9; Rom. 12:1-2; Mt. 16:21-27

The first reading is from the book of the prophet who has left us more than any other in the way of biographical data, Jeremiah. This remarkable man lived during and after the final, tragic years of Israel. He was born about a century after the northern kingdom had succumbed to its Assyrian conquerors, and he died, an unwilling refugee in Egypt, sometime after the southern kingdom had fallen to Assyria's own conquerors, the Babylonians, in the early part of the sixth century. Jeremiah's career was a stormy one even by the standards of such tumultuous times. His prophetic audacity earned him some very harsh treatment, and his life was frequently in danger. Jeremiah had an especially hostile relationship with Jehoiakin, the next to last ruler of the independent southern kingdom of Judah. It was probably by the authority of this king that the prophet was flogged and put into stocks by the chief official of the temple. This action was in retaliation for Jeremiah's denunciation of the corrupt temple worship and his prediction that Jerusalem would be destroyed. Far from being intimidated by his punishment, Jeremiah, immediately on being released, directed at his captor, the temple official, a prediction of divine punishment ending only with death as a friendless exile in Babylon. This episode is immediately followed by the passage from which the reading is taken, and the contrast is striking. Whereas the narrative describes the irrepressible wrath of a dauntless prophet, the poetic passage that follows it displays the private side of this remarkable life. He addresses God with the same bluntness that characterizes his prophecies, telling God that he lured him into the position in which he now finds himself, an object of detestation and derision, so tormented that he strives even to keep himself from prophesying. But, however exasperated and exhausted he becomes, Jeremiah finds that the divine fire within him cannot be quenched and must, despite the consequences, burst forth into speech.

The second reading comprises the first two verses of a long section of the letter to the Romans which is devoted to practical Christian holiness, or the living of a distinctively Christian moral life. The background of this material is Paul's famous discussion, earlier in the same letter, of the meaning, and the means, of justification, understood as the achieving of a right relationship with God to replace the wrong relationship which is called sin. Paul has insisted that the person who is justified, not through obedience to the law but through faith in Jesus Christ, acquires not simply a new formal status, but a genuinely new life, intimately united with the life of Christ himself, and thereby to the principle of divine life which he calls the Spirit of God. This new life, like any real life, is to be and indeed has to be lived, actively, inwardly and outwardly. The outward living of it is Paul's basic idea of Christian morality. He makes no attempt to prescribe such a life in legislative detail, considering it to be the spontaneous expression of an interior spiritual principle that makes it possible to "judge what is God's will," what is good, pleasing and perfect. He does reflect on some examples of what such a life entails, but mainly he exhorts his readers to live their lives on this basis. These introductory verses are typical of his exhortation, appealing for holy lives, in the sense of lives consecrated by the Spirit that directs them. Such living is for Paul the most authentic kind of worship, and persons who live such lives fulfill in the deepest sense the meaning of sacrifice.

The third reading is an episode which marks a decisive turning point in the narrative of the Gospel according to Matthew. The new direction of the story is pointed clearly by the first verse, which tells us that "from then on" Jesus told of his imminent destiny, in the city of Jerusalem, where he was to suffer and die at the hands of the Jewish leaders, and on the third day to rise again. That the meaning of the last phrase was unperceived at the time is made clear by Peter's intensely negative reaction, which envisages only the tragic outcome of the forthcoming journey to Jerusalem. In the rather vehement exchange between Jesus and Peter which follows this reaction we are shown both the seriousness of Peter's misconception of Jesus' mission, and the indispensably central importance attributed to the events commemorated in Holy Week. The profundity of their disagreement is expressed in Jesus' final accusation: "You are not judging by God's standards but by man's." The evangelist has made this crucial argument a point of departure for Jesus' instructions to his disciples, in which he assures them that his own destiny cannot be escaped by those who would follow him. Just as self-saving preoccupations would frustrate his own messianic mission, so too they would frustrate the mission of his disciples. The significance of this exhortation, like the mention of the resurrection, depends on the experiences after Good Friday from which the apostolic Church emerged.

TWENTY-SECOND SUNDAY OF THE YEAR

Cycle "B" Readings: Deut. 4:1-2, 6-8; Jas. 1:17-18, 21b-22, 27; Mk. 7:1-8a, 14-15, 21-23

It is difficult for modern people to understand and almost impossible for them to assume the attitude toward divine law that is so frequently and so eloquently expressed in the Old Testament. Among us, the necessity of law and the importance of good laws are commonly acknowledged. But this recognition of law's rightfully important place in society seldom carries with it any notable enthusiasm. Whereas in Israel, the sense of the law's importance comes across to us in the Bible as a sense full of reverence, admiration, and actual pride. Thus, in today's first liturgical reading, from the book of Deuteronomy, we find the law regarded as a thing of such conspicuous excellence that it is expected to make Israel the envy of its largely hostile neighbors. The basic explanation of Israel's pride in the law is, of course, Israel's conviction that the law was neither contrived nor discovered by people, but was a gift bestowed directly by God. The law was, moreover, a very special gift, uniquely bestowed on Israel, as part of that covenant whereby Israel became the people of God, chosen by God for a uniquely exalted destiny. To keep the law meant for the Israelites to do their part in preserving the covenant. And to preserve the covenant meant keeping in vital touch with that God by whose love Israel survived and prospered. The dependence of Israel's blessings on Israel's adherence to the law is initially expressed, as in the present passage, in terms of a condition for entering the promised land. Subsequently, Israel's security and prosperity in that land were regularly interpreted as functions of Israel's fidelity to the law given by God to Moses. The fact that all the formulations and elaborations of the law given in the Old Testament are attributed to Moses is historically indefensible but religiously and culturally quite understandable. For this attribution of the law to Moses, who received the covenant, preserves the law's essential connection with the covenant, and thereby its fundamental position in the life of Israel.

The place of law in the religion of the New Testament, the issue often referred to in terms of the relationship between Gospel and law, has been a subject of much thought and much debate throughout Christian history and especially since the Reformation. Protestants have sometimes insisted that law has no place whatever in Christian religion, which consists of God's assurance of forgiveness and humanity's response of faith, and has nothing to do with setting up rules of behavior by following which salvation is somehow earned. Catholics have often favored an opposite emphasis, that Christ has called us to be his active followers by living in the way that his example shows us and his words teach us. Both of these emphases can find support within the New Testament itself. The former one is most evident in the principal letters of St. Paul, which had so strong an influence on the theology of the Protestant Reformers. The latter one is especially characteristic of the letter of James, for which, it may be recalled, Martin Luther had an undisguised dislike. It is not unlikely that the letter of James, from which our second liturgical reading is taken, was aimed in part at correcting an exaggerated interpretation of the opposite emphasis found in St. Paul's writings. In any case, the letter of James clearly perceives in the doctrine of "salvation by faith" a danger of supposing that humanity can hope to be reconciled with God merely by believing certain doctrines, quite regardless of how one leads one's life. Consequently, the letter, while clearly attaching the hope of salvation to the acceptance of the Gospel, tends to stress that the Gospel itself has an obligatory aspect, and that genuine acceptance of it entails obedience to it as what the letter calls "the perfect law, the law that makes us free." The practical emphasis characteristic of the letter of James is well expressed by the phrase "be sure that you act on the message and do not merely listen; for that would be to mislead yourselves."

In the life and teaching of Jesus Christ as we find it in the New Testament an attitude toward the law appears which is at the same time critical and respectful. On the critical side, this attitude appears most clearly as a resolute opposition to legalism, especially in the form of a punctilious outward observance of regulations in disregard of, or even in opposition to, interior morality. Jesus tends to deal with the obligations imposed by rabbinical tradition in a way that emphasizes the human, and therefore perfectly fallible origin of these obligations. Far from being elucidations and applications of divine law, the teachings of these moral theologians were criticized by Jesus as constituting serious obstacles to doing the authentic will of God. Both Jesus' insistence on interior morality as opposed to external formalities, and his effort to rescue the truly divine imperatives from a morass of misleading human interpretations appear clearly in the third liturgical reading from the Gospel according to Mark. Thus, apropos the contemporary teachers, he charges that they "neglect the commandment of God, in order to maintain the tradition of men." And apropos their teachings about purification, he insists that "nothing that goes from outside into a man can defile him . . . It is what comes out of a man that defiles him."

TWENTY-SECOND SUNDAY OF THE YEAR

Cycle "C" Readings: Sir. 3:17-21, 28-31;
Heb. 12:18-19, 22-24; Lk. 14:1, 7-14

The first reading of today's liturgy is taken from the Book of Sirach. Often called Ecclesiasticus, this is a work of wisdom literature that was extremely popular in the early Christian Church. It was not part of the Hebrew Bible, and Protestants accordingly classify it among the apocrypha, whereas Roman Catholics still regard it as part of the Old Testament. The book as we know it is a Greek rendering done late in the second century of a Hebrew book composed by the translator's grandfather, Jesus ben Sirach, earlier in the same century, as is explained in a prologue which accompanies the text in our Bibles.

The book's content is mostly short essays and discourses devoted to advising on a great many subjects pertaining to morals and manners. Practical philosophy of life is thus what the book has mainly to offer, and much of it has no particular religious or theological significance, though much of the moralizing is expressed as the kind of personal deportment God approves of. The reading has put together in a somewhat confusing way portions of two successive passages dealing with quite different topics. Thus the first verses of the reading belong to an exhortation calling for a modest, gentle manner of life, free of pretentiousness or excessive ambition. The final verse is an appeal for docility to such wisdom teachings as the book itself contains, offered as the positive implication of a denunciation of mental stubbornness or being opinionated. Common to both passages is a commendation of what in general might be called humility or deference.

The second reading is taken from the letter to the Hebrews, and the verses it contains touch very closely the basic theme of that document. Expressed in the broadest possible terms, that theme is the relationship of Christianity to Judaism, understood in such a way that Judaism is understood to be simply obsolete, totally and permanently superseded by the religion based on faith in Jesus Christ. It is clear that this theme is part of a vigorous controversy, and that the writer is reacting against what he judges to be a serious danger to Christians from Jewish or pro-Jewish influences. It is not clear precisely how this danger was envisaged, or precisely who were considered to be its source. Possibly the writer anticipated defection from Christianity to Judaism on the part of some believers. Possibly what he feared was rather that Christianity might become encumbered with Jewish religious obligations. In any case, he never tires of contrasting Christianity with Judaism as the new and perfect are contrasted with the old and imperfect.

This recurrent pattern of contrast is exemplified in the verses selected for the reading. In this instance, the basic contrast is drawn between the presence of God to the people of Israel and the presence of God to the people of Christ. The former is represented by the theophany at Mount Sinai, when the covenant took the form of Mosaic Law. The event is recalled as a terrifying experience of the closeness of God, expressed in fire and darkness and trumpeting and words of revelation. With this account of God's presence on the sacred mountain, there is contrasted an account of Christians as a people who stand before the heavenly city of God. Thus, whereas Israel's God comes down into the presence of his people, as the Christian God he rather brings the people up into his own celestial presence.

The third reading is a parable peculiar to the Gospel according to Luke, said to have been occasioned by the scrambling of Jesus' fellow guests to occupy positions of honor at a dinner. Elsewhere in the same Gospel we read that Jesus directly criticized the scribes for the same kind of behavior and for other conduct similarly rooted in personal pride. The lesson is one that, at least on a certain level, belongs to a tradition of proverbial social wisdom. On that level, the wisdom consists in recognizing that one who puts himself forward too brashly risks the embarrassment of being snubbed, whereas unpretentious behavior maximizes one's chances of being singled out for honor. A neat proverb to this effect is the saying, found in several different New Testament contexts, "Everyone who exalts himself shall be humbled and he who humbles himself shall be exalted."

Jesus' words could be interpreted as simply echoing this tradition of social tact, but the passage that follows them, as well as the whole pattern of Jesus' teaching, makes it clear that he refers primarily to the status of human beings not before their fellow human beings, but before God. It is not social acceptance, but divine acceptance, that calls for humility. Accordingly, the humility is no more appropriate for guests with respect to their host than it is for a host with respect to guests. For guests and hosts are in the same position before God, and the humility of the one is no less essential to divine acceptance than the humility of the other.

TWENTY-THIRD SUNDAY OF THE YEAR

Cycle "A" Readings: Ezek. 33:7-9; Rom. 13:8-10; Mt. 18:15-20

Ezekiel was one of a group of Israelites deported to Babylon ten years before the final destruction of Jerusalem, and his prophetic charism was exercised among his fellow exiles. The passage in today's liturgy corresponds to the time just before the great catastrophe of 587 B.C., and its imagery seems to reflect the prophet's consciousness of Jerusalem's besieged condition and apprehensive mood. For the passage is introduced by a reminder that, in time of war, people appoint sentinels to keep sharp watch for the first sign of invading forces and to sound the alarm for emergency defense measures. This is a situation which implies two levels of obligation: the sentinel's duty to perceive the danger and sound the warning, and the citizens' duty to heed the warning and oppose the danger.

Ezekiel represents his own situation as analogous to that of the sentinel. For his duty is precisely to sound a warning, loud and clear, of impending disaster. Only the danger the prophet warns against is not military but moral. It is the menace which the just God inevitably represents in an unjust society whose sins cry to heaven for vengeance. And Ezekiel's job is to warn of that menace, as God's sentinel, appointed to wake out of their complacent torpor a people who, in the world of a just God, cannot go forever unpunished. It is notable that Ezekiel's fidelity to this joyless task of public admonition is based on motivation which characterizes him as a prophet. It is not primarily compassionate concern for the people which impels Ezekiel to strive for their reform. Rather it is obedience to God, who makes prophets, not for their reasons, but for his own, to deliver messages, not of their devising but of his. The words of a prophet are, to be sure, words of love. But the love they are words of is God's love, and of that love the prophet is merely an instrument, whose service depends on unquestioning obedience to God.

The second reading is taken from that concluding section of Paul's letter to the Romans which mainly comprises a series of moral exhortations to the Christian community. And in reading this section one cannot but notice the distinctively Christian difference of Paul's conscious motivation from that of an Old Testament prophet like Ezekiel. Paul, no less than Ezekiel, conceives his role as that of one called by God to be his spokesman, and fulfills his role as the instrument of God's love. And yet it is conspicuous how much more closely in Paul's case responsiveness to God's mission is associated, and even identified with responsiveness to humanity's need. For in Paul's theology one finds a habitual sense of continuity between what God provides and what people require. And as a result, within the framework of that theology, responsiveness to the spiritual or material poverty of other people becomes inseparable in principle from responsiveness to the abundant generosity of God. The apostolic position is, in other words, that of a kind of middleman between divine supply and human demand. And so St. Paul, like Jesus his Master, has no hesitation about simply equating fulfillment of the law, which means, of course, obedience to God, with love of one's neighbor. For obedience to God means doing God's will in this world. And it is the belief of Christians that God's will in this world is the healing and saving of all people.

The selection in today's liturgy from the Gospel according to Matthew invites us to identify the kind of job we have seen Ezekiel doing with the kind of doctrine we have seen Paul expounding. For this well-known presentation of the Christian attitude towards fraternal correction is a reminder that the kind of message God entrusted to the prophet Ezekiel is a kind of thing that any Christian may at times be obliged to say because God wants it said. But God wants it said because there are those who need to hear it said. Christians have at times, with respect to their neighbor, that same duty which Ezekiel's sentinel had with respect to his endangered fellow-citizens. There are times, in other words, when what is owed by "the debt that binds us to love one another" is precisely a warning. "If your brother should commit some wrong against you, go and point out his fault, but keep it between the two of you." The object of this embarrassing interview is not retaliation. It is reconciliation. "If he listens to you, you have won your brother over." It is for the sake, not of the offended, but of the offender. It is not to extort an apology but to restore a vital relationship. It is an act in one's neighbor's behalf out of the conviction that "If anyone says 'My love is fixed on God,' yet hates his brother, he is a liar." Fraternal correction is a task undertaken for the sake of opening one's brother or sister to the love of God and the life of the Church. And if all efforts fail, both alone and with the help of others, the offender is alienated from the community by a refusal to love and be loved. It is this danger, the greatest of all dangers, which obliges the Christian, like Ezekiel's watchman, to give warning, kindly but clearly, before it is too late.

TWENTY-THIRD SUNDAY OF THE YEAR
Cycle "B" Readings: Is. 35:4-7a; Jas. 2:1-5; Mk. 7:31-37

The first reading of today's liturgy is part of a lovely Hebrew poem which comprises a chapter of the book of Isaiah that could be appropriately entitled Paradise Regained. From start to finish it is a lyrical celebration of the renewal of life and strength, beauty and wholesomeness. Its initial and recurrent imagery is that of an arid wasteland which has been suddenly irrigated and is fairly bursting with fertility. This theme of dramatic rehabilitation is carried on by a series of images of human recovery, from feebleness to strength, from anxiety to assurance, and from blind, deaf, dumb unresponsiveness to a fullness of sensation and expression. The context of these exuberant verses indicates that their literal subject matter is one of the most eagerly anticipated events in the entire Old Testament narrative, namely the return of the Israelites to their native soil from the exile known as the Babylonian Captivity. One noteworthy feature is that in this joyous context God is referred to chiefly under his title as judge. And we are thereby reminded that to think of God as judge was, in the perspective of the Old Testament, to think of him in heartening rather than in menacing terms. For as judge God was conceived of as the bringer of justice, the righter of wrongs, and therefore as the ultimate basis of hope for all victims of injustice. Consequently, for patient sufferers God the judge was for all practical purposes equivalent to God the savior, and to celebrate the saving acts of God was to celebrate his acts of judgment. The contrast familiar in Christian usage between God's dreaded justice and his longed-for mercy is not, therefore, a conspicuous feature of Old Testament thought. And by the same token, the eager hopefulness with whom Israelites prayed to God precisely as judge and prayed to him precisely for judgment is likely to impress Christians as presumptuous.

The letter of James, from which the second liturgical reading is taken, is almost unique among New Testament writings in being exclusively occupied with moral exhortation, without any real preaching of the Christian Gospel or explanation of Christian belief. The section read in this liturgy is part of a larger section devoted to the subject of social discrimination. The behavior it denounces as irreconcilable with Christianity is the showing of special honors to the rich and, as the other side of the same coin, the dishonoring of the poor. The scene it depicts is the still sadly familiar scene of supposedly religious people acting with fulsome obsequiousness toward those who are conspicuously wealthy, while treating the poor indifferently or patronizingly. Christians who behave in this way are sharply reprehended as persons who "judge by false standards." The completely opposite orientation of the Gospel is called to mind by the reference to God's having "chosen those who are poor in the eyes of the world to be rich in faith and to inherit the kingdom." As the letter proceeds, this orientation is manifested more strongly in a positive hostility to the rich who are collectively stigmatized as "oppressors." At the same time, those Christians to whom the letter of James is addressed are themselves identified with the poor. Attitudes toward riches and those who possess riches are cool at best in the New Testament writings, but in certain documents, such as this one, the opposition between Christian love and wealth is expressed in the most radical terms. Correspondingly, New Testament attitudes toward poverty vary in intensity, but are consistently favorable. And, in view of the rather technical conceptions of so-called "evangelical poverty" which were developed later in the history of the Church, it may be necessary to recall that, as in the present reading, so throughout the New Testament, poverty is understood primarily in its ordinary sense of grave economic deprivation and consequent insecurity, and never as a merely dependent economic status, however comfortable and secure.

The third reading, from the Gospel according to Mark, contains distinct echoes of the first reading, from the book of Isaiah. It is highly probable that the evangelist formulated his narrative of Jesus' curing the deaf mute in such a way as to emphasize the episode's correspondence with a celebrated Old Testament prophecy. The actions performed by Jesus in curing the man, which may seem bizarre or ostentatious to modern readers, are known to have been employed by Greek and Jewish healers. They are gestures which, by strongly implying the possibility of a cure, might serve to enlist the power of suggestion in the healing process. In this episode, as so often in Mark's Gospel, the fact that Jesus "forbade them to tell anyone" is, under the circumstances of a cure which could scarcely go unnoticed, a rather perplexing feature, considered by some interpreters to have been supplied after the event. If this is an editorial addition, it might well be accounted for as an effort by Christian writers to indicate why Jesus' messianic character was not widely acknowledged during his lifetime.

TWENTY-THIRD SUNDAY OF THE YEAR

Cycle "C" Readings: Wis. 9:13-18; Phlm. 9-10, 12-17; Lk. 14:25-33

The first reading is from a book which Jews and Protestants exclude from the biblical canon, while Catholics continue to regard it as part of the Old Testament. Its title, "Wisdom of Solomon," is a literary fiction, and the book was actually written nearly a millennium after Solomon's reign. The reading is part of a passage represented as addressed in prayer by Solomon to God. This portion of the prayer strongly reflects popular Greek philosophy in its explanation of humankind's inability to penetrate divine intentions because "the corruptible body burdens the soul and the earthen shelter weighs down the mind." This sharp distinction between soul and body and the conception of matter as detrimental to mind are alien to typically biblical thought and represent the influence on Judaism of that Platonic philosophy that was to become so much a part of Christian theology.

The next-to-last verse of the passage anticipates Christian theology in its reference to God's sending of the "holy spirit from on high" to enlighten human minds in their effort to grasp the divine will. Although later applied by Christians to trinitarian theology, the "holy spirit" referred to here is wisdom itself, the main theme of this book, which refers to wisdom as both a divine attribute and a divine gift, and refers to it at times with a high degree of personification. Although it would be a mistake to read Christian theology into this passage, it is a passage in which currents of thought are vigorously at work that would later greatly influence Gentile Christian theology.

The letter of Paul to Philemon, from which the second reading is taken, is the only example in the New Testament of what most of us think of as a personal letter, from one individual to another, focused on private concerns. Paul wrote from Rome, where he was under arrest, to three persons at Colossae who may have been members of a single household, that of Philemon, at whose home the local Christians regularly convened. He wrote on behalf of a slave of Philemon's, named Onesimus, who had run away from his master and come to Rome, where he had been serving Paul. A fugitive slave was liable to very severe penalties, and the main purpose of the letter is to enable Onesimus to return to Philemon without fear of the consequences. Paul's reference to the slave as "my child, whom I have begotten during my imprisonment" implies that he has made a Christian of him during their time together. Thus his conciliatory letter is greatly facilitated by the fact that he is sending a Christian slave back to a Christian master and can appeal to their common Christianity as the basis for a kind reunion.

Paul seems to hint that he would be pleased if Onesimus could remain with him, but he does not want to presume on Philemon's generosity, and he recognizes that the best thing of all might be for the slave and the master to remain together in a new relationship, based on their brotherhood as Christians. Commentators on this shortest book of the Bible almost invariably discuss the fact that Paul does not seek to persuade Philemon to free Onesimus, nor does he express any misgivings about the institution of slavery. We are reminded thereby that a transformation of social institutions, in the sense of replacing certain institutions by others, was no part of Paul's program. For Paul, if human relationships were fashioned in the spirit of Christ, it made little difference whether the persons involved were, technically speaking, slaves or free men.

The passage which the third reading cites from the Gospel according to Luke is a notoriously strong statement of the "cost of discipleship," of what it means, in terms of suffering and deprivation, to be a committed follower of Jesus Christ. Basically, what the passage asserts is that the only valid commitment to Jesus is unconditional commitment, that discipleship with limits or reservations is no real discipleship at all. Accordingly, to give this lesson concreteness, the passage first lists what is most precious to good people, parents, spouse, children, siblings, and life itself, and declares that to be a real follower of Jesus is to make these an object of "hatred," as the term is literally but misleadingly rendered. The meaning is obviously not that one should foster actual animosity toward those who are normally nearest and dearest, but that in one's order of priorities even these cannot take preference over the following of Jesus Christ.

Discipleship cannot be deterred even by such extreme suffering as is represented by a daily carrying of the cross. No doubt this particular figure of speech points to the fact that when this Gospel was written down the manner of Jesus' own death was well known. The passage goes on to develop two homely illustrations of the importance of knowing clearly what one is "getting into," namely construction plans and military strategy. As essential as adequate materials are to a builder, or adequate troops are to a commander, self-dispossession is essential to a Christian disciple.

TWENTY-FOURTH SUNDAY OF THE YEAR

Cycle "A" Readings: Sir. 27:30—28:7; Rom. 14:7-9; Mt. 18:21-35

The first reading is taken from the second century wisdom book named for its author, Sirach. It is known also as Ecclesiasticus, and that title may remind us of how popular a book it was for ecclesiastical use among early Christians. Roman Catholics continue to include it in the canon of Holy Scripture, while Jews and Protestants class it among the apocrypha. Its doctrinal content anticipates both Christian and later rabbinical teaching at a number of points. This is well illustrated by the present passage, given entire in the reading, which agrees strikingly with one of Jesus' most characteristic and emphatic teachings. Throughout the passage one basic idea is reiterated, both negatively and positively, in a series of parallel verses. That basic idea is well summarized by the petition in the Lord's Prayer to "forgive us our trespasses (or: debts) as we forgive those who trespass against us (or: our debtors)." Virtually a commentary on such prayer is the verse, "Forgive your neighbor's injustice; then when you pray your own sins will be forgiven." The initial verse introduces the negative aspect of the same idea by its statement that wrath and anger, detestable in themselves, are cherished traits of sinners. Throughout the entire passage, one's expectation of divine forgiveness is represented as conditioned upon one's own readiness to forgive. A theological rationale of this doctrine is suggested in two exhortations which point to appropriate motivation. First, the reader is exhorted to think of his own death, when his need of forgiveness will be most urgent. He is likewise urged to think of God's covenant, which expresses the divine character of mercy and compassion.

The second reading, from the letter to the Romans, comprises three verses which are part of a much longer discussion of a problem that troubled the consciences of some of Paul's readers and had occasioned hard feelings among them. This discussion comes just after Paul's general exposition of Christian morality, and brings his moralizing from the level of generalities to that of particular cases. The issue is one that reappears, and is treated more fully, elsewhere in Paul's writings. It is the question of whether Christians should consider themselves obliged to adopt certain observances, in the way of diet and special holy days, as did the Jews and certain pagan sects as well. Paul consistently makes it clear that he does not regard practices of this kind as generally obligatory for Christians. But it is not this opinion that he is chiefly concerned to communicate. He knows that some of his readers share his liberal view of the matter, but he also knows that others sincerely hold a different and much stricter opinion. His main interest is to persuade both parties to live together peacefully in an atmosphere of mutual respect. If in one sense he defends liberty of conscience, what he defends more strongly is the right to follow one's conscience without incurring the scorn or recrimination of those whose consciences are differently convinced. Thus he insists that all who act conscientiously, even though differently, are serving God, and are answerable for their conduct to God alone, and not to critical neighbors. It is in this context that he reminds his readers that in all they do, whether living or dying, they belong and are responsible not to themselves, but to the Lord who has dominion over living and dead.

The third reading, from the Gospel according to Matthew, is a parable whose significance is indicated by the episode by which the evangelist introduces it. Peter asks Jesus how often one should forgive, suggesting that one ought to do so repeatedly. Jesus replies with a formula which says in effect that what is required is not frequent, but limitless forgiveness. By way of explanation, he describes a servant who, having been forgiven an enormous debt by the extraordinary generosity of his master, is nevertheless brutally insensitive to the pleas of a fellow servant who owes him a trivial sum of money. On learning of this grotesquely ironic development, the master retracts his former generosity, and applies to the first servant the same harshly inflexible standard that the servant had seen fit to impose on his own debtor. The parable ends with a blunt warning that the master's action in this case represents the way that God himself will deal with human beings who are unwilling to forgive. We have here one of the plainest statements in the Gospel of Jesus' repeated insistence that to be forgiving is the indispensable condition of being forgiven, that divine generosity can be effective only insofar as it is allowed to enkindle a like generosity in its human recipients. It is this fundamental principle of Christian morality that is strikingly anticipated by the wisdom text given as the first reading.

TWENTY-FOURTH SUNDAY OF THE YEAR

Cycle "B" Readings: Is. 50:5-9a; Jas. 2:14-18; Mk. 8:27-35

The first passage read in today's liturgy comprises all but the first verse and half of the last verse of the third of four famous Old Testament poems known as "servant songs." These poems, which came into the Bible as later additions to the book of Isaiah, owe their name to their frequent references to a mysterious figure called "the Lord's Servant," who is described as one singled out by God to transmit his revelation at the cost of bitter humiliation and acute suffering. These poems date from the time of the Babylonian Captivity, and they represent a message of hope in that time of great misfortune for Israel. It is highly probable that, in their original context, the poems represent Israel itself under the figure of the Servant, perhaps combined with other connotations. Among Christians, the correspondence between passages of these poems and details of Jesus' passion were noted from earliest times, and it is not unlikely that Jesus applied these passages to himself. In the liturgical selection, the Servant is represented first as one who heard God and obeyed him. The suffering which this obedience entails is here described in terms strongly reminiscent of the New Testament passion narratives: the lashing, the spitting, and the insulting words. What is emphasized in the final verses of the passage is the dauntlessness of the Servant throughout this ordeal. This dauntlessness is attributed to his unshakable confidence that "the Lord God stands by to help." Because of his assurance of God's support, the Servant is represented as confident not only of his capacity to endure abuse, but also of his ultimate vindication. His treatment is the treatment of one who is gravely guilty, the treatment given to the worst of criminals. At the same time, since all that befalls him results from his obedience to God, his innocence is perfect. And his faith in the justice of God leaves no doubt that in the last analysis his innocence will prove triumphant, and his persecutors will be overcome.

The second reading in today's liturgy is part of a passage in the letter of James which seems to be a reaction against the misapplication of St. Paul's doctrine of salvation by faith. The point of view which is here being attacked is what is called "antinomianism." It amounts to inferring from the sufficiency of faith that the moral quality of one's behavior makes no real difference. This inference was certainly not part of Paul's own teaching which, on the contrary, makes rigorous ethical demands precisely on the basis of faith. The error refuted here is shown later in the same passage to be based on a conception of faith as a mere intellectual adherence to certain doctrinal beliefs, notably the belief in monotheism. The letter of James insists, as Paul himself insisted, that real faith is inevitably manifested in a distinctive way of life, whose dominant characteristic is love. Possible though it doubtless is to hold certain true religious beliefs while continuing to live a totally uncharitable life, that kind of believing is clearly not what Paul means by faith. However, by the time, perhaps a century later, that the letter of James came to be written, faith apparently had, in some Christian circles, taken on this shallow meaning. Such faith, which in Paul's vocabulary would not have deserved the name, is described very aptly by the letter of James as "dead" faith. Subsequent Christian history has many times seen the Pauline doctrine of salvation by faith rather than by "works of the law" distorted in a way that undermines Christian ethics, and the argument of the letter of James has often proved timely.

The third reading, from the Gospel according to Mark, records words spoken by Jesus in a context that represents the central moment and turning point of the earliest account of Jesus' public life. The setting of this episode is near the northern town of Caesarea Philippi, which is the point of departure for the final journey that brings Jesus to Jerusalem and to his passion and death. The verses read in the liturgy deal with two matters of great importance which are highly appropriate to this point in the narrative of Jesus' career. First is the acknowledgment by Peter of Jesus' messianic status, by the words "You are the Christ." And second is Jesus' own prediction of his imminent passion and death. Immediately connected with this solemn announcement are the famous words in which Jesus then insists that his own courageous acceptance of mortal suffering sets a pattern which must be followed by all who claim to follow him. No passage in the Gospel deals more pointedly than this one with the crucial and inseparable questions of who Jesus is and what it means to be his disciple. The words which here express what a famous modern theologian has taught us to call "the cost of discipleship" occur almost identically in all three Synoptic Gospels and in closely equivalent terms in the Gospel according to John. On the basis of this and other evidence there are probably no other words in the New Testament which we have better reason to believe were spoken by Jesus himself. And there are probably no other words of Jesus which better epitomize the distinctive character of Christian morality. The image of courageous suffering in fidelity to God that this passage introduces into the Gospel narrative is undoubtedly related to that Old Testament image of the "Suffering Servant" which appeared in the first reading.

TWENTY-FOURTH SUNDAY OF THE YEAR

Cycle "C" Readings: Ex. 32:7-11, 13-14; 1 Tim. 1:12-17; Lk. 15:1-32

The first reading of today's liturgy is taken from the second half of the book of Exodus, which deals with Israel's sojourn at Sinai, where they received the divine covenant after the escape from Egypt and travels across the desert, recounted in the first half of the same book. The second half begins with Moses' ascent of the mountain, where God told him that if he and his people would obey God and keep his covenant, they would be God's favored people. Moses transmitted this message to his people, who responded, "All that the Lord has spoken, we will do." After reporting this response, Moses prepared the people by a ritual purification for the dramatic promulgation of the Ten Commandments which shortly followed. Part of what is generally regarded as the first commandment includes the injunction not to "make for yourself a graven image, or any likeness of anything that is in heaven above or that is in the earth beneath; you shall now bow down to them or serve them; for I the Lord your God am a jealous God." Moses then reascended the mountain for "forty days and forty nights."

The present reading describes how on his return he discovered that the people who had promised unreserved obedience to a God whose very first commandment prohibited all forms of idolatry had already lapsed into idolatry of the grossest sort. The God of Moses, who had described himself as a "jealous God," reacts accordingly to this betrayal, but in response to Moses' plea he agrees to keep his promises even to a people who so readily break their promises to him. The pattern here illustrated of an encounter between human infidelity and divine fidelity is one of the most basic motifs of biblical morality.

The second reading is from the first portion of the first letter to Timothy, supposed to have been written by St. Paul according to a tradition upon which modern scholarship has cast considerable doubt. It is, in any case, written as though Paul were its author, and it contains passages which appear to be very personal statements by Paul. Today's reading opens with one such passage, in which not only the content but the very wording has a distinctly Pauline flavor. It begins with an expression of deeply felt gratitude to Jesus Christ who has entrusted Paul with his evangelical mission and enabled him to carry it out effectively. This gratitude is greatly intensified by Paul's recollection of how extraordinarily unworthy of such a favor was a man who had bitterly persecuted Christ by persecuting his followers. The best Paul can say of himself is that his unbelief was rooted in ignorance. His main concern, however, is not to make excuses, but to exemplify by his own experience that unmerited divine generosity which is called grace.

Paul's private recollections form the basis of his public exhortation, which appeals to the reader to understand that the way Christ showed himself to be in his treatment of Paul is the way he is with respect to all his potential followers. Paul's case is important not because it is Paul's but because it is typical. The outline of his experience is the very outline of the Gospel, the good news that God's benevolence is extended, through Jesus Christ, to those who deserve it least, to sinful unbelievers, so that they may have "faith in him and gain everlasting life."

The third reading comprises a whole chapter of the Gospel according to Luke, which contains the famous parable of the "Prodigal Son," as it is usually but rather misleadingly called, two much shorter and simpler parables which precede and introduce it, and an initial description of an episode in Jesus' ministry which determines the significance that this Gospel attributes to all three of the parables. The episode, which is the key to interpretation, is one in which, as so often happened, morally and socially disreputable people, typified by "tax collectors and sinners," flock to Jesus, while morally and socially reputable people, typified by "the Pharisees and the scribes," criticize Jesus for his indifference to bad company.

The three parables that follow are clearly intended as a retort to this criticism. The first two tell of the anxious seeking and joyous finding of one out of a hundred sheep and one out of ten silver coins, and they explicitly apply to God the character of one who eagerly seeks and joyously finds one human being who is lost to him by sin. God's love and mercy are thus conceived in terms so strong that God is represented as positively preferential in his treatment of sinners. The same theme is developed, with much greater artistry, in the third parable, which is again a story of loss and recovery. Since, however, it is now the loss of a son, through his hardness of heart, to a father, despite his kindness of heart, that the parable describes, its applicability to the condition of sinners before God is greatly deepened, and the divine significance of the father's exuberantly forgiving love is greatly heightened. The attitude of the elder son is precisely that of Jesus' critics: contemptuous self-righteousness.

TWENTY-FIFTH SUNDAY OF THE YEAR

Cycle "A" Readings: Is. 55:6-9; Phil. 1:20-24, 27; Mt. 20:1-16

The portion of the book of Isaiah which contains the passage read in today's liturgy has been appropriately subtitled "The Book of Israel's Consolation." It is a much later composition than the chapters which precede it, and the remarkably different mood it expresses reflects momentous changes in the situation of Israel. The long-dreaded conquest and destruction of Jerusalem had taken place. Its unhappy survivors were exiles in pagan Babylon. But political events in the Middle East had taken further dramatic turns, and with the ascendancy of Cyrus, the Persian emperor, great changes were clearly under way. For Israel, these changes represented the dawn of a new hope, which was in fact fulfilled under Cyrus, of restoration to their ancestral homeland with all that that implied. That hope is everywhere perceptible in the prophecies of what has come to be called Second Isaiah, and constitutes the theme of some of the most beautiful poetry in the Bible, poetry filled with the imagery of hope. Our present text exemplifies the optimism of the time when it was formulated. It is a prophecy of reassurance that God had not abandoned his people and that, if they would turn to God they should find him still their saviour. God's promises are not annulled. God's intentions are not frustrated. But God's designs are on too vast a scale for us to comprehend them.

It is remarkable, and hardly insignificant, how much of what is most beautiful in the Bible was written or spoken or inspired by exiles, fugitives, convicts, or prisoners. St. Paul's letter to the Philippians, written from a prison probably in Ephesus, is no exception. As the passage selected for today's liturgy implies, the letter was composed at a time when Paul had already been charged, arrested, and jailed, but before he had been tried and sentenced. The details of Paul's legal predicament are obscure, but the letter makes it quite clear that its outcome might well be the death penalty. And it is the anticipation of death which shapes the thought of the present passage. Ought Paul to fear the prospect of death? Obviously not, if his feelings are consistent with the conviction he had always preached, that Christ had conquered death. Ought he then to look forward to death with joyful eagerness? That is a less simple question, and Paul answers it less simply. From a sheerly individual point of view, death means for Paul exchanging a painful and toilsome life for the inexpressible peace and joy of final union with Christ. Nevertheless, Paul's basic point of view is not a sheerly individual one. Paul is an apostle, a preacher of the Gospel, an instrument chosen by God to be used in the service of humankind. Paul states his motivational dilemma plainly. On the one hand "What I should like to do is to depart and be with Christ." But on the other hand, "For your sake there is greater need for me to stay on in the body." And since Paul is above all an apostle, it is the apostolic motive which weighs most heavily in his mental balance, and he will not court a martyr's death. His choice is to live on. And whatever practical implications that choice may have had for him, it is clear that he expects to live on.

That God's Ways are higher than humanity's ways and God's thoughts higher than humanity's thoughts is a theme which takes on new depth of meaning in the New Testament. What Jesus Christ says and does was and is for many a disappointment, a scandal, an absurdity. Christians, of course, believe that this sense of perplexity and disenchantment testifies to a profound misconception of God, and that Jesus Christ, by revealing God, corrects that misconception. A basic issue here is the assumption that God's dealings with humankind are governed by essentially the same principles as human beings have established as normative for their dealings with one another. Among the most universally respected of these principles is an idea of justice which measures what is given by what is had in return—more for more, less for less, and nothing for nothing. It is a principle which regulates such vital areas of social behavior as honest trade and fair employment. But Jesus never ceases to insist that if we apply this principle to God we shall tragically misunderstand God. For God does not deal with humankind according to fairness. He deals with us according to love. The measure of what God gives is not what he receives in return—which is always nothing—but rather what he has in himself. And what God has in himself is inexhaustible, irrepressible goodness. This is the point of the parable—the story of an employer who could hardly be described as "fair." His standards are not the standards of fairness. But neither are they below those standards. Rather they are above standards of fairness. The employer gives what is certainly not deserved. Good men are puzzled and annoyed. And well they might be, for by ordinary decent human standards the employer's behavior is indefensible. And that, of course, is the point. His ways are higher than their ways. His thoughts are higher than their thoughts.

TWENTY-FIFTH SUNDAY OF THE YEAR

Cycle "B" Readings: Wis. 2:12, 17-20; Jas. 3:16—4:3; Mk. 9:30-37

The Wisdom of Solomon is one of those writings, called "deuterocanonical" or "apocryphal," which are received by Catholics as part of the Old Testament, but which are not included in Jewish or Protestant Bibles. It is a theological work, written in Greek, probably at Alexandria in the first century B.C., apparently for the purpose of reenforcing the faith of Jews whose religion had been attenuated by over-accommodation to Hellenistic culture. The work begins by identifying Wisdom as a divine spirit devoted to humanity's good, and insisting that only by a righteous manner of life can people have access to this Wisdom. It then proceeds to describe an attitude, apparently widespread at the time, of practical despair over the prospect of human destiny. A consequent sense of the ultimate meaninglessness of human life fosters, on the one hand, unmitigated sensual self-indulgence and, on the other, ruthless antagonism toward those inhibited by more delicate consciences. This is the context of the initial verse of the liturgical reading: "Let us lay a trap for the just man; he stands in our way. . . ." The subsequent verses, omitted from the reading, show this "just man" to be an object not of disdain merely, but of bitter hatred on the part of those whose corrupt lives contrasted so repulsively with his own. The final verses of the reading continue the reviling of the "just man" in terms which Christians have always found strongly suggestive of elements in the story of Jesus' passion. In particular we find here persistent mockery of the "just man" with the apparent futility of his reliance on divine support. Cruelty is intensified as a test of its victim's extraordinary patience, and as a demonstration of God's powerlessness to save those who have the greatest faith in him.

One of the characteristic features of the letter of James is its being made up of a number of largely self-contained units, roughly comparable to short sermons, which are not closely related to one another. Today's second liturgical reading begins about halfway through one of these units and ends about a quarter of the way into the next one. The first of the two units is introduced by the question, "Who among you is wise or clever?" The second one is introduced by another question, "What causes conflicts and quarrels among you?" The first question probably reflects the problems, frequently alluded to in early Christian writings, of groups of people who prided themselves on possessing a special kind of wisdom, of a divine character, which was denied to more ordinary Christians. Claims of this sort, and the coteries which grew up around them, were a frequent source of division and disharmony among Christians, and a grave obstacle to the real progress of the Gospel. Here, accordingly, the claim of being "wise or clever" is said to find its proper test in social behavior. Where such behavior was benevolent, constructive, generous, and serene, real wisdom was manifested. Where opposite conditions prevailed, protestations of wisdom could only be delusions or deceptions. The second question is the basic one of where, why and how human hostility and aggression originate. The answer given to this question is the basic one which attributes animosity and discord to the combination of cupidity and competition, the immoderate, insistent craving of certain things by more than one person. From this combination of cupidity and competition proceed both inner attitudes and outward acts of malice.

The third reading is one of three passages in the gospel according to Mark which are characterized by the same basic structure. First, there is a prediction by Jesus of his approaching passion, death, and resurrection. Second, there is in each instance a misunderstanding of Jesus' words on the part of his disciples. And third, a lesson is taught by Jesus concerning the implications of discipleship. In the second of these three Markan passages, which is the one read in today's liturgy, Jesus once again announces, as they travel southward through Galilee toward Jerusalem that he is to be betrayed and slain and that after three days he is to rise again. To the disciples this announcement is incomprehensible, and their only response is silence. On arrival at Capernaum, however, Jesus reveals his awareness that they have been arguing among themselves about their relative greatness. Jesus initially responds by saying that the only way really to be "first" is by being the last servant of all. He then takes a small child and says that to receive such a child in Jesus' name is to receive both Jesus and God who sent Jesus. If, as some scholars have doubted, the latter verse occupies its proper context, the little child presumably represents those weak, socially insignificant persons whom Jesus, and therefore the disciples of Jesus, are sent to help and serve. On this understanding, receiving a little child would be symbolically equivalent to being the servant of all, including the very humblest.

TWENTY-FIFTH SUNDAY OF THE YEAR

Cycle "C" Readings: Amos 8:4-7; 1 Tim. 2:1-8; Lk. 16:1-13

The first reading is from the Book of Amos, one of the earliest of the prophets whose message has come down to us in writing. Amos, who identifies himself as a shepherd from Judah, responded to a divine call by undertaking a career of prophecy in Israel during the eighth century. He is a prophet of divine judgment, warning a disobedient, presumptuous, self-sufficient people that the divine sovereignty they ignore will indeed be vindicated. This proclamation of impending doom is directed to various categories of people. The passage which constitutes this reading is directed to fraudulent tradesmen or tradeswomen whose unscrupulous pursuit of profit inflicts deadly suffering on the poor.

In a few verses, the objects of this warning are portrayed with dramatic vividness. Those who "trample upon the needy and destroy the poor" are heard in conversation, impatient for the passage of holy days when work, including commerce, was forbidden, and eager to resume their predatory operations at the grain market. It is significant, of course, that these ruthless and dishonest men should deal in a commodity as basic and indispensable as wheat, the proverbial "staff of life." Their plans are to manipulate the market scales so as to inflate the weight of what is sold. Thus a shekel will be "added to" in the sense that the ephah measure of grain for which shekels are paid will in actuality contain considerably less than a standard measure. "Less for your money" is the concealed maxim of these all-too-typical businessmen. The final verses of the passage turn from considerations of what these men are doing to why they are doing it, and with what consequences. They are doing it to enrich themselves—doing it for silver, for a pair of sandals, for property. And the cost of their property, the consequence of their rapacious greed, is quite simply the destruction of human lives.

The second reading, from the first letter to Timothy, reflects the condition of the Church at the time when it was written. It was a Church that had begun to develop definite organizational structure within a Roman society that was largely pagan. The passage reflects both of these features. It has almost the tone of a modern pastoral letter issued from a diocesan chancery, giving quite definite directions for religious practices in the light of existing circumstances. The directions pertain to public prayers of Christian congregations and require such prayers to be offered for all men and in particular for high government officials.

It is a well-known fact that deep mutual distrust existed between early Christians and Roman officialdom. Christians were subject to recurrent persecution, and the persecutors were generally convinced that Christians were very deficient in what Romans esteemed as civic virtues. No doubt the insistence in this passage on public prayer for the political leaders of a pagan state is aimed at counteracting official suspicions that Christians represented a dangerously unassimilated and uncooperative segment of the population. The hope expressed that such prayer might ensure "undisturbed and tranquil lives" is based as much on diplomacy as on piety.

The parable from the Gospel according to Luke that comprises most of the third reading is one that often perplexes Christian hearers. Like a number of the parables, it describes a crisis in human life that calls for a quick and radical response. What signalizes the parable is the fact that the crisis is a crudely secular economic plight, and the quick and radical response with which it is met is not only crudely secular and economic, but dishonest as well. The manager who is about to lose his job on account of his bad reputation provides for his future security by manipulating his employer's accounts to the advantage of his employer's debtors. The debtors are thereby made to incur a debt of gratitude to the unscrupulous manager who has saved them a great deal of money. It is expected that the debtors will be prompted to reward their benefactor by providing him, after his discharge, with a style of life more comfortable than that of a beggar or laborer. The point of the parable is made in the concluding observation that worldly people tend to deal more swiftly and shrewdly with their worldly crises than less worldly people do with crises of a much more profound and ultimate nature. Much of Jesus' preaching was, of course, aimed at presenting the Kingdom of God as the present crisis of all humankind, and warning against apathy and inertia in the face of such a crisis. The point of the parable is not to be found in its details, as though it were approving the dishonest behavior of a cleverly selfish man. Its point is simply that crises demand quick thinking and resolute action, and no less so when the crisis is spiritual in nature.

TWENTY-SIXTH SUNDAY OF THE YEAR

Cycle "A" Readings: Ezek. 18:25-28; Phil. 2:1-11; Mt. 21:28-32

The whole eighteenth chapter of Ezekiel, one portion of which is read in today's liturgy, is a tightly-built logical structure which represents a major development in the religious ethics of the Old Testament. The chapter begins by recalling an ancient proverb which is also quoted in Jeremiah, who, anticipating the restoration of Israel from its Babylonian captivity, proclaimed that "In those days it shall no longer be said 'The fathers have eaten sour grapes and the children's teeth are set on edge.' " Ezekiel carries this prophecy a farther step in declaring the same proverb to be formally repudiated by God. What the proverb was taken to mean was that successive generations of descendants are punished by God for sins committed by their ancestors. This idea, often reflected in mythology by the idea of a "family curse," finds a human counterpart in the hereditary vendetta which is widely practiced in relatively uncivilized societies and by no means unknown even to supposedly civilized ones. Ezekiel's message is that hereditary vendettas have no place with God, and that such conceptions are unworthy of God, who deals with each individual person according to his or her own unique moral condition. Ezekiel applies this basic insight in considerable detail to particular cases. The consistent underlying motif is: life for the righteous, death for the unrighteous. And this moral norm applies not only regardless of one's family history, but regardless also of one's own past, if one has really put that past behind one.

The second reading in today's liturgy is a theological moral exhortation which occupies a very different point of view from that of the famous passage in Ezekiel. The essential contrast appears in the very first words of Paul's appeal: "If then our common life in Christ yields anything . . ." One has no need to read beyond these words to perceive that Ezekiel's elaborate insistence on the unique moral situation of each individual before God is certainly not in the foreground of Paul's thought. What Paul emphasizes is not what is proper to each but what is common to all. And what is common to all, in Paul's theology, is one life in union with Jesus Christ. This is, of course, no return to the crude ideas of human solidarity which approved the slaughtering of children to punish their ancestors, or conceived of God as one whose justice included the imposition of family curses for ancient misdeeds. But neither is it a view according to which morality has only individual dimensions. What Paul is asking for is a kind of moral behavior which gives outward expression to the belief of Christians that their salvation is achieved through their union with Jesus Christ, and that being united to Jesus Christ entails being united to one another.

The little parable which is the final reading in today's liturgy is found only in the Gospel according to Matthew. In that Gospel, moreover, it seems to have acquired an application to John the Baptist, occasioned by questions raised about the Baptist in the early Church, which was not part of its original significance. In its original form it seems highly probable that the story simply contrasted the responses of the two sons, asked the question which of them was the really obedient one, and concluded with Jesus' shocking assertion that "tax-gatherers and prostitutes are entering the kingdom of God ahead of you." The context is undoubtedly accurate in presenting this parable as spoken to the kind of audience we associate with the "priests and elders," that is, an audience representing religious authority as well as social prestige among the Jews of Jesus' time. With such an audience in mind, we can readily associate this parable with a persistent theme of Jesus' preaching. For what we find almost invariably in Jesus' words to such people as these is his insistence that God's grace is more effective with frankly sinful people than with self-righteous paragons of legal virtue. Jesus echoes Ezekiel, though in a different sense, by his emphatic denial that a sinner's fate is sealed irrevocably by his or her past. Rather, it is that very past which makes sinners the special objects of divine grace. And by the same token that a sinful history is no reason for despair, a virtuous past constitutes no warrant for presumption. God's grace is indeed for all. But it is sadly possible that those whose moral estimate of themselves is highest will be the least inclined to acknowledge their need for that grace and to accept it. Whereas others—the kinds of others represented by tax-gatherers and prostitutes—may be much freer from illusions of spiritual self-sufficiency, the lethal folly of religious pride.

TWENTY-SIXTH SUNDAY OF THE YEAR

Cycle "B" Readings: Num. 11:25-29; Jas. 5:1-6; Mk. 9:38-43, 47-48

The first reading in today's liturgy, from the book of Numbers, recounts an episode which supposedly occurred during the Hebrew desert wanderings between the time of escape from Egypt and that of settlement in Palestine. The episode is introduced by one of the many occasions during that time when the Hebrews complained bitterly about their austere circumstances, and berated their leader, Moses, as one who had led them, so to speak, out of the frying pan into the fire. On this occasion Moses finds his plaintive and recalcitrant followers exasperating beyond all endurance, and he in turn complains to God about the overwhelming task of leadership which God has imposed upon him alone. His cry for help is heard, and the help is provided by God through a divine instruction to "Assemble seventy elders from Israel." God then proceeds to declare that "they will share with you the burden of taking care for the people." It is the carrying out of this divine plan that is described in the passage read in today's liturgy: The spirit that is shared is the spirit of prophecy, or what was later called the prophetic charism. The possession of this spirit or charism was manifested by distinctive behavior of an ecstatic nature which was apparently regarded as public evidence of being a prophet, although prophecy itself did not consist primarily in such behavior, but rather in transmitting meaningful messages from God.

The second reading in today's liturgy is a passage from the letter of James which consists entirely of a resounding denunciation of those "who have great possessions." Scarcely anywhere in the New Testament does one find any very kind words about the rich, who are repeatedly, even within this short letter of James, strongly reprehended. It is consistent with this that in the New Testament the poor are regularly referred to in terms of esteem, and even, as in the Beatitudes, of the very highest religious praise. Perhaps the most general idea underlying these sharply contrasting attitudes toward rich and poor is the notion that, whereas poverty encourages reliance upon God, riches foster self-reliance and self-esteem, thereby impeding the wholesome realization that one is both entirely dependent upon God and extensively depended upon by fellow human beings. On this account, riches are inimical to both the love of God and the love of one's neighbor, which comprise the essence of New Testament ethics. In the passage read from the letter of James, the rich are presented as persons who, on account of their preoccupation with wealth, ignore the coming judgment of God, while, by that same preoccupation they prepare their own condemnation by neglecting their neighbor's needs to the point of defrauding their laborers and penalizing the innocent. Although this passage seems to anticipate that the end of the world as we know it is imminent, its moral perspective retains its validity in view of the shortness of individual lives and the impermanence of all material prosperity as contrasted with the eternity of God and of humanity's ultimate destiny.

The third liturgical reading is a section of the gospel according to Mark which comprises four distinct elements having no logical relationship to one another, but having verbal linkages in the Greek text. The first is a conversation between Jesus and John, which mentions having tried to stop a person who was not one of the disciples from performing exorcisms in Jesus' name. Jesus' reply, that "he who is not against us is on our side" points to the validity of a positive relationship with Jesus based on sharing his work and appealing to his authority, regardless of visible adherence to his following. The statement which follows this, that benefactors of Jesus' disciples will be rewarded, occupies a different context in Matthew's Gospel and seems to be out of place here. The next statement introduces another quite independent idea, that to cause spiritual downfall to the weak is an evil deserving punishment worse than death. Finally, the occasion of causing one's own spiritual downfall is presented as one to be avoided at all costs, even to sacrificing things as precious as hand, foot or eye. The danger of doing otherwise is here represented as the peril of "Gehenna," which is often translated as "hell." Actually, it is the name of a valley near Jerusalem, anciently associated with human sacrifice, and later used for the burning of refuse. Gehenna thus came to symbolize the rejection and destruction of what is worthless, and therefore to represent the fate of worthless human lives, damnation.

TWENTY-SIXTH SUNDAY OF THE YEAR

Cycle "C" Readings: Amos 6:1, 4-7; 1 Tim. 6:11-16; Lk. 16:19-31

The Book of Amos, from which the first reading is taken, derives from the preaching of a prophet to the people of Israel at a time, in the middle of the eighth century B.C., when that northern kingdom was bigger, richer, and stronger than at any previous or subsequent period of its history. And yet, scarcely twenty-five years after the prophetic career of Amos, that kingdom had been ravaged by war, conquered by the Assyrian empire, and despoiled of the outstanding elements of its population by the victor's policy of deporting potential resisters and replacing them with colonists. Such events were by no means unforeseeable at the time of Amos, and Amos did foresee the general shape of them. That others were less far-seeing must be credited to the false sense of security, fostered by the luxury and wealth of the privileged classes of a nation that was unconsciously fattening itself for the kill.

Hindsight makes it clear that Israel's fate might have seemed likely enough to any objective and politically astute observer at the time of Amos. Amos himself based his anticipation of Israel's doom not on political astuteness, but on the religious sensitivity of a prophet. What might have seemed to another a politically unstable situation seemed to Amos a divinely intolerable situation. Accordingly, what Amos proclaimed was not a political analysis, but a divine judgment, directed by God against a people whose opulent self-indulgence had blinded them to the realities of religion and morals no less than to those of politics. Thus in the passage read in the liturgy we hear Amos denounce, in tones saturated with disgust, the complacency of a sinful people who are blinded to their danger by the very features of their life that most endanger them. What Amos offers them is a word, not of hope, but of irrevocable judgment.

The second reading comprises the entire concluding passage of the first letter to Timothy. It is a passage of exhortation, and its formal structure and solemn tone are more suggestive of a liturgical exhortation than of personal and private advice. Indeed, elements in its structure have persuaded many scholars that it incorporates portions of a baptismal liturgy or, less probably, a ceremony of ordination. In any case, it is an injunction, very much in the manner of a consecration, to live an impeccably Christian life based on the Christian faith that has been professed. It is an appeal to understand the practical implications of a Christian commitment and to live up to them.

Christian commitment is here identified with the commitment of Jesus Christ himself, and specifically refers to Jesus' testimony before Pilate on the eve of his crucifixion. The only biblical passage that makes this reference meaningful is that of the Gospel according to John which represents Jesus as declaring to the Roman governor: "For this was I born and for this I have come into the world, to bear witness to the truth." Thus the witness that Jesus bore, preeminently through his death, is the witness to be borne in turn by his disciples, and in this case specifically by the official leader of a local church. In this passage the witness that is called for is not the testimony of teaching, but the testimony of example. What is called for is a life that manifests in conduct the faith on which it is founded, a life of "integrity, piety, faith, love, steadfastness and a gentle spirit."

The third reading is the well-known parable of the rich man and Lazarus, which is found only in the Gospel according to Luke. Like several of Jesus' parables, this one has two very distinct parts, and its purpose is to make two related but distinct points. The first part of the parable belongs to a tradition of stories that are concerned with the fate that befalls people in the after-life and which may be in sharp contrast with the condition of their life in this world. In the case of this parable, the situations of two men are absolutely reversed in the after-life. One of them, left nameless, is a typical figure of rich self-indulgence. Although his fate after death is to undergo torment, we are given no account of his judgment nor any specification of his sin. The other character in the story is a beggar, whose name, Lazarus, means "God helps," and is presumably symbolic. Although his fate after death is a happy one, his judgment too is left to our imagination, and there is no suggestion that he is conspicuous for sinlessness or virtue.

The whole contrast is between luxury and misery, not between moral failure and moral success, and the after-life simply reverses the relationship between the "haves" and "have-nots" of this world. Thus the story makes the point, so typical of Jesus, that worldly status is no index of divine favor nor any guarantee of salvation. The second part of the parable, in which God refuses to show the rich man's fate to his surviving brothers, makes the further point that refusal to hear God's word cannot be altered merely by a more sensational mode of revelation.

TWENTY-SEVENTH SUNDAY OF THE YEAR

Cycle "A" Readings: Is. 5:1-7; Phil. 4:6-9; Mt. 21:33-43

The first reading is an eloquent parable from the prophecies of Isaiah. Perhaps only someone who has gone out of his Way to help another, and been bitterly cursed for the trouble, can understand the psychology of the story of the vineyard. Note that initially the presentation is in the third person: the vineyard belongs to a friend. But soon it shifts into the more direct first person, in the plaintive question later exploited in the Good Friday liturgy: "What more ought I do for you that I have not done?" Finally, the parable is manifest: the vineyard is Israel, the cherished plant Judah.

God is patient, the vignette suggests, as he painstakingly prepares his vineyard; nevertheless, evil will not always have its way, and the time of reckoning comes. "Now, I will let you know what I mean to do to my vineyard."

Like a shaft of sunlight in these darker meditations is the passage from Philippians. The Christian life comprises the sum of everything good, honest, admirable and virtuous. Such a life is based on prayer, and is known only to those who live in the awareness of God's love. Contrasted to the "wild grapes" of the first reading, the fruit of living the model of the Gospel is God's own peace.

Jesus tells a story of a vineyard too, and the similarity between Matthew and Isaiah cannot be missed. Here however the poignancy is heightened to a keener pitch. In the first place, the mute and unresponsive ground of the earlier account becomes the tenants, which underlines the personal reference. Next, the outrage is not one of mere non-response, but of positive and gratuitous evil, as the tenants seize and kill the servants who are sent. Finally, the parable shifts abruptly into allegory, and Jesus himself comes into tragic focus as the son sent with the assumption that he at least will surely be respected. But the tenants' thinking is entirely warped: "Let us kill him and then we shall have his inheritance!" Incomprehensible as this rejection of God's gracious initiative is, it continually recurs.

Somber indeed is the burden of the opening and closing readings; yet they are not without hope. The second reading declares that some fields are far from barren. In the Gospel the kingdom will be taken away from the wicked servants, but only to be given to a nation that will yield a rich harvest.

TWENTY-SEVENTH SUNDAY OF THE YEAR

Cycle "B" Readings: Gen. 2:18-24; Heb. 2:9-11; Mk. 10:2-16

The first reading in today's liturgy is taken from the second or so-called Yahwistic account of creation, given in the book of Genesis. The particular selection is a mythological account of the origin of woman which, on closer observation, is seen to be more precisely a mythological explanation of human mating behavior. The point of the story, which is told in a shrewd and somewhat whimsical fashion, becomes evident if one notes that it begins with God saying "It is not good for the man to be alone," and ends with him saying "Therefore a man leaves his father and mother and cleaves to his wife, and they become one flesh." The myth, in other words, begins by dramatizing a hypothetical problem—how lonely and unfulfilled men would be if there were no women. It then proceeds to dramatize the divine solution of that problem—the female human creation. And it concludes by observing that the satisfactoriness of the divine solution is constantly attested by the fact that men, once they are mature, generally go off and get married. Within this structure, the story develops the idea that the human female is, so to speak, "just right" for the human male. (And, one might wish to add, vice versa, but Israel like most ancient cultures had a strongly masculine bias which is evident throughout its literature, sacred as well as profane.) The unique "rightness" of woman for man is introduced first of all by noting that nothing else in the whole animate creation could possibly serve the same purpose. The man "named" the other animals, meaning that, in a sense, he made them his own, but none of them was the "helper fit for him." The description of God's fashioning the woman out of the man's rib is a quaint way of conveying the idea that she is made of the "same stuff" as he—roughly the same idea we express as genetic identity of species. Once the man sees the woman, his perplexity is resolved. And once he is united with her, his inadequacy is removed. Basically, what the myth is intended to affirm is the correspondence of marriage, as it is normally experienced, with the creative design of God.

The second liturgical reading, from the letter to the Hebrews, has been taken somewhat out of context. In the preceding verses, it is asserted that dominion over "the world to come" was given by God, not to angels, but to man, and it is conceded that "we do not yet see everything in subjection to" man. In saying, in the first verse of the reading, that Jesus "for a little while was made lower than the angels," the writer refers to the earthly life of Jesus, which he then contrasts with Jesus' present condition, "crowned with glory and honor because of the suffering of death, so that by the grace of God he might taste death for everyone." This terse account of the redemptive death of the earthly Jesus is then developed in one of the major themes of Hebrews, that of the priestly sacrifice of Jesus, which is here briefly introduced, and extensively developed in later passages. At this point, what is emphasized is that Jesus, by his humanity, is of the same kind as those fellow human beings whom he consecrates or sanctifies by his sacrifice. Underlying this assertion is the idea of the priest as representative of those whom his priesthood serves, and therefore as necessarily "one of them." Thus Jesus, our priest *par excellence*, is unequivocally "one of us" in virtue of the incarnation. Thus the author of Hebrews, in conceiving of Jesus' redemptive death as a sacrifice, conceives Jesus himself as a priest, and on the basis of Jesus' priestly relationship to his people he links the incarnation, by which Jesus is one of us, with the redemption, in which Jesus sacrifices himself for our sanctification. The background of the understanding of priest and sacrifice which is here assumed is to be found in Israelite traditions of worship.

The third reading, from the Gospel according to Mark, contains the account of Jesus' response to Pharisaic questioning about the legitimacy of a man's divorcing of his wife—a practice whose legitimacy was generally admitted in principle, although there was much controversy about what constituted sufficient grounds for divorce. (It may be noted that among the Jews divorce was entirely a husband's prerogative, without any corresponding provision for discontented wives, as the wording of the Pharisees' question implies.) The acceptability of divorce was considered to be justified by Scripture, inasmuch as the Mosaic law called for a "certificate of divorce" to be given by a divorcing husband, apparently in order to free the woman for possible remarriage, and thereby the Mosaic law clearly implied that divorce itself was not necessarily wrong. Jesus was therefore placed in the position of having to contradict the highest authority acknowledged by his Jewish coreligionists, that of Moses himself, if he wished to take a position of unqualified opposition to divorce. Jesus did take precisely such a position, according to this account, but he did so by an ingenious turn of theological argument. For he based his anti-divorce doctrine on the only authority which a Jew could represent as superior to Moses, the authority, namely, of God himself. Jesus appeals from the judgment of Moses (which he regards as a concession to human malice) to the creative intention of God that in marrying a woman a man becomes in union with her a new composite being. Divorce is thus condemned as a violation of God's basic plan of creation, tearing apart what the Creator himself puts together.

TWENTY-SEVENTH SUNDAY OF THE YEAR

Cycle "C" Readings: Hab. 1:2-3; 2:2-4;
2 Tim. 1:6-8, 13-14; Lk. 17:5-10

The book of Habakkuk from which the first reading is taken is a notoriously obscure work, and there is much uncertainty concerning the identity of the prophet for whom it is named and the precise circumstances of his preaching. It is clear at all events that his message reflects impending danger from foreign enemies. The first chapter contains a vivid description of the new military threat of the Chaldeans (last of the Babylonian dynasties), but it is not clear whether at that point this power was seen as a threat to Judah itself or to Judah's enemies the Assyrians, whom the Chaldeans conquered before attacking the Judean remnant of what had been the kingdom of Israel. This ambiguity complicates our understanding of the issue raised by the prophet at the beginning of the book, the question of how, under such circumstances, the justice of God could be vindicated. Regardless of historical particulars, the basic religious question is clear: How could belief in an all-just, all-powerful God be reconciled with the brutal triumph of ruthless imperialism over peoples more righteous than their conquerors? The prophet represents himself as a sentinel posted in a watch-tower, scanning the scene for some clue as to how this dilemma might find hopeful resolution. The answer comes to him from God in the form of a vision which he is directed to write down so that it can be transmitted like a field dispatch to the anxious people. This message, which St. Paul later adapted to his own theology of faith, is one of reassurance but not of explanation. Its basic import is that appearances are deceptive, and that life—that is, the future—belongs after all rather to religious fidelity than to military boldness. "The rash man has no integrity" refers to an inner weakness of the bold invader which will be his undoing. Whereas "the just man" (he who obeys God) "because of his faith" (his loyalty to God) "will live." It is a message of hope which depends on faith for its persuasiveness.

The second reading is from the second letter to Timothy, whose authorship by St. Paul is unlikely, although Pauline inspiration is very evident. Timothy is referred to in Paul's writings and in Acts as a friend and missionary collaborator of Paul's. Here he is presented as the leader of a local church, and the document implies that by the time of its writing, Christian churches had developed a definite institutional structure with a recognized pastoral officialdom. Timothy can thus be thought of as a bishop if one separates that title from the elaborate juridical and theological connotations of a later date. The first part of the letter, from which the reading combines two separate passages, is mainly an exhortation reminding Timothy of the virtues required by his office and urging him to preserve and deepen them. The first of the cited passages is an appeal for courage to proclaim the Gospel with a fearlessness inspired by love and confirmed by self-discipline, at a time when persecution, which had led to Paul's own imprisonment, was a constant threat. The second passage turns from the question of courageous preaching to that of correct preaching. It calls upon the church leader to keep as a standard the Gospel message as he heard it from Paul himself. The final verse, directing him to "guard the rich deposit of faith," has been a watchword of the Church's magisterial duty to insure the authenticity of doctrinal tradition against heretical distortions.

The Gospel reading is the conclusion of a long section in the Gospel according to Luke which is a collection of passages, often unrelated in meaning, most of which are sayings of Jesus, and many of which are found only in this Gospel. The reading presents the last two of these passages dealing with distinct subjects and probably derived from different occasions. The former passage is confusing inasmuch as it is introduced by the apostles' request that their faith be increased, whereas the reply rather extols the power of faith than says anything about how to increase it. The saying makes better sense in Matthew's context, where it is used to make the disciples aware of their weakness of faith. The last portion of the reading has the form of a parable, the point of which is to liken a disciple's fidelity to that of a servant (or better, a slave) to his master. Discipleship is not a matter of favors done but of duties executed. It is a matter for approval but not for gratitude. An obedient disciple is simply fulfilling his own function, not assuming some function of his master's. In doing as he is obliged by his master, he does not make his master obliged to him. In serving he is being what he is, not becoming what he is not. The very notion of an irreducible inequality between superior and subject that makes the institution of slavery repugnant to us, makes the idea of slavery faultlessly applicable to the contrast between human beings and God. Accordingly, the later application of this text to the relationship between divine sovereignty and human contingency is in basic harmony with its conceptual structure. God the kind, forgiving master, is still God the master.

TWENTY-EIGHTH SUNDAY OF THE YEAR

Cycle "A" Readings: Is. 25:6-10; Phil. 4:12-14, 19-20; Mt. 22:1-14

The meal that friends share becomes in the "messianic banquet" a favorite scriptural image for God's communion with humanity, as in the first reading from the prophecy of Isaiah. The heavily-laden table of Isaiah shimmers in apocalyptic vision, a totally ideal state. Note the location: God provides his feast on the mountain, the special locus of his presence. Moses meets God on the mountain, and there the covenant is given; to the same height Elijah returns in his search for God. In the New Testament, the favored disciples glimpse the transfigured Jesus once more on the mountain. Even in Greek mythology, the gods inhabit Mount Olympus. Thus the presence of God is signified: "For the hand of the Lord will rest on this mountain."

Death, the ancient enemy, will be destroyed; God will wipe away every tear, signifying that suffering is banished. In other words, this is a return to the garden of Eden. God has familiar intercourse with people, food is readily available, suffering and death are unknown. In this usage the banquet stands for God's final and unrestricted giving of himself to humanity; the image is other-worldly.

The earthly hardships of Paul are unmistakable in the second reading, but seeing in his discussion of want and plenty a continuation of the banquet theme is stretching a point. Paul seems to have arrived at a state of holy indifference. The external circumstances of eating well or going hungry mean little to him; what is paramount is his inner detachment, founded in his dependence on the divine strength.

Matthew evokes once again the banquet image, but now it seems to reflect division and conflict more than peace. The presence of God is here "the reign of God," and its appearance among people demands a response. Obviously, the royal invitation is not to be trifled with! The existential import of human living is heavily underlined in this parable, as the divine initiative divides people according to their acceptance or rejection.

There are three groups that refuse the invitation. Some simply ignore it, attracted by other cares and preoccupations. Others actively resist the message and interfere in its announcement. These receive the severest retribution. Finally, there is the hapless guest without the wedding garment, perhaps meant to signify that even entrance into the Church is not an assurance of salvation. He too is excluded.

There are also those who accept, however, and the parable highlights the gratuitous and unexpected nature of their invitation. The servants fan out into the byroads and ask in whomever they come upon. The new guests are suddenly urged to receive the privilege abandoned by those originally invited. For God is not restrained by human priorities or expectations.

God's salvation is communicated in developing phases. In the present, terrestrial phase, the reign of God lays a demand upon human life. Some refuse the invitation; others respond. To these latter God's strength and protection are available. But there will be another and final phase. There the intimate divine presence will banish suffering and death, wiping away every tear.

TWENTY-EIGHTH SUNDAY OF THE YEAR

Cycle "B" Readings: Wis. 7:7-11; Heb. 4:12-13; Mk. 10:17-30

The book from which the first liturgical reading is taken is called the Wisdom of Solomon, for although it was written many centuries after the reign of King Solomon it is set down as though it were actually composed by that king, who had long been associated with wisdom in Jewish thinking. The passage selected for this reading clearly hearkens back to the episode narrated in the first book of Kings, when God in a dream offered to give Solomon whatever he asked, and was pleased that Solomon chose wisdom rather than longevity or wealth or vengeance. Indeed, so pleased was God that Solomon asked only for wisdom that he promised to give him, in addition, riches, honor, and, if he behaved well, long life. This episode is here developed in a soliloquy, attributed to Solomon, in praise of wisdom. It begins by emphasizing that wisdom was Solomon's first choice by listing a series of attractive alternatives to which it was preferred, a whole catalogue of traditional royal luxuries, along with money, health, good looks, and even the very light of day. However, the final verse makes the point that Solomon was destined to have "all this and wisdom too." The passage, like much of the Bible's wisdom literature and much of its other literature as well, reflects a view of wealth and material luxury which the prophetic literature and above all the New Testament strongly opposed, an interpretation of material prosperity as a blessing of God which implies the special favor of God. Such a view of wealth naturally entails a view of poverty which interprets it as a sign of divine disfavor. Quite different religious attitudes toward wealth and poverty co-exist in the Old Testament. And although the New Testament is remarkable for its uniform disesteem of wealth, post-biblical Christianity has shown great ethical diversity in this respect.

The second reading is the well-known passage from the letter to the Hebrews which describes the word of God as "living and active, sharper than any two-edged sword," an instrument capable of penetrating to the most hidden recesses of human personality and of laying bare the thoughts and feelings of the heart. This striking passage about the word of God is introduced at a point before which the word of God, understood as divine revelation, had already been established as a major and recurrent topic. It will be recalled that the very first verses of Hebrews declare that whereas the word of God had been spoken in the past in a great variety of ways through the prophets, it has now been spoken through the very Son of God himself. Similarly in the present context the word of God may be understood generally of all instances of divine revelation, but is to be understood primarily of God's consummate self-revelation in the Son who bears the likeness of his very nature. The idea associated with the imagery of the two-edged sword is the very important, though somewhat subtle idea that the word of God is revealing in two quite different senses. It is revealing, first of all, of God himself, as conveying some understanding or experience of the divine to its human recipients. But it is also revealing of the moral and religious dispositions of the human beings to whom it is presented. For as they react to divine revelation, so they show themselves to be with respect to God. This is most evident where the word is God incarnate, whose encounter with the world of men so dramatically divides that world into the friends and the enemies of God, the accepters and rejecters of his supreme self-manifestation in Christ. This theme of the profound significance of opposite human reactions to the Word Incarnate is extensively developed in the Gospel according to John.

The third reading, from the Gospel according to Mark, comprises three closely related passages having to do with the positive relationship between poverty and the following of Jesus Christ. The first passage, which has inspired some of the noblest behavior in the annals of Christian sanctity, tells of the rich young man whose moral uprightness endeared him to Jesus but whose affluence prevented him from accepting Jesus' invitation to sell his possessions, give to the poor, and be one of Jesus' followers. It should be noted in this passage that it is not simply poverty which is advocated, but rather a social beneficence and a committed discipleship, with neither of which the retention of wealth can be reconciled. This episode serves to introduce two conversations, each of which is designed to emphasize a distinctive pronouncement of Jesus. The first of these is the famous statement likening the ease of a rich man's entry into the Kingdom to that of a camel's passage through the eye of a needle. This severe figurative assertion of what can only be interpreted as sheer impossibility is followed by the obscure but consoling reassurance that the scope of divine possibilities far exceeds that of human possibilities. In the final conversation devoted to this theme, the voluntary acceptance of poverty for the sake of discipleship is assured of abundant rewards, both temporal and eternal, which do not, however, exclude the prospect of persecution.

TWENTY-EIGHTH SUNDAY OF THE YEAR

Cycle "C" Readings: 2 Kgs. 5:14-17; 2 Tim. 2:8-13; Lk. 17:11-19

The first reading comes from a rather disorganized cycle of legends concerning the ninth-century prophet Elisha which is preserved in the second book of Kings. Miracle stories are frequent in these legends, as in the story from which the reading is taken. Since the reading itself contains only the climax of the story, the vigor of the well-constructed narrative is hard to appreciate. It is the story of Naaman, a military leader greatly esteemed by the king of Aram, a people hostile to and feared by Israel, who, on being stricken with leprosy, hears from a captive Israelite girl of a prophet in Samaria who might cure him. When the king of Israel is informed that his enemy king is sending a military commander to be cured, he is dismayed at what he assumes to be an impossible demand, intended as a pretext for aggression. Sharply contrasted with the diffidence of the king is the confidence of Elisha, who is quite ready to demonstrate "that there is a prophet in Israel." This lofty self-assurance is further manifested when, without so much as personally receiving his intimidating visitor, Elisha merely sends him word that he will be cured by bathing seven times in Israel's very unimpressive river, the Jordan. Persuaded at last, despite his suspicions of being mocked, at least to try this preposterous remedy, Naaman is cured instantly, and thereby converted to worshiping the God of Elisha. That the convert takes his leave with a cargo of Israelite soil is an interesting reminder of prevailing ideas of geographically bounded local deities. And there is a note of winsome realism in Naaman's asking pardon in advance from the God of Israel for those visits to a pagan temple which will occasionally be made unavoidable by his attendance upon a pagan king.

The second reading, from the second letter to Timothy, is a distinctive passage which seems to interrupt a series of rather prosaic bits of advice on how Timothy, as official leader of a Christian church, ought to conduct himself. Thus the passage immediately follows recommendations to the effect that ecclesiastical office is a full-time employment, entitled to be supported without dependence on secular commerce. The passage immediately precedes warnings against loose, controversial talk. The passage itself is mainly a declaration of basic Christian doctrine, expressed in a formal way suggestive of liturgical sources, perhaps a hymn and a credal formula. "Remember Jesus Christ, risen from the dead, born of David's line" nicely epitomizes the basic Christian assertion of Jesus' messianic lineage and the consummation of his mission in his death and resurrection. The author emphasizes that this, being what Christianity is all about, is what evangelists undergo persecution for, confident that the divine message cannot be suppressed by human violence. The final verses are a credal statement which focuses on the ultimate redemptive significance of the Christian's fidelity to Christ. To have "died with him" recalls a familiar Pauline conception of baptism. The warning note that "if we deny him he will deny us" has seemed to some commentators contrary to the following assertion that "if we are unfaithful he will still remain faithful," which is further intensified by the explanatory "he cannot deny himself," implying that Jesus' dedication to his mission is unalterably intrinsic to his very being. The apparent inconsistency of these final verses may be resolved by understanding Jesus' faithfulness as fidelity to his Father and his Father's mission, rather than as a kind of indiscriminate loyalty to mankind.

The story from the Gospel according to Luke which comprises the final reading is commonly understood as a moralizing example, commending gratitude and reminding us of how often recipients of God's blessings fail to express thanks. Although implications of this sort are certainly not alien to the narrative, it contains a further intimation which ought not to be lost sight of. What makes the story different from many other miracle stories of Jesus' healing the afflicted is, of course, that it follows the subsequent behavior of those who have been healed up to the point where one of them does and the others do not express their gratitude. It is noteworthy, however, that the sole example of gratitude is explicitly identified as a Samaritan. And this point is further emphasized by Jesus' concluding reflection that none expressed thanks "except this foreigner." It is also noteworthy that the thanks Jesus refers to are thanks, not to himself, but "thanks to God." Clearly, a strong contrast is intended here not simply between the grateful and the ungrateful, but between foreign gratitude and native ingratitude precisely to God. In view of Luke's strong orientation toward the Gentile Christianity whose vigorous development he depicts in Acts, which also emphasizes the alienation of Christianity from Judaism, it is natural to see in this passage, and especially in the symbolism of the grateful Samaritan, an allusion to that same contrast between native rejection and foreign acceptance of the Gospel. Jesus' final words, "your faith has been your salvation," can thus be understood as referring to much more than a physical healing.

TWENTY-NINTH SUNDAY OF THE YEAR

Cycle "A" Readings: Is. 45:1, 4-6; 1 Thes. 1:1-5; Mt. 22:15-21

The gods of the ancient near East were usually associated with a people and its land. Thus when Naaman the Syrian is converted to Yahweh, he takes back to his country an amount of Israelite soil so that he can worship the new God (2 Kgs. 5:17). Yahweh was originally the powerful personage who led the tribes of Israel out of Egypt, making them a nation. But as Jewish thought developed, Yahweh became identified as the creator of the whole world, as in the first part of Genesis. The passage from Isaiah is a daring further step in this universalization of the God of Israel. Here his providence extends to Cyrus, the ruler of a powerful pagan nation. All unknown to him, God has called Cyrus by name, taken him by the hand, subdued peoples before him. The purpose of this orchestration of history is specified: it is for the sake of Israel, the chosen of Yahweh.

The opening verses of 1 Thessalonians form the second reading. There is some echo of God's universal dominion in the salutation to the Christians "who belong to God the Father and the Lord Jesus Christ." The chosen people of the Old Testament now include this Gentile Church, and Paul goes on to detail the manner of their choice. "We know . . . how you were chosen. Our preaching . . . was carried on in the Holy Spirit." Thus Paul neatly fills out the trinitarian schema.

A conflict story appears in the Gospel. Approaching Jesus with insincere praise, the Pharisees attempt to place him in a dilemma with a question about paying tax to the emperor. If Jesus says yes, he will seem to be capitulating to the hated Romans and accepting the legitimacy of their occupation. But if he says no, he can be reported to the governor for treason, and some Herodian sympathizers are brought along just in case he may make any such statement.

Jesus however sees right through their game. Having been shown the coin with Caesar's image, he replies, "Give to Caesar what is Caesar's, and to God what is God's." The response can be read on a number of levels. On the first level, it is simply a crafty answer. Jesus does not take it upon himself to justify Roman dominance; he bases himself merely on the recognition that his questioners have already implicitly accorded to Rome. For clearly, by the very fact that they carry around the Roman coinage, they are already involved in the Roman system of government.

A theory of politics may be sought on a second level. That some recognition is accorded civil government by Jesus' statement is hard to deny. He positively states that there are some obligations toward Caesar; he does not simply denounce Rome. Still, to seek to justify the medieval theory of the two swords or the American doctrine of separation of Church and state from this one remark loads too much interpretation on a single statement in a polemical context.

Finally, on a third level, an underlying irony appears when the response is examined more closely. Consider the concluding clause: Give to God what belongs to God. Is anything excluded from that? Obviously, nothing. Recalling the first reading, all the nations are in the hand of God; he creates all, and nothing escapes his providence.

The relation of Church and state is still a pressing question. On the one hand, preachers sometimes presume to pronounce in the name of the Church on delicate questions of political and social fact, for which the Church possesses no special charism. On the other hand, too many Christians believe that religion has nothing to do with social or political questions, which denies that ultimately everything "belongs to God."

TWENTY-NINTH SUNDAY OF THE YEAR

Cycle "B" Readings: Is. 53:10-11; Heb. 4:14-16; Mk. 10:35-45

The first reading of today's liturgy consists of two verses extracted from the last of four extraordinary poems called "servant songs" which were among material added at a later time to the original book of Isaiah. The designation commonly applied to these poems refers to the mysterious character, identified only as "the Lord's servant," who appears in all of them. The servant is represented as one singled out by God to bring divine enlightenment to the Gentile world. But, although there is assurance of the servant's ultimately glorious success expressed throughout these poems, they carry no less assurance that the servant's mission will be carried out under circumstances of the most extreme suffering and humiliation. It is thought by many interpreters, and with good reason, that the servant is a personification of Israel itself, whose sense of a universal mission was mainly acquired during the time of the Babylonian captivity, which seems to be the time when the servant songs were composed. Christian readers of these passages, however, can scarcely fail to be impressed by the applicability to Jesus Christ of a number of the references to the anonymous servant. There are unmistakable echoes of the servant songs in the Gospel accounts of Jesus' passion, and verses like those read in today's liturgy are strongly suggestive of the theological interpretation of Jesus' passion and death as a sacrifice, offered in obedience to the will of God, for the sins of humankind. There is considerable evidence in the Gospels that Jesus himself drew on the servant songs for the interpretation of his own mission. The relationship of the servant songs to the Christian Gospel has been generally considered by Christians as a prophetic foreshadowing. To this idea, however, it is necessary to add that the servant songs not only anticipated but positively shaped the way in which vital elements of the Christian Gospel were conceived and formulated.

The second reading comprises three verses that constitute an excellent summary of the principal theme of the letter to the Hebrews, from which they are taken. At the very beginning of that work its author introduces a contrast between the imperfect revelations of the Old Testament and that perfect revelation which has now come to us through Jesus Christ. This pattern of contrast underlies the basic thought of the entire work, and it is expressed most elaborately in terms of priesthood. Thus, the religion of the Old Testament, with its recurrent sacrifices offered by priestly officials who alone might enter the sanctuary, is regarded as a dim foreshadowing of the Gospel message of one unique sacrifice offered by the great high priest, Jesus Christ, whose sanctuary is heaven itself, which he has entered once and for all, empowered to bring all his human followers in after him. Evidently, the letter to the Hebrews was written at a time when Christians were sorely tempted to abandon their faith, perhaps under pressure of persecution; apparently it was addressed to Jewish Christians who contemplated a return to the Judaism of their past. Against these tendencies, the author appeals to his idea of Jesus as "a great high priest who has passed through the heavens" for motivation to "hold fast to our confession." Following this verse of exhortation, he develops the priestly conception of Jesus by pointing out that he is the kind of priest who can truly represent his people before God because he is truly one of them, "who in every respect has been tempted as we are, yet without sin." Finally, on the basis of this reassuring message, he summons his readers, instead of shrinking away from their religion in fear, to "with confidence draw near to the throne of grace, that we may receive mercy and find grace to help in time of need."

The Gospel reading, from the Gospel according to Mark, tells of a naive request by James and John for positions of first and second rank in the "glory" of Jesus. The request implies that these disciples shared the common expectation of a messianic kingdom constituted along lines of power structure analogous to earthly political arrangements. Jesus' reply clearly refers back to the announcement recorded only a few verses previously that it was his destiny to go to Jerusalem and there be condemned by the Jews and tortured and executed by the Gentiles, only to rise again after three days. This destiny of Jesus, he reminds them, is the pattern also of his followers' destiny. Beyond that, questions of divine honors must be left to God. The discussion is then carried further in response to the other disciples' indignation at the presumptuousness of James and John. They are reminded that their ideal as followers of Christ must be one of humble service and not of proud dominance. The passage is concluded by a verse which has had great influence on theological speculation, and which is apparently borrowed from the servant song quoted in this first reading. This verse describes the significance of the death of the Son of Man as an act of ransom, or redemption, which means literally an act of liberation by purchase, as in the buying of freedom for a slave. The idea developed by Christian theologians of a debt paid by Christ to the devil is an example of the over-literal interpretation of this figurative expression of the liberation gained by Christ's atoning death.

TWENTY-NINTH SUNDAY OF THE YEAR

Cycle "C" Readings: Ex. 17:8-13; 2 Tim. 3:14—4:2; Lk. 18:1-8

The first liturgical reading, from the book of Exodus, recounts an episode during the Hebrews' eventful and suspenseful journey from their land of enslavement in Egypt to their land of promise in Canaan. It is situated in what would have been by far the most difficult part of such a journey, the crossing of the Negeb desert, northeast of Sinai. At a point no longer identifiable, called Rephidim, the Hebrews, under their military leader Joshua, successfully repulsed a raid by desert tribesmen called Amalekites. A conviction that this victory was owed rather to divine assistance than to martial prowess is expressed dramatically by the observation that the defensive combat proved effective only as long as their leader and prophet Moses kept his hands upstretched in an attitude of prayer. The implications of this symbolism are deeply consistent with theological convictions that shape the entire narrative. The Hebrews' salvation, preservation, and progress are to be accounted for, not by their own valor and skill, but by the benevolent intervention of an invincible God. Moreover, their principal, divinely appointed link with that God, is their intermediary spokesman, Moses. A specific nationalistic reason for including this episode comes to light in the final verses, omitted from the reading. Here God is represented as determined to wage continual warfare against the Amalekites, and ultimately to destroy them. Here we see the literary anticipation of what, by the time our Bible was put together, was remembered as an ancient feud, carried on according to the primitive ethic of a relentless vendetta, aimed at the ultimate extermination of a people stigmatized as ancestral enemies.

The second reading, from the second letter to Timothy, is occupied, like most of that letter, with exhortation and instruction addressed to the leader of a Christian church, on what sort of tasks he should perform, and what sort of person he must be to perform them rightly. In the passage cited here, it is the preaching function that is chiefly in view, and the exhortation touches on what is to be preached, and on how and when it is to be preached. As for the content of preaching, it is to be solidly traditional, clearly comprehended doctrine. There is no place in a Christian preacher's function, for material innovation. Neither is there any place for what is only doubtfully held or only obscurely understood. The main resources to which Timothy is referred in order to identify and clarify his religious message are his own teachers, and those "sacred Scriptures" which Timothy has known from childhood. The reference is, of course, to what we now call the Old Testament, with which Timothy, as the son of a Jewish mother, would have been acquainted from his earliest years. As among early Christian writers generally, the Old Testament is here understood as prophetically anticipating the coming of Jesus as Christ, or Messiah, and therefore as leading the way to Christian faith. A general endorsement is here given to the pastoral usefulness of all those writings which are called, by a word found nowhere else in the Bible, "inspired." Here, apparently, the Greek idea of divine forces controlling the writing of religious books is imported into Christian theology, where it has had a long and complex history. The last verses of the reading remind Timothy that the work of preaching is to be constant, not intermittent, and that what is a bad time from the preacher's viewpoint, is still the right time for the permanently indispensable message of the Gospel.

The third reading, from the Gospel according to Luke, is a very homely parable, the use of which reflects this writer's particularly strong interest in matters concerning prayer. The story, which has a very realistic flavor, describes a widow who in so male-dominated a society was characteristically a very poor and uninfluential person. She is trying to get a judge to decide a case that must clearly be concluded in her favor. Her one resource is that which has so often succeeded when all else failed in stagnant bureaucracies and slovenly tribunals of both church and state—sheer relentlessness. She will not let up or be put off until mere importunity penetrates by exasperation the thick skin of a boorish magistrate whom no considerations of human need or divine justice could have affected. The story is applied to prayer as a parable. And as with parables generally, the point is limited to the conclusion, to which the rest of the story merely draws attention. In this case, accordingly, the point is not that the God the reader prays to is like the judge the widow appealed to. Rather the point is simply that the reader should do at prayer what the widow did at court—keep it up, even when it seems to be futile, in full confidence that good results will follow. The final verses relate this lesson in perseverance to the expectation of divine judgment when Christian hope is fulfilled.

THIRTIETH SUNDAY OF THE YEAR

Cycle "A" Readings: Ex. 22:20-26; 1 Thes. 1:5-10; Mt. 22:34-40

Christianity is not first a message to be taught, but a way of life to be lived. It is pictured as a warm and intimate relationship between God and the believer which flows over immediately into a life of love for other human beings.

In the reading from Exodus, God is presented above all as "compassionate." His concern embraces particularly the unprotected and the helpless. He has a special ear for the cry of the widow and the orphan when they are wronged, and the punishment is swift and severe. The poor, and those who possess only one cloak, must be given special consideration by their neighbors. The whole passage reflects the central revelation of Yahweh to Moses later in the same book: "The Lord, a merciful and gracious God, slow to anger and rich in kindness . . . for a thousand generations" (Ex. 34:6-7).

The life-style of faith is again the focus of the second reading, but now more from Paul's point of view. There seems to be a succession of imitation here. Jesus is the prime model, and Paul molds his conduct on that of the Lord. The Thessalonians in turn have become imitators of Paul and the Lord, having seen how Paul acted among them on their behalf. Now the Thessalonians have become models for all the believers of Macedonia and Achaia.

The Christian life is described as one of conversion, service and hope. The conversion is a turning from idols. The service is of the living and true God. The hope is an awaiting from heaven of the risen Jesus. All of this is done, finally, in the joy of the Holy Spirit.

Matthew's Gospel presents as a conflict story an incident which in the Marcan and Lucan narratives occurs in a friendlier tone. In any case, the context is one of a rabbinical discussion about the most basic of the commandments recognized in the law. Jesus' response is not original. If the first occurs prominently as the Shema, recited daily by the devout Jew, in

Deuteronomy 6:5, the second can also be found in Leviticus 19:18. What is original is that Jesus places both together on an equal footing. Thus what in Leviticus is just one of a number of rules of conduct is ranged alongside the commandment which stands at the head of the covenant provisions in Deuteronomy.

This exaltation of the law of love of neighbor is reflected throughout the New Testament. John states unambiguously that he who claims to love God while hating his neighbor is a liar. The practical James asks pointedly: What good will it do to wish your neighbor the peace of God, while refusing to clothe him when he is naked, and feed him when he is hungry? In Matthew's great judgment scene, whatever is done to the least of the brethren is also done to Christ. The further question of the lawyer "And who is my neighbor?" takes on larger and larger implications as the contemporary world shrinks. It remains one of the unfinished challenges of the Church to communicate effectively that the second commandment is like the first.

THIRTIETH SUNDAY OF THE YEAR

Cycle "B" Readings: Jer. 31:7-9; Heb. 5:1-6; Mk. 10:46-52

The first reading in today's liturgy comes from a section of the book of Jeremiah which has been aptly named the "book of Israel's consolation." It pertains to a time when Israel sorely needed consolation, the time when Babylon, having become the major power in the Middle East, had overrun Palestine, besieged Jerusalem itself, and driven the people into exile in the homeland of their invaders. Jeremiah held the politically unpopular conviction that these tribulations were richly deserved punishments inflicted by God for the chronic infidelity of his chosen people. Accordingly, he regarded the Babylonian aggressors less as a national enemy to be resisted than as an instrument of divine chastisement to be patiently endured. Moreover, once the exile had become a fact, Jeremiah's unworldly interpretation of the events enabled him to look forward with great confidence to a time when the Israelites should have discharged their divinely appointed penalty for past sins, and might therefore be restored to freedom and to that homeland which represented for them the special favor of God. It is the happy anticipation of this eventual release which finds expression in the liturgical reading. The verses have the form of a hymn, in praise of God who "has saved his people" and who "will bring them from the north country." There follows a graphic portrayal of the homecoming, from all the scattered places of their exile, of a whole people: healthy, blind, lame, women in pregnancy, at the point of childbirth—the whole realistic diversity of a people sharing in the common salvation bestowed upon them by the God who is their common Father.

The second reading is the first part of a notable passage that develops the principal theme of the letter to the Hebrews, the high priesthood of Jesus Christ. In expounding the thesis that Christianity represents the perfection of what was only imperfectly anticipated by the religion of the Old Testament, the author of this document gives symbolic concreteness to that idea by contrasting the Old Testament's imperfect priesthood with the perfection of priesthood realized by Jesus Christ. In order to develop the contrast between inadequate and adequate priesthood, it is necessary to establish an accepted notion of what priesthood in general implies, and then to show the propriety of applying this notion to Jesus, who was not, of course, a priest in the ordinary official sense of the word. This is what is done in the present passage, and succinctly in its opening verse, which characterizes a high priest as one who is "chosen from among men" to "act on behalf of men in relation to God" by offering "gifts and sacrifices for sins." In the remaining verses of the passage, two of these points are separately emphasized. First the representative character of Christ is indicated by pointing out that he fully shared that sin-ridden environment of his fellow human beings for which he offered effective sacrifice. And then it is stressed that the priestly role of Jesus belonged to him, not by self-appointment, but by divine choice. The authenticity of Jesus' priesthood is thus vindicated insofar as he is both representative of his people and designated by God. Other elements which define priesthood are similarly attributed to Christ as the argument proceeds to demonstrate the superiority of his priesthood to that of all the priests who preceded him.

The third reading is a simple but striking narrative, taken from the Gospel according to Mark, of Jesus' cure of a blind man. It has often been pointed out that one of the noteworthy aspects of this narrative is the extent to which it enables the reader to contemplate the episode from the standpoint of the blind man who is cured. Also impressive, and the more so when one compares this passage with its parallel versions in Matthew and Luke, is the realistic vividness and detail with which the circumstances of the episode are described. Both the name of the man. Bartimaeus, and the location, at the edge of Jericho, are supplied. The blind beggar sitting at the roadside is no uncommon sight in that part of the world. He hears that Jesus of Nazareth is passing and hails him as Son of David, a phrase with messianic implications, appealing for compassion. The crowd first tries to silence him, but then, when Jesus sends for him, their tone becomes one of encouragement. Even the detail of his throwing aside his cloak as he jumped up is recorded. Asked what he wants, he states his hope: the restoration of his sight. Jesus answers with the typical assurance that his faith—that is, his confident reliance—has saved him. It is interesting to note that, in contrast with the other cure of a blind man narrated earlier in the same Gospel, this story does not report any curative action on Jesus' part, and that whereas in the earlier story Jesus sent the cured man home with a warning not to talk about what had happened, in this story the cured man immediately becomes one of the group of Jesus' followers. The latter feature is consistent with the more public, definite, and assertive character which Jesus' ministry assumes in the latter part of this Gospel as he approaches Jerusalem and the climax of his ministry.

THIRTIETH SUNDAY OF THE YEAR

Cycle "C" Readings: Sir. 35:12-14, 16-18; 2 Tim. 4:6-8, 16-18; Lk. 18:9-14

The book of Sirach, from which the first reading is taken, is one of those which, because they were not part of the Hebrew Bible, are placed by many Christians among the Apocrypha rather than included, as they are by Catholics, in the Old Testament proper. It is a work of wisdom literature, dating from the second century B.C., and it enjoyed great popularity in the early Church. The contents of the book have little organization beyond a grouping of related sayings. The passage chosen for the reading comes from a section directed against those who appear to think that the mere offering of ritual sacrifice can keep them on good terms with God. On the contrary, it is insisted that obedience to his law is what God chiefly requires, and that such obedience has in itself the virtue of sacrifice. Moreover, such obedience is an indispensable condition for ritual sacrifice to have any religious value whatsoever. The assertion that there is no value to a bad man's sacrifice, or an offering of ill-gotten goods, introduces the theme of God's impartiality. Thus those who are socially of low degree do not on that account have inferior claim on divine attention. The basic idea is that one gets from God what one deserves, and that what one deserves is unaffected by worldly status and determined entirely by how conscientiously one serves God. In sharp contrast with New Testament theology, what is affirmed here is a rigid merit system. God is conceived as exercising justice, impartially and inflexibly. The measure of divine justice is human merit, and the standard of human merit is divine law. Thus mankind's position before God is seen as determined by a rigorously single standard of legal justice which, while excluding on the one hand any reliance on privileged treatment for "important" people, also excludes any significant hope of divine mercy in the form of unmerited grace.

The second letter to Timothy, from which the second reading is taken, although probably not in its present form actually composed by Paul, is put together as though Paul had written it. It thus includes much Pauline phraseology and refers to events of Paul's life. The reading combines two passages from the final portion of the letter, which alludes to Paul's imprisonment and expectation of death, and contains several echoes of authentically Pauline writings. Some scholars believe that we have here part of an original letter of Paul's, to which other material was later added. The first three verses, which liken Paul's death to a sacrificial libation, and compare his approach to death with that of a winning runner to the finish line of his race, resemble similar figures of speech in the letter to Philippians. The last three verses allude to legal developments in Paul's case. The "first hearing" was a preliminary session for the purpose of determining whether or not the case should be brought to trial. Apparently there had been some hope that with the right testimony the case might have been dismissed at that point, but the necessary witnesses failed to present themselves. What followed is not altogether clear, but at least there does not seem to have been any immediate conviction and sentence. Paul attributes the postponement of his fate to the intervention of God, who can be relied upon to preserve his apostle as long as his evangelical mission requires him.

The third reading, from the Gospel according to Luke, is the famous parable of the Pharisee and the publican. Its point is made clear from the start by observing that it was addressed "to those who believed in their own self-righteousness while holding everyone else in contempt." Background assumptions that must be kept in mind are well exemplified in the first reading, from Sirach, where God is presented as a rigidly impartial judge who deals out rewards and punishments in strict accordance with meritorious observance of his law. The Pharisee believes in such a God. He also believes in himself, in the sense that he is conscious of having an excellent record of obedience to the law. Accordingly, he can present himself as a deserving subject to a just Lord, in full confidence of receiving a reward consistent with his virtuous life, which, as he points out, not only meets but exceeds legal requirements in such crucial areas as fasting and almsgiving. The publican, on the other hand, is painfully conscious of not measuring up to divine standards of justice. He knows and admits himself to be one who violates God's law, a sinner. And yet he is convinced that a sinner's case before God is not the hopeless one it would be if justice alone prevailed. And he accordingly appeals to God, not for justice, which would inevitably condemn him, but for mercy, the only thing that can save him. Jesus contrasts the two as persons, one of whom misunderstands both God's nature and his own, and the other of whom is basically right on both scores. The prayer of one is based on what is false; that of the other is based on what is true, the central truth of the Gospel.

THIRTY-FIRST SUNDAY OF THE YEAR

Cycle "A" Readings: Mal. 1:14—2:2, 8-10;
1 Thes. 2:7-9, 13; Mt. 23:1-12

The first reading is taken from the book of Malachi, which seems to be simply a word meaning "my messenger," rather than, as is often assumed, the name of a particular prophet. Whoever the prophet was, he exercised his ministry during the period after the exile had ended and the Jerusalem temple had been rebuilt, but apparently before the major religious reforms of the fifth century. The disorder of the times was attributed by this prophet above all to negligence in public worship. Since public worship was entrusted to a special class of people, the priests of the tribe of Levi, much of the strongest denunciation contained in this book is directed against an irresponsible priesthood. The reading comprises the intermediate and closing verses of the book's first passage condemning the behavior of the priests of the time, but omits those verses which make it clear that it is precisely priests who are being addressed, and who are being blamed for the failings of the people they have misguided. The omitted verses also make it impossible to tell what is being referred to as "it" in the repeated injunction to "lay it to heart" or else suffer the curse of God: it is in fact the divine command to perform conscientiously the priestly duties of sacrifice and religious instruction. It is through their dereliction of these sacred duties that the priests are said to have "made void the covenant of Levi," whereby the priesthood itself was instituted. The final verse of the reading, about the divine Creator's universal fatherhood, which seems to have no logical connection with what precedes it is, in fact, the opening verse of a new passage deploring infidelity.

In the second chapter of the first letter to the Thessalonians, Paul turns from his introductory remarks on the Gospel and its warm reception by the Christians of Thessalonica, to more specific and personal issues. The defensive tone which characterizes the first section of this chapter makes it evident that Paul's personal reputation was at the time somewhat insecure among these people whom he himself had converted from paganism. He reminds them, therefore, from his present distance, of his original visit to them, and of the candor, courage, and impartiality with which he had discharged his mission. In the verses included in the reading, Paul especially emphasizes the kindness of his conduct. Although his apostolic authority might have justified a certain severity, he describes his behavior as positively motherly in its gentleness. So thoroughly loving was his evangelical motivation that his giving of the Gospel was inseparable from his giving of himself. The unselfishness of his motivation was very practically demonstrated by the fact that during his mission he earned his own living by ordinary labor, rather than demand pay for his preaching or accept charity from his converts. Presumably Paul's craft of tentmaker, referred to in Acts of the Apostles, was his means of self-support during this time. The final verse of the reading resumes the introductory theme of the letter, once again expressing gratitude to God for the way that the Thessalonians responded to the Gospel.

The third reading, from the Gospel according to Matthew, begins by representing Jesus as enunciating a teaching which the New Testament as a whole hardly prepares us to expect, the teaching that the scribes and Pharisees are to be obeyed by Jesus' followers. This startling injunction is explained by reference to the fact that these Jewish authorities functioned in the synagogue as teachers in the tradition of Moses. They were indeed interpreters of what Jesus and his fellow Jews regarded as divine revelation and perhaps, as in the Sermon on the Mount, what we have here is basically an affirmation of the validity of that revelation, which was to be part of the Christian no less than of the Jewish Bible. The main force of the passage, however, is not to legitimize the public function of these religious teachers, but to criticize them for public behavior inconsistent with the very teaching they professed. The dominant motif of this criticism is the familiar charge of hypocrisy combined with oppressive legalism. The Jewish teachers are represented as imposing on their hearers the heaviest burdens of the law, while making adroit exceptions in their own favor. Their ministry is regarded as a ceaseless quest for personal religious and social prestige. But this denunciation, finally, is intended mainly as a warning to Jesus' own disciples, whose ministry is to be one of humble service to their people, in complete subordination to their Lord, uncorrupted by self-importance. The whole context of this passage strongly suggests that period in the early Church when Jewish and Christian teachers had become hostile competitors, and when the latter were subject to the same temptations as the former, to exercise a self-serving ministry.

THIRTY-FIRST SUNDAY OF THE YEAR

Cycle "B" Readings: Deut. 6:2-6; Heb. 7:23-28; Mk. 12:28b-34

The first reading in today's liturgy contains a passage which came to occupy a position of great importance in Jewish piety, as indicated by its incorporation in the Jewish daily morning and evening prayer called the *Shema*. The name, which means "Listen," derives from the verse in this passage of Deuteronomy which reads: "Hear, O Israel: the Lord our God is one Lord." This verse expresses the central religious tenet of Judaism, the uniqueness of God and his identity with the Yahweh of Israelite history, and might therefore be likened to a very concise kind of creed. That the statement is not conceived as a mere abstract formulation of monotheism, however, is made clear by the fact that it is immediately followed by a verse which states its practical meaning, in the form of a supreme moral and religious imperative that sets an ultimate standard for the lives of Jews and Christians alike: "And you shall love the Lord your God with all your heart, and with all your soul, and with all your might." Each of the Synoptic Gospels represents this verse as an expression of the greatest of all commandments, recognized as such by Jesus as well as by his Jewish contemporaries. The two verses together, proclaiming faith in one God and promising to love that God above all else, richly express what has been called by an outstanding modern theologian "radical monotheism." It creates a worldview in which there is only one absolute and all the rest is relative, and it generates an ethic in which the only worthy human life is that in which every action is subordinated to the wholehearted service of God. For the love of God which is here demanded is not, of course, an attitude of simple fondness or a sentiment of warm affection, but an unwavering policy of devotion which finds its practical expression in the constant endeavor to know and to do God's will.

The second reading, from the letter to the Hebrews, continues that document's lengthy argument that the imperfect priesthood of the Old Testament is a mere foreshadowing of that perfect priesthood which is found only in Jesus Christ. In preceding verses the author has applied to Jesus the words of a psalm, "Thou art a priest forever, after the order of Melchizedek." He then argues that Melchizedek (who is mentioned in only one other Old Testament passage) represents a priesthood superior to the hereditary priesthood traditionally belonging by divine appointment to the tribe of Levi. In the context from which the present reading has been taken, the author carries his argument a step further, in contending that the priesthood of Jesus (who is not descended from the tribe of Levi, and would not therefore be recognized as priestly by ordinary Jewish criteria) is likewise superior to the levitical priesthood. Still relying on his rather gratuitous assumption that the psalmist was referring to Jesus as a "priest forever, after the order of Melchizedek," the author maintains that this "new priest" (namely, Jesus) "is one like Melchizedek, owing his priesthood not to a system of earth-bound rules but to the power of a life that cannot be destroyed." It is on this basis that the author reaches the conclusions expressed in today's reading. In the first place, the Old Testament priests were many, because their functioning ceased with their death, and they had to be replaced, whereas Jesus' priesthood is everlasting because Jesus lives forever. Moreover, the Old Testament priests, being themselves sinners, had to offer sacrifice first for their own guilt and then for the failings of their people, whereas Jesus, being himself absolutely sinless, had no need to offer repeated sacrifices for his own repeated failings, and could offer instead a single, permanently efficacious sacrifice, "once for all."

The third reading, from the Gospel according to Mark, is a passage which has profoundly influenced the formation of Christian ethics. It represents Jesus' answer to a kind of question which was often presented to rabbis of his time, the question of how to express succinctly, without the protracted legalistic commentary which flourished among Jewish teachers, the very gist or essence of God's law. It is this sort of demand which is expressed by the scribe's asking Jesus: "Which commandment is the first of all?" In answer, Jesus first of all cites that verse, so well known to all Jews from its daily recital in the *Shema*, which was included in the first reading, from Deuteronomy: "Hear, O Israel! The Lord our God, the Lord is one: and you shall love the Lord your God with all your heart, and with all your soul, and with all your mind, and with all your strength." Given the status of these verses in Jewish piety, one may assume that Jesus' use of it to epitomize the primary commandment of God would have commended itself readily to his hearers. Jesus, however, amplifies his teaching by immediately adding what he calls the "second" commandment. This he cites from a different Old Testament context, in the book of Leviticus: "You shall love your neighbor as yourself." The joining of these commandments, with the added observation that "there is no other commandment greater than these," has tended to set Christian ethical teaching within a habitual framework based on the love of God and of one's neighbor.

THIRTY-FIRST SUNDAY OF THE YEAR

Cycle "C" Readings: Wis. 11:23—12:2; 2 Thes. 1:11—2:2; Lk. 19:1-10

Wisdom of Solomon, from which the first reading is taken, is considered part of the Old Testament by the Catholic Church, but classed among the apocrypha by others, as not having been part of the Hebrew Bible. It was written in Greek less than a century before Christ, and its title's reference to Solomon is a literary fiction. The section from which the reading is taken is a series of historical illustrations of the power of God's Wisdom, which this book personifies, as though it were a distinct agent rather than an intrinsic attribute of God. The verses selected for the reading follow a summary account of the exodus in which the misfortunes of the Egyptians are contrasted with the Hebrews' good fortune. An account of the divinely sent plagues is followed, rather surprisingly, by the observation that even for the Egyptians things could have been worse—God might have sent bears, lions, or specially contrived monsters to annihilate them totally! With this rather cold comfort, the theme of divine mercy is introduced with the reflection that God proceeds moderately, restraining his immense power which dwarfs the whole created universe. This divine restraint is applied to human beings in the form of a merciful readiness to overlook sinful offenses. God's gentleness is interpreted as manifesting his love for all existing things. He loves them because they are his creatures, and it is unthinkable that he should create anything he himself hated. This idea is otherwise expressed by saying that God's immortal spirit is in all things, recalling the reference in the first creation account to God's spirit, or breath. God's benevolence toward his creatures is consistent with the suffering he sometimes inflicts on human beings, because this is a corrective measure, leading to repentance and a renewal of trust in God.

The second reading is taken from the second letter to the Thessalonians. The first part of the reading is a prayer that God will enable the Thessalonians to make continual progress in the practical living of the implications of the faith to which they are called. That this prayer has in view a specific situation is made clear by the verses that precede it, but it remains obscure just what the situation was. In any case, the Thessalonian Christians were experiencing opposition severe enough to be called persecution. Paul expresses his confidence that God will not leave the persecutors unpunished, along with his gratitude that the Christians' faith has proved firm. Another issue is also involved, which is a major theme of this letter, and it is introduced by the last two verses of the reading. Here Paul attempts to calm the Thessalonians' anxious anticipation of an imminent second coming of Jesus Christ. An earlier message from Paul himself had given rise to a belief that the "Day of the Lord" was at hand. This phrase, derived from the book of Daniel, refers to the occasion of God's final judgment, and it was much used in early Christian discourse. To dispel this misapprehension, Paul proceeds to make use of the traditional Jewish belief that a great rebellion against God must precede the decisive Day, and he argues that this rebellion had not yet taken place.

The final reading, from the Gospel according to Luke, is the story found only in that Gospel of Jesus' encounter with a man named Zacchaeus, who exercised the intensely unpopular occupation of tax collector. Never very popular people, tax collectors were doubly despised by the Jews: first, because they were so devoid of national spirit as to become agents of Roman imperialism; and second, because they operated on a commission basis which made it a matter of self-interest to make oppressive and relentless demands on their fellow-countrymen. Thus, the observation that this Zacchaeus was very rich says a great deal about how he must have discharged his duties. It is noteworthy, and literarily vivid, that the little man is described as sufficiently interested in seeing Jesus to climb a tree. But much more significant is the fact that Jesus directly seeks him out and urgently requires his hospitality. Here we find the motif, so strongly present in this Gospel, of Jesus' explicit and virtually exclusive mission to typically sinful persons. And as usual, this motif is closely associated with another, that of the more respectable Jews' incomprehension and resentment of favorable attention's being shown to sinners. The story is a concise dramatization of the Gospel itself, the good news of God's saving love for sinners. And Zacchaeus' response in welcoming Jesus, and in setting about immediately to reform the most sinful aspect of his life, his avarice and dishonesty, is a concise dramatization of that response to the good news which Christians call faith.

THIRTY-SECOND SUNDAY OF THE YEAR

Cycle "A" Readings: Wis. 6:12-16; 1 Thes. 4:13-17; Mt. 25:1-13

King Solomon was for Israel the traditional patron of wisdom. The wisdom book from which the first reading is taken was accordingly attributed to Solomon, despite the fact that it was written centuries after not only Solomon's own death, but even the ultimate extinction of his kingdom. Written in Greek, and evidently addressed to Jews living in a Hellenistic environment, this book is not part of the Hebrew Bible nor of Protestant Bibles, but is regarded by Catholics as belonging to the Old Testament. The literary fiction of Solomonic authorship is further developed in some passages by presenting the author's words as addressed to kings, as though Solomon were acting as the sage mentor of his less enlightened fellow-monarchs. The passage given in the reading is one of these. It is an exhortation to seek wisdom, in the confidence that it really is not hard to find, provided one is genuinely devoted to the quest. To make this idea more vivid, the author personifies wisdom as a lady (the Hebrew word being feminine in gender) who, even as she is being sought after, is herself actually seeking to be found. But in this representation of wisdom as one who eagerly puts herself in the way of those who seek her, there is more involved than a mere literary trick of personification. To appreciate this it is necessary to recall that, for Israel, wisdom is, in the final analysis, not simply a human discovery but a divine gift. The pursuit of wisdom is thus normally understood not as a secular academic undertaking, but as a religious quest. Consequently, in representing wisdom as making herself readily accessible to earnest seekers, divine graciousness is implied.

The second reading is a portion of the first letter to the Thessalonians in which Paul deals with a problem that was evidently keenly felt among the first Christians, but which for later readers had much less urgency. The question about "those who sleep in death" is not simply the familiar question of whether or not, or under what conditions, there is life after death. The Thessalonians were worried about those Christians who had already died, and what worried them was the fear that these dead might "miss" the second coming of Christ. For in the earliest years of Christianity it was expected that Christ would return very shortly, and that his coming would bring the completion of salvation, when Christians would be enabled to share in his risen life. This view of the matter seemed to imply a tragic untimeliness about a Christian's dying before this climactic event occurred. It is this concern that Paul seeks to dispel by assuring his readers that those who die before Christ's coming will indeed be taken care of. He presents, as equivalently the Lord's own teaching, an explanation to the effect that at the Lord's coming the dead Christians rise, to rejoin their surviving brethren, before all are united with their glorified Lord. It is noteworthy that Paul seems to expect himself and his readers to be still alive on this supreme occasion, for which, therefore, he cannot anticipate any long delay. Nevertheless, in the verse which immediately follows the reading, Paul insists that the day of the Lord, whenever it arrives, will come with startling suddenness.

The third reading, from the Gospel according to Matthew is, like the second reading, about the sudden and climactic Day of the Lord, which the evangelist, like other early Christians, identified with the second coming of Jesus Christ. One aspect of this event is conspicuous here, as it was also in Jewish apocalyptic tradition, which was not part of the Thessalonians' problem, namely the divine judgment by which the ultimate fate of human beings is to be determined. The idea of judgment as a sudden and decisive event is clearly basic to the structure of this parable. In essence, it is the story of ten people of whom all shared the same eager expectation, whereas only half of them were prudent enough to remain in constant readiness, while the others missed the very thing they were waiting for as a result of their unpreparedness. One can easily imagine such a story, conveying such a message, as part of Jesus' own public preaching. And one can easily see also how certain details of the story would have assumed special significance for early Christians such as the evangelist himself. The fact that the awaited event was the arrival of a bridegroom strongly suggests the nuptial imagery used to describe Christ's relationship to his Church. The additional circumstance that "the groom delayed his coming" recalls the Thessalonians' problem about the return of Christ being much less prompt than they had expected. In that connection, Paul's reference to "those who have fallen asleep," meaning the already deceased Christians, come inevitably to mind when we read of the bridesmaids' falling asleep while waiting for the groom.

THIRTY-SECOND SUNDAY OF THE YEAR

Cycle "B" Readings: 1 Kgs. 17:10-16; Heb. 9:24-28; Mk. 12:38-44

The first reading in today's liturgy is an early episode in what has come to be known as the "Elijah cycle," a series of consecutive anecdotes, beginning in the first and ending in the second book of Kings, dealing with events in the life of that prophet. The cycle begins by introducing Elijah very abruptly, rather as though he had already been properly identified. He appears first as announcing to Ahab, the contemporary king of Israel whom the Bible portrays as monumentally wicked and impious, that there would be a drought for years to come, which would only end at Elijah's bidding. Presumably to protect him from angry reprisals when his prediction should begin to be verified, God tells Elijah to hide, first by a stream, which provides him with water while a regular food supply is brought to him by ravens, and later, when the stream dries up, at the house of a widow in the Phoenician town of Zarephath. This is the scene of the story told in the liturgical reading of how the widow, herself on the brink of famine, was assured by Elijah that if she shared with him her scanty remaining provisions, she could rely on God's promise to keep her little stock of oil and flour constantly replenished as long as the drought continued. The story is quite typical of the Elijah cycle, which favors legends of the miraculous. It also brings out an idea, which seems to have characterized Elijah, that Yahweh, the God of Israel, exercises dominion over what we should call the laws of nature. This emphasis is consistent with the fact that much of Elijah's prophetic career was a sustained struggle against the danger of Israel's apostasy to Canaanite religion, which enjoyed royal favor under Ahab and his pagan queen Jezebel. Since the Canaanite deities were especially associated with control of fertility and related natural phenomena, the vindication of Yahweh's dominion in this sphere of life was a vital element in Elijah's mission.

The second reading continues the series of passages read on previous Sundays and concluded next Sunday, dealing with the high priesthood of Christ as understood in the letter to the Hebrews. The present passage moves from considerations of the priestly office itself, in which Christ's position has been represented as superior to that of Israel's traditional priesthood, to a discussion of how Christ exercises the main function of priesthood, which is the offering of sacrifice. The background of the passage is taken from the temple ritual in which the priest is directed to enter the sanctuary and there offer animal sacrifices to God in expiation of the sins of the people whom he represents. This ritual is conceived, in accordance with the fundamental thought of this document, as a prefigurement, wholly inadequate in itself, of what has been accomplished with complete and final adequacy by Jesus Christ. Accordingly, the man-made temple sanctuary entered by the Israelite priests is constrasted with that only true sanctuary, heaven itself, which Jesus Christ has entered. Similarly, the periodic repetition of the traditional priestly rite, necessary because of its inadequacy, is contrasted with the unique sacrifice of Christ, never again to be repeated because of its total and permanent adequacy. Again, the animal blood shed by the priests of the past is contrasted with Christ's shedding of his own blood in a perfect act of sacrifice. And finally, the repeated emergence of the temple priests from their sanctuary after their repeated sacrifices is contrasted with the anticipated return of Jesus from the real sanctuary of God's abode in heaven, when at his second coming he will bring the fullness of salvation to those who await him.

The third reading is a selection from the Gospel according to Mark which includes two very different samples of Jesus' ethical teaching. Although they are only loosely connected logically, and probably of separate origin, they fit well into a scene somewhere in the vicinity of the temple during Jesus' last visit to Jerusalem. The first passage is a harsh denunciation of "the scribes" for the conceitedness of their behavior and the deceitfulness of their careers. Their representation as both pompous asses and avaricious hypocrites is undoubtedly a caricature, and one inapplicable to the better examples of this class of religious teachers. Reliable Jewish writers give a much more favorable impression, and the Gospels themselves elsewhere contain references to a much more respectable type of scribe. And yet the faults ascribed to them are so typical of those observed in other religious elites with similarly legalistic tendencies, even among Christians, that the passage is not hard to credit with the sort of veracity appropriate to justifiable satire. Probably it was mention of the scribes' exploitation of widows that caused this story to be linked with the beautiful account which follows of a widow who, having little, gave all, and thus was judged from a point of view whose values transcend economics to have given more than anyone else.

THIRTY-SECOND SUNDAY OF THE YEAR

Cycle "C" Readings: 2 Macc. 7:1-2, 9-14;
2 Thes. 2:16—3:5; Lk. 20:27-38

The first reading is a Jewish example of the kind of religious literature called, in early Christianity, acts of the martyrs, a kind of courtroom report of the trials and executions of those who gave the strongest possible witness to their faith by their readiness to suffer and die rather than betray it. The second book of Maccabees, which furnishes the reading, is one of four books by that name, only the first two of which are included in Roman Catholic bibles, and none of which are considered canonical by Jews or Protestants. They are named from a Greek word meaning a hammer, which was the nickname of a revolutionary Jewish hero of religious nationalism, applied also to his brothers, in the second century B.C. The beginning of their revolutionary career is described just after the atrocities recorded in the section from which the reading is taken. The latter were part of a persecution launched by the Syrian tyrant, Antiochus III, against devout Jews, in an effort entirely to replace Jewish tradition with the usages of Hellenistic paganism. To conservative Jews, even more distressing than the persecution itself was the readiness of many of their liberal brethren to welcome and assist the paganizing of Judaism as something civilizing and progressive. The entire episode, of which the reading gives us two fragments, was a very famous one in which seven brothers were in turn hideously mutilated and, along with their mother, brutally executed for refusing to violate Mosaic dietary laws. Each of the brothers, like those whose fates are described in the reading, not only refuses to perform the impious act demanded of him, but boldly seizes the occasion to declare his faith in a God who will both preserve his faithful ones and destroy their enemies. Theologically, these professions of faith are especially noteworthy for expressing clearly a doctrine of personal resurrection, which became a religious tenet only late in the history of pre-Christian Judaism. Disagreement about this doctrine persisted among the Jews, and is referred to in Gospel references to Jesus' involvement in current Jewish theological debate.

The second reading consists of the final verses of St. Paul's second letter to the Thessalonians apart from a concluding exhortation. The verses quoted contain two prayers of Paul for the Thessalonians and, in between them, his request that they should pray for him, to which he adds expressions of confidence. Having reiterated the thanks with which the letter began, for God's calling of the Thessalonians, Paul appeals to them to preserve their faith in difficult times, and calls upon God to keep encouraging their fidelity. The prayer Paul then requests for himself is basically a prayer for the continued success of his mission to spread the Gospel, for which he hopes to be spared from the assaults of his enemies. Having reaffirmed his trust that the Thessalonians will continue following his directions, Paul again intercedes for them in a brief and eloquent prayer that the Lord might direct their hearts toward God's love and Christ's fidelity. The three short prayers contained in this passage are rich expressions of distinctively Christian faith and distinctively apostolic concern. Along with other passages in the Pauline writings, they offer valuable models of pastoral prayer.

The third reading, from the Gospel according to Luke, narrates an episode which involves Jesus in a current theological debate about whether or not there is a resurrection. Foremost among those who denied resurrection was the sect called Sadducees, who originated at the time of the Maccabees. They came, for the most part, from aristocratic and priestly circles. Politically, they pinned their hopes for Israel's survival on collaboration with, rather than rebellion against, foreign imperialism. Theologically, their conservatism took a fundamentalist direction, hostile to the Pharisees' belief in a kind of development of doctrine and their corresponding interest in applying biblical faith in new ways to changing social circumstances. That the Sadducees should have disbelieved in the resurrection is consistent with their doctrinal conservatism, for there is no very clear support for that belief in the Hebrew Bible. Long experience in debating this theological issue had undoubtedly armed the Sadducees with many rhetorical devices, like the story about the woman who died after surviving seven husbands, intended as a *reductio ad absurdum* to confute believers in a resurrection. Jesus, in answering, comes down squarely on the side of the Pharisees, as he probably would have done with regard to most current Jewish theological questions. But he is represented as going farther than simply affirming the resurrection. In refuting the Sadducees' argument, he takes a position on a question that is still often heard, of whether the risen life is to be understood more or less as a resumption, freed from death and evil, of the kind of life we already experience in worldly society. In this passage he is represented as teaching, like St. Paul, that the risen life is unimaginably different and radically new.

THIRTY-THIRD SUNDAY OF THE YEAR

Cycle "A" Readings: Prov. 31:10-13, 19-20, 30-31; 1 Thes. 5:1-6; Mt. 25:14-30

The first reading, from Proverbs, is part of the portrait of an ideal wife. But, in fact, the good qualities ascribed to her in the verses read today are applicable to and must be attained by all, while the final verses enunciate values that are fundamental if life is be successful in God's sight.

All of us, like the ideal wife, must do good and not evil, with the good taking the form of concrete actions for the benefit of others. Like her, we must be hardworking, and generous and helpful to the poor (there are many kinds of "poverty" that are not met by giving money to good causes).

The last two verses call for alertness and sobriety. Right judgment would be easier if the choice were always between the clearly good and the clearly bad. It is more difficult to establish a proper hierarchy among good things and to judge accordingly. Charm and beauty are good, but they are of limited value: beauty is transient; charm may be lasting but for that very reason may delude its possessor into thinking he or she is made good by that fact. For "beauty and charm" we can substitute anything that is transient or can lull its possessor into a false sense of security. The true source of an authentic life before God and in relation to others is that reverent fear of the Lord which finds its expression in practical religion and makes us sensitive to moral truth.

In the second reading, Paul raises the question of the precise time of Christ's coming. His answer (a reminder of Christ's own teaching) is that the precise moment cannot be foretold. The important thing, however, is that Christ will surely come, and will come unexpectedly. Christians must therefore be watchful and not let themselves be tricked into unpreparedness by a false sense of security. As people reborn in Christ, they share the nature of him who is the light of the world. This means that they, like Christ, are to live holy lives, free of the darkness and opaqueness that sin creates in the minds and hearts of people, and that they are to have the alertness and sobriety of people who profit by the light of day. "Sobriety" is a freedom from excess of every kind and from all confusion of mind, a balance and self-control. Alertness and sobriety enable Christians to live in accord with their true nature, because they are aware of the end and the coming judgment, and thus can pass true judgments on the various values that solicit their adherence. When the end comes, they will already have judged themselves for good or for ill.

In the Gospel according to Matthew the parable of the silver pieces presents a picture of the ideal servant. Though less detailed than the picture of the ideal wife, it does point out a basic attitude without which the service of God will be sporadic and to that extent a failure. The parable inculcates a realistic understanding and acceptance of God's gifts to us. We must not bemoan the fact that less has been given to us than to others, so that we become paralyzed by pride and envy, nor regret that God has "burdened" us with his gifts, so that we become paralyzed by resentment or fear of failure and take refuge in an inactivity we try to disguise as humility or piety. Realistic acceptance requires genuine humility and objectivity, and passes over into responsible action.

The parable brings us up against two paradoxes. One is explicit: our reward will not be "rest" in a retirement home but greater responsibility. Yet that responsibility, far from being a source of anxiety, will be our way of sharing "the master's joy." We are here given a veiled glimpse of the inner life of God, whose "rest" on the seventh day is unwearying, joyous activity. The second paradox is implicit: when God comes to require an account of us, we will be forced to say: "We are unprofitable servants" (since we will have nothing really our own to give but will simply be returning his gifts), yet, at the same time, our good works must go with us.

THIRTY-THIRD SUNDAY OF THE YEAR

Cycle "B" Readings: Dan. 12:1-3; Heb. 10:11-14, 18; Mk. 13:24-32

The book of Daniel, which furnishes today's first liturgical reading, represents a special class of literature, found both inside and outside the Bible, called apocalyptic. Although actually written in the second century B.C., this work is constructed as though it had been a sixth-century production. It thus seems to foresee a sequence of events which were, in fact, already matters of history. Thus, the second major section of the book of Daniel narrates a series of symbolic visions that represent the rise and fall of increasingly corrupt regimes, the empires of the Babylonians, Medes, Persians, and Greeks, and the fragmentary kingdoms which emerged from power struggles following the death of Alexander the Great. At that point, which is contemporary with the writer of this book, the visions depart from a resume of political history and look forward beyond history to an ultimate divine victory over all the forces of human wickedness, whereby the Kingdom of God would be established. As described in the verses read in today's liturgy, the arrival of this Kingdom, to be preceded by an interval of great tribulation, would mean the definitive rescue of all the living who were true to God. It would also mean the raising up of "many" of the dead, "some to everlasting life, and some to shame and everlasting contempt." We thus find in the book of Daniel a conception of history and of its eschatological climax which brings us much nearer to the mentality of early Christianity than is generally the case with Old Testament writings. Especially important in this regard is the anticipated resurrection of the dead and of a final judgment which situates the vindication of divine justice not within human history, but at or beyond the end of human history, on the threshold of a "life of the world to come."

The second reading, from the letter to the Hebrews, is the concluding passage of that document's prolonged comparison of the Old Testament's priesthood and sacrifice with the priesthood and sacrifice of Jesus Christ. Here, once again, points of contrast are used to reinforce the basic contention that Old Testament religion was an imperfect foreshadowing of the perfect reality achieved by Christ. The opening verses concisely express this view by a series of contrasts, all having the same basic significance. Every other priest is contrasted with the one unique Christ. Their repeated sacrifices are contrasted with his single sacrifice. Their continued offerings are contrasted with his completed offering. Their inadequacy to remove sin is contrasted with his perfect act of consecration to God. Even the standing posture of the other priests at their altar is contrasted with Christ's position as seated at the right hand of God. The final verse of the reading summarizes the main point of the entire passage: since sacrifice is for the forgiveness of sins, as long as sins remain unforgiven, sacrifices must continue, but once sins have been forgiven, no further sacrifice is required. Everything about the Old Testament sacrifices is thus invoked as evidence of their inadequacy, while all the contrasting features of Christ's sacrifice are indicative of its total efficacy. Although the mode of argumentation and the manner of interpreting Scripture of the author of Hebrews is not likely to commend itself to modern standards of logic or exegesis, the conclusion of the argument, expressed in terms of an all-sufficient sacrifice resulting in universal forgiveness, clearly corresponds to basic Christian belief in the atonement brought about by Jesus Christ through his passion and death.

The thirteenth chapter of the Gospel according to Mark, from which the last reading is taken, has often been referred to as the "little apocalypse." It differs strikingly from most of the Gospel material by its graphic and rather sensational representation of events which are foreseen as marking the climax of the world's history. Like the section of the book of Daniel from which the first reading was taken, these verses purport to lift the veil, as it were (the word "apocalypse" means an unveiling), from the scene of ultimate destiny. As in other apocalyptic literature, a time of extensive tribulation is foreseen as just preceding the end. Indeed, the readers are admonished to watch for these catastrophic events as indications that the end is imminent. A great deal of speculation has been occasioned by one verse in particular, which seems quite clearly to assert that these climactic events would come to pass within the lifetime of Jesus' contemporaries. Events surrounding the destruction of the Temple by the Romans in 70 A.D. certainly constituted a time of great tribulation, and presumably encouraged the assumption, evidently widespread in the first generation of Christians, that the final judgment would occur within their lifetime. It is not impossible that Jesus at some point in his career tended to share this opinion. But that the opinion, even for Jesus, could be no more than a conjecture is insisted upon in the final verse of the reading, which declares that "of that day or that hour no one knows, not even the angels in heaven nor the Son, but only the Father."

THIRTY-THIRD SUNDAY OF THE YEAR

Cycle "C" Readings: Mal. 3:19-20 (4:1-2); 2 Thes. 3:7-12; Lk. 21:5-19

The book called Malachi, from which the first reading is taken, derived its name from a Hebrew word meaning messenger which, transcribed into Greek, looked like a proper name of the prophet who remains in fact anonymous. The work dates from the fifth century, after the rebuilding of the temple, and during the re-establishment of the Jewish community and its religion after the exile. Throughout the book, the prophet is concerned with religious and moral abuses which characterized this period of reconstruction, and he exhorts the community to reform its worship and its social morality. Among the social failings of the time, as of earlier times, economic injustice was conspicuous, and for religious Jews this problem pertained not only to ethics but also to faith. Given the sovereignty of God, and the known will of God, a special difficulty was presented by the undeniable fact that goodness and prosperity were very far from coinciding. Among the Jews, no less than elsewhere, riches and power seemed to accumulate precisely in the hands of those who most disregarded God's demands for justice and compassion. Thus the very people who appeared least to respect God's commandments seemed most to enjoy his blessings in the form of worldly prosperity and success. Like earlier prophets, the author of this work points to the future as holding the solution to this problem. Ultimately, the solution is conceived as the final divine judgment, when the tables will be turned on those who have defied God's known will and, to all appearances, gotten away with it. One of the characteristic features of this book is its forecast of a return of the prophet Elijah on a mission of reconciliation, prior to the definitive Day of the Lord when "the proud and all evildoers" will be burned up like waste stubble after the harvest, and for the God-fearing "there will arise the sun of justice with its healing rays."

The second letter to the Thessalonians, like the first letter of Paul to the same community, contains evidence that one of the results of the Thessalonians' expectation of Christ's imminent return was that some of them had, for all practical purposes, given up all productive work and assumed the roles of pious busybodies. It is not difficult to understand how, for persons of a certain type, the conviction that the world was approaching its end was construed as a license for social irresponsibility. Why, after all, should one devote more than minimal energy to a social and economic order of things that was already doomed and soon to disappear altogether? Those who developed this line of religious thought into a practical policy could easily be induced to a kind of premature retirement, and those who did so became inevitably both a nuisance and a burden, existing as parasites among their more industrious brethren. Paul strongly reproaches this behavior, reminding the Thessalonians first of all, of his own example. Paul made it a point throughout much of his missionary career to be self-supporting, and not to ask for contributions from the communities he served. At the same time, he frequently insisted that there would be nothing unfair about his expecting some material assistance in recompense for his ministry. Thus he is in a position to contrast his own readiness to take on extra work rather than burden the community with the attitude of those whose religiously rationalized indolence made them expect something for nothing. That the same problem later recurred in other Christian communities is recalled by the adoption of Paul's rule "that anyone who would not work should not eat" among the Puritans of the Massachusetts Bay Colony.

The final reading, from the Gospel according to Luke, is part of a longer section dealing with the early Christian preoccupation about the Day of the Lord, which is here identified with the coming of the Son of Man. The section begins with an anticipation of the destruction of the temple, and a later phrase, about "Jerusalem encircled by armies," so vividly suggests the Roman destruction of the city in 70 A.D. that a number of scholars infer that the passage was written after that event. In response to questions about preliminary signs of when the end will come, Jesus is represented as warning against false alarms and premature reactions. His answer anticipates that false claimants to be the Son of Man are certain to appear, and cautions that they must not be heeded. In general, the passage tends to push the anticipated final Day farther into the future, to discourage efforts at predicting its exact occurrence, and to redirect attention toward the events of a nearer future. Before the end, there will be great catastrophes both in the natural order and in the political order. But even more imminently, there will be grievous persecution for faithful Christians. Accordingly, the main emphasis of exhortation is to courageous constancy during a time when Christians will experience not only the hostility of religious and political authorities, but also the treachery of those who are closest to them. In all of these tribulations, they are to see their opportunity to testify to their faith, confident of divine assistance and of their ultimate salvation.

CHRIST THE KING

Cycle "A" Readings: Ezek. 34:11-12, 15-17; 1 Cor. 15:20-26, 28; Mt. 25:31-46

In the first reading, the passage from Ezekiel presents God as the true shepherd or king of his people. The two titles are interchangeable in the Old Testament, with "shepherd" showing the meaning and function of "king". He is the shepherd who, unlike people, does not act from selfish interest nor fail in his task. In what does his shepherding or ruling consist? It consists essentially in protecting, nurturing, and rescuing his flock and, finally, in judging it. This description would, if isolated, be too narrow to express the full relationship between God and people in the Old Testament. The images of shepherd and king in the Old Testament tend to emphasize the passivity of those who are shepherded and ruled, and the power, concern, and care of the shepherd and ruler.

In the second reading, the passage from 1 Corinthians speaks of the kingship of Christ at the climactic moment of its exercise: the resurrection of the dead. Here the power to protect and nurture and rescue finds its supreme expression; by that act the other powers that seek to exercise rule over people—sin and death—will be definitively conquered and eliminated. Then, having effectively manifested his kingly power in its fullest form, Christ will hand over to the Father, the supreme king, the kingdom (the adherents) he has won. In this act, Christ, with the whole of redeemed creation, will pay homage to the Father and make it clear that the Father is the source and goal of all reality outside himself.

This picture of God and Christ ruling creation and humankind could well give the impression that they stand apart, over against people who are primarily the passive recipients of their gifts and the beneficiaries of their power. Christ's kingship certainly does mean that he is the source of all blessings and that in the end he will crown his gifts with the resurrection and make us an eternal kingdom for his Father. But what of the interval between beginning and end? Does he rule in us as well as over us? How does Christ (God in Christ) rule in us now?

In the third reading, from the Gospel according to Matthew, the answer given in the description of the Last Judgment is that through our selfless love for others Christ rules in us and, through us, in the world about us, especially in our fellow human beings. Insofar as this love is lacking, God's rule remains external and is to some extent frustrated; his gifts are offered but rejected. Moreover, where people do not love, the Spirit does not dwell and will not be able to raise them up as members of the eternal kingdom. On the other hand, the more perfect the love, the more perfectly God rules and the more a person becomes the translucent image of the creator and redeemer, anticipating in the opaqueness of the flesh and the ambiguity of the world something of the "glory" of heaven: the inner life of the Trinity shaping and shining through the being and life of the creature.

As God rules the universe through the love he pours out on it to create and sustain it, so he rules through love in the specifically human world of free will. Nor is it one-sided and incomplete to equate his rule in us with our sharing in his love for people. For this love can only be built on faith and thus on God's rule in the mind no less than in the heart and will. This love depends, moreover, for its purity and intensity on the moral quality of the person who loves. If Christians lack the vision of faith, if they do not pray and worship God, if they do not live according to the evangelical principles of morality, they will not be able to see Christ in others or to see others with the eyes of Christ.

CHRIST THE KING

Cycle "B" Readings: Dan. 7:13-14; Rev. 1:5-8; Jn. 18:33b-37

The first reading in today's liturgy consists of two Old Testament verses whose echoes in New Testament writings have given them a unique significance for Christian readers. They occur in one of the apocalyptic visions that abound in the book of Daniel. This particular vision opens with a spectacle of four monstrous beasts, representing four pagan empires of the ancient Middle East. The verses which follow introduce a colossal courtroom scene, presided over by an "Ancient," evidently representing God, on a throne of fire surrounded by innumerable attendants. Judgment is pronounced on all of the "beasts," and one of them which symbolizes the most immediate danger, the Seleucid Hellenistic dynasty, is immediately put to death. The sequel of these visionary episodes is the description read in today's liturgy, of "one like a son of man coming on the clouds of heaven," who is presented to the "Ancient," and receives from him a universal and indestructible dominion, for all time and over all humankind. Although in ordinary Hebrew usage "son of man" is simply an alternative way of saying "man," the context of the phrase in these passages gave it special exchatological connotations in the religious language of Judaism. Although the eschatological interpretations of the phrase varied considerably in Jewish thought, they included two notions that have particular relevance to Christianity. One notion of the "son of man" was of a heavenly being who would come at the end of time to establish the reign of God's holy people. Another notion of the "son of man" understood it as referring to a heavenly man who is mysteriously identified with the primordial representative of the human race. In view of the application of this title, "son of man," to Jesus in the Gospels, it is easy to see a connection both with the expectation of Jesus' coming at the end of time which finds frequent expression in the New Testament, and also with the conception of Jesus as being a "second Adam" which plays an important part in the theology of Paul.

The New Testament book of Revelation, from which the second reading is taken, is, like the book of Daniel, an apocalypse—that is, it takes the form of a visionary anticipation, expressed in symbols, of the final episodes of the world's history, culminating in the definitive judgment of God. Such literature is characteristically composed during times of grave suffering or danger, and is designed to foster courageous endurance based on confident hope. The New Testament's apocalyptic book owes much of its structure and imagery to Old Testament models, especially Ezekiel and Daniel. In the passage read in today's liturgy, Jesus is referred to in terms which strongly suggest the eschatological conception of the "son of man" described in connection with the first reading. Thus Jesus is looked forward to as one who is to come, and whose coming will affect all the peoples of the world. Moreover, his coming is closely related to his role as universal ruler— "ruler of the kings of the earth." And at the same time, Jesus is referred not only to the world's destiny but also to the world's origin—he is both first and last: Alpha and Omega, "the one who is and who was and who is to come."

The third reading recounts the conversation on Good Friday between Jesus and Pontius Pilate, as described in the Gospel according to John. Jesus has just been brought from the house of Caiaphas to the headquarters of the Roman governor. Pilate first goes outside to talk with Jesus' accusers, who will not enter his pagan house for fear of defilement, and who make it clear that they are demanding a death penalty. The precise charge is not specified, but in the conversation which follows, between Pilate and Jesus, it is implied that the Jews have accused Jesus of sedition, and that they have related this accusation to allegations that Jesus has made claims of kingship. Pilate, to whom the Jewish religious language of kingship would be largely if not entirely unfamiliar, appears to have been seriously apprehensive about dismissing charges, however far-fetched, which, at a notoriously uncertain time in local imperial government, carried overtones of rebellion. At the same time, he seems to have perceived at once Jesus' manifestly unpolitical character, and to have carried out his perfunctory questioning as an official going through official motions, in cynical awareness of a foregone conclusion that, in the last analysis, questions of politics must drown out questions of justice. His initial cynical question "Are you the King of the Jews?" evokes an equally cynical response, "Are you asking this on your own, or have others been telling you about me?" As the conversation proceeds, Pilate clings tenaciously to what for him is the only relevant and material question in the case, whether or not Jesus claims kingship. And Jesus' answer is, in effect, yes and no. Yes, in the sense of kingship which should be most familiar and most important to the Jews. No, in the only sense of kingship which could be familiar or important to the Roman governor. The dialogue is fruitless, and the conclusion is inevitable.

CHRIST THE KING

Cycle "C" Readings: 2 Sam. 5:1-3; Col. 1:12-20; Lk. 23:35-43

The first reading is taken from the second book of Samuel, which was originally the second half of a single book. The first half, or book, narrates the story of Samuel and the reign of Saul, and introduces the career of David, the story of whose reign occupies the entire second half. According to this account, shortly after Saul's death David became king of Judah, which had a separate national existence, probably in vassalage to the Philistines. At the same time, Ishbosheth, Saul's son, with the assistance of Saul's general, Abner, succeeded to the kingship of Israel. Subsequently, Ishbosheth antagonized Abner by rebuking him for taking a wife from Saul's harem, and this proved to be a fatal error. Abner retaliated by transferring his allegiance to David. During the ensuing struggles, first Abner and then Ishbosheth lost their lives as victims of murder, leaving David as the only serious contender for the throne of Israel. An Israelite delegation came to David at his capital city of Hebron, to acclaim him as their king. David responded by proposing a covenant agreement, on the basis of which he was duly anointed as Israel's king, thereby uniting that northern territory with the southern one, Judah, already under his rule. This union of Israel and Judah, which only came to be after David had ruled the southern kingdom more than seven years, survived only until the death of David's son, Solomon, after which the original division reappeared. By all indications the separateness of the two territories was a more natural state of affairs than their union as a single state. To the extent that the modern state of Israel has historical precedent for its geographical scope of sovereignty, that precedent existed for less than a century, nearly three thousand years ago.

The second reading is from the letter to the Colossians, whose traditional attribution to St. Paul has been challenged by a number of modern scholars on plausible but debatable critical grounds. Some of the theological characteristics which make this letter quite different from earlier Pauline writings are closely related to its main purpose, which was to settle questions of doctrinal error. These issues had been raised owing to the influence of some kind of Gnostic teaching. The details of the controversy are obscure, but they involved a belief in some kind of "powers" or "elements" intermediate between the divine and the human, and the adoption of special ritual and ascetical practices. In the perspective of Pauline theology, the crucial issue was not the reality of these super-human beings, but the primacy of Christ. In asserting that primacy, the letter strongly affirms Christ's unique supremacy. In the process of developing this line of thought, the theology of Christ's role is greatly expanded, as may be seen in the passage quoted in the reading. Here Christ is presented as the image of God, not simply in the historical lifetime of Jesus, but from before the dawn of creation. Thus, whatever superhuman powers might exist, they too are entirely subordinate to Christ as being mere creatures. This universally sovereign Christ is likewise "head of the body, the Church." And as he is the foundation of the original creation, so too he is the foundation of that new creation which is manifested in the resurrection of the dead and accomplished by the atonement, conceived as the reconciliation of the entire universe with God.

The final reading for this final Sunday of the year which is celebrated as the feast of Christ the King, is taken from the passion narrative of the Gospel according to Luke. The scene is from the final moments of the crucifixion, and its theme is indicated by the ironic inscription, attached to an instrument of capital punishment, identifying its victim as "king of the Jews." The irony is exploited ruthlessly by some of the onlookers, who mock the powerlessness of a so-called king to escape from an ignominious death, taunting him as a self-proclaimed messiah, a word meaning anointed, and combining the connotations of king and savior. Luke has organized this passage in such a way that the irony perceived by Christ's enemies serves as a kind of backdrop for the contrary irony perceived by Christ's followers. The two contrasting motifs are brought into dramatic conjunction in the final episode of the reading, where they are represented by the two criminals crucified along with Jesus. For one of them, as for the hostile onlookers, the spectacle of Christ's suffering is, in view of his reputation, a supreme anticlimax. For the other, however, it is an occasion that engenders first a sense of justice, and then an insight of faith. The admittedly guilty victim turns, in a spirit of faith, to the obviously innocent victim, and asks for help from this seemingly helpless source. And as always in the Gospel when faith seeks help from Jesus, that help is promised, salvation is assured.

BIBLICAL INDEX

GENESIS
2:7-9; 3:1-7 — 1st Sun. of Lent, A
2:18-24 — 27th Sun. of the Yr., B
3:9-15 — 10th Sun. of the Yr., B
9:8-15 — 1st Sun. of Lent, B
12:1-4 — 2nd Sun. of Lent, A
15:5-12, 17-18 — 2nd Sun. of Lent, C
18:1-10 — 16th Sun. of the Yr., C
18:20-32 — 17th Sun. of the Yr., C
22:1-2, 9, 10-13, 15-18 — 2nd Sun. of Lent, B

EXODUS
3:1-8, 13-15 — 3rd Sun. of Lent, C
16:2-4, 12-15 — 18th Sun. of the Yr., B
17:3-7 — 3rd Sun. of Lent, A
17:8-13 — 29th Sun. of the Yr., C
19:2-6 — 11th Sun. of the Yr., A
20:1-17 — 3rd Sun. of Lent, B
22:20-26 — 30th Sun. of the Yr., A
32:7-11, 13-14 — 24th Sun. of the Yr., C
34:4-6, 8-9 — Trinity Sun., A

LEVITICUS
13:1-2, 44-46 — 6th Sun. of the Yr., B
19:1-2, 17-18 — 7th Sun. of the Yr., A

NUMBERS
6:22-27 — Octave of Christmas, A, B, C
11:25-29 — 26th Sun. of the Yr., B

DEUTERONOMY
4:1-2, 6-8 — 22nd Sun. of the Yr., B
4:32-34, 39-40 — Trinity Sun., B
5:12-15 — 9th Sun. of the Yr., B
6:2-6 — 31st Sun. of the Yr., B
11:18, 26-28 — 9th Sun. of the Yr., A
18:15-20 — 4th Sun. of the Yr., B
26:4-10 — 1st Sun. of Lent, C
30:10-14 — 15th Sun. of the Yr., C

JOSHUA
5:9, 10-12 — 4th Sun. of Lent, C
24:1-2, 15-17, 18 — 21st Sun. of the Yr., B

1 SAMUEL
3:3-10, 19 — 2nd Sun. of the Yr., B
16:1, 6-7, 10-13 — 4th Sun. of Lent, A

26:2.7-9, 12-13, 22-23   7th Sun. of the Yr., C
2 SAMUEL
   5:1-3   Christ the King, C
   7:1-5, 8-11, 16   4th Sun. of Advent, B
   12:7-10, 13   11th Sun. of the Yr., C
1 KINGS
   3:5, 7-12   17th Sun. of the Yr., A
   8:41-43   9th Sun. of the Yr., C
   17:10-16   32nd Sun. of the Yr., B
   17:17-24   10th Sun. of the Yr., C
   19:4-8   19th Sun. of the Yr., B
   19:9, 11-13   19th Sun. of the Yr., A
   19:16, 19-21   13th Sun. of the Yr., C
2 KINGS
   4:8-11, 14-16   13th Sun. of the Yr., A
   4:42-44   17th Sun. of the Yr., B
   5:14-17   28th Sun. of the Yr., C
2 CHRONICLES
   36:14-16, 19-23   4th Sun. of Lent, B
NEHEMIAH
   8:2-4, 5-6, 8-10   3rd Sun. of the Yr., C
2 MACCABEES
   7:1-2, 9-14   32nd Sun. of the Yr., C
JOB
   7:1-4, 6-7   5th Sun. of the Yr., B
   38:1, 8-11   12th Sun. of the Yr., B
PROVERBS
   8:22-31   Trinity Sun., C
   9:1-6   20th Sun. of the Yr., B
   31:10-13, 19-20, 30-31   33rd Sun. of the Yr., A
ECCLESIASTES
   1:2, 2, 21-23   18th Sun. of the Yr., C
WISDOM
   1:13-15; 2:23-24   13th Sun. of the Yr., B
   2:17-20   25th Sun. of the Yr., B
   6:12-16   32nd Sun. of the Yr., A
   7:7-11   28th Sun. of the Yr., B
   9:13-18   23rd Sun. of the Yr., C
   11:22; 12:1   31st Sun. of the Yr., C
   12:13, 16-19   16th Sun. of the Yr., A
   18:6-9   19th Sun. of the Yr., C
SIRACH
   3:2-6, 12-14   Holy Family, A, B, C
   3:17-18, 20, 28-29   22nd Sun. of the Yr., C
   15:15-20   6th Sun. of the Yr., A
   24:1-4, 8-12   2nd Sun. after Christmas, A, B, C

27:4-7   8th Sun. of the Yr., C
27:30—28:7   24th Sun. of the Yr., A
35:12-14, 16-18   30th Sun. of the Yr., C

ISAIAH

2:1-5   1st Sun. of Advent, A
5:1-7   27th Sun. of the Yr., A
6:1-2, 3-8   5th Sun. of the Yr., C
7:10-14   4th Sun. of Advent, A
8:23—9:3   3rd Sun. of the Yr., A
9:1-6   Christmas Midnight, A, B, C
11:1-10   2nd Sun. of Advent, A
22:15, 19-23   21st Sun. of the Yr., A
25:6-10   28th Sun. of the Yr., A
35:1-6, 10   3rd Sun. of Advent, A
35:4-7   23rd Sun. of the Yr., B
40:1-5, 9-11   2nd Sun. of Advent, B
42:1-4, 6-7   Baptism of the Lord, A, B, C
43:16-21   5th Sun. of Lent, C
43:18-19, 21-22, 24-25   7th Sun. of the Yr., B
45:1, 4-6   29th Sun. of the Yr., A
49:3, 5-6   2nd Sun. of the Yr., A
49:14-15   8th Sun. of the Yr., A
50:4-7   Passion (Palm) Sunday, A, B, C
50:4-9   24th Sun. of the Yr., B
52:7-10   Christmas Day, A, B, C
53:10-11   29th Sun. of the Yr., B
55:1-3   18th Sun. of the Yr., A
55:6-9   25th Sun. of the Yr., A
55:10-11   15th Sun. of the Yr., A
56:1, 6-7   20th Sun. of the Yr., A
58:7-10   5th Sun. of the Yr., A
60:1-6   Epiphany, A, B, C
61:1-2, 10-11   3rd Sun. of Advent, B
62:1-5   2nd Sun. of the Yr., C
63:16, 17, 19; 64:2-7   1st Sun. of Advent, B
66:10-14   14th Sun. of the Yr., C

JEREMIAH

1:4-5, 17-19   4th Sun. of the Yr., C
17:5-8   6th Sun. of the Yr., C
20:7-9   22nd Sun. of the Yr., A
20:10-13   12th Sun. of the Yr., A
23:1-6   16th Sun. of the Yr., B
31:7-9   30th Sun. of the Yr., B
31:31-34   5th Sun. of Lent, B
33:14-16   1st Sun. of Advent, C
38:4-6, 8-10   20th Sun. of the Yr., C

BARUCH
  5:1-9   2nd Sun. of Advent, C
EZEKIEL
  2:2-5   14th Sun. of the Yr., B
  17:22-24   11th Sun. of the Yr., B
  18:25-28   26th Sun. of the Yr., A
  33:7-9   23rd Sun. of the Yr., A
  34:11-12, 15-17   Christ the King, A
  37:12-14   5th Sun. of Lent, A
DANIEL
  7:13-14   Christ the King, B
  12:1-3   33rd Sun. of the Yr., B
HOSEA
  2:16-17, 18, 21-22   8th Sun. of the Yr., B
  6:3-6   10th Sun. of the Yr., A
AMOS
  6:1, 4-7   26th Sun. of the Yr., C
  7:12-15   15th Sun. of the Yr., B
  8:4-7   25th Sun. of the Yr., C
JONAH
  3:1-5, 10   3rd Sun. of the Yr., B
MICAH
  5:1-4   4th Sun. of Advent, C
HABAKKUK
  1:2-3; 2:2-4   27th Sun. of the Yr., C
ZEPHANIAH
  2:3; 3:12-13   4th Sun. of the Yr., A
  3:14-18   3rd Sun. of Advent, C
ZECHARIAH
  9:9-10   14th Sun. of the Yr., A
  12:10-11   12th Sun. of the Yr., C
MALACHI
  1:14—2:2, 8-10   31st Sun. of the Yr., A
  3:19-20   33rd Sun. of the Yr., C
MATTHEW
  1:18-24   4th Sun. of Advent, A
  2:1-12   Epiphany, A, B, C
  2:13-15, 19-23   Holy Family, A
  3:1-12   2nd Sun. of Advent, A
  3:13-17   Baptism of the Lord, A
  4:1-11   1st Sun. of Lent, A
  4:12-23   3rd Sun. of the Yr., A
  5:1-12   4th Sun. of the Yr., A
  5:13-16   5th Sun. of the Yr., A
  5:17-37   6th Sun. of the Yr., A
  5:38-48   7th Sun. of the Yr., A

6:24-34	8th Sun. of the Yr., A
7:21-27	9th Sun. of the Yr., A
9:9-13	10th Sun. of the Yr., A
9:36—10:8	11th Sun. of the Yr., A
10:26-33	12th Sun. of the Yr., A
10:37-42	13th Sun. of the Yr., A
11:2-11	3rd Sun. of Advent, A
11:25-30	14th Sun. of the Yr., A
13:1-23	15th Sun. of the Yr., A
13:24-43	16th Sun. of the Yr., A
13:44-52	17th Sun. of the Yr., A
14:13-21	18th Sun. of the Yr., A
14:22-33	19th Sun. of the Yr., A
15:21-28	20th Sun. of the Yr., A
16:13-20	21st Sun. of the Yr., A
16:21-27	22nd Sun. of the Yr., A
17:1-9	2nd Sun. of Lent, A
18:15-20	23rd Sun. of the Yr., A
18:21-35	24th Sun. of the Yr., A
20:1-16	25th Sun. of the Yr., A
21:28-32	26th Sun. of the Yr., A
21:33-43	27th Sun. of the Yr., A
22:1-14	28th Sun. of the Yr., A
22:15-21	29th Sun. of the Yr., A
22:34-40	30th Sun. of the Yr., A
23:1-12	31st Sun. of the Yr., A
24:37-44	1st Sun. of Advent, A
25:1-13	32nd Sun. of the Yr., A
25:14-30	33rd Sun. of the Yr., A
25:31-46	Christ the King, A
26:14—27:66	Passion (Palm) Sun., A
28:16-20	Ascension, A; Trinity Sun., B
MARK	
1:1-8	2nd Sun. of Advent, B
1:7-11	Baptism of the Lord, B
1:12-15	1st Sun. of Lent, B
1:14-20	3rd Sun. of the Yr., B
1:21-28	4th Sun. of the Yr., B
1:29-39	5th Sun. of the Yr., B
1:40-45	6th Sun. of the Yr., B
2:1-12	7th Sun. of the Yr., B
2:18-22	8th Sun. of the Yr., B
2:23—3:6	9th Sun. of the Yr., B
3:20-35	10th Sun. of the Yr., B
4:26-34	11th Sun. of the Yr., B
4:35-41	12th Sun. of the Yr., B

5:21-43	13th Sun. of the Yr., B
6:1-6	14th Sun. of the Yr., B
6:7-13	15th Sun. of the Yr., B
6:30-34	16th Sun. of the Yr., B
7:1-8, 14-15, 21-23	22nd Sun. of the Yr., B
7:31-37	23rd Sun. of the Yr., B
8:27-35	24th Sun. of the Yr., B
9:2-10	2nd Sun. of Lent, B
9:30-37	25th Sun. of the Yr., B
9:38-43, 45, 47-48	26th Sun. of the Yr., B
10:2-16	27th Sun. of the Yr., B
10:17-30	28th Sun. of the Yr., B
10:35-45	29th Sun. of the Yr., B
10:46-52	30th Sun. of the Yr., B
12:28-34	31st Sun. of the Yr., B
12:38-44	32nd Sun. of the Yr., B
13:24-32	33rd Sun. of the Yr., B
13:33-37	1st Sun. of Advent, B
14:1—15:47	Passion (Palm) Sun., B
16:15-20	Ascension, B

LUKE

1:1-4; 4:14-21	3rd Sun. of the Yr., C
1:26-38	4th Sun. of Advent, B
1:39-45	4th Sun. of Advent, C
2:1-14	Christmas Midnight, A, B, C
2:16-21	Octave of Christmas, A, B, C
2:22-40	Holy Family, B
2:41-52	Holy Family, C
3:1-6	2nd Sun. of Advent, C
3:10-18	3rd Sun. of Advent, C
3:15-16, 21-22	Baptism of the Lord, C
4:1-13	1st Sun. of Lent, C
4:14-21	3rd Sun. of the Yr., C
4:21-30	4th Sun. of the Yr., C
5:1-11	5th Sun. of the Yr., C
6:17, 20-26	6th Sun. of the Yr., C
6:27-38	7th Sun. of the Yr., C
6:39-45	8th Sun. of the Yr., C
7:1-10	9th Sun. of the Yr., C
7:11-17	10th Sun. of the Yr., C
7:36—8:3	11th Sun. of the Yr., C
9:18-24	12th Sun. of the Yr., C
9:28-36	2nd Sun. of Lent, C
9:51-62	13th Sun. of the Yr., C
10:1-12, 17-20	14th Sun. of the Yr., C
10:25-37	15th Sun. of the Yr., C

10:38-42	16th Sun. of the Yr., C
11:1-13	17th Sun. of the Yr., C
12:13-21	18th Sun. of the Yr., C
12:32-48	19th Sun. of the Yr., C
12:49-53	20th Sun. of the Yr., C
13:1-9	3rd Sun. of Lent, C
13:22-30	21st Sun. of the Yr., C
14:1; 7:14	22nd Sun. of the Yr., C
14:25-33	23rd Sun. of the Yr., C
15:1-32	24th Sun. of the Yr., C
15:1-3, 11-32	4th Sun. of Lent, C
16:1-13	25th Sun. of the Yr., C
16:19-31	26th Sun. of the Yr., C
17:5-10	27th Sun. of the Yr., C
17:11-19	28th Sun. of the Yr., C
18:1-8	29th Sun. of the Yr., C
18:9-14	30th Sun. of the Yr., C
19:1-10	31st Sun. of the Yr., C
20:27-38	32nd Sun. of the Yr., C
21:5-19	33rd Sun. of the Yr., C
21:25-28, 34-36	1st Sun. of Advent, C
22:14—23:56	Passion (Palm) Sun., C
23:35-43	Christ the King, C
24:13-35	Easter Sunday, A, B, C
24:13-35	3rd Sun. of Easter, A
24:35-48	3rd Sun. of Easter, B
24:46-53	Ascension, C

JOHN

1:1-18	Christmas Day, A, B, C
1:1.18	2nd Sun. after Christmas, A, B, C
1:6-8, 19-28	3rd Sun. of Advent, B
1:29-34	2nd Sun. of the Yr., A
1:35-42	2nd Sun. of the Yr., B
2:1-12	2nd Sun. of the Yr., C
2:13-25	3rd Sun. of Lent, B
3:14-21	4th Sun. of Lent, B
3:16-18	Trinity Sun., A
4:5-42	3rd Sun. of Lent, A
6:1-15	17th Sun. of the Yr., B
6:24-35	18th Sun. of the Yr., B
6:41-51	19th Sun. of the Yr., B
6:51-58	20th Sun. of the Yr., B
6:60-69	21st Sun. of the Yr., B
8:1-11	5th Sun. of Lent, C
9:1-41	4th Sun. of Lent, A
10:1-10	4th Sun. of Easter, A

10:11-18	4th Sun. of Easter, B
10:27-30	4th Sun. of Easter, C
11:1-45	5th Sun. of Lent, A
12:20-33	5th Sun. of Lent, B
13:31-33, 34-35	5th Sun. of Easter, C
14:1-12	5th Sun. of Easter, A
14:15-21	6th Sun. of Easter, A
14:23-29	6th Sun. of Easter, C
15:1-8	5th Sun. of Easter, B
15:9-17	6th Sun. of Easter, B
16:12-15	Trinity Sun., C
17:1-11	7th Sun. of Easter, A
17:11-19	7th Sun. of Easter, B
17:20-26	7th Sun. of Easter, C
18:33-37	Christ the King, B
20:1-9	Easter Sun., A, B, C
20:19-31	2nd Sun. of Easter, A, B, C
20:19-23	Pentecost, A, B, C
21:1-19	3rd Sun. of Easter, C

ACTS OF THE APOSTLES

1:1-11	Ascension, A, B, C
1:12-14	7th Sun. of Easter, A
1:15-17, 20-26	7th Sun. of Easter, B
2:1-11	Pentecost, A, B, C
2:14, 22-28	3rd Sun. of Easter, A
2:14, 36-41	4th Sun. of Easter, A
2:42-47	2nd Sun. of Easter, A
3:13-15, 17-19	3rd Sun. of Easter, B
4:8-12	4th Sun. of Easter, B
4:32-35	2nd Sun. of Easter, B
5:12-16	2nd Sun. of Easter, C
5:27-32, 40-41	3rd Sun. of Easter, C
6:1-7	5th Sun. of Easter, A
7:55-60	7th Sun. of Easter, C
8:5-8, 14-17	6th Sun. of Easter, A
9:26-31	5th Sun. of Easter, B
10:25-26, 34-35, 44-48	6th Sun. of Easter, B
10:34-38	Baptism of the Lord, A, B, C
10:34, 37-43	Easter Sun., A, B, C
13:14, 43-52	4th Sun. of Easter, C
14:21-27	5th Sun. of Easter, C
15:1-2, 22-29	6th Sun. of Easter, C

ROMANS

1:1-7	4th Sun. of Advent, A
3:21-25, 28	9th Sun. of the Yr., A
4:18-25	10th Sun. of the Yr., A

5:1-2, 5-8	3rd Sun. of Lent, A
5:1-5	Trinity Sun., C
5:6-11	11th Sun. of the Yr., A
5:12-15	12th Sun. of the Yr., A
5:12-19	1st Sun. of Lent, A
6:3-4, 8-11	13th Sun. of the Yr., A
8:8-11	5th Sun. of Lent, A
8:9, 11-13	14th Sun. of the Yr., A
8:14-17	Trinity Sun., B
8:18-23	15th Sun. of the Yr., A
8:26-27	16th Sun. of the Yr., A
8:28-30	17th Sun. of the Yr., A
8:31-34	2nd Sun. of Lent, B
8:35, 37-39	18th Sun. of the Yr., A
9:1-5	19th Sun. of the Yr., A
10:8-13	1st Sun. of Lent, C
11:13-15, 29-32	20th Sun. of the Yr., A
11:33-36	21st Sun. of the Yr., A
12:1-2	22nd Sun. of the Yr., A
13:8-10	23rd Sun. of the Yr., A
13:11-14	1st Sun. of Advent, A
14:7-9	24th Sun. of the Yr., A
15:4-9	2nd Sun. of Advent, A
16:25-27	4th Sun. of Advent, B

1 CORINTHIANS

1:1-3	2nd Sun. of the Yr., A
1:3-9	1st Sun. of Advent, B
1:10-13, 17	3rd Sun. of the Yr., A
1:22-25	3rd Sun. of Lent, B
1:26-31	4th Sun. of the Yr., A
2:1-5	5th Sun. of the Yr., A
2:6-10	6th Sun. of the Yr., A
3:16-23	7th Sun. of the Yr., A
4:1-5	8th Sun. of the Yr., A
5:6-8	Easter Sun., A, B, C
6:13-15, 17-20	2nd Sun. of the Yr., B
7:29-31	3rd Sun. of the Yr., B
7:32-35	4th Sun. of the Yr., B
9:16-19, 22-23	5th Sun. of the Yr., B
10:1-6, 10-12	3rd Sun. of Lent, C
10:31—11:1	6th Sun. of the Yr., B
12:3-7, 12-13	Pentecost, A, B, C
12:4-11	2nd Sun. of the Yr., C
12:12-30	3rd Sun. of the Yr., C
12:31—13:13	4th Sun. of the Yr., C
15:1-11	5th Sun. of the Yr., C

15:12, 16-20	6th Sun. of the Yr., C
15:20-26, 28	Christ the King, A
15:45-49	7th Sun. of the Yr., C
15:54-58	8th Sun. of the Yr., C

2 CORINTHIANS

1:18-22	7th Sun. of the Yr., B
3:1-6	8th Sun. of the Yr., B
4:6-11	9th Sun. of the Yr., B
4:13—5:1	10th Sun. of the Yr., B
5:6-10	11th Sun. of the Yr., B
5:14-17	12th Sun. of the Yr., B
5:17-21	4th Sun. of Lent, C
8:7, 9, 13-15	13th Sun. of the Yr., B
12:7-10	14th Sun. of the Yr., B
13:11-13	Trinity Sun., A

GALATIANS

1:1-2, 6-10	9th Sun. of the Yr., C
1:11-19	10th Sun. of the Yr., C
2:16, 19-21	11th Sun. of the Yr., C
3:26-29	12th Sun. of the Yr., C
4:4-7	Octave of Christmas, A, B, C
5:1, 13-18	13th Sun. of the Yr., C
6:14-18	14th Sun. of the Yr., C

EPHESIANS

1:3-14	15th Sun. of the Yr., B
1:3-6, 15-18	2nd Sun. after Christmas, A, B, C
1:17-23	Ascension, A, B, C
2:4-10	4th Sun. of Lent, B
2:13-18	16th Sun. of the Yr., B
3:2-3, 5-6	Epiphany, A, B, C
4:1-6	17th Sun. of the Yr., B
4:17, 20-24	18th Sun. of the Yr., B
4:30—5:2	19th Sun. of the Yr., B
5:8-14	4th Sun. of Lent, A
5:15-20	20th Sun. of the Yr., B
5:21-32	21st Sun. of the Yr., B

PHILIPPIANS

1:4-6, 8-11	2nd Sun. of Advent, C
1:20-24, 27	25th Sun. of the Yr., A
2:1-11	26th Sun. of the Yr., A
2:6-11	Passion (Palm) Sun., A, B, C
3:8-14	5th Sun. of Lent, C
3:17—4:1	2nd Sun. of Lent, C
4:4-7	3rd Sun. of Advent, C
4:6-9	27th Sun. of the Yr., A
4:12-14, 19-20	28th Sun. of the Yr., A

COLOSSIANS
1:12-20   Christ the King, C
1:15-20   15th Sun. of the Yr., C
1:24-28   16th Sun. of the Yr., C
2:12-14   17th Sun. of the Yr., C
3:1-5, 9-11   18th Sun. of the Yr., C
3:1-4   Easter Sun., A, B, C
3:12-21   Holy Family, A, B, C

1 THESSALONIANS
1:1-5   29th Sun. of the Yr., A
1:5-10   20th Sun. of the Yr., A
2:7-9, 13   31st Sun. of the Yr., A
3:12— 4:2   1st Sun. of Advent, C
4:13-17   32nd Sun. of the Yr., A
5:1-6   33rd Sun. of the Yr., A
5:16-24   3rd Sun. of Advent, B

2 THESSALONIANS
1:11—2:2   31st Sun. of the Yr., C
2:16—3:5   32nd Sun. of the Yr., C
3:7-12   33rd Sun. of the Yr., C

1 TIMOTHY
1:12-17   24th Sun. of the Yr., C
2:1-8   25th Sun. of the Yr., C
6:11-16   26th Sun. of the Yr., C

2 TIMOTHY
1:6-8, 13-14   27th Sun. of the Yr., C
1:8-10   2nd Sun. of Lent, A
2:8-13   28th Sun. of the Yr., C
3:14—4:2   29th Sun. of the Yr., C
4:6-8, 16-18   30th Sun. of the Yr., C

TITUS
2:11-14   Christmas Midnight, A, B, C

PHILEMON
9-10, 12-17   23rd Sun. of the Yr., C

HEBREWS
1:1-6   Christmas Day, A, B, C
2:9-11   27th Sun. of the Yr., B
4:12-13   28th Sun. of the Yr., B
4:14-16   29th Sun. of the Yr., B
5:1-6   30th Sun. of the Yr., B
5:7-9   5th Sun. of Lent, B
7:23-28   31st Sun. of the Yr., B
9:24-28   32nd Sun. of the Yr., B
10:5-10   4th Sun. of Advent, C
10:11-14, 18   33rd Sun. of the Yr., B
11:1-2, 8-19   19th Sun. of the Yr., C

12:1-4	20th Sun. of the Yr., C
12:5-7, 11-13	21st Sun. of the Yr., C
12:18-19, 22-24	22nd Sun. of the Yr., C
JAMES	
1:17-18, 21-22, 27	22nd Sun. of the Yr., B
2:1-5	23rd Sun. of the Yr., B
2:14-18	24th Sun. of the Yr., B
3:16—4:3	25th Sun. of the Yr., B
5:1-6	26th Sun. of the Yr., B
5:7-10	3rd Sun. of Advent, A
1 PETER	
1:3-9	2nd Sun. of Easter, A
1:17-21	3rd Sun. of Easter, A
2:4-9	5th Sun. of Easter, A
2:20-25	4th Sun. of Easter, A
3:15-18	6th Sun. of Easter, A
3:18-22	1st Sun. of Lent, B
4:13-16	7th Sun. of Easter, A
2 PETER	
3:8-14	2nd Sun. of Advent, B
1 JOHN	
2:1-5	3rd Sun. of Easter, B
3:1-2	4th Sun. of Easter, B
3:18-24	5th Sun. of Easter, B
4:7-10	6th Sun. of Easter, B
4:11-16	7th Sun. of Easter, B
5:1-6	2nd Sun. of Easter, B
REVELATION	
1:5-8	Christ the King, B
1:9-11, 12-13, 17-19	2nd Sun. of Easter, C
5:11-14	3rd Sun. of Easter, C
7:9, 14-17	4th Sun. of Easter, C
21:1-5	5th Sun. of Easter, C
21:10-14, 22-23	6th Sun. of Easter, C
22:12-14, 16-17, 20	7th Sun. of Easter, C